SIDESWIPED

LESSONS LEARNED COURTESY OF
THE HIT MEN OF CAPITOL HILL

ROBERT W. NEY

CHANGING LIVES PRESS

CHANGING LIVES PRESS
50 Public Square #1600
Cleveland, OH 44113
www.changinglivespress.com

Excerpts from *Into the Sun*, Volz, Neil (2011) Author House, used by
permission of the author.

Library of Congress Cataloging-in-Publication Data is available
through the Library of Congress.

ISBN: 978-0-9843047-7-6

Editor: Shari Johnson
Cover and Interior design: Gary A. Rosenberg • www.thebookcouple.com
Author's photo courtesy of Tim Ritter

Printed in the United States of America

10   9   8   7   6   5   4   3   2   1

CONTENTS

PART III   The Slippery Slope of Politics

PART IV   Post-Congress

PART V   Moving On

I dedicate this book to my friend, Ellen Ratner.
You have been my friend, mentor, psychiatrist,
specialist, enforcer, tough-love implementer,
travel and adventure partner, and many more
aspects that one human being brings to another
along their journey. *"To the world you may be one
person, but to one person you may be the world."*
You are the world to me, a gift to many others,
and you are famous among those who know
and love you for your rare ability to do
what you say you will.

☆ ☆ ☆

ACKNOWLEDGMENTS AND THANKS

In this section of the book there are so many that can be included (and many I have probably forgotten to include) who have been all-important to my life. I am forever thankful to all of my family, both here and departed; friends; acquaintances; even some who may not be friends; and for the experience and lessons learned.

Thank you . . .

First and foremost, to my wonderful, loving parents, Dorothy and Bob Ney, who brought me into this world, nurtured me and gave me absolutely the best guidance (that I, unfortunately, did not always follow). I love you and cherish your unconditional love for me.

To my beloved children, Bobby Ney and Kayla Kidd, I have lived a thousand lifetimes of happiness due to your love, support, and the blessings that you have bestowed on your mother and me. You have turned into fantastic adults. I appreciate also the support of your spouses, Julie and Adam.

To Aaliyah, my loving, beautiful granddaughter—you have constantly filled my days with joy and wonderment.

To my Sister Emmy Lou, brother-in-law, Rick Charlton, and my nieces and nephews—for being with me through my toughest times.

To my wonderful aunts, uncles, and cousins.

To my grandparents who have passed on, Marguerite and Elmer McCloud, Mildred and Charles Ricer, and William Ney.

To Bruce Velt, thanks for all the years of support.

To my college friends Tim Ritter, Deborah Akers and husband, Sami Shubaily.

To Warren Papas—from Saudi Arabia to America, I appreciate everything.

To Dr. Renato and Nancy Dela Cruz, thanks for being there for me and for my family.

To Matt and Marina Parker, special thanks and God bless you!

To Bob Wallace and Terry Wallace, thank you.

Thank you, Corey Lewandowski.

To Howard Monroe at WVLY, a voice of reason in the wilderness.

To Cholene Espinoza, who has been there to encourage me and, when needed, stepped in to be a voice of reason to make things better.

To my Ohio State House friends: Neil Clark, Stanley J. Aronoff, Mike Morrison, Pat Sweeney, Harry Meshel, Nick Zimmers, Greg Haas, John Climaco, the late Verne Riffe and many more.

To the Members of Congress I served with—there are so many good people on both sides of the aisle, and great moments that the media has *not* covered. Thank you for your patience, understanding, and the memories you have given me.

A special note to Congressman Steve and Jennifer LaTourette—your support has meant the world to me.

To all of the staff from the Ohio House, Ohio Senate, and Congressional days: You served the people of the nation and I thank you for it. My deepest sorrow for how it ended, because of me.

To the constituents of the 18th District: You are amazing people who have had to endure tough economic times. You are what America is about. My deepest apologies again for the disgrace I brought you and for breaking your trust in me. You are truly exceptional people, and I thank you for supporting me over the years.

To the Vinson and Elkins Law Firm: Mark Touhey, Bill Lawler, David Hawkins, and Craig Margolis. Your legal prowess was amazing.

Special thanks to Bill Lawler—your ongoing friendship is so appreciated.

To Neil Volz, as we turn new pages as friends.

To Judge Huvelle—you have helped me in my new path.

To my friends who helped me in recovery—Russ P., Tim H., John P., Steve C., Justin J., Kevin I., Brian I., Michael D., Rich J., Joe B., Bill and Judy M., Scott R., Cody C., Denny M., Judy E., Daryl M., Jan and John W.,

Trisha P., Dixie, Sue and many more friends I have met in the rooms, who have educated me.

To my Texas Hold 'em buddies who made my entry back into the world fun, although not profitable—Ethan P., John "Doc" D., Stephen R., Chris S., Andrew M., John P., Mitch K., Trevor B., Steve and Trisha W., and Michael T.

To Francesca Minerva and the staff at Changing Lives Press, who published this book.

To my editor, Shari Johnson. As I struggled nearly a year ago to write this book, holed up in a hut in India, you playfully dubbed me "Ernest Hemingway." I literally could not have written this—without not only your command of the "King's English," but also your guidance, tough love when needed, prayers, and encouraging e-mails when I felt like stopping. You are truly a magnificent human being and I cherish the relationship that the Internet helped us develop over nearly a year's time.

Throughout all of this, I am humbled and thankful to the Master of Grace—The Bread of Life—Our Lord.

*Three times I pleaded with the Lord about this, that it should
leave me. But he said to me, "My grace is sufficient for you,
for my power is made perfect in weakness." Therefore
I will boast all the more gladly of my weaknesses,
so that the power of Christ may rest upon me.*

—II CORINTHIANS 12:8–9

☆ ☆ ☆

PROLOGUE/PURPOSE

This book has been in the making for over five years. I first thought about writing my ideas down while in federal prison—or, as I refer to Morgantown Federal Correctional Institution, "The Bush Housing Program." I quickly concluded that writing a book while incarcerated was not a good way to win friends and/or keep a low profile. To put one's candid, honest thoughts (or any thoughts) in writing while incarcerated is not only foolish, but would provide delightful entertainment for the guards if they were to read it. Remaining low key is essential—especially for high-profile persons such as Jack Abramoff and me. (I was amused to see Jack give Rod Blagojevich, convicted former Governor of Illinois, advice about that.) Jack had Kevin Spacey, the actor who played the role of Jack in the movie *Casino Jack*, visit him in prison—and although I am a big Kevin Spacey fan, it wasn't exactly a low-profile move.) Besides, writing a book in prison was out of the question in the legal sense of not profiting from one's crime while incarcerated.

After prison and upon my release from the Alvis House, a halfway house in Columbus, Ohio, the last thing on my "to do" list was to write my life history. I was simply trying to pick up the shattered pieces, work, get on my feet, think things through, stay sober, and find out if life would again find me or I would bump into it. I was truly doing the "white knuckle" existence. Reestablishing normal life with my family was a challenge for me, but not because of them. They were wonderful while I was in prison; they visited me, they weren't mad at me, they were understanding—they were just waiting till I got out. Then when that time came, for them I was back and everything was okay. For me, having been in prison was my problem alone, not a strain between me and my family. It required relating to them and getting back to my real life, leaving the whole prison scenario behind. Paramount on the list was my hope to put together a decent living condition and absorb myself in my "program" (12 Step) in order that all else would fall in line. Digesting what had happened, facing people, and surviving a very nerve-racking federal probation period became my number-one goal— not regurgitating on the written page all that had happened to me or how broken the system is.

Besides, I wondered, *Who really gives a damn anyway? Who besides my family would want to purchase the book? What credibility could it have?* An even bigger question for me following the aftermath was, *What good would it do for the general public?* That is why I began government service in the first place; it was a higher call to help people. That went down the rat hole of conceptions with the merger of "Ney World" (as Neil Volz, my former Chief of Staff, referred to it) and Team Abramoff.

I continued to struggle with the common good of writing versus the selfish desire to spill my guts and tell "my side," whatever that was. "My side" in 2008 was surely different from "my side" today after self-analysis and many months of rehab. I received golden advice: "Write the book." "Don't write it." "Put the past behind by writing." "Put the past behind by not bothering to write it." "Write it for the money." "Write it for revenge." "Write it to screw a bunch of people" (except for the one giving the advice). "Write for therapeutic purposes." "Unload to show what those bastards did to you." Some friends in 12 Step recovery even said it would really be a "fearless and moral inventory" (the Fourth Step).

Despite the urging from friends and people who had good intentions in their desire for me to "tell my story," I once again decided to can the idea.

In 2010 a longtime friend of mine, Jim Owen, convinced me that a lot of good and some personal closure could and should come out of a writing endeavor. Knowing that my parole was soon coming to an end, I worked out a deal, through Jim, to begin with a professional writer of sorts who was really interested in helping me write my book. Ellen Ratner, my friend, boss (she hates that), and book cheerleader, was ecstatic. I spent countless days the summer of 2010 taping hours of thoughts, intimate stories, feelings, and secrets. In August after serving the full probation period, which almost no one does unless you take a leak on your parole officer, I was finally finished with the two-year post-prison parole. I was awaiting the outline and first two chapters of my book, and then I would be off to India to finish the book over the next few months by e-mail.

The entire deal fell apart due to personal reasons on the part of the ghostwriter and my tapes were not returned. I again concluded that the book was toast and what is, is.

The year 2011 was a blur of going to 12 Step meetings, working with a sponsor, working for Talk Radio News, and constantly debating whether to write the book or shelve the idea.

Ellen Ratner asked me to go to a luncheon after a radio event in New York that she hosted. "Just a luncheon, that's all." The lunch morphed into a conversation with Francesca Minerva, CEO of Changing Lives Press, a very charismatic, Italian-American who really is a no-BS lady, and after talking with her for an hour, convinced me that Ellen was right; a book was a good thing and we just needed to get on it, *subito!*

Finally, I was again headed to India. My two children were married and settled and I trekked off to Dharamsala, India, specifically Sarah College, the Tibetan College nestled in the foothills of the Himalayas, right in the shadow of His Holiness the Dalai Lama's residence of McLeodganj.

Before I left for India, I filmed, with the joint decision of Neil Volz, my former Chief of Staff and Team Abramoff staffer, a *60 Minutes* segment on Jack Abramoff. I was in India when I saw the show.

As I watched and listened closely to Jack talking with Leslie Stahl on *60 Minutes*, my thoughts were varied. I knew he went through a lot, I sympathized with his prison time, and I understood how he had to be all over the board with his thinking. We shared some similarities: responsibility for our crimes, guilt, shame, wrongdoing, and atonement.

As I watched him try to explain himself, I wondered—was this the Jack that he wanted us to see or the Jack that no one sees—Jack the transparent, or Jack the showman? Keeping an open mind, I sent him a private Facebook message—a very simple, "God Bless, wishing you the best." He responded equally as short and proper. I assumed he called his probation officer as one cannot talk to another felon while on probation, and he may have thought I was setting him up. Who knows? Our mutual trust was not Grade "A" at this point.

I had some more false starts and stops on the book, including losing my *muse*—and then some events transpired that set me back on track.

Neil Volz had written his honest, personal story in his book, *Into the Sun*, and I thought it was good; he was able to unload, but he also shared how people can change—as his life was changed for the better. Jack Abramoff's book *Capitol Punishment* was out, and although not much was stated about the book itself, Jack became the media celebrity for "personal change." Even Melanie Sloan, the head of an ethics "watch-dog" group, CREW, bought into Jack's venture by attending an event with him that gave him credibility while losing some of the little she had left.

As I watched Jack "share," as Volz had done, I began to think that telling my story was important. I felt that Jack was twisting and manip-ulating the facts; not trying to set the record straight, but rather setting Jack in motion for future pursuits—a sort of "Jack's back."

It became a goal of mine not to give my version versus Jack or Neil's, but simply to give my insight and add something to it beyond my life story and my prison woes.

Jack made the statement in a Texas paper, "I don't know why Bob is trying to rewrite history" in reference to something that I recalled dif-ferently than he. I realized then that Jack had not learned much. He has the right to his version of history, but his observations and statements were similar to wearing a coat—when it gets a bit too hot, you simply take it off. He would comment whenever comfortable, but when con-fronted by Tom Rodgers, the Abramoff Affair whistleblower, at the National Press Club about his inside, unethical collusions with power-ful reporters, he took the coat off.

I simply concluded that I could, and had to, do better. I needed to atone, to give a point of view, and not only shed light on some unknown facts, but send a message that people could understand and utilize in their own lives. I needed to help them understand what is really going on in the halls of the shiny Capitol that I so love.

I proceeded with the book like a man on a mission. I pray that it leaves you with not only an idea of what happened to me, but more important, what really goes on in government. The slippery slope of ethics and life can take me, you, or anyone else down a dark road where we can be sideswiped through our own carelessness, that of others, or both.

Hopefully my message will help to clean up the system and illumi-nate the fact that things are still not totally kosher—even after a few people got locked up from 2005 to 2006 and some window-dressing in the nature of Ethics Legislation hit the floor of the House to "drain the swamp," as then Speaker Pelosi called it.

With a few exceptions, this book consists of my own perspective and interpretation of events. When quoting conversations, I have endeavored to be as accurate as possible.

On a personal note, I found my purpose in sharing personal situations and demons to be not only therapeutic and as a way to atone for my sins, but also as a way for me to give you a personal warning: Think about, analyze, and question your behavior. Be aware and have a sharpened sense about what you do, who you spend your time with, what bed you lie in. Be mindful of what you ingest into your body and what you feed your soul; care for both with love and common sense.

That is my purpose. This is my story.

☆ ☆ ☆

HELPFUL TIPS
FOR READING THIS BOOK

Even though this book is essentially a chronicle of my life, it hasn't been possible to adhere to a strict chronological order. Each chapter deals with a period of time or events, but it is often necessary to look to past or future events within that chapter. To avoid confusion such as: *Is this now, or was that then, or is this going to happen at a later date?* I have indicated these parts with italics and/or parentheses.

Because "member" is a commonly used word, when referring generically to U.S. Representatives it is capitalized in this book. Grammatical license has been taken in some areas for purposes of clarity, such as references to the U.S. Congress are capitalized—Congress, Congressman, Congresswoman, Congressional, and so forth.

There is a Resource section in the back of the book with links to further reading of incidents mentioned in the text. The links are divided according to chapters.

☆ ☆ ☆

TIMELINE

To facilitate your reading further, below is a timeline of events should you get lost along the way:

November 1976—Started Bureau of Motor Vehicles (BMV) job

December 1976—Graduated from Ohio State University

December 1977—Quit BMV job

January 1978—Went to Iran

July 1978—Left Iran

Fall of 1978—Worked in Appalachia Job Development Department, Columbus, Ohio

November 1979—Quit Appalachia job, left Columbus, and returned to the Ohio Valley

January 1980—Became Safety Director of City of Bellaire for Mayor Fitch

February 1980—Filed for state representative, Belmont County, Ohio— no primary

November 1980—Elected to Ohio House of Representatives

December 1980—Resigned as Safety Director, City of Bellaire

January 1981—Sworn in as Ohio state representative

March 1981—Met Candy Taggart, my future wife

November 1982—Lost reelection to Jack Cera

January 1983—Left office as Ohio state representative

January 1983—Took a job with Amerigard in Wheeling, West Virginia

March 1983—Went to Saudi Arabia as a joint venture with Amerigard

August 1983—I returned to the states and married Candy—two days
later returned to Saudi Arabia

December 1983—Returned to U.S. to enter my name as an
appointment for Senator Speck's vacated seat

January 13, 1984—Appointed to replace Senator Sam Speck and sworn
into the Ohio State Senate

January 23, 1984—Bobby, our first child, was born

November 1984—Candy, Bobby, and I moved from Bellaire, Ohio, to
Barnesville, Ohio

January 1985—Sworn in for first complete term as state senator

1987—Became Chairman of the Banking and Insurance Committee

November 1988—Won reelection to the Ohio State Senate

December 31, 1988—Our daughter, Kayla, was born

1990—Became Chairman of the Senate Finance Committee

1991–1992—Foreign exchange student from Sweden, Trita Parsi, lived
with us

1992—Reelected to the Ohio State Senate (four-year term)

August 1992—Candy, Bobby, Kayla, and I moved to St. Clairsville,
Ohio

1994—Ran for the U.S. House of Representatives from Ohio's 18th
District

November1994—Elected to U.S. House of Representatives

January 1995—I left the Ohio State Senate, was replaced by Jim Carnes
for the Senate Seat. Sworn into the U.S. House of Representatives

February 1996—Candy and I divorced (dissolution)

November 1996—Reelected to the U.S. House

November 1998—Reelected to the U.S. House

2000—Met my second wife-to-be

2000—Reelected to the U.S. House

January 2001—Became Chairman of the House Administration Committee

June 2001—Married my second wife

2002—Unopposed for the U.S. House

2004—Reelected to the U.S. House

2004—Redistricted

August 2005—Moved from St. Clairsville to Heath, Ohio, due to redistricting

January 2006—Resigned as Chairman of House Administration Committee

June 2006—Won primary for U.S. House

August 2006—Stepped out of election

September 13, 2006—Last drink

October 13, 2006—Pled guilty

November 3, 2006—Resigned as a U.S. Congressman

December 2006—Moved out of my house in Heath, Ohio, put all items in storage; Daughter, Kayla, moved into an apartment in Newark, Ohio, to complete her senior year

January 19, 2007—Sentenced to thirty months in Morgantown Federal Correctional Institution Morgantown, West Virginia

March 1, 2007—Started my sentence

February 15, 2008—Released from Morgantown Federal Correctional Institution

February 15, 2008–August 15, 2008—Alvis Halfway House Columbus, Ohio; Started working for Ellen Ratner, Talk Radio News Service

August 2008–June 2009—Lived with Kayla, her husband Adam, and granddaughter Aaliyah in Newark, Ohio

January 2009—Was divorced from my second wife (dissolution)

June 2009—Kayla, Adam, and Aaliyah move; I stayed in the Newark rental house and got two roommates

April 2009–April 2010—worked for Talk Radio News Service and had my own radio show on WVLY, *Bob Ney News and Notes*

September 2010—Moved to another rental house in Newark, three different roommates

September 1, 2010–Dec 19, 2010—India

March 2011–May 2011—India

September 23, 2011–December 22, 2011—India

March 23, 2012–May 29, 2012—India; wrote the first draft of this book

At this writing—Living in Newark, Ohio

PART I

★ ★ ★

PRE-CONGRESS

"There are only two ways to live your life.
One is as though nothing is a miracle.
The other is as though everything is a miracle."

—ALBERT EINSTEIN

Chapter 1

☆ ☆ ☆

VALLEY BOY

"If growing up is the process of creating ideas and dreams about what life should be, then maturity is letting go again."

—MARY BETH DANIELSON

My mother and father were born in the city of Bellaire, Ohio, and their families had been in this area known as the Ohio Valley since the 1800s.

Mom and Dad were high school sweethearts, and continue to be sweethearts as I write this. While in prison, I heard stories from other inmates about their families—stories of fighting, violence, drugs, alcohol and divorce. All of these backgrounds can play a part in the behavior that leads to criminal activities by those who came from those environments.

In my case, when I "shared" in rehab sessions, I could only talk about a 100 percent *normal*, ideal, upbringing. My parents were poor, but happy. We (my sister, Emmy Lou, and I) had no idea we were poor. Until I was four, my mom, dad, sister, and I slept in the same room. When my sister was twelve, she moved up to the attic. It was tiny, but it was "her own room." I continued to sleep in the same room as mom and dad until I was seven, when they saved enough money to buy a modest house that they still live in. To me, it was a castle in which I had my own room and my own closet versus the closet under the attic stairs that we all shared.

My grandparents, aunts, uncles, cousins, all lived within less than a mile of each other. Raised in Bellaire, Ohio, a bustling town of 10,000 people at that time (4,900 today), in a nice family, surrounded by cousins and a lot of friends was idyllic. My future mistakes can't be blamed on "bad family environment."

The Ohio Valley was a fun place. The "all-American" town of Bellaire was about 85 percent Italian Catholic. Living within the Italian community was an amazing experience that not only brought the great taste of Naples to our plates, but a lot of friendships with loving people who enjoyed life to the fullest—good, hardworking people who, like my German and Irish ancestors, immigrated to Bellaire to be part of the exploding textile, glass, coal, and steel industries. Life was good, one did not need a college degree to feed their families, and all could have a wholesome, God-fearing life in the "all-American" town.

My sister, Emmy Lou, was eight and a half years older than I was and had a lot of friends. She took me many places with her, and I think this opened up a large world to me. Being around my aunts, uncles, and older cousins, I learned a lot. I started first grade with the ability to read and, through listening to so many adults, developed a good ear for memorization of issues, which helped me later in my political life.

I enjoyed high school and was not too concerned about a career. I worked at Cook United grocery store, and that job enabled me to, with the help of my parents, buy a new, modestly priced car. In the Valley in those days, when you were aged sixteen through eighteen and the drinking age was twenty-one, it was not a problem to get into bars, nightclubs or to purchase carryout packages—and my friends and I took advantage of that.

In February of 1972, my parents noticed in the newspaper that various colleges were organizing a College Night in the gym at St. John's. After school that day my dad asked me, "What time are you going to College Night tomorrow?"

"I'm not."

"Yes you are."

My dad is very kind and never was one to put a lot of demands on me, but he put his foot down on this one. My sister had a nursing degree. My thinking was: *Why the hell would I want to spend four years in college and come out with debt when I can get hired in a New York minute in the coalmine or steel mill?* That's what all my friends were doing; that's what some of my relatives had done; that's what their fathers before them had done. In order to humor my dad, I went to College Night (he came along to make sure), and Dad won—I would get a college degree.

Before I graduated from high school in June of 1972, my parents gave me a choice: go to the local branch of Ohio University (Eastern), get my new car, continue to work and in two years transfer to the main campus, Ohio University Athens, *or* no new car. Option one sounded good.

I went to college at the local branch of Ohio University and damn near failed the first two quarters, until a light bulb went off. The Branch was a cool place. People called it "high school on the hill," but I had fun. I played euchre (a card game big in the Midwest) in the lounge with some of my friends. Students could smoke in class (my buddy Greg Bosold gave me a cigarette during a boring history class); and we could go to Gasper's Bar down the road. What more could a person want? Life was good and politics was the last thing on my mind.

Before Nixon's resignation, I'm not sure why, but I wrote him a letter. I got a response and he said, "I know the American people have a desire to become involved in the energetic give and take of public debate." I learned much later that John Kasich (former U.S Congressman and at this writing governor of Ohio) wrote him a letter too and ended up being invited to the White House. Nixon must have really paid attention to young voters.

I finished (barely) my first year of college at Ohio University Eastern. Then a news blurb on my dad's car radio on the way to church and a conversation on the church steps that same day fatefully coalesced to change the course of my life.

★ ★ ★

I was still working at Cook United grocery store, planning on finishing my second year at Ohio University Eastern (the local branch) in 1974 and then move to the main campus of Ohio University in Athens, Ohio, to pursue a pre-law degree.

A turn of events in late 1973 changed my plans about moving to Athens. I was in the car with my parents on our way to the mandatory St. John's Sunday noon mass. My dad turned the car radio on for the news. John Gilligan, a Democrat elected in 1970, was the first term governor, and the State of Ohio was in a budget crisis. As I listened, something caught my ear. Governor Gilligan was proposing that anyone who attended law school or medical school would have to pay back a portion of what the state subsidized for students. I didn't catch the entire broadcast, but I caught enough of it to decide that the governor who had visited my high school a couple of years earlier, and for whom our band had played (I was a drummer), was no longer in my favor. I had just decided to be a lawyer, and here was a damned politician trying to make me pay more.

After mass, as we stepped down the stone church steps to the street, my dad's longtime friend Dom Pulito stopped us to say hello. Dom was a very nice, jovial, Italian guy from Bellaire. He had made it to the big time, working eight years at the Division of Liquor Control for Republican Governor Jim Rhodes' first two administrations. Even though Dom was a Republican from my home town of Bellaire, which had a 3 percent Republican registration, he managed to keep his job under the new governor, Gilligan. Politics are politics and Bellaire had a connection to Governor Gilligan—his son was married to a Bellaire girl.

Mr. Pulito, as my parents taught me to address him, asked me what I would be doing in college. I told him that after going to the local branch of Ohio University for two years, then two years at Ohio University Athens, I wanted to go to law school at the Ohio State University, College of Law.

He then asked me if I liked Governor Rhodes or the current governor, John Gilligan. I answered that I did not know Rhodes, although I remembered that he and Governor Arch Moore of West Virginia, let me sit in their limousine when I was a kid and my dad was covering a story. *(My dad was the news photographer for WTRF Wheeling, West Virginia, for 36 years. Governor Moore was a U.S. Congressman at one time, served time in a federal prison for bribery, and is the father of West Virginia Congresswoman Shelley Moore Capito.)*

Now a few things need to be put into perspective. First, my father who never says anything ill of anyone, used to chide the only Republican in the family—my brother-in-law, Rick Charlton, about Rick's Republican registration. We would be going to the beach, all in one car, and my dad would say to me, "Bobby, what is a good Republican?" I would answer, "An invisible one, Dad," and smile at Rick. He also used to say, "Remember—Republicans will do little for the common people." Having had this ingrained in my mind, I had attempted to work for the Young Democrats, but no one really showed interest when I tried to volunteer.

In addition to my dad's feelings about Republicans, there was another problem with Rhodes—he had sent the National Guard into Kent State

University. (On May 4, 1970, the National Guard shot into a crowd of students who were protesting the Vietnam War, killing four and wounding nine.) This was an issue for me, because I was against the Vietnam War. So, balancing my personal wants versus what I believed in, my question back to Dom was this: "I don't have to register Republican to work for Rhodes, do I?" Dom's answer was classic Good Politics 101, was how Rhodes operated, and was why he was successful. Dom said, "Jim Rhodes doesn't care if you are rich or poor, black or white, Republican or Democrat, or in between. As long as you work for him, he will be loyal to you." Okay, that was good enough for me.

Something extraordinary happened next—Dom actually passed my name, the name of a nineteen-year-old kid, to the Belmont County Republican Party Chairman, James A. Carnes. *(Jim has remained a friend and eventually took and held my state senate seat when I went to the U.S. Congress.)*

Within a week I received a letter from Rhodes. His face was water-marked into the letter (it seemed as though he were personally addressing me), and then I received a phone call from Chairman Carnes. I was an absolute rookie in politics, but I sure was getting some attention. I thought *They may be Republicans, but hey—I'm getting into law school!*

While still working at Cook United grocery store in 1974, I became the "Belmont County Youth for Rhodes Coordinator." I was teased by co-workers with, "Hey, take me to the White House when you make it big." They weren't teasing me so much for working on a campaign as much as they were harassing me because I was working for a Republican. Have I made it clear yet? The Valley was big-time Democrat—overwhelmingly Democrat.

Among other things, I handed out stickers and other political paraphernalia for Rhodes. I was supposed to transfer to Athens, Ohio, but in the fall of '74, I was so into the Rhodes' campaign that I transferred to Ohio State University in the capital city of Columbus so I could work on the campaign and see it through to the end. I was compelled to make the transfer despite everyone else's telling me to go to Athens.

It was my first quarter at Ohio State and my friend Tim Ritter from Bellaire was my roommate at Harrison House. My mother and father and Tim's mother, Julia, dropped us off at Ohio State and my campaign career was about to go into full swing.

Campaigning for Rhodes was not easy. Students across Ohio despised him for the Kent State tragedy. Election eve, I attended the downtown

Columbus victory party with Tim. Rhodes was losing, and did not attend the party. He then conceded. I went back to my room on campus, pretty "bummed out" about the loss of the first big election I was involved in.

The next morning, Tim and I went to the Ohio State cafeteria for breakfast, and I picked up the *Columbus Dispatch* newspaper along the way but didn't open it. Tim and I got our food and had just sat down when I heard a loud voice at a nearby table say, "I can't believe that bastard won!" Then another student said, "Yeah, can you believe after Kent State that Rhodes won?" I opened my paper and there it was—he had won by a slim margin of about 10,000 votes statewide. I was told later that even Rhodes himself was shocked when they woke him up to tell him he had won!

Chapter 2

☆ ☆ ☆

POLITICS 101

"Whoever said, 'It's not whether you win or lose that counts,'
probably lost."

—MARTINA NAVRATILOVA

W hen I became involved with the Rhodes campaign in 1974, while
I was still at Ohio University Eastern Campus, I received a phone
call from Terry Kundert who was with the Ohio Republican State Headquarters.

Terry and a man named Karl Wolfe drove down to Bellaire in Belmont County, Ohio, to meet with me. Terry was very aggressive and
sounded like a political "big man on campus." He asked me if I would
like to form a college Republican chapter at the Ohio University Eastern branch in Belmont County. He said I could do it simultaneously
while working for the Rhodes campaign. So I did. I enlisted every friend
I could, Republican or not. (It wasn't easy finding someone in Belmont
County who was actually a Republican.)

Terry had an ulterior motive for my becoming the chairman of the
Belmont County College Republican Club. In 1975 he asked me to come
to the State Convention of College Republicans in Findlay, Ohio, where
elections for officers of the Ohio State College Republicans would be
held. One week before I arrived in Findlay, Terry, Karl Wolfe, Bob (Robert
R. Cupp, former Ohio Supreme Court Justice) his wife, Libby, and a few
others planned my run for state chairman. When I found out about it,
the problem as I saw it was this: I was brand new to politics; I was the

unseasoned chairman of a new College Republican Club from a rural county that was Democratic; I was running against three other people who had been involved in politics for a lot longer than I had been; and probably most important, I wasn't even sure that I was a Republican. I just wanted to help Rhodes and get some political push to go to law school.

After some persuasion, I headed to Findlay, Ohio, for the College Republican State Convention. Accompanied by my college roommate, Tim Ritter, and some friends from Bellaire and Columbus, I was on my way to throwing my hat in the ring for something I probably wouldn't win. However, voilà! By the end of the weekend, through pamphlets and a courtesy bar arranged by Terry and Karl Wolfe, I had won. I was overwhelmed. I got in my car and headed home. I turned on the radio and with Elton John's *Philadelphia Freedom* blasting in my ears, I decided that I was on my way to something big—I was just not sure what. I was young and the big thing for me was that I drank some booze, slept with some rich Republican college girl from Columbus, and got elected to something. Life was good.

My political life kicked into high gear. I made an enormous number of friends, established myself in an inner circle, and got my picture on the cover of the *Ohio Republican* newspaper with my vice-chair, Janet Parkhurst, and the current Governor at the time, James A. Rhodes. I also met Karl Rove who was the National Chairman of the College Republicans. He was a longhaired, skinny kid that had a mystical aura that surrounded him . . . the word going around was that he was abandoned as a baby, found in a dumpster and raised by foster parents—yet he went on to become driven and oh, so powerful. *Back in the day,* we all worked for Karl; we just didn't call him "the architect"—not yet. I still have the letter where I was asked to support his campaign for chairman of the College Republican National Committee. (Imagine that; the days when Karl Rove needed letters of support instead of giving them out.)

It wasn't long before Hal Duryee (executive director of the Ohio Republican Party) called me to his office on behalf of Kent McGough, the Chairman of the party. Hal said that I would have an office for the College Republicans, a key to state headquarters, a small budget (large to me), and I was to build the College Republicans. That we did. The team was Janet Parkhurst, vice-chair (now the wife of a Columbus judge), Jim Owen as executive director (now a well-known attorney in Columbus, Ohio, who has successfully obtained the release of several innocent people from prison), Alex Arshinkoff (now a political power-house in Ohio), Ed Brookover (who has worked extensively with the National Republican Congressional Committee, the Republican National Committee, and the National Republican Senatorial Committee, to name but a few), and a wide variety of College Republican presidents who have gone on to various careers—all led by Karl Rove, the superstar.

It was 1975 and I was Ohio State Chairman of College Republicans, popular, drinking for free at events, having a great time, learning a lot, getting a plum of a summer political job, meeting representatives and senators . . . what more could a college guy from Appalachian Ohio ask for?

In 1976, Hal Duryee again called me to his office. Now in those days, Hal was an intimidating man. He was a great person, ran a very tight ship, knew politics, was a Rhodes loyalist and was a very effective right-hand man for the chair of the Ohio Republican Party. He wore "granny glasses" that sat way down on the tip of his nose, and he had a tendency to look at a person over them that sent chills down this person's spine.

He very quickly got to the point and said, "How would you like to be a delegate at large to the 1976 Republican National Convention in Kansas City?" I really wasn't sure what all a delegate did. I had learned a lot about Robert's Rules of Order, politics, government and campaigns, but delegates? Kansas City? Not really sure. I wondered how long the drive was to Kansas City. I had never been on an airplane.

Then my mind focused back on the question at hand and I said, "I guess so, if you want me to." Hal leaned forward, slowly; his glasses seemed to be on the very tip of his nose and about to fall off on the top of my head. Then, in a bit of a raised and a definitely mocking voice he said, "I guess so, if you want me to?!!!" He then went into a rapid dis-course starting with "Do you have any idea how many people since this democracy was formed strive and struggle all of their lives to be a del-egate—and a delegate at large is beyond the reach of most of them—and you say, 'If you *want* me to?'" By this time I knew that he hadn't liked my answer. After apologizing profusely and accepting his gracious offer, I found out later that only 26 of Ohio's 99 delegates at that time were *at large*. They were basically appointed by the governor or Repub-lican party, and they did not have to competitively run for the slot—they were "ordained" and on their way to the convention.

That year in Kansas City, Gerald Ford was being challenged by Ronald Reagan. Ohio delegates were not legally bound by whom the head of the party supports, but they were ethically bound if they went as a Ford delegate. All of the delegates at large were hand-selected, so I was "ethically bound" for Ford, and quickly understood why I had been selected. The Ford nomination was going to be close. The party was hand-selecting people who would vote *their* way—for Ford. I was now involved with the Republican Party of Ohio as a College Republican Chairman and would be more inclined to vote their way.

The competition became so tough for that nomination that the White House invited groups of delegates to dinner. I got to choose three other people to go with me. I took Jim Owen, Mirah Khan, and Ed Brookover. We headed to D.C. in my Chevy Chevette, changed our clothes in Karl Rove's apartment and camped out there that night. His place seemed disorganized and had the appearance of an apartment where the occupant doesn't spend much time.

First, it was lunch with Nelson Rockefeller at the famous Mayflower Hotel. Like a buffoon, I parked my car out front in a no-parking zone! When we left the hotel, the car was gone. I mentioned it to Mayor Ralph Perk of Cleveland who was at the luncheon. He promptly ordered his aid to call the office of D.C.'s mayor to get our car back, which he did. Using politicians to defy local laws would get you in the press these days, but the 70s were a different bag.

Dinner that evening was in the State Dining Room of the White House. It was mind-boggling to me that I—a "Valley Boy"—was walking into the White House. I marveled at the size of it. I was awestruck with thoughts of Abraham Lincoln strolling down the same hallways, entering the same beautiful rooms I was entering.

The waiters wore white gloves and the tables were laden with food—some of which I didn't even recognize. The President of the United States was announced, and in walked a very calm, distinguished-looking President Gerald Ford. He greeted all of us with a kind and personable demeanor. We were invited to take a seat at the dinner tables. President Ford welcomed us to "Your house" and spoke briefly about the upcoming convention. We had one of the best meals I could recall having. I remember that we stayed till the last. The marine on guard politely came over to our group of four, as we were still having cocktails, and said, "Hope you all had a great time. Good night."

We went on to pay a midnight visit to the Capitol. Jim Owen had an ID because he was an intern for then Congressman John Ashbrook, an amazing, famous, conservative Congressman from the Johnstown, Ohio, area. We walked through the Capitol and went underground, which of course today would be quite impossible due to security. Then as we walked into the gorgeous Rotunda and were on our way to the Senate side, we heard bells that continued to go off—not like sirens, but like small chimes.

Soon, a Capitol Hill policeman sternly asked, "What the hell are you people doing?" He took Jim's ID, we left without being cuffed, and Jim got a "mild" *no, no* from the Ashbrook office. The private tour was pretty nice while it lasted. Later in my life, I sometimes strolled through the Capitol or took friends on midnight tours without being told to leave. It was as glorious and magnificent then as it was that night, walking with Jim.

The year 1976 went into hyper gear. Just like seasons won, it became seasons lost. I went to Kansas City in August, and Ford won the nomination. I did some advance work for Jack Ford, President Ford's son; met Bob Dole and did some events with him; worked on the campaign for Senator Robert Taft, Jr. and had a pending job with him if I wanted it. At the same time, I worked with Dick Stobbs on some of his plans for his sheriff's race in Belmont County. However, Gerald Ford lost to Jimmy Carter and Senator Taft lost to Howard Metzenbaum. Shell-shocked by the Republican losses, and realizing I was nearing my graduation in December, I keenly felt the need to find a job.

I took a position at the Bureau of Motor Vehicles (BMV). I decided to cool my jets with politics. I had gone a bit too fast and all of my candidates lost. I graduated from college, started 1977 in my own apartment on Hudson Street in Columbus, Ohio, worked for the BMV and took a hiatus from campaign life.

Chapter 3

☆ ☆ ☆

IRAN

"The most beautiful adventures are not those we go to seek."

—ROBERT LOUIS STEVENSON

No school, no politics, and a good job—1977 was going well. The job with the State of Ohio, Bureau of Motor Vehicles (BMV) came about from a conversation I had in 1976 with the late Curt Andrews who was at that time registrar of the Bureau of Motor Vehicles, at a politically oriented party after the Kansas City Republican National Convention. He was retired from the Air Force, and we all called him Colonel Andrews. The Colonel was a short, mustached, no-nonsense man, who had the presence and bravado of a fearsome, axe-wielding giant. Although he was rather new to the Ohio Governor Rhodes' *machine*, he had been appointed registrar of the BMV. Technically, his superior was Don Cook, who was the head of the Department of Highway Safety, which had authority over the Bureau of Motor Vehicles.

In my conversation with Colonel Andrews, he made it clear that I had made the "liberal" choice in supporting President Ford, and that Ford would lose the presidency—which he did, in November. However, he also said that I was a loyal Rhodes guy and if I wanted a job, I could call him the next day at the BMV and I could have one.

I thought that after four years of college good paying jobs would surely be there. Then reality and stark fear set in and "Where's the beef?" became "Where's the job?" Although my soon-to-be achieved degree would qualify me to be a certified social studies teacher, a job (albeit a temporary one) was a good thing. I called Colonel Andrews and went down to see him the following week.

Upon arriving in the outer waiting area, I saw an attractive, older woman (hey, 30 is older when you are 22) go into the Colonel's office. She then came out and asked the secretary to get the Xerox man on the phone. She went back in, and then back out with the same request. In again, out again, making another request for a call to the Xerox man. At that point, the Colonel stepped out of his office, looked directly at her and said, "Tell that bastard that if he is not out here in exactly forty-seven minutes to fix the Xerox machine, I will have the machine put on rollers and I'll shove it down Kimberley Parkway myself!"

He then turned to me, said hello, and told me to come into his office. I thought, *Damn! I'm glad I'm not working for Xerox!*

The Colonel offered me a coffee, we talked politics, and then he asked me if I wanted a job. He then asked what time my classes were this final quarter before graduation. I told him that the last class was at 5 p.m. He said, "Good." He then called some guy on the intercom who promptly came into the office looking nervous, but then seemed relieved when the Colonel said, "This is Bob Ney. He is a good Rhodes man and a friend of mine. Have him start the midnight accounting tomorrow." (This was a different era—in today's political world, telling someone who works in government that a person is hired because he is a friend or perhaps had worked for the governor could result in some jail time—or at least wind up on the front page of a newspaper or Web site!)

I thanked the Colonel, did not ask about the salary, did not ask about the job, just started to leave. He said, "By the way, do a good job no matter how trivial it is, and be my eyes and ears." As I left, two maintenance men from the Bureau of Motor Vehicles were putting the Xerox machine on rollers.

The next night was fascinating. I reported to the bureau at 11:30 p.m. and walked into a second floor room where there were about 70 people, all at separate small desks, furiously going through green application after green application. These were pre-computer days, so everything was done by hand. Against the wall were multiple boxes—some were being filled with completed applications and some just being opened to start the night's work. All desks faced front toward an office with glass windows where the night supervisor, a quiet, unassuming man, sat watching us. Who he was, where he came from, and any other details about him were not known.

One night in particular, halfway through the shift at about 3:30 a.m., Colonel Andrews showed up. He saw a cup of coffee on a man's desk, looked straight at all of us as he stood in front of the man, and yelled, "I said no liquids on these desks" (which had been clearly stressed on two occasions since I had been there). Without taking his eyes off of us, or looking down, he swept the cup of coffee and its contents onto the floor. He then proceeded to tell us that this was a war; that the Democrats who ran the license plate bureaus had embezzled money from the plate fees and it was our job to catch them and put them in prison. If liquid were spilled on these (pre-computer-day) registrations, we would not be able to catch these people. He then looked down at the stunned man and said, "Get a mop and bucket and clean this up."

I was assigned a job to put millions, and I mean millions, of documents in order in a warehouse so that at any time we could physically get our hands on any application we needed. Ironically, a good guy from Bellaire, Bruce Massa, held the job before I did. The person who really should have had the job when Bruce left was Trena Duchene. She was a nice person, talented and deserved the position. On day one, she told me honestly that she felt it was not right that I got the job, but she would work with me, and she did.

Eventually my boss, Colonel Andrews, and Rhodes' longtime friend Don Cook got into a huge fight that spilled into the newspapers. Rhodes fired both of them, but Andrews was given a number two job at the Ohio Department of Transportation. The political talk around town was clear: Cook was a longtime Rhodes ally, Andrews was new; Andrews got a lateral promotion, Cook got thrown out. Andrews' money-raising ability had a lot of kick to it.

After the Colonel left, things changed rapidly for me. A job opened up and the new registrar, Dean Dollison, gave it to a man named Frank Stauffer instead of to me. Frank was a nice man, but a Democrat, so I considered myself passed over for the position and realized why—if you were an Andrews man, too bad. Upon hearing about it, the Colonel called me up and offered me a great job at the Ohio Department of Transportation, doubling what I was making. I thought about it. Then, as a young, carefree person would do, I decided to trek off to Iran—by myself—no job—and not enough money for a return ticket.

★ ★ ★

All news broadcasts in 1978 started with the broadcaster saying, "Aryameh shahanshah," the king of kings, light of light—the Shah of Iran. President Jimmy Carter and Rosalynn were spending New Year's Eve of 1977 in Teheran. On January 2, two days later, I was on my way to Iran, leaving from New York. My mom and dad traveled to New York with me to see me off. They felt bad about my leaving, which I could not understand at the time, but now I can. If one of my kids had been going off to a Middle East country by themselves at the age of twenty-four . . .

You might be wondering, "Why Iran?" I had met Vahid Ghobadian (now a famous architect and professor), on an elevator in Harrison House at Ohio State University in Columbus, Ohio. He had a darling little girl with him and I said hello to both of them, having no idea where they were from. From time to time, I would see him and the cute little girl going out of the building. One summer day I got in the elevator carrying a rug scrubber. In order to have my room in the summer, I scrubbed rugs and painted rooms for free rent. Vahid asked me how the "ultra-modern" machine worked. He said he was engineering oriented and was curious. After giving him my limited electrical knowledge of the device, he said that he and his sister were in room 709 and invited me to lunch that day.

At the time I thought Arabs, Persians, and Lebanese were the same people. They all made a guttural sound when they spoke their language, and that was as much as I knew about Iranians. I quickly found out more than I thought I would ever know, and it came to be an integral part of my life.

One of the reasons I felt comfortable with the Iranians is that there was a sizable Lebanese population in Wheeling, West Virginia, and there seemed to be some similarities. I used to eat lamb, kibbee, and Lebanese bread with the Bosolds in Wheeling. Mark Bosold was a friend of mine whose mother, Virginia, was Lebanese. We would visit with Virginia's mother who spoke Arabic and was from the "old country" of Beirut, Lebanon.

The Iranian food Vahid served, the cultural similarities and even his looks made me somehow feel that I was in a comfortable surrounding where I needed to be. Soon, when I moved to another apartment, I became roommates with Vahid and several of his Iranian friends. At that time many universities across America, including Ohio State, enrolled Iranian students by the thousands. Ironically, these students in America became a hot spot of dissent against the Shah. If we were smart today, we would again encourage students from Iran to come and observe our democracy; maybe it would help to do something toward building a democracy in Iran.

Vahid told me that a friend of his had a brother who wanted to come to the United States. I mentioned it at a family dinner and eventually the student, who was about 14 years old, came and lived with my sister. Between knowing this young man and my roommates speaking Farsi exclusively, I rapidly learned Farsi (Persian), the language of Iran.

Something else—in 1976 when I was invited to dinner at the White House as an Ohio Delegate to the Republican National Convention, the Shah of Iran and his entourage were leaving as I was going in. I saw him and was tremendously impressed with his piercing eyes and the stature with which he carried himself. Everything I did, everywhere I went, everything I saw—learning Farsi, my Iranian friends, being in D.C. at the same time as the Shah—pointed in an ominous way to Iran. After returning from that Washington D.C. trip, I soon discovered that my Iranian roommates and friends were no fans of the Shah whatsoever.

After the lack of a promotion at the BMV, I tried to find a teaching job. At that time history teachers were a dime a dozen. It was also August and past the school starting date. Unless a teacher died or was fired, I was out of luck. I expressed my frustration to Vahid and he simply and calmly said, "You speak Farsi, you get along with the Iranians, you can easily teach in Iran, go there."

I sold what little I owned, a used car and some furniture, bought a one-way ticket to Iran and had four hundred dollars in my pocket. I had abandoned the idea of law school, wanted a break from politics, had been soured on the state job I had, and Iran was calling me to one of the biggest adventures of my life—then or since.

Of course, I didn't tell my parents the truth. I told them that I had enough money for a return ticket, had a job and a place to live all awaiting me. Having a place to stay was partially true. I wasn't sure what it would be like, but my friend Masoud Hamounnavard said his family would love to have me stay with them. In those days in Iran (and even privately now to some extent) Americans were liked. Having an American in their homes was prestigious and their children could learn English.

I moved in with the Hamounnavards and started my journey of exploration in Iran. They lived in the wonderful city of Shiraz—a beautiful city known as the City of Flowers. There was a clock in the city made of flowers and it was the "trademark" of Shiraz. It is home to the tombs of Hafez and Saadi, two famous Persian poets. In the city at that time was the original House of the Bab, the leader of the Bahá'i faith, but it was destroyed by Revolutionary Guardsmen after the revolution. However, the most famous site, within twenty minutes of Shiraz, is Persepolis, or Takht-e Jamshid, as the Persians call it. It was the great Library of King Darius that was sacked by Alexander the Great.

I got a job as a translator for a group of British people who ran a pub located up a small street. It was off a large thoroughfare called Ghasrodasht, and across from a type of military barracks. I took them down to the bazaar and translated for them with the *bazaarees*, who then and now run the economy of Iran. These were 700-year-old stone bazaars that wound around the city like tunnels, full of merchants in small shops selling spices, rugs, home goods, food, and just about anything else one would want.

On Wednesdays, the British owners opened their club up to any Brit who was not a member and they could get a drink there. The American club was open to any nationality including the Iranians, but the Iranians and Americans were not welcome to have a drink at the British club. I figured if I couldn't have a drink there, why work for them? My decision to quit was made on Easter Sunday 1978.

The people I worked for rented the fifth floor of Mr. Hamounnavard's house, where I lived. By three in the afternoon on Easter they were in their apartment, loaded, and doing the Bunny Hop to loud music. The chandeliers were shaking and an angry Mr. Hamounnavard and I went upstairs. When the British club managers opened the door it was Easter *booze it up and party* time. Everyone was wearing party hats and about thirty people were snaking around the room in a line, doing the Bunny Hop. Right after the door opened, all the people in the line did a hop, hop, hop, and the chandeliers shook in unison.

They said, "Come on in."

I said, "No thanks, but Mr. Hamounnavard wants the music turned down."

The renter said, "Hey now, it's Easter—you know, that Christian holiday?" (I guess I lost something in the translation or culture, but I thought it had more to do with Jesus than getting loaded and doing the Bunny Hop.) I told him again that it needed to be turned down.

The man looked at me and said, "Isn't this strange? We are in a country of pigs and they do not eat pork."

Whether it was the gin talking or not, I was horrified. Mr. Hamounnavard asked me to translate. I hesitated and started to make something up, but although he could not speak English, he just knew that the guy said something else. I took a breath, translated and watched as Mr. Hamounnavard broke a flowerpot on the floor. That got their attention, as did his throwing their clothes out the window into the alley that led to the club that they owned. When I left Iran, the fifth floor of Mr. Hamounnavard's house was still vacant.

Iran was an amazing country. For a Middle Eastern country, it was quite progressive and developing further. Many women didn't wear the chadors, and they drove cars; worship by Bahá'i, Christians and Jews was very open and public. Iran was a jewel of the Middle East—like the new Beirut after it was out from under the siege—the "Paris of the Middle East."

After abandoning the British job, I took a teaching position at the Iran-America Society in Shiraz, Iran. Mrs. Barbara Hekmat, who was married to an Iranian officer, was the director/principal. There were four of these schools: Teheran, Shiraz, Mashhad and Isfahan. The last director of the main school in Teheran, Katherine Koob, was taken hostage and held at the U.S. Embassy for 444 days. She was one of only two women not released until the end, when all the hostages came back.

The Iran-America Society was a cultural center that promoted friendship between the Iranians and the Americans, and was an extremely popular place. It provided classes in English, which is what I was hired to teach. The classes ranged from levels one through six, and Iranians of all ages were in the classes—not according to ages, but according to their English language skills. Passing the course boosted an Iranian's chances of getting a student visa to the United States. Part of the purpose of the school was to teach American culture. It was a wonderful school—well accepted, well liked, and prestigious. American teachers were called "doctors" and were well paid. The Iranian parents were very exceptionally interactive with us and with their children. Education was a priority for the Shah and for the average parent. At one time Iran had a huge illiteracy rate. The Shah brought about a dramatic drop in that rate.

Change was occurring in Iran—maybe a bit too fast. Couple that with the American policy of human rights at the time, which was one of Jimmy Carter's main initiatives, and change was forced even faster. The Shah had to comply or lose military weaponry from the U.S. He had a fear of Russia, and rightfully so, given what was happening in Afghanistan in 1978, so he complied.

I am not saying that the Shah was to be revered. His secret police force, SAVAK, was trained by our CIA, but then took torture to an entirely different level. Also, in 1953, going against the wishes of the Iranian people, the intelligence agencies of the U.S. and the United Kingdom managed to overthrow the popular Iranian Prime Minister Mohammad Mossadegh, and put the Shah back on the throne. But when one looks at what came later and the heinous fundamentalists that rule Iran today, then maybe our human rights, self-righteous policies forced change a bit too rapidly.

Iran was going through a nervous breakdown of sorts, and I eventually realized that it was falling apart. One day when I asked the students in my class to define intelligence (meaning smart) a student answered, "Oh, your vicious CIA." Just the day before, we teachers had received instructions that if there were any problems in class—comments that didn't seem quite right or were unseemly—we were to avoid any trouble and promptly dismiss the class. I did as instructed and dismissed the class for the day. Riots and protests were escalating and our school was closing. But an incident that scared me beyond belief told me what I needed to know—it was time to go.

Chapter 4

☆ ☆ ☆

GET A JOB!

"When you come to a fork in the road . . . take it."

—YOGI BERRA

My mother had at last convinced my dad to come see me in Iran. I didn't get it at the time, but I now understand a parent's desire to visit his or her child no matter where they might be. In July of 1978, Mom and Dad were on a plane headed to Iran. Trouble broke out at just about the time their plane was airborne. I tried to call them and tell them to forget the trip, but it was too late.

A warning was issued against travel to Teheran from the provincial cities such as Shiraz, where I lived. I was unable to go to Teheran and meet them at the Mehrabad Airport. The family of my friend Homa Zhartofsky from Ohio State lived in Teheran, so I called them and asked for their help. One of Homa's sisters went to the airport and met Mom and Dad by holding a sign that read, Mr. and Mrs. Ney. She then made sure they got on a flight to Shiraz that evening.

There was a 10 p.m. curfew in effect, so I told a cabbie to pick them up at the Shiraz airport. He met them holding a sign. (They must have been sign-weary by this point.) I waited for them at Hamounnavard's residence where I was living. I walked outside the gate of the walled home. It was a decent night, not too hot. I walked about fifty feet, heard a loud smack and a man screaming at the top of his lungs. About twenty-five feet away from me was a soldier holding an automatic weapon—leveled at me. He wasn't moving and he was still screaming. Although

I spoke Farsi, I was so stunned, alarmed, and scared that I froze and could not understand one single word he was saying. A hundred thoughts flashed through my mind: My parents arriving and finding me in a pool of blood; the hills of southeastern Ohio; an American summer day; children I would never have; my sister and her family. It seemed like a week, and even though he was standing before me, I saw only those images in my mind.

Then I just looked at him and he looked at me. I wondered what he was thinking. *Foreigner, terrorist, agitator?* I came to the full realization that I was going to be killed—shot dead there on the street in a foreign country by a person I didn't know. I wanted to say, *I have a family, do you have a family? I am a son, are you a son of someone?* Instead, I said nothing. I closed my eyes and turned around with my hands up, my back to him. I didn't want to see the gunfire coming. I stood for what seemed an eternity. I heard nothing, no words no sounds, no breathing, no screaming . . . absolutely nothing in the Iranian night air.

Then, still holding my hands up in the air, I walked slowly back toward the gate, and with every footstep I thought surely I would hear a shot, feel the pain—praying that the first shot would end it all. I have never been so sure of death, so terrified, since that night. I continued walking slowly until finally I entered the safety of the gate, closed it behind me, stood back against the wall, breathed intensely at first, then slowly, thinking nothing—then I collapsed slowly down to the ground and sat on the soil totally stunned, zombie-like, unable to speak, cry, or move.

Later, when I returned to the U.S., Jimmy Mountain, a trusted, talented, "old time" reporter in Ohio for the Martins Ferry newspaper, the *Times Leader,* captured my story about that night in amazing detail and published it in the local paper. Decades later, that incident in a faraway place remains a vivid memory.

Within a few minutes I heard the taxi outside. I opened the gate and my parents were there, exiting the taxi, the cabbie carrying their bags. They were happy to see me, of course, but they seemed dazed, a bit subdued. They told me that when they arrived at the airport, the taxi drivers started fighting over the Americans. (The Americans paid well and tipped well in Iran.) My driver whisked my parents into his cab, and as they sped down the road, one of the angry cab drivers chased them and played chicken all the way up the Ghasrodasht road to the house.

After Mom and Dad finished relaying the nightmare cab ride I said, "Well, my night topped yours."

We visited some of the sites: shrines, mosques, the Persepolis, but the times grew more and more tense. I recall the shock of seeing the Shah of Iran himself appear on television, actually admitting that there were problems and disturbances in Iran. He said, "I took you from camels to cars, dirt to asphalted highways, illiteracy to education. If you want to let these outside forces and communists control the county, they will ruin it."

From my brush with death and my parents' timely visit, I knew that even though I loved it there, it was time for me to leave. My dad and I had to borrow a phone, and it took hours to get a call through to Pan American Airlines. Eventually we got the first flight out, which was to Istanbul, Turkey. When we arrived at the Mehrabad Airport in Teheran, it was chaotic. Even then, many people were trying to leave Iran and get their money and relatives out, fearing the worst was to come. The deskman at Pan Am said that I didn't have seats. I demanded to see the manager, as I knew from friends that the desk people were selling seats under the table for big money to panic-struck people who wanted to leave. I told the manager, "I am an American and I want my seats." They complied.

Getting our luggage through the crowd was a nightmare. We had to hold it above our heads. I asked a porter to help us. He saw my gold Dunhill lighter, a gift from Adbul Rahman Al Shubaily, the father of my friend Sami Shubaily, who was a student at Ohio State. He and his father were and are good friends of mine. I refused to give the lighter up. It was from a friend and, frankly, a lighter that at that stage of my life I could have never afforded.

Stubbornly, we dragged our luggage through the crowded, chaotic airport. There was tension in the air—people looked as though they were in a panic to leave. Although the revolution had not replaced the Shah of Iran, there was still a sense of urgency on the part of some people to leave the country while they still could.

It was eerie at the end, sitting in a room waiting for our flight. A couple of Iranian men started asking me a lot of questions, but I evaded them for the most part, not knowing who these people were. I suspected that they were the Shah's secret police or the Ayatollah's people; either way, they were not friends. We finally boarded the plane and we sat . . . and sat. The three of us couldn't help but wonder if the revolution had taken place. *Has the airport been taken over?* Those days in Iran, you never knew what was around the corner. (Within six months of that time, the powerful Shah himself was on a plane out of Iran.)

We arrived in Istanbul, and then transferred to Rome. After all the turmoil in Iran and seeing soldiers everywhere, we were looking forward to being able to chill out and relax. However, a few months before our arrival in Rome, the body of Aldo Moro, Italy's prime minister, had been found in the trunk of a car. Security must have still been on heightened alert, because the Leonardo da Vinci Airport had more soldiers walking around with machine guns than Iran did! We stayed at the Excelsior Hotel up from the American Embassy in Rome, had a pleasant few days, and then headed back to the United States. When we arrived back in Bellaire, my dad turned to me and said, "If you move anywhere beyond your home county, we are not visiting you!"

★ ★ ★

I went through a period of culture shock when I returned. Although I was back in my beloved America, I was not used to the order of things. The familiarity of my surroundings was, in a way, extremely boring and unchallenging. Plus, I was unemployed and had absolutely no idea of what I was going to do. My great adventure that was to last at least five years overseas came to an abrupt end at the hand of a 90-year-old cleric living in France.

My answer to *What do I do now?* was to play Backgammon with friends, live with a couple I knew (I had no job, after all), drink beer, contemplate, and find my calling. After six weeks, my *calling* was an elusive phantom and I decided that anything jobwise would be better than what I was doing. A friend from politics suggested that since I was a Rhodes loyalist, I should go see the governor's main man, Roy Martin and seek his help in getting a job. I tried in vain to find a teaching job—that's what my degree was for, that's why I went to Iran, so why not do it here in the U.S.? I searched from Columbus to Shadyside, Ohio, near my home area. In the late 70s a history teacher barely out of college didn't have much of a chance. I followed my friend's advice about contacting Roy Martin, but swore to myself that this would be a state job, not politics. I needed to steer clear of politics.

Off I went to Roy Martin's office. Roy had been Governor Rhodes' right hand man for years. Nothing happened dealing with Rhodes that Roy didn't know about or approve. He was the *hub* of the wheel that drove the entire Rhodes operation. He was far from a warm, touchy-feely political guy, and he was a man of few words. I arrived at my appointment, talked to the secretary, Betty Pappas, whom I knew, and was then taken into Roy Martin's office, which was just outside the governor's personal office. I said, "Hello, Mr. Martin, thanks for seeing me." He said hello and the conversation was then up to me. I told him that I was seeking a job.

He pulled out a state application from his drawer, handed it to me, and said, "On the back it says three references. Fill out one only, James A. Rhodes. Drop it off at DAS [Department of Administrative Services]."

I said, "Thanks." He said nothing.

I said, "Bye." He said nothing.

I did as I was told and met a guy named Web Davis, who seemed not to like me or care that I knew anyone, or care that I needed a job. He said he would call me back. About six weeks passed. I called Web several times and he said nothing was out there.

I went to see a woman I was referred to, Rose Piloseno. Rose had "Valley" connections. Her husband Dan was from my city of Bellaire, Ohio. She said, "Go back and see Roy Martin again." I thought I would rather have a root canal. He made me squirm; he made everyone squirm. Back I went. Roy asked if I had dropped the application off, did I put James A. Rhodes' name down, and who did I talk to? He then asked me to step out. In about five minutes, I was taken back in.

He said, "At two today, go see Phil Hamilton. Good bye."

At 1:30 p.m., I was in the reception area outside Phil Hamilton's office. I was nervous, having been given a directive to see Mr. Hamilton by Roy Martin, one of the most powerful people in Ohio at that time. As a young person, I was wondering what the job would entail, would it pay enough and could I make a career of it. I seemed to think that my entire future hinged on what this meeting with Phil Hamilton would bring— he was the governor's Director of the Department of Administrative Services. He was a big deal; he ran the workings of the state and, most important, the jobs. Phil was a smart, very charismatic man. I was escorted in, and seated in a chair to his left. In front of him in this spacious office at the Rhodes Tower was none other than Web Davis, looking pretty pissed off.

This was 1979 and the first time I had ever seen a computer. Mr. Hamilton was surfing through screens full of jobs listings. As he would come across a job, he would ask Web about it, but there was always a reason why I wasn't hired—not qualified; promised already; not appropriate; not in his field, etc.

Phil turned to Web and talked about me as though I were not in the room. "This man was sent to me and the back of his application says James A. Rhodes. Find a job, create a job, or shit a job, I do not care which, but do it now."

The next day I was presented at the personnel office to Rose Piloseno as the new Appalachian Education Program Manager for Ohio's twenty-eight-county Appalachian area. I was a planner—really made me wish I had studied planning or grants writing in college!

From that day forward, whenever I would meet Web Davis in the hallways he would give me a look that clearly said, "You caused me problems!" We never spoke again and I think he disliked me.

During that self-determined *non-political time*, I did work as a volunteer on the "Kasich for State Senate Committee." It was John's first venture into elective office. (After leaving the Senate in 1983 he was elected to the U.S. House of Representatives. I joined him in 1995 and we shared Licking County —he had part of the county in his Congressional district, and I had the other part in mine. At a party one night I told him that working on his 1978 state senate campaign gave me the stimulus to run. When he looked a bit proud I quipped, "If you could win at that age [26], anyone could!") At this writing he is serving as the Governor of Ohio.

Chapter 5

☆ ☆ ☆

1980–1994

"Life is what happens to you
while you're busy making other plans."

—JOHN LENNON

I was twenty-six years old when I filed in 1980 for Ohio State Representative, Belmont County against the living legend, Wayne L. Hays. I had gotten a job as Safety Director of the City of Bellaire for Mayor Fitch through the efforts of former Sherriff Richard (Dick) Stobbs, and I was into it so completely that I was ignoring the race. My friends made me focus.

I relentlessly went door to door, and volunteers for my campaign did the same. I went to the steel mill gates and entrances to the coal mines during shift changes and stopped at the guard shacks to meet people on duty, sometimes at two, three, and four o'clock in the morning. I knew we were doing well when two weeks before the election I went through the line at Kmart and saw a lady who was wearing my button, "Ney for State Representative." I asked her about it. She looked at me and said, "I don't know who he is but my friend Kathy Wallace speaks well of him." This was the type of campaign you rarely see these days. We had a huge volunteer base.

At first, even though they were supportive, my dad and family said variations of, "Don't be disappointed. It's Wayne Hays. Most likely, you won't win." However, the last two weeks before the election my dad and others were saying, "Wow, it's going to be close, but you might make

27

it." The election was iconic. People marveled at it. We had no money for the campaign and I should not have won. Hays was shocked. Yet he called me on election night to congratulate me—one of the few to do that in my entire political career. He was amazing. The *Washington Post* called me "giant killer." *(Within a few decades, they called me "disgraced.")*

January of 1981 I was sworn in as State Representative for the 99th Ohio House of Representatives—the first Republican elected to that office from Belmont County in 100 years. I was the youngest that year in the legislature and one of the youngest ever elected as of that time. I liked my job. I shared one secretary with three State Representatives and had an office so small I had to move the chair out to close the door.

I sported a moustache due to my young-looking face. I kept it through most of my Ohio Senate years. I looked so young that one day I visited State representative Mike Fox's office when Dave Hobson (then County Commissioner Dave Hobson, later U.S. Congressman Dave Hobson) was there. Mike had ordered coffee from a page, and when I walked in he mistook me for the page and said, "I'll have cream in my coffee." We laughed about that for years. *(It shocked my kids when I shaved my mustache on Halloween of 1992, I believe it was.)*

Lori Hall, my secretary, told me one day that I should meet her roommate. "She just graduated from high school and moved here from Wellsville," which was near my home in the upper Ohio Valley. So I met her. *(And in August of 1983 Candy Taggart became my wife.)*

Things went well in the legislature. At that time in Ohio legislative history, the community and working relationships transcended politics. The legislature was a place where laws were made, in many cases, by cooperation between the two political parties. Friendships were created versus the poisonous attitude prevailing in today's political reality. Art Bowers and Bill Hinig, two Democrat state reps from back home, were good to me. Dan Jones, then a page, who later became my staffer in the Ohio Senate, was also a good friend. You might say we were all growing up together in the House. I made political friends and garnered support at home, but did not have a resounding career in sponsoring laws. The legislature was Democrat-controlled; we were six seats short of taking it over. Ohio State Representative Mike Fox was a great help and stuck his neck out for me. I worked hard at my job, dated my wife-to-be and had fun.

Unfortunately, it ended for me as quickly as it began. I only served two years. In 1982 I was narrowly defeated by Jack Cera in my reelection bid by 126 votes. Cera came out of nowhere. He had been in Florida and moved back to run. His winning the election was as much a surprise as mine had been two years before against Wayne Hays. It was a bad, bad year for Republicans. I had done zero advertising—no television, no radio—nothing. Jack Cera did a good job of campaigning and paying attention to people. I believed that people knew my record, so no need to raise money and spend it. That was the last time I thought like that! Of course later in my life, raising money led to Jack Abramoff.

In January of 1983 I left the Ohio State House of Representatives and took a job for minimum wage in Wheeling, West Virginia, with Amerigard, a security alarms company owned by Dick Crane. I lived in Bellaire with my parents and Candy stayed in Columbus. I had bought a house there after I got elected in 1980. It was a wild ride in those post-Carter days, with interest rates at 14 percent.

Because the election had been so close, I thought I would bide my time for a year and then run again. However, I changed my plans when one day a man at Rigas restaurant in Bellaire said to me, "I know your family . . . great people. I think you did a great job, and the new guy, Cera, I'm angry at him. But I voted against you because I was mad at Republicans. You have to run again."

True to my compulsive nature, I immediately switched to a totally different mindset. I said, "You could have said that you hated me, my family or the way I voted and I would have run again to change your opinion. But when people vote against me because I am Republican, it is the same as someone who is White saying, 'You are a good person, but because you are Black, I don't support you." I then said, "Thanks. I am not running again." He stared at me with a puzzled expression on his face.

Due to hearing this man and other remarks very similar to this, that very week I decided to pursue something else with my boss, Dick Crane. I would go overseas, use my Saudi contacts, create a joint venture—and get rich.

This came about with the help of my Saudi Arabian college friend, Sami Shubaily, who lived in Jeddah, Saudi Arabia. I had been his best man in his wedding to Deborah Akers.

There had been a fire somewhere in Saudi Arabia and overnight, the kingdom posted some new laws, as kingdoms do, about having fire protection and safety systems. In addition, Saudi Arabia, which was virtually crime free, wanted to keep it that way, so even burglar alarms were desired. Sami knew of a friend who had acquired a security/safety license.

I moved to Jeddah in March of 1983 to set up and run the company. It was a new start for me and I was going to make a ton of money. Things were going well in Saudi Arabia. I found it to be very interesting, and was learning Arabic.

I was looking forward to Candy coming over and our starting out new. We had a lot of plans; we would raise kids in Saudi Arabia, and then return to the U.S. when they were in middle school and we would be financially set. I would be out of politics, which was fine from Candy's perspective and mine—so I thought. I was living in a crime-free, alcohol-free environment. (Of course, my friends and I managed to get the bootlegged scotch. I hated Scotch—still do—but the Arabs bought it at 256 dollars a fifth and we bought the one-dollar sandwiches for Thursday night poker at my place.)

I made friends with a great Indian guy, Gulam Ahmed, who still lives there with his family. He made my stay and the business go well. I learned a lot about India from Ahmed, who coined the term, "Mother India."

In August of that same year I returned to the states and married Candy Taggart—two days later I went back to Saudi Arabia. Candy and I made plans for her to come over in 1984.

Late in the fall, just a few months of my returning to Saudi Arabia, State Senator Sam Speck from my home area was made Deputy Assistant of the Federal Emergency Management Agency (FEMA) under President Reagan, and he resigned as an Ohio State Senator. I received calls from several people who urged me to come back for the senate seat that had been opened up. Neil Clark, at that time Chief Operating Officer of the Ohio Senate Republican Caucus, orchestrated the calls to me. I said no.

In December, I needed to renew my visa so I could continue to work in Saudi Arabia. In order to do this I would have to fly to Bahrain. I needed Sami Shubaily's paperwork as my sponsor, so I went to see him. Sami said, "You can stay here and get rich, but you belong in politics."

For someone from another country who is working in Saudi Arabia, it normally takes two or three days of clearance to get out of the country—if all your debts have been paid and everything else is in order. Yet Sami said, "If you want to go, I can have you out of here on a flight tonight."

I said yes, and he did. The only person who knew was Neil Clark, the main staffer for the Senate Republicans—even Candy didn't know I was coming back. She was pregnant, and was so shocked when I walked into the house in Columbus, I thought she might have the baby right then!

The next afternoon I called the senate president's office in order to tell them I was coming to the senate to be screened. The staffer said, "Do we need to arrange a conference call from Saudi Arabia?" I said, "No, I am here in Columbus."

The screening committee was considering someone else, a seasoned state representative. I had lost the previous election, so it only made sense that they would go with someone else. They asked me what I would do if I were not picked. Although some Republicans had told me to answer, "I will still be a team player," I said instead, "Gentlemen, I quit my good job, flew halfway around the world, and have given up a lot of money. No offense, but I will run and I will defeat whoever you appoint—I have nothing to lose."

I was sworn into the Ohio State Senate on January 13, 1984, to replace Senator Sam Speck.

Our son Bobby was born ten days later, on January 23, 1984. Candy, Bobby, and I lived with my mom and dad from January through November of 1984 as I ran for the senate seat. We geared up for a tough race, as the control of the Ohio Senate hinged on the seat I was running for and a couple of other key races. I put together a strong team with Mike Morrison, my sharp Legislative Chief of Staff, and Joel Potts, a local Belmont County man who was a smart and dedicated Campaign Manager. Neil Clark put the pieces together for funding and strategy, and we pushed forward. I won the primary in June, and won the seat in a fierce election against Bob Olexo in November of 1984. The Ohio State Senate went from a Democrat majority of 17–16 to a Republican majority of 18–15.

Richard and Kay Keyser, friends of ours, put their house on the market, and in November of 1984, Candy, Bobby and I moved from Bellaire, Ohio, to Barnesville, Ohio, into their 1885 French empire home. In January of 1985, I was sworn in for my first complete term as an Ohio State Senator.

When Bobby was a year old, I became Chairman of the Senate Local Government Committee. When I took the oath, I was holding Bobby (looking so dapper in his little bow tie), and held his hand up. The picture made national news.

Candy and I settled into Barnesville and started a long process to restore the Victorian house.

Ohio State Senator Buz Lukens became a U.S. Congressman in 1987, and I became Chairman of the Banking and Insurance Committee. This was a powerful committee, as Ohio is big in both banking and insurance.

I won reelection to the Ohio Senate in November 1988.

December 31, 1988, our daughter, Kayla, was born, and we now had a boy and a girl. We had miscarried a couple of pregnancies in between Bobby and Kayla, but now we had the house, two cars, two kids and two dogs. All was well.

In 1990 I became Chairman of the Senate Finance Committee, a very powerful position.

From 1991 to 1992, a foreign exchange student from Sweden, Trita Parsi (now Dr. Parsi), came to live with us. When Candy and I were asked to take in a "Swedish" student and we met him for the first time, he didn't look Swedish. He said he was an Iranian whose family had moved when he was three years old to Sweden from Iran. I told him I lived in Iran in 1978 and I could speak Farsi. He was shocked. Trita was seventeen at the time. Our kids liked him and he became a part of our family. He went to Barnesville High School, and graduated from there. *(He returned to Sweden and eventually came back to the U.S. and worked in my Congressional office on an educational internship. He married a wonderful woman, Amina, and has three children. He formed the National Iranian American Council [NIAC] to educate people about Iranian issues.)*

Candy, Bobby, Kayla and I moved to St. Clairsville, Ohio, in August of 1992. We had our fill of redoing an old house and moved closer to the Ohio River where I was from. We settled into a nice house and had great neighbors. It was utopia. St. Clairsville was a great place to raise kids.

There are a lot of memories from living in that house. I am so fortunate to have the kids that Candy and I have. Bobby was ornery and funny. He called my Capitol office in Washington, D.C., one time, saying that he had to speak to me because it was an emergency. I always left instructions that family was to be put through no matter what. On this occasion, I was meeting with the president of one of the *stans* (Kazakhstan or some other *stan,* as I called them) along with Congressman Dennis Kucinich. I told the president of the country that I had to go, but that Dennis and I would fly over to his country and visit.

I took the call and the "emergency" was that Bobby needed to order bearings for his inline skates and he needed my credit card. To him, that was an emergency. Dennis later got a kick out of why I had to leave to help Bobby out—and my promise that we would fly over to see that president, which we did not do.

Bobby also once called on April Fools' Day and said the house was on fire. I bought it for a minute or so, including the fake sirens in the background. I didn't get mad, because Bobby had a different sense of humor.

Kayla was a mild-mannered child, and although independently minded she was a little less ornery. However, in the first few days after she got her driver's license, I got a call about an hour after she had left the house from a police officer who said he had clocked her at 80-something. He said she was not ticketed, but I told him she should have been. He just wanted me to know. When she got home, I asked how things were and she didn't tell me so I took the keys away for a month. I found out just a few years ago that she had a spare!

Both kids really were great. They put up with a lot of hassle when parents got mad at the way I had voted on something and expressed it through their kids. Nevertheless, they have been strong and have pushed on to build their own lives. Neither one was ever enthused about politics, but I think they appreciated some of the education and advantages it provided.

PART II

☆ ☆ ☆

CONGRESS

*"We could certainly slow the aging process down
if it had to work its way through Congress."*

—WILL ROGERS

Chapter 6

☆ ☆ ☆

NEWT GINGRICH RECRUITMENT PLAN

*"Dream your dreams but be willing to pay the price
to make them come true."*

—LANGSTON HUGHES

It was 1993 and I was an Ohio State Senator. All of a sudden my office became a revolving door of sorts, with people wanting to talk to me. Paul Gilmor, who is now deceased but had at one time been President of the Ohio Senate and at this time was a member of the U.S. House of Representatives, came into my office and said, "You've got to consider running for [United States] Congress." He was a friend of mine, so he wanted me to run; and he wanted a Republican majority in the House after a forty-year dry spell. Paul was a really nice and interesting guy. He gave me reasons why I should run, but mainly focused on the pension system and some of the benefits.

The next guy who came through my door was David Hobson, a sitting member of the U.S. Congress, a former Ohio State Senator and a friend of mine. David talked about the POWER. I could be all-powerful. Everything with David had to do with power and how to use it wisely for constituents. It also paid better than the money I made.

Then John Kasich came through my door. John was also in Congress at the time. He talked about the future generations and how he was going to build the frame for a diverse, balanced budget. He needed support to do that, and my running for the U.S. House of Representatives

36

would be a wonderful thing that we could do to balance this nation's budget—if we could attain a majority in the U.S. House.

So, each came to impart wisdom and give me their reasons to motivate me to run.

Soon after the "courting" by the Members, I went to a college graduation dinner for Greg Petersen, an intern of mine who later became a law student. The party was at Lindy's in German Village, Columbus, Ohio. Bob Bennett, a friend of Greg's family and sitting chairman of the Ohio Republican Party was there. In the course of our conversation that night, Bob said that I should run for U.S. Congress. He said they were going to put a big team together and take back control of the U.S. House. I told Bob that it was never going to happen in my lifetime, that they were never going to take back control and that I wasn't interested. The conversation didn't go any further.

The next day Bob Bennett called me and said, "Look, is it okay if I use your name in a political poll?"

I said, "Sure. If you want to use my name go ahead and do it, but I'm not running." The political gurus who were to analyze the survey were Neil Clark, owner of the powerful NSC lobbying firm in Ohio, and Kurt Steiner, a prominent lobbyist and friend who worked for another Ohio lobbying firm.

Bennett called me with the results. The survey showed that the sitting member of Congress, Doug Applegate, who had been sitting in Congress for eighteen years, was very weak. He had only about 25 percent in strong support (the "I will go to the wall for you and die" kind of support). I then met with Chairman Bennett and the two lobbyists. They were excited about the results and said, "Look at this—you can win this seat!"

I said, "I think I *can* win this seat, but frankly I don't want to run."

Some time passed and I let it be known I wasn't going to run. It was already fall of 1993 and the elections were going to be in 1994. If a person were going to run, it had to be planned immediately. It leaked out that I wouldn't be running and people were gearing up to run because they could smell that 1994 was going to be a big year.

Newt Gingrich was the minority leader in the U.S. House of Representatives and he was what we call a bomb thrower (someone who launches political *grenades* into the process). Chairman Bennett came to me and said, "Look, just do me a favor. I want you to go out and see Newt Gingrich and talk to him."

I said, "Bob, why should I do that? I'm not going to run."

"Because I promised Newt that you would talk to him about this race."

"Well, you will just have to tell him no, because I am not going out to see him."

Bob said. "Just do me a favor—go out, spend ten minutes with the guy and you tell him no."

My thinking was, *How do I fly out there* [Washington, D.C.], *spend ten minutes with him and tell the guy no?* I didn't think that would be too cool, but Bob insisted on it. I finally said that I would go. Bennett said I could take somebody with me and that the Republican Party would pay for nice hotel rooms, any food or drink that I wanted, and dining in any restaurant that I desired.

I said to Dave Distefano, my Ohio budget staffer, "Do you want to go to D.C.?" I described the situation to him. Distefano had wanted me to run for Congress in the worst way for a very long time. I think it was because he viewed it as a pay raise for himself, but he knew I wasn't going to run.

He said, "Sure."

On the plane on our way to D.C., he asked, "What's the plan?"

I said, "I've never met Newt Gingrich. I go in, I spend ten minutes, I tell him no, and then we'll just go out and get loaded."

The next morning, Distefano and I headed to the Capitol. We went into the South House side door and told the Capitol Police officer that I was there to see Congressman Hobson in the Members' Dining Room. We went through a security-screening machine, a wand was swept around our bodies, and our briefcases and pocket contents were x-rayed. *(This would be the last time this would ever happen to me, because when I returned after the election I was "exempted" as a Member of Congress from ever being screened at the Capitol.)* We proceeded on to the House Dining Room to meet Congressman Hobson for breakfast. It was an amazing, ornate room; dark blue walls, wood framing painted white, and a huge brass chandelier hung from the ceiling in the middle of the room. The waiters were dressed in black suits and the ambiance sang out that power ate in these rooms!

Congressman Hobson gave us the background on Newt—what type of leader he was and noted that he was aggressive. We then said good-bye to Congressman Hobson and headed up the elevator to the second floor where the stately House Chamber sits, awaiting the debates that take place there.

I went into the Capitol, and I will never forget it. I was told to go to room 209, which is right behind the floor of the House. It is a secured area for members and designated staff only. The hallways were shining with black and white squares of worn, but gorgeous, marble from the 1870's. The walk to room 209 seemed to be endless, and again I envisioned Abraham Lincoln walking down the same corridor that I was.

We went to room 209 and I knocked on the door. A young woman opened the door, and I could see that it was one room, not very big, and Newt was sitting on the couch. The room was filled with people. There was beautiful Duncan Phyfe furniture surrounded by newly reupholstered Victorian couches and several overstuffed chairs. Two desks, both small, were on each end of the room with what appeared to be staffers, intensely engaged in telephone conversations. The room would have comfortably held maybe three or four people, but there were about ten people in the room working at whatever their assignments happened to be.

I said, "I'm sorry, I thought this was the reception area. Where is the receptionist?"

The young woman said, "There is no receptionist. This is it. Can you please wait for a second?" She shut the door, and I was left standing in the hallway, a bit taken aback.

In the Ohio Senate, I had a very luxurious, spacious, newly redone Victorian style office and conference room. One could open a door and walk out onto the floor of the Finance Committee, which I Chaired. The entire Annex for the Ohio Senate was completely restored and had space for a Legislative Body. (Despite what the majority of the public thinks, most legislatures are "space challenged.") I looked at Distefano and said, "Look at this! What a joke—this guy is the minority leader and look at the type of office he has. This is unreal. This whole thing is ridiculous—they aren't going to win control, this is a pipedream. They aren't organized and their offices are terrible." I repeated what I had said before: "We'll just go in, tell him no, get out of here, and get loaded."

Eventually I was called into the office. I sat down on a large couch with Distefano to my right. Then Newt Gingrich, who had been in another area, joined us and sat on a small chair right next to us. This was the first time I saw Newt in person. I had only seen him on television before this. He had more white hair than I expected, but he had a boyish look to his face. He beamed a pleasant, wide smile and definitely had a charismatic presence about him. His dark blue suit was accompanied by a starched, white shirt and a bright, "political" red tie—the color of tie that seemed to proliferate into every corner of the Capitol. Newt said hello, and before we began talking about why I was there he said, "Let me thank you for something. You took care of a job for my brother in-law."

Distefano looked at me in surprise because I had kept it to myself. I had never told him that I received a call about a year before from David Hobson (U.S. Representative from Ohio) who said, "Look, can you do me a favor? Newt's brother-in-law is up against the wall. He's got three kids and he lives in Columbiana County, Ohio. Can you get the guy a job?" (Newt's brother-in-law was the sibling of Marianne Gingrich, Newt's wife at that time, who was from Columbiana County, Ohio. Marianne had been introduced to Newt by former Member Lyle Williams at a Republican Dinner in the Youngstown, Ohio, area where Newt was the speaker.)

I told him that I would. I really pushed hard on the Highway Department to hire him, and they did. Newt was thanking me for that, which made me feel somewhat important.

I said, "Well, that's no problem—happy to do it. How's he doing?" We talked about that for a short while and then Newt got to the point.

"You know, I'm glad you came out here. You're a seasoned legislator, you're a professional, and I need to chat with you today about something very, very important."

I looked at him and said, "I don't think you are going to win control of the House, but if you do win control of the House, I just don't see how this structure is going to be conducive for me to do anything. Right now I'm Chairman of the Appropriations Committee in the Ohio Senate; I have a lot of political power and ability to get things done; I can snap my fingers and get results for the district; I like what I do; I make decent money, and I will receive a pension sooner if I stay with the state because I now have years invested. I don't understand where this is all going."

Suddenly, Newt started talking. He didn't speak about money or pensions or power. He talked about opportunity for change—how he was going to change the welfare system as we know it; how he was going to empower people; how we would give them a step up instead of a hammock. He talked about how we were going to change the education system to make it functional for children; he talked about families, workers jobs, and he went down this whole list of what we were going to do for the country. He focused on the out of control deficit and the large "bill" we were handing future generations to pay for the "drunken sailor" spending.

He then said, "The country is nearly lost. This is our small window of opportunity, and then it's going to be gone. You have a seat that we technically cannot win; your seat is in a thirteen or fourteen percent Republican index and we can't win it. There are about twenty people like you in this Country with impossible seats for us to win, technically, and if today you tell me yes, that you will be part of this contract with America that we are developing—if you tell me yes, then I only have to find maybe nineteen more people to save America. If you want to be part of that system, I need you—if you tell me no, you may be part of that one missing vote that could have made the change in this small window of opportunity we have for your children and your grandchildren and future generations. It's in your hands."

I looked at him, and in a snap of a second, I said, "I'll run."

Newt said, "Great! I'll be in to help you."

I told him frankly, "I'm not sure I want you in the district. They really don't like you. You're pretty polarizing and I'm not sure that we even want you in, but thank you."

He said, "Okay, I will give you some contact points, and we will help with any amount of resources we can for you."

I said goodbye, we walked out of the office, and I turned to Distefano who looked as though he had seen a ghost. He said, "What the fuck do we do now?"

I said, "We stay to the game plan and we get drunk." And we did. That was the last time I saw Newt Gingrich until I went to Washington in 1994 to be part of the Freshman Orientation.

I felt as though Newt had hypnotized me. He's very charismatic, and when he laid out his vision for me, I would have felt like a traitor if I had said no.

Chapter 7

☆ ☆ ☆

FORTY YEARS
IN THE (POLITICAL)
WILDERNESS ENDS

*"I'm willing to lead, but I'm not willing to preside
over people who are cannibals."*

—NEWT GINGRICH (WHEN HE STEPPED DOWN AS SPEAKER IN 1998)

The election process of 1994 in the United States was amazing. I took on an extremely difficult campaign. It had been fifty-five years since a Republican had won the 18th District of Ohio Congressional seat. It is called a *river seat* because it started up near Steubenville, Ohio, in Jefferson County and ran down the river to Monroe County where my step-grandfather Ricer's family was from. It was a Democrat seat and had only a 13 percent Republican index.

I was running against a tough opponent, Senator Greg DiDonato. He served in the Ohio State Senate and he was the first of two State Senators that I would run against down the road, but this was undoubtedly one of the most difficult campaigns I had to go through for the United States House of Representatives. From day one, it was as though the pistols had been fired and we were off and running—sort of like one of those movies that seems to be one long, fast-paced car chase that never ends. At the same time, I was embroiled in the Pay to Play/Honoraria scandal in Ohio.

According to the dictionary, an honorarium is "a payment for a service (as making a speech) on which custom or propriety forbids a price to be set." In plain English, if you are a lawmaker and you give a speech, whatever money you receive as a "thank you" for that speech, you get to keep. Some would call it bribery, while others would say that's how legislators supplemented their income. Whatever way you looked at it, it was a lucrative way to do business—on both sides.

Let's say that a lobbyist wants a legislator to speak for as special group, and he says something like, "Hey, Bob, come and give a speech for my group—and by the way I'm going to give you five hundred dollars." Practically everyone gave these honorarium speeches—a very nice term, *honorarium*, versus "I think that's touchy money and it doesn't smell good."

Honorarium sounds like it's the honorable thing to do—and it turned out to be considered one of the biggest scandals of the 1990's in the Ohio State House of Representatives. It encompassed members of both the Ohio House and Senate and was given the name "Pay to Play" by the media. The Akron Beacon Journal homed in on it and they had reporters assigned full time to this thing—Andy Zajac and later, John Craig.

The rules in those days in the State House were very unclear. Basically, you could accept dinners, trips and so forth, and you didn't have to file anything. It was wide open and rules and regulations were laid by the wayside.

There were two powerful Ohio lobbyists, Neil Clark and Paul Tipps. Neil Clark was a former staffer for Republican Ohio State Senator Stan Aronoff and, essentially, for the Ohio Senate Republicans. *(Stan Aronoff is a charming, classy man who had a long political history in Ohio. Known as a power broker in Ohio politics, he was a wonderful mentor to me. Through Stan's guidance, I quickly rose to prominent positions that helped me gain momentum for the U.S. Congressional race.)*

Neil Clark was the guy who single-handedly changed the majority in 1984 from a 17/16 Democratic majority in the Senate to an 18/15 Republican majority. (Neil was such a "junk yard dog," as I would say when I was in politics, that when his apartment burned down while the campaigns were under way, he never even went up there—he sent some pages to get the remainder of items that were salvageable and had them brought down to him—that's how focused he was. He had only one site in his scope; to win control—and he did.) As a result of Neil Clark's wresting control from the Democrats, the Ohio Senate went Republican, which made it the only Republican entity in the state. The governor at the time, Dick Celeste, was a Democrat, every statewide office holder was Democrat, and it was a Democratic House.

By the time we were into the mid-90s the entire state was going Republican, all because of the Ohio Senate and, in no small part, thanks to the efforts of Neil Clark who had become a very powerful lobbyist. Paul Tipps was the former Chairman of the Democratic Party and Neil Clark was almost like a son to Republican Senator Aronoff (one of the most powerful men in Ohio Government at the time). They were long-time power players and had both sides covered. Tipps and Clark ran a successful, powerful, lobby shop together, and these two were never far from the big issues.

Dinners were held at Paul Tipps' house. For going to those dinners and giving a brief speech, honorariums were given to legislators. It got the attention of high-profile newspapers, and they began to look into it. I got caught up in it, as did Senator Aronoff, Vern Riffe (Democrat, Ohio State Speaker of the House), and former Ohio State Representative Paul Jones (who has now done some federal prison time for other issues).

I was spared of any charges. When I ran for Congress in 1994, I was required to file ALL honoraria at the Congressional filing, so I had done that. However, at the Ohio forums I didn't file all of them because instructions stated that you would file ONLY if they came from the same entity and were for an amount above 500 dollars. I did not consider them from the same source so I didn't file all of them. If I had not been running for U.S. Congress and had been required to file all of them on federal forms, I most likely would have had to take the misdemeanor plea like the rest of the legislators.

I was pressured to plea, but my attorney, Rocky Saxbe, and I made the decision not to plead anything. The hotshot special prosecutor came after all of us. He wanted to make a big name for himself because he wanted to run for judge. (He did run later and lost.) Before my interview with him, my attorney told me not to talk too much. He said, "You guys are politicians and they like for you to talk, but just answer yes or no."

The prosecutor grilled me about the Blue Cross honoraria. I had received 500 dollars from the Blue Cross attorney, 500 dollars from the Blue Cross Insurance Company and 500 dollars from Clark and Tipps, which fit the criterion—only honorariums over 500 dollars from any one source had to be filed. He argued that I should have filed all of those as one because they were all from Blue Cross. I argued that they were from three separate entities.

I was offered the same plea and fine as the others—two hundred and fifty dollars for a reporting error—almost like a parking ticket, a minor misdemeanor. I refused.

The grand jury was convened while the U.S. Congress was in session. Concerning my appearing, and as a ploy to save face (his), the prosecutor called my attorney and said, "Since he's in Congress now, we can't compel him on a misdemeanor to come to the grand jury." I wasn't about to let him get by with that, so I called the prosecutor and said, "Convene a grand jury on Saturday and I will be there."

My attorney was furious with me, but I was more than antagonistic with the prosecution because they had spent thousands of dollars, backed themselves off the diving board, and at the end got nothing of any value or substance on anyone for the money they spent. Because the special prosecutor wanted to be a judge, that drove the investigation more than any legal violations.

No action was continued against me—it was all dropped. Yet that cloud was hanging over our heads and my fierce opponent, Greg DiDonato, used it to the hilt—it was a nonstop barrage.

We started putting our team together for the campaign. I heard of Glen Bolger of Public Opinion Strategies. He was a tremendous pollster who eventually did the polling for George W. Bush. I also added the first consultants, Neil Clark and Kurt Steiner. I went internally for the campaign manager.

About two years prior to my 1994 run, I had hired Dave Heil as my Legislative Assistant in the Ohio Senate. It's interesting how that came about. Hang with me as I digress:

Dave Heil was working for Clarence Miller, a Republican U.S. Representative from Ohio's 10th District. We were redistricting at the time. Ohio had lost population and two of the U.S. Representatives were going to have to go.

Vern Riffe, a Democrat who was a very fair but tough Speaker of the Ohio State House of Representatives said, "Look, we have to get rid of two people because Ohio has lost population, so you Republicans get rid of one and I, as a Democrat, will get rid of the other."

I knew that Clarence Miller had been targeted because I had been privy to some private conversations. This is how one of them went down:

The President Pro Tempore of the Senate, Richard Finan from Cincinnati, had asked how they should proceed. Someone piped up and said, "Well, John Boehner has the least seniority. He's the newest member, so we get rid of the person that has the least seniority on the Republican side." [Boehner was an Ohio State Representative at the time and ran against Buz Lukens, who was involved in a sex scandal, but refused to resign his seat. In 1990, Buz lost the Republican primary race to John Boehner.]

State Senator Dave Hobson [later became U.S. Representative from Ohio's 7th District] said, "Wait a minute. No, no, no, we can't do that," although Dave was not wanting his involvement to be publicly known. He liked to make the bullets, not be the one who pulled the trigger—he liked to keep his hands clean. He had multiple faces and he probably told Boehner that he was protecting Boehner, and told Clarence Miller that he was protecting Clarence.

They decided to get rid of the oldest in seniority, who was Clarence Miller. Having served in the U.S. House since 1967, he was the dean of the delegation. But Clarence had never, played ball; he never supported people [including me in my election for the Ohio State Senate, until the final week]. Clarence was an old time politician. He did not like controversy and was concerned first about Clarence Miller and his own reelection. I am not saying that he wasn't a good man and certainly not trying to indicate that other Members are selfless and not "reelection" paranoid, it's just that Clarence took it to new heights. He always operated that way—with many candidates and with the Republican Party in general. He was a good Republican and had a great voting record, but never played the modern day political money-giving game.

In my own situation, in a critical election for the Senate seat when having a Republican State Senator should have been on Congressman Miller's agenda, it simply was not. He would speak to me at events and was cordial, but no campaign contributions were forthcoming and he waited until the very last moment to endorse me—when it was too late for us to utilize it. This was his style, which finally came back to bite him. Although looking back, it was refreshing to see a Member who wasn't a political money-raising machine.)

Back to Dave Heil: I had observed Dave at a couple of county fairs down in the district. I then saw him and his wife, Monica, at a Lincoln Day Dinner in Morgan County. I talked with Dave and he was very impressive. He and his wife were both nice people. After the dinner that night I said, "Dave, have you ever thought about working for the State Senate."

He looked at me, rather puzzled, and he said, "No, I work for Congressman Clarence Miller." I told him that maybe he ought to work for the Senate, and he said he would be up to see me the next day.

Dave Heil came to Columbus the next evening, and a staffer and I took him out to eat at Mario's Restaurant across from the State House. I knew that Dave had brought Clarence Miller up before this to meet with Stan Aronoff, and that Clarence had brought a five thousand dollar-campaign contribution check for the Senate Republican Caucus, but it was a little too late. I was honest with Dave that evening and I said to him, "Look, Clarence is not going to survive this and they are going to get rid of him. You ought to come with me."

Within two weeks, Dave Heil came to work for me as my Legislative Assistant. Prior to his running for City Council in a tough race in Lancaster, Ohio, Dave came to me and said, "Are you running for Congress?"

This was 1993 and I said, "No, I am not going to run for Congress."

He said, "Okay, because I don't want to battle for this council seat if I have to give it up."

I said, "No, no, you're safe. Go ahead and run because I'm not going to Congress." *(Dave Heil actually won the race, but later when my plans changed, Dave Heil's plans changed too and he became my Campaign Manager.)*

Dave Distefano, who did the budget for me in the Ohio Senate, was my finance man for the campaign, Dave Heil became the campaign field manager and Mike Carey, who started as a page and then worked for me as a legislative staffer, became the campaign guru. Mike is a brilliant political guy. After the election he became my District Office Director, and later on went to work for the Ohio Coal Association. We had our team together, but soon into the process we realized that we couldn't afford additional consultants. Although Neil Clark and Kurt Steiner were the best in the business, we just couldn't afford them—we couldn't raise enough money. They continued to help on the election, however, at no cost to us in an as-needed advisory role. We put together a grassroots campaign, and it was masterfully done. We broke the district into three parts with four counties per part. Each person functioned as their own Campaign Manager. Dave Heil oversaw the field reps.

(As the campaign got underway and throughout the election process, I believe that Distefano wanted Dave Heil out of the way. However, he just said that Heil wasn't doing his job; that he was too lazy; that we were wasting money with him and needed to send him back to the State Senate office or get rid of him. There was no way I was going to fire Dave Heil, so upon Distefano's

urging I talked him into going back up to the Senate. I told him I needed some-
one to run the office up there, which was partially true, but it was because of
Dave Distefano's urging that I took Dave Heil out of the campaign manager's
slot and Mike Carey became the fulltime Campaign Manager. I am now con-
vinced Distefano did that to get Heil completely out of the way so he could lock
up Chief of Staff if I won the election, and that Dave Distefano's motives were
entirely self-serving.)

We had garnered the support of so many people. One "average man"
(non-politico), a Democrat who was not only influential, but gave me
tremendous personal and political guidance was Earl Cramblett. He ran
his own BP Gas Station in Steubenville, Ohio. Jefferson County/Steuben-
ville is overwhelmingly democrat. We did so well there it was tough for
a democrat to defeat me in the rest of the region.

We went through the campaign process, designed the perfect grass
roots effort, hit it hard, developed a huge mass of volunteers—and so
did DiDonato. It was a slugfest; if we weren't at an event, we had a
representative there; if DiDonato wasn't at an event, he had a representative there. We went into debates. DiDonato ran some very nasty commercials—*if you wanted to talk to Bob Ney, you had to pay his staffers, who*
were lobbyists. It was all based on ethics, which, ironically, is what I went
down for later on in Congress. My personal belief was that we could not
run negative ads, and for six weeks I would not counter DiDonato's negative ads. Then Glen Bolger, my pollster from Public Opinion Strategies,
called me up and Dave Distefano, Mike Carey, and I met with him. Bolger
said point blank, "You are going to lose—you are tanking. DiDonato's
ripping you apart. If you do not respond, and we have responded with
a *nice* ad, but if you do not respond hard-hitting, you're done."

We got with our media consultants and put together an ad that, honestly, made me shiver. It seems that my opponent, Senator DiDonato,
had a roommate who was a lobbyist, of all things, so as he was yelling
at us, he was having a rent situation with the lobbyist. You can read
between the lines that maybe he wasn't paying the full rent . . . the lobbyist owned the place . . . blah, blah, blah. The situation was on the up
and up and the lobbyist was a great guy, but in the world of politics,
ethically, it made him look bad. We ran the ad, which turned the campaign into an even bigger slugfest. It got very, very nasty and at the end
of the last two weeks we were going at it. We were calling him filthy, he
was calling us filthy—so I changed tactics and I started asking Greg
DiDonato to meet me and we would sign a clean campaign pledge. He

avoided me, because DiDonato knew what I knew; we had to keep running the dirty ads—that's just the way it is. People say, "I hate those dirty ads!" But guess what? They really work. I actually started following him to events to try to get him to sign it for publicity purposes, and he would either not be at the event or make sure he wasn't near where I was.

Election Day finally came. This was major—the big leagues—the United States House of Representatives. When I woke that morning, I felt as if I were in a dream; not really running for election, but that the last year of constant work and pressure was just a dream. My feelings were mixed. There was wanting something so badly, putting full effort into it and feeling somewhat confident, but there was also knowing that this could go the other way—against me.

I decided to live in the moment, enjoy the day, and for sure keep busy to avoid Election Day jitters. I sat for a while with my family, then Candy and the kids went about their normal routine and I headed out to stand near some election voting sites to say hello and ask for some last minute votes. Most of the voters I saw that day seemed friendly.

I headed home, ate a light meal with Candy, Mom, and Dad, took a shower, and prepared to head to the Sheraton Inn, where we would all be when the results came in.

Early in the evening I felt that we were on solid ground for a win, but I still had butterflies. As the early returns came in and I saw that my very Democratic home county, Belmont, had held for me and that we were doing remarkably well for a Republican in overwhelmingly Democratic Jefferson County (Steubenville, Ohio), I knew that the election was headed our way. My parents, my wife, Candy, my kids, Bobby and Kayla, my entire extended family, friends, campaign staff, and supporters packed the Sheraton Inn Ballroom in St. Clairsville, Ohio. I entered the ballroom to music, chanting, tears, whistling, and smiles. We had a huge celebration. The excitement and happiness surrounding all of us was overwhelming. I gave an upbeat speech and the dancing, mingling, and laughter continued well into the morning hours.

The people of Ohio's 18th District had elected the first Republican Congressman in over fifty-five years—yours truly.

Chapter 8

☆ ☆ ☆

THERE'S A NEW KID
IN TOWN

"Either you set your goals and, in doing so,
have your life governed by choice or you do nothing
and have your life governed by chance."

—ROBIN SHARMA

I can remember driving back home in my car after the 1994 victory party at the Sheraton, where I held all my victory parties. We lived within about six miles from there. My wife, Candy, and the kids had left ahead of me. As I drove, Mike Carey, my Campaign Manager, looked at me and said, "You just got a pay raise." I asked him what he meant and he said, "You're going to make one hundred thirty-two thousand dollars." And then it struck me—I was going to make $132,000 a year! (Although I knew I would be making more money even before meeting Newt Gingrich and deciding to run, the money had simply never been a factor in my decision to run for Congress. In fact, it would cost me, because had I remained in the State Senate I would have collected about 75% of around $66,000 per year, payable starting in 1998 for the rest of my life.)

We were so delighted—I remember the thrill of being part of the Newt Gingrich Congress, as we called it: Contract with America. (I never went to the Contract with America signing—Neil Volz, my former Chief of Staff, recalls in his book that I did, but actually, I didn't. Dave Distefano, Mike Carey, and I made a decision never to go out and be part of that Contract with America photo op. We were running our own show.

Although I supported the philosophy of the contract with America, my overwhelming Democratic District had other issues of concern and we did not want to "nationalize" the election by focusing on the D.C.-generated Republican Contract. We were running as a Republican, but an independent voice, and Contract with America wasn't part of our gig. Although, after being elected, I supported every aspect of the Contract with my votes.

In the days following the election, the calls poured in. Tom DeLay was running for House Majority Whip, and he called to ask me for a vote. It was a three-way race among Bob Walker, DeLay, and Bill McCollum. Each of them had come in and campaigned for me. DeLay came to Newark, Ohio, and said, "I'm happy to be in Newark, New Jersey." It created a few laughs. Gingrich was unopposed for speaker, but I still got the phone calls on the contested races.

The big race was Tom DeLay's for Majority Whip and I committed to DeLay early, without any direct response or reciprocity from him for anything. Early on, I was asked to be one of his thirteen deputy whips. That was a big deal. I was officially part of the "leadership."

Within days I had to be in D.C. for the freshman orientation. I was allowed to bring one potential staffer with me. Our rooms would be paid for at the Hyatt on Capitol Hill. I took Distefano with me—he had asked to go, of course. He asked me point blank to be my chief of staff—something that should not be done. Nor was I to commit to anyone before the election. Once he got Dave Heil out of the way, he made it very clear that he wanted to be my chief of staff and I told him he could be. Therefore, with a wink and a nod before the election, Dave Distefano became the Chief of Staff.

From day one, Distefano and I were in conflict. The first agenda he promoted when he moved to D.C. was to hire his sister, Paula. He wanted Paula hired for the District Office. I had tried to get Paula a job before, during the 1994 election year. I contacted Chet Kalis who was Director of Human Services (we called it Welfare at the time) for Belmont County, my home county. Chet had run the Bob Olexo State Senate election against me, but we were friends and neighbors so I asked Chet about Paula. She took the test and flunked simple, basic math three times.

Again, Distefano wanted me to do something—call Human Services for Paula. We had a bad argument. I essentially said, "Dave, you know she can't pass simple math."

His response to that was, "What? Are you calling her stupid?"

All my calls in the world to Chet weren't going to make up the difference. Chet made it clear, and rightfully so, that if she couldn't pass simple math they couldn't hire her.

Then Distefano started on, "She would be good in your District Office, as your scheduler." Finally I yielded and agreed to hire her as my scheduler and she did a superior job in that position. Thus, Paula was the second person hired. This wasn't about Distefano looking out for his sister—this was Distefano making sure that he took care of Distefano. (Much more on Dave Distefano later in the book.)

We went through the freshman orientation, and even though I was excited, I was a bit on the depressed side. I think this probably happens to a lot of people who win—there is a letdown of sorts. Yes, you're excited about serving, but now you are looking at all the responsibility. Running through my mind also was that I had a young family and if I needed to get home quickly, it was a five-hour drive, not the hour and a half commute from Columbus.

Congress was definitely the big-time. This wasn't a little local race—there was national attention, national focus. Everyone was interested in how I won the seat. Requests were coming in for special interviews. I, like many of the new "Contract with America class," had interview requests from the *New York Times,* the *Washington Post,* CNN, magazines, and so forth. The media was very focused on what my goals were, what I thought of Newt, how it felt to win an overwhelmingly Democratic seat, my plans and what committees I wanted, just to name a few of the endless topics I was quizzed about. The interviews and freshmen orientation kept us busy and Distefano and I were hitting it pretty hard. We spent the three or four days we were in D.C. at freshman orientation all day long, and then we hit the drinking sites at night.

Distefano hooked up one night with some girl in a bar and came in the next morning ten minutes before we were to go to the Capitol, looking like hell. I didn't think he was going to make it. We went to the orientation and I must say he did a good job. He set up computer services and started hiring people. Barry Jackson, John Boehner's Chief of Staff, was fond of Dave and guided him, making sure that he was taken care of and had the right information. We were the first to file our computer items, and line up committees. Through Barry Jackson's help we were way ahead of the curve, which enabled us to get up and running, *boots on the ground,* early.

The Democrats went after me furiously the day after the 1994 election—I had taken what they considered a "for sure" Democratic seat. They targeted my seat, meaning that they would start raising money and aggressively search for the right candidate to run against me. They would talk to special interest groups they were close with in order to encourage them, even before the election, to run TV and Radio spots disparaging me. Being "targeted," means just that—you walk around with a *bull's eye* on the back of your business suit. We needed to be organized and prepared immediately—we couldn't afford any delay in responding to our constituents

I recall that in February 1995, one month after being sworn in as brand-new freshmen Members, Frank Cremeans, Republican from southern Ohio, and I were on the elevator when Democrat Dick Gephardt, House Minority Leader, got on the elevator and said, "Hello, Frank. Hi, Bob." When he got off the elevator, Frank turned to me and said, "Wow, we are pretty powerful already—all these new Members here and he knows us!"

I said, "Frank, he knows us because we are on his target list for extinction next election!" (Frank lost his next bid to Ted Strickland, a Democrat, who later became Governor of Ohio. Frank passed away in 2003 of respiratory disease.)

The Ways and Means Committee is a very powerful committee where all the money is raised, and that's what we wanted. Distefano and I had to meet with Congressman Tom Bliley (R-Virginia), who was to be chairman. He was a crafty old guy—one of the old bulls who had been around a long, long time. He had been a mortician, so I think he probably paid attention to details, like clothes and such. When we met with him, I talked about what a professional I was, about how I knew the ropes and I knew what was going on. As we were leaving his office I noticed that Distefano was getting a little squirmy. When we got out into the hallway, he just burst out laughing. For some unknown reason, I was wearing a jacket to one suit, but the pants to another. I was into my "I'm a professional speech" when Distefano noticed that my clothes didn't match. Now I don't know if that was what cost me the Ways and Means seat—I doubt it—but it had to have given Congressman Bliley a good chuckle about the brand new freshman who didn't even know how to dress himself!

Chapter 9

☆ ☆ ☆

GROUNDHOG DAY 1996

"The trouble with the rat race is that even if you win,
you're still a rat."

—LILY TOMLIN

One of my favorite movies is *Groundhog Day* in which Bill Murray's character awakes every morning in Punxsutawney, Pennsylvania, and no matter what he does, the same day occurs over and over. I felt like the year 1996 and the daily fight to survive was casting me in the Bill Murray character role.

The 1996 election was hell on earth—it was a bad year for Republicans due to a midterm election [near the mid-point of the presidential term], I had a "junk yard dog" opponent, and on a difficult, personal note, Candy and I divorced. I take the blame and view divorce as a failure, but throughout that painful time we worked together to be sure the kids knew they had two parents who loved them.

The divorce was in the early part of my first reelection. I went to Sonny Bono to talk to him about it and seek advice, as I trusted him. Sonny and I were both freshmen Congressmen in 1995 and had become good friends. I also told Newt Gingrich. Dave Hobson, U.S. Congressman from Ohio's 7th District, found out and he didn't want me to file the divorce until after the filing deadline. I decided to go contrary to that and announce that I was getting divorced before I actually filed and before the closing of the filing deadline. My theory, which prevailed, was this: If I didn't make it public before the filing deadline closed, and then

54

within days afterward I announced that a pre-planned divorce was in process, it could and should be used against me for the general election. I figured that if some Republican thought the divorce was enough to take me out, let them file—or as George W. Bush would later say, "Bring it on."

The divorce itself went smoothly. We shared the same attorney and with two Sunday sit-downs at the house, it was all concluded. Thirteen years dissolved in about eight hours on two different days. Candy made up a complete and fair list, and all personal goods were split. However, one strange situation happened at the end.

We were to go to the Belmont County Courthouse to meet our attorney Frank Fregiato (later, Judge Frank Fregiato). He and his wife, Cynthia, were longtime friends of ours. We were in the law library on the third floor, waiting to enter Judge Knapp's office to finalize the agreed-to dissolution. It was a sad moment. Candy and I were both a bit numb, and felt like the air had been knocked out of us. The differences we had had with each other were over, and we were ready.

Frank explained the procedure. We had kept everything under wraps, and although Judge Knapp was a Democrat, he could be trusted to keep this to himself. When we had first walked into the law library, the building was empty, but when Frank opened the door to go to the judge's office, he came right back in and said the hallway was packed full of reporters. Candy and I took a breath, then walked out to face the onslaught. As we walked toward the press battalion, I saw Brenda Danehart, a television reporter from WTRF. She said hello and asked me how I was doing. I warily responded that I was fine, waiting for her to ask the divorce question. As I looked around, a couple of reporters waved but no one was gathering around us. Brenda said she was waiting on the arraignment of a young man for killing his parents. It suddenly struck me; they weren't here for us—they were here about the murder of my dad's mailman. His son had murdered him and his wife. Dad's mailman was decapitated and his head had been placed in a bowl on the family's dining room table. It was a high-profile, grizzly murder that had the entire local press corps out in force that morning.

We were relieved, and just kept walking into the judge's private office. As the judge asked us if this is what we wanted, and if we were sure, we simply responded that it was over. Then Judge Knapp looked at me, and with a slight grin on his face said that the House Democratic Campaign Committee had called him the day before. They had heard that we were getting a divorce and they wanted a copy of the divorce right away. He said he didn't respond to them, but would send a copy today. He then said, "It's a pretty boring divorce."

Although it was civil, boring, and contained nothing derogatory toward either one of us, it made no difference in the world of politics. The rumors abounded. Candy and I had each heard several varieties of rumors about both of us. The best one (or worst one, depending on how you viewed it), was the Sonny Bono rumor. When Sonny and I were in our first terms as U.S. Representatives, we became close friends. Sonny had come to the Valley for my fundraiser, and I got divorced soon after that. The rumor was that he arrived in Belmont County and stayed overnight at our house (which he did not—the government shut down during that time and we had to fly right back to D.C.). Version number one was that Candy caught Sonny and me in our house in bed with a prostitute. Version number two was that she caught just Sonny and me in our bed. I liked version one better. However, if I were running in a more liberal area, version two would have been the one we promoted.

I even had a call from Dick Farrell of the New Philadelphia Times wanting a statement from me to "squash" the rumor about me and Sonny and the prostitute. I refused to comment. As I told Dick, it would be like trying to answer the old question, "Do you still beat your wife?" I tracked the rumor to an official within the Democratic Party from the nearby village of Shadyside. He was a longtime operative known for vicious political campaigning.

There were other rumors abounding about a war between the two of us—that we were in a full-fledged battle similar to the couple portrayed by Michael Douglas and Kathleen Turner in the movie *War of the Roses*.

One Ohio newspaper, the *Zanesville Times Recorder*, actually said the divorce should be an issue in my campaign. There was also a disturbing incident with the Christian Coalition that says more about its "politics" than its "Christianity." I had called Chuck Cunningham, who at that time was with the Christian Coalition (and later with the National Rifle Association). My opponent, Ohio Senator Burch, was breathing down my neck in a tough election and I asked Chuck for help. I was at a 100 percent rating with the Christian Coalition and Burch was under 50 percent. (The Christian Coalition rates politicians and candidates on their records concerning "pro-family" issues.) Chuck had me call the local Coshocton, Ohio, Christian Coalition representative for the district. When I called the guy for help, he asked me why I was divorced, what happened, and had Candy and I repented. He then wrapped it up by—not offering help, of course—but by sending me a book about remarrying your spouse. When it arrived, I swiftly *filed* it in the wastebasket. I said a prayer for the guy personally and moved on in an attempt to win the election.

Eventually we were able to focus on the issues of the campaign.

After coming off a relentless campaign with Senator DiDonato of New Philadelphia, Ohio, in 1994—the Newt Gingrich contract year and my first U.S. Congressional election—I naively thought that 1996 wouldn't be as bad. Senator Rob Burch, a Democrat and a friend of mine while we served in the Ohio State Senate, was out front to run against me. While in the Senate together, we spent many a night in Columbus hanging out at Zeno's bar and a bar called Club 185. It was a "union" Democrat bar and I frequented it a lot with Burch and union friends.

Burch had run for governor mid-term of his Senate seat. He produced a disastrous result for the Ohio Democrat Party by getting only 25 percent of the vote against incumbent Governor George Voinovich (later Ohio U.S. Senator Voinovich). If a political party's candidate gets less than 25 percent of the vote in Ohio's gubernatorial race, it is possible that the party can be invalidated for four years.

We felt confident that due to his dismal performance and his clear-cut, partisan thinking that Democrat was good, Republican was bad (there were a lot of Independents in the district) he would be someone to watch, but not the toughest candidate.

This was our thinking nine months before the election, but as deceased British politician and Prime Minister Harold Wilson said, "A week is a long time in politics." By the end of October, we were mid-term (presidential term) and hanging on for dear life.

I had been caught on tape saying Hillary Clinton, First Lady at the time, had big hips (didn't help with the female vote). I had received a phone call from someone saying that they were working for a teen Republican magazine and wanted to ask questions about politics and about being a Member of the Contract with America class. The caller went on to ask if I could say something personal about Hillary Clinton. I said that what I could say could not be printed in a magazine, and then went on to say it—about her hips. This turned out to be a setup to get several Members to say derogatory things about Hillary by a group that loved to "punk" or set up new Members. When Kathy Rizzo with Associated Press at the time called about it, I tried to bounce around the issue as I had done with other news outlets until she said, "I heard the tape." I then gave her the interview and started my apologies. I sent flowers to the White House and could kick myself for being so stupid. By the way, I really like Hillary Clinton!

As if that weren't enough, my opponent, Burch, was well financed and was a political "Pit Bull." The stars were aligning and it looked like a supernova was coming my way.

The national media was beyond focused on our race, as it was the "contract with America" class reelection. This would be the test of how Newt's time as Speaker of the House would hold up. Television ads heavily funded by unions and left-wing groups were *morphing* people into Newt. Even the teachers union turned on me. In one of the worst districts in America for a Republican (13 percent), I had never denied Newt. At every event and every opportunity, Burch relentlessly pointed at me and said, "He is Newt Gingrich, out to take away your Social Security." I finally started debates with Burch by saying, "Senator Burch, I am Bob Ney. If you want to run against Newt, move to Georgia."

The race was an hour-by-hour, knuckle-biter for months—an aggressive, back and forth race between Senator Burch and me. Neither of us held back any political punches and we were not civil to each other. It was an aggressive match between two very aggressive contenders that was too close to call, and we both knew it.

By election night we were limping to the victory post. In St. Clairsville, Ohio, upstairs at the Hampton Inn, I sat with Mike Carey, my Campaign Manager; Dave Distefano, my Chief of Staff; Neil Volz, my Press Secretary; my cousin John Ney; and a few selected campaign staff. Downstairs were about 500 people—family and friends. Also on hand was Howard Monroe, a local long-time TV host and, in my opinion, a political expert with great analytical capabilities. At one point, local television channels were reporting that we were finished, but I think Howard sensed that it was a close race before we did.

Kathy Rizzo of *Associated Press* called me in our control room at around one a.m. Even with that acknowledgement from a seasoned reporter such as Kathy, I was still hesitant to claim victory. I went downstairs to a tired, scared crowd, but we all limped together into a 5,000-vote margin of victory. The next day Burch made his reelection announcement that he was right back at it from day one—onward to 1998. In his mind, he needed only 5,001 more votes.

Chapter 10

☆ ☆ ☆

HERE WE GO AGAIN

"When a scorpion stings without mercy,
you kill it without mercy."

—ASHANTI PROVERB, GHANA, AFRICA

We came into Congress 1997 on crutches. Nevertheless, Senator Burch, true to his word, didn't miss a beat and came right back at us. Everything went into high gear in an atmosphere of paranoia, thinking that Washington held the key to reelection. The campaign staff in Ohio was dissolved and the D.C. staff took over by focusing on our voting record and what we did in D.C. I told Distefano that this could not be a good way to operate.

Soon, the instincts that had gotten me that far kicked in and moved me to decide to get a new campaign manager before May of 1999 or we would have a repeat, or worse, of 1998. We put the word out and received about eighty résumés for the position of campaign manager. Of those, sixty were weeded out and the remaining twenty were scrutinized and whittled down to ten. Distefano and I, with the assistance of Mike Carey (who had moved on to become a candidate for another office at this time), reviewed those ten carefully. Calls were made and through those phone conversations, we narrowed it to three. At that juncture, Distefano and I met with all three outside of the Capitol. They were all superior candidates with previous campaign experience. One stood out to me and that was Corey Lewandowski. He met us for dinner and we spent hours going over the campaigns, what we expected, what he thought, and strategies. We talked about relentless work hours, additional staff, and the salary. There were some things about Corey that stood out. He had a heavy, and I mean heavy, Massachusetts accent. We thought this could be a downer, as our Appalachian constituents could be pretty unaccepting of "foreigners" or someone that is not "one of us." However, Corey's style, charm, humor, and his ability to handle a beer and discuss any subject allowed him to fit into our area despite the lack of a "twang" in his voice.

It's strange how small details can make the difference. It was tough to choose among the three candidates, but at some point during the dinner with Corey I looked down and saw a small fray on the cuff of his white shirt. This was a working man, not a guy from money. He also said, "Let me make it clear; I am not some weak-kneed guy. I can take one for the team." We appreciated this well-used saying in politics that one will do whatever is needed to win. Corey was well liked by our inner circles. He rebuilt the campaign volunteer base that we had not used in a while, and pushed the newly hired additional staff. He was a bull in a china shop at times, irritating our traditional D.C. staff—including a few of our top brass in the office, but he got the job done.

Meanwhile, Burch made news every week by his latest bashing. I had voted against Clinton's anti-terrorism Oklahoma Bombing bill. I believed that it contained language that overstretched and led to the loss of liberty for America's citizens. However, it was still hard to justify that vote back home.

We hit Burch through a television ad that John Brabender (the owner of Brabender/Cox, our media firm) had masterfully created. It was based on Burch's being the only member of the Ohio Senate, on either side of the aisle, who voted against my bill to make assaulting a police officer or firefighter a felony in all cases. The ad depicted Burch as not knowing the difference between the good guys—the cops (picture of men in blue) and the bad guys—the criminals (a rough looking guy with a beard, lurking around, looking sinister). "Good guys, bad guys—Burch does not know the difference" hit the screen over and over.

Something else happened that was quite bizarre. I got a call from Rick Homrighausen, the Republican Mayor of Dover, Ohio, Burch's hometown. Rick said Burch was involved in some sort of carbon monoxide situation. He was not sure of the details, but someone said he might not make it. Now politics is really a blood sport, and I have personally heard statements of all kinds. When a political figure dies, immediately people say "I feel bad," then in the next breath, "Who is going to replace him?" These conversations often occur in close proximity to coffins. I, as well as others, understand and accept these types of thoughts. In this case, our politico friends were saying, "God, I hope he lives; you want to beat him, not win by default or they will come after you again." Burch survived, but for a while was a bit tame, unlike his usual, Pit Bull self.

After Burch physically recovered, the election took on an Attila the Hun, take no prisoners tone by both of us. I even had an Attila the Hun quote on a t-shirt that I wore around my house: "It is not enough to defeat my opponent, we must destroy him."

The U.S. House was not able to finish budgets and we were kept there week after week, so I was not able to show up for scheduled debates at the end of the campaign. Burch was really frustrated when we sent a stand-in by having Bob Olexo take my place. Bob was my 1984 Ohio Senate opponent, a popular Democrat and a fine person. I hired Bob to do development for our District Office. When he showed up, Burch flipped. At one of the major debates, right before the coin toss, Burch went into a tirade about my not being there. "Where's Ney? Does he exist?" he yelled. "Why doesn't he show up?"

When the campaign finally ended, we had beaten Burch unmercifully. He made the grave mistake of those who come close; he assumed that because the last election was a 5,000-vote difference, he would start out that close. I knew that the public changes, the political climate changes, and the campaigns change. We ran a textbook campaign with Corey as manager and John Brabender as the media guru. We went back to Congress with the Democrat National Committee saying under their breath that their chance was gone for now. Former Senator Burch, an attorney by profession, started a totally new career as a truck driver.

Something strange happened the Thursday after the election. Our home phone rang, and it was Newt calling me. I said, "Hello Speaker, we had a close one."

He said, "Well, you're back and that's what counts. You can get the margin higher next round—you are a seasoned professional." This is something Newt had said to me before and had said in front of the caucus concerning our ability to "retail campaign," as we called it. Newt's tone then took a serious and shocking turn when he asked, "Are you going to vote for me for Speaker?"

I was taken aback—speechless. At one point during the election Newt had privately said to me, "If you need to distance yourself from me or hit me a bit, I understand." My response was, "Thanks, but I don't need to attack you in order to save myself. I appreciate it, but I am loyal to you and I will fight this without falling down that rat-hole of making you the entire election."

I firmly believe that once you react to "You are Newt's clone" or "You are Pelosi's clone" by distancing yourself, the opponent smells blood and keeps getting you to disagree with other points or positions raised by your leader until the entire election becomes *you and your leader* instead of *you and your vision*.

I responded with a question of my own: "Speaker, why on earth would you ask me that? I am always loyal to you, and did not badmouth you in the election."

He again asked, "Will you vote for me for Speaker?" Something was going on that I wasn't aware of and it could not be good. A bit angry for being questioned, I simply and forcefully answered, "Yes, absolutely!"

Newt then said, "Thank you. We have six members who have told me I need to step aside. After losing seats this time, it's close enough that losing these six could cause a problem."

I enthusiastically responded with an affirmation and a suggestion: "Again, yes, I am voting for you. Also, why don't you set up a calling drive to Members? You can break up regions, assign Members, and whip this thing!"

I was excited about the challenge and knew that Newt could get this moving. He agreed to do this; however, I knew from the sound in his voice that he was not optimistic. The rest is history. With a Republican Caucus ready to rebel against him, Newt resigned as Speaker of the House on November 5, 1998 and resigned his Congressional seat on January 3, 1999. The man who led his political party out of the forty years in the desert was self-exiled. It didn't take ten plagues to descend on him, just six gutless, politically terrified Members.

Chapter 11

☆ ☆ ☆

CRY ME A RIVER

"Nothing dries sooner than tears."

—SAMUEL RICHARDSON

John Boehner, a relatively new Ohio State Representative at the time, ran in the 1990 U.S. Congressional race and defeated the incumbent, Buz Lukens.

As for the new Congressman from Ohio, John Boehner's life in Congress seemed like a maintenance job. I say this because although people thought he was a nice guy, he was considered a bit lazy. Nevertheless, many felt that his money-raising focus would make up for his lack of concern about legislation—he was considered a man who was all about winning and money. He was a chain-smoking, relentless wine drinker who was more interested in the high life—golf, women, cigarettes, fun, and alcohol. He was well liked but not very politically connected. As I mentioned previously, not long after he took office redistricting in Ohio spared Boehner and took out the senior Republican Representative, Clarence Miller.

John didn't like controversy—he was more of a good old boy or "don't rock the boat" kind of guy. He was quite bright in some domestic policies, especially fiscal. John often mentioned that he had worked in his dad's bar and that it was a "union" bar. He mentioned this particularly to the building trades unions when he was an Ohio State Representative. Boehner liked to, and still does, give the "I am one of multiple kids and my dad and family are working people" spiel. Even the union guys used to comment on it. Because of his upbringing, they often said they couldn't understand why he wasn't more sympathetic to the average working man. To them (and many other people) John presented himself as a "country club" type.

Having assumed office as a U.S. Congressman in January of 1991, when the "Contract with America" idea first came up, Boehner and his longtime Chief of Staff, Barry Jackson, went into leadership mode. In 1995 Boehner won the Communications position of the Republican Conference. This was one of the "big four" positions. Each Party in Congress has different leadership slots, but the four most important on the Majority Party side are the Speaker of the House, Majority Leader, Majority Whip (vote counter), and Communications Chair. The latter one is the position Boehner sought. His plan was to start there and work his way up to Speaker when Newt moved on. I vividly remember Boehner winning that day. He stood before the conference with his wife, biting his lip in an effort to stem the flowing tears. I had seen John become tearful upon occasion, but this was the first time I saw him lose it in public, in front of a group.

John quickly began to proceed on several fronts. First, Barry Jackson considered Tom DeLay to be the enemy and did all he could to discredit him by being an anonymous "leadership mole" for the media. (These are the anonymous sources the media quote to show they have a high-up source.) It was an open secret that the mole was Barry Jackson, and it was confirmed to me by my Chief of Staff, Dave Distefano. Distefano knew everything about Barry and how he operated. He told me about Barry one evening when he was drunk or I would never have known positively that the mole was Jackson.

Within a few years all hell broke loose; it was 1999, Newt was out as Speaker and there was dissention among the ranks. The anger was extreme. We lost seats in the House and someone was at fault. That "someone" was the leadership of the Republican Conference, or "The Big Four" as they are called.

Someone had to go. Dick Armey and Tom DeLay had hung on to their leadership positions, despite the blame assigned to them. John Boehner as Chairman of the House Republican Conference was a marked man due to the fact that someone had to pay the price, and Boehner was the last man standing. To add to Boehner's woes, his position was challenged and won by a popular Member, J.C. Watts, a former Oklahoma football player and prominent African American Republican Congressman. And just as he had done when he won Communications Chair, Boehner's eyes watered and he became emotional. His voice cracked as he conceded before the entire Republican Conference. According to Dave Distefano, he heard that John broke into all-out wailing when he reached his office after the conference voting session.

That night, Distefano suggested we go to Smith and Wollensky's, a prominent D.C. steakhouse, to console John. Barry Jackson arranged for some of Boehner's friends, some Ohio lobbyist-types and some Members to be there. John, I must say, was upbeat.

Barry Jackson and Distefano had a lot to drink, and the more Barry consumed, the more vocal he got about all the "motherfuckers" he was going to get. Distefano was cheering him on, indicating that he could be of help; that he was *in.* I thought at the time that Distefano seemed to be more loyal to Barry than to me. I was to find out later that you couldn't separate Distefano and Barry with a *political* crowbar.

When John was Communications Chair, he spent almost all of his time on fundraising, not policy. The Communication Chair is a no-win position because some Members foolishly believed that one person in our conference, the Communications Chair, could represent our views in the media and the people in all of our districts would listen and believe. Good politicians realized that it had to be done by them—it has to be spun locally by the Members to their individual districts. It doesn't hurt to have the message given nationally, but the Members themselves have to get the message out—not depend on a magical leader within our Caucus.

As J.D. Hayworth, an enjoyable, talented, former Member from Arizona used to say, "It's retail politics." One time in a conference meeting, J.D. used me as an example of how to conduct campaigns. He said, "Bob Ney is the best retail politician in America."

I responded, "Yes, Kmart style." My district was very Appalachian—blue collar, non-pretentious, average American type of people, so I always liked to say Kmart politics versus Tiffany's.

Boehner did not become the TV darling, but instead he golfed, drank constantly and took the easy way legislatively, letting Barry Jackson organize the mechanics of the Republican message. Boehner's fundraising focus was legendary, second only to Tom DeLay in its push. John didn't care how it looked, how it smelled, or who cared. One famous film shows John getting off a private plane and the media asking, "Is that an R.J. Reynolds tobacco plane?" John responded while smoking a cigarette, "No it's Phillip Morris." He was then heard to say, "Barry, do we have the golf clubs? Make sure they get into the trunk." This famous clip got around and made many members laugh and say, "That John!"— but it made others nervous.

Another famous moment that got Boehner into trouble was when he handed out campaign checks on the floor of the House, which is totally against the rules. He did it constantly, and I have to admit that he gave one to me. One day he gave it to the wrong Member. After he passed a check from a tobacco lobbyist to Steve Largent, Congressman from Oklahoma, Largent publicly complained.

Other occurrences have never been publicly mentioned, but have been known by a few. I was told, point blank, that I could get certain brands of cigarettes—in particular, Barclay, John's brand—by going to the Communication Chair's Office (Boehner's office). I did that every three weeks or so, only when I ran out of my brand. I really didn't care for Barclay cigarettes. The procedure was to go to the office in person and a staffer (in my case, Barry Jackson—special treatment by the top dog for us) would open a large drawer, and take out a couple of packs. They were free, courtesy of a tobacco company passed through Boehner to me and other Members.

Later, a Jack Abramoff-type of scenario was established when former Boehner staffers bought a restaurant, Cantina Marina. Boehner, staff and friends could drink and eat at will, for free. It is located by the Gangplank Marina where my boat was docked. (I purchased a boat because my roommates had begun to move on, and keeping my children in an apartment when they spent the summer season with me in D.C. was neither safe nor fun for younger kids. The boat purchase seemed to make sense; it was behind a locked security fence, and there was full-time security.)

The Cantina Marina is a small, out of the way restaurant/bar on the Potomac, convenient to the Capitol but not directly downtown so not as easily scrutinized as Jack Abramoff's restaurant, Signatures. This was another open secret in D.C—no staffers paid when they were with "Boehner" friends or with Members of Congress. Lobbyists would visit the Cantina awaiting a chance to buy drinks. It wasn't a much different concept than Signatures, just a bit lower key and not packed nightly, as was Signatures. The press also frequented the haunt, and although they didn't necessarily benefit from the lobbyists' generosity, they surely witnessed others who did.

The most open, direct, *out there* violation took place during the Bush Administration, and it was never seized upon by the Justice Department with Attorney General Alberto Gonzales (2005–2007) at the helm. This concerned the well-known "Boehner Table" at the Capitol Hill Club. (It was also called the Republican Club because it was located inside the Republican Building that housed the National Republican Committee.) The club was across the street from the Cannon House Office Building where Members' offices were located. Two to three nights a week for years, either after or in between votes, Boehner sat with prominent, powerful tobacco lobbyists, and a lobbyist who was also his landlord. Boehner drank red wine, smoked cigarettes and snacked on hors d'oeuvres. If someone had held a gun to Boehner's head and told him to produce receipts proving that he paid for all those years of drinking at the Republican Club or he would be shot, he would have wound up in a body bag. It amounted to thousands of dollars. Boehner was equally well known for his constant, non-stop golfing, which for years was paid for by lobbyists. (He is still an avid golfer, and has played with President Obama.)

A trust situation of sorts developed between Boehner and me that involved the two of us and two women who worked on the Hill. It started innocently enough at the Capital Grille, a restaurant and local Hill hangout. I was there with a few people having a drink. Boehner was there that night but didn't have his entourage with him. It was just John, me, and a couple of other people at a table.

I spotted a friend of mine, Bess, who was speaking to another staffer. I walked over to her, as I hadn't seen her in quite a while. We had a lot of mutual interests and had spent time together over the last year. She was interested in boats, had been on mine and was trying to decide whether to purchase one and dock it at Gangplank Marina.

Bess is a good person. She's bright, and has been on the Hill for a while. At that time she worked for a fairly senior Republican Senator. We drank, talked, and then I invited her to the table to meet John. We sat for quite a while and he threw the usual John Boehner smooth style and humor around. It was a good time. The drinking increased, as did the level of noise in the room. Bess's friend, a staffer in the Senate for another Republican Member, waved at Bess, then came over to the table and was introduced to John and me. After a few minutes she sat down and it ended up to be just the four of us at the table next to the bar. For two more hours we drank, laughed, and carried on toward the one a.m.

hour. For Boehner to be out this late, publicly anyway, was not a standard. John loved to tell everyone that it was past his bedtime when it was 10:30. This became the running joke—that when John did leave around 10:30 it was because he had a more "private party" to attend. This night he surprised me because he was out later than usual and drinking even more than his usually large allotment of red wine. The bar emptied and Bess said, "Let's go."

We all got into her car—she had tempered her drinks and was driving okay. I sat up front with Bess, Boehner and Bess's friend were in the back. We all decided to head back to my boat because her friend really wanted to see it. Boehner said that he wanted to be dropped off at his place, but Bess's friend said she still wanted to see the boat. I looked back and saw him whisper in her ear. Bess was looking in the rearview mirror and saw it too. We both laughed and Bess nudged my arm.

The young lady was pretty loaded, as were John and I. She smiled a beautiful smile, tossed her stunning, long, black hair back and to the left, smiled at John and nodded. Bess nudged me again and asked Boehner his address. The place he rented from the lobbyist was near the Hill. We dropped them off, watched them walk into the apartment, and then we left.

The next morning John himself called me. He asked if I could come to his office. I went down to his personal office, was escorted in, and then the door was closed. John didn't appear to be his normal self. He appeared a bit distressed and uncomfortable. To stop the awkwardness I said, "What happens at the Grille, stays at the Grille."

He smiled a bit, waved his hand and said, "Nothing happened."

"Yeah, right," I said.

He got a more serious expression on his face and said, "No, really, I called her a cab."

I then looked him in the eye and said, "John, I have known you a long time, and I understand that you trust very few. I am not out to get you."

He smiled, waved his hand in the air, and said, "Goodbye, get out of here." He then took a puff on his cigarette and laughed. I never raised the subject again but I was fully aware that John was trying to treat the situation lightly, as though it hadn't occurred, versus trusting me. He didn't fool me for a second—his attempt at lightheartedness didn't cover the look of worry that was on his face.

I was involved in a situation at one time that later turned into a "Boehner myth." Newt Gingrich at the height of his über popularity as

Speaker of the House, agreed in 1995 to come to Columbus, Ohio, for a major fundraiser at the Aladdin Shrine Hall. As I was standing around in the back area with several hundred people who had paid upward of five thousand dollars to get a book autographed and a picture with Newt, there was a medical emergency. Right next to me a man collapsed as he was talking to my friend Ohio State Senator Gene Watts. Senator Watts immediately went down on his knees and cupped the man's head in his hands as I elevated the man's feet. John Hamlin, who had worked for the Republican Senate at one time and was working for then Ohio Governor Voinovich (later U.S. Senator Voinovich) had just that day taken a state course in CPR. John instantly started to push on the man's chest. Senator Watts told him that it wasn't needed. Eventually the EMTs came in and took him away. I got the gentleman's name, took it back to D.C. and gave it to Newt, who promptly wrote him a note and sent it with a signed copy of his book.

Then, politics being what it is, the story got around D.C. that John Boehner, who was there, did CPR and saved the man's life. "John Hamlin" became "John Boehner." One of Boehner's staffers and a lobbyist stopped me in the halls of the Longworth Building and asked me if it was true. I responded, "No, it was John Hamlin, but Boehner was standing there, looking over at the guy, smoking a cigarette saying, "We got his check, didn't we?" That joke became reality as D.C. goes, and it was easy to believe because people could envision John Boehner as more concerned over receiving the check than he was about the man's life.

John's personal style was simply bizarre at times. He could be praising a staffer, then switch immediately to condemnation or an off-base comment. This happened one time when we were on an official Congressional Delegation trip to Jordan. Distefano and I were talking with Boehner when an extremely loyal staff guy of his walked by. I commented to John, "That guy does a great job for you."

Boehner looked at him, sipped on a drink, took a drag of his cigarette and said in a very nonchalant tone, "Yes he does. I think he might be a fag but he does a good job." He then took another sip, another drag on his cigarette and stared straight out the window.

On a few of John's famous golf parties, he blatantly stayed in condos with lobbyists. If the Justice department were ever to make John produce receipts for his addiction to golf just for the years from 1995 to 2004, he would be hard pressed to comply. John got away with more than any other Member on the Hill. First, he is a likeable person; second, he always had the powerful, Rove-connected Barry Jackson to shield his wrongdoings. Barry was better than anyone else on the Hill at focusing attention on some other Member—and still is. (More on Barry Jackson to come.)

Two final interactions with John sealed my fate. I'm not complaining, because God, Higher Power, karma, or whatever you want to call it has a way of bringing it all about for good. These two events were significant and are related in Part III of this book.

Chapter 12

☆ ☆ ☆

THE "GOOD" SENATOR MCCAIN

mav · er · ick *n.*

1. An unbranded range animal, especially a calf that has become separated from its mother, traditionally considered the property of the first person who brands it.

—THE FREE DICTIONARY BY FARLEX

As a young man, I admired the "Maverick" in many ways. Not only was he a war hero, but he was a Republican who stood firm to his ideas and was unwavering in his convictions. In my mind at that time, nothing could have dislodged my high opinion of "The Good Senator." It was inconceivable that he could play politics or use others for his own personal gain. Later, my thoughts, opinions, and perceptions proved to wash away as quickly as the rain melts children's chalk drawings in the driveway.

My contact with Senator McCain after taking office was to see him here and there at events. Then I saw more of him when John Kasich decided to run for president in 1999 amid the early search for candidates to take up the sword as the magical Teflon Clinton years were coming to an end. (Eventually Kasich faded out and I went with Bush. As Karl Rove had told me in a conversation, "Once Kasich folds, fades, and exits, we will gladly have you on the Bush team," which is exactly what took place.)

I distinctly remember seeing McCain at Congressman John Boehner's infamous "beach party," held in a Veteran's Hall within one block of the Capitol. It is a popular place, and is rented out for fundraisers. This was a winter fundraiser full of beach balls, so-so food, plenty of free-flowing booze, hook-up possibilities for many, and lobbyist conversations for all.

Senator McCain came in and immediately was the spoke for the lobby wheels at the event. He was charming, cussed a bit, showed the Maverick smile and made his rounds. Young Hill staffers were especially impressed and, frankly, I was too.

Later, my interactions with McCain were not so admiring, pleasant, or upstandingly honest. McCain was attempting to build the presidential base. He knew in his mind he had to overcome the "open secret " in D.C., which was that not only could the Maverick be shot down over his past Keating scandal due to his personal sensitivity to it, but that he could have definitely done prison time over the scandal.

(In 1989, five United States Senators, including McCain, were accused of corruption, which ignited a major political scandal as part of the larger Savings and Loan crisis. The five senators were accused of improperly intervening in 1987 on behalf of Charles H. Keating, Jr., Chairman of the Lincoln Savings and Loan Association—the target of a regulatory investigation by the Federal Home Loan Bank Board (FHLBB). The FHLBB subsequently backed off taking action against Lincoln, but it collapsed in 1989, at a cost of over three billion dollars to the federal government. Some 23,000 Lincoln bondholders were defrauded and many investors lost their life savings. The substantial political contributions Keating had made to each of the five senators, totaling 1.3 million dollars, attracted considerable public and media attention. After a lengthy investigation, the Senate Ethics Committee determined in 1991 that McCain was one of the two senators cleared of having acted improperly but was criticized for having exercised "poor judgment." In April 1986, McCain's wife, Cindy, and her father invested $359,100 in a shopping center project with Keating. This, combined with her role as a bookkeeper who later had difficulty finding receipts for family trips on Keating's jet, caused complications for the "good senator" during the Keating Five scandal. McCain used his wife's addiction to pain medication at the time as an excuse to take the heat off himself.)

In 2001 McCain linked up with the liberal senator from Wisconsin, Russ Feingold, and embarked on a high-profile adventure into "cleaning up" the campaign corruption that everyone knew existed and, in McCain's mind, participated in—except him, of course. On the House side in a brilliant move, McCain enlisted the support of Congressman Christopher Shays. Chris Shays, a Republican Congressman from Connecticut, was an extremely empathetic, sensitive type who was a constant conscience of the House. He drew the wrath of many, but existed in a district that liked him and accepted his being a liberal—and I mean liberal—Republican. They did not always like it, but he survived conservative challenges. It was known that McCain privately not only made fun of his "lap dog," but would boast that Chris was so blindly loyal to him and so naïve that he had undoubtedly been a blessing sent McCain's way in order to get his "clean-up" bill passed. It turned out that Senator McCain was correct.

There were times in the final days before the bill was to go to the floor of the House when Chris Shays would turn to us as we cut deals (or tried to) and say, "Let me check with Dick Gephardt," who happened to be, of course, the Democrat Minority Leader. Gephardt, like all the money whores in D.C., had the same need as both sides did (and still do)—to acquire as much campaigning cash as humanly possible. The need for money is insatiable.

(Despite his perseverance, Shays would have been driven into the ground in the House if it had not been for one factor: No matter what Chris did, no matter how he betrayed the Party, no matter how he took his direct marching orders from McCain and Gephardt, no matter how he badmouthed Republicans in the media—at the end of the day he had the unequivocal, total protection of Scott Palmer, Speaker Hastert's Chief of Staff. Scott was not only famous for his mean-spirited, ruthless, controlling, vengeful style; he was also famous for having a total, unrequited, almost obsession for Chris Shays.)

I was Chairman of the House Administration Committee by this time (more on how that came about later in the book). Shays could do as he pleased, whatever he pleased and Palmer would directly order me not only to work with him, but to satisfy Chris's legislative needs. This was totally impossible and out of line with the vast majority of the Republican Caucus. Tom DeLay was fit to be tied and expressed to me that "Chris must have some pictures of Scott tucked away somewhere."

As Chairman of the House Administration Committee, I had a great private working relationship with Congressman Steny Hoyer and the Democrat side. One of the other Democrat minority Members, Congressman Bob Brady of Pennsylvania, was a gregarious, easy to get along with former political "boss" within the Democrat party. None of the leaders on either side of the aisle and none of the leaders within the Democratic National Committee, Republican National Committee or state parties wanted this bill of McCain's. This bill would dry up their money-raising abilities. The key term was *soft money*. McCain successfully made "soft money" a four-letter word, although none of the public really knew what it was.

All of us wanted this bill dead, but didn't want to admit it to the public, so I privately conveyed to the Committee Members that I would take the heat and announce that I was personally not bringing this bill up for a vote. They could then tell their constituents that they couldn't do anything because the Committee Chair wouldn't bring it up. The Republican Members, especially John Doolittle and John Mica, were an easy sell. The Democrats secretly liked it also. However, I let all of them know that if they accused me of any wrongdoing (such as pandering to special interests) I would bring it to a vote. They understood the game plan and the bill came to a halt.

Staffers said I would be challenged politically and damaged; that this was a hot issue. Two things happened. First, I was unopposed that election. Second, McCain was beyond hysterically pissed *(which would later cost me dearly through the Senate Indian Affairs Abramoff hearings)*. Even Scott Palmer with his salivating, unending support for whatever Chris Shays wanted could not stop me. Tom DeLay lit up a victory cigar—his prayers were answered—and the *soft money* still existed. It was fundraising debauchery with no limits or end in sight.

Eventually, McCain passed his campaign finance measure.

Chapter 13

☆ ☆ ☆

FREEDOM FRIES

"We can't all be Washingtons, but we can all be patriots."

—CHARLES F. BROWNE, 1835–1867

Early in January of 2003, while I was Chairman of the House Administration Committee, we received a request from Walter Jones, a Republican U.S. Representative from North Carolina, stating that he would like the House food system to rename French fries, Freedom fries. We really didn't pay too much attention to it at the time. I thought it was rather trite. Walter Jones stopped me on the floor of the house one day and said, "Look, I sent you a letter about a month ago about Freedom fries, and I would really like for you to consider this."

I said, "Okay, I'll take a look at it once again when I get back to the office."

To help you understand that I wasn't just blowing Walter off, the House Administration Office has several duties. It oversees federal election law, the Library of Congress, the Smithsonian, budgets of House Committees, and has other significant duties.

In addition to these important functions, it also oversees the minutiae of the House; the drapes, the rugs, whether the Members get their offices painted, their phone lines, their computer equipment, their newsletter, and these things don't require a vote of the committee. It was required of me as Chairman of the House Administration Committee to decide whether to approve these requests. (An official list of the duties is included at the end of this chapter.)

Walter Jones's request was not high on the priority list. However, that changed. Not long after speaking with Walter, I went to McConnelsville in Morgan County, Ohio, where some troops were being readied for deployment, very possibly to Iraq, as the Iraq war seemed imminent. This was an emotional event; these were National Guard Reservists and the families were crying. Governor Taft was there, and it all struck me pretty hard.

I returned to D.C. with these images in my mind, and coupled with French President Jacque Chirac's refusal to vote for a United Nations' resolution authorizing war in Iraq and the American anti-French sentiment and the rhetoric that went with that, I was ready to act on Walter's request. I asked the office staff what was required, and they told me that I just needed to sign a letter, and order the House CAO (Chief Administration Officer) who oversees this to change the menus and it's done. It took a few seconds of my time to sign the letter. It was that simple.

Walter Jones called me and I told him I was going to do it. He asked me how I wanted to go about it. I said, "I will send out a notice, and then you and I will go down to the cafeteria and present a little plaque, renaming these [French fries], Freedom fries." Walter and I agreed that it was strictly symbolic. We were sticking it to the French for all their rhetoric over Iraq. He had some pressure from constituents in his district to do it and he thought it was a good idea. I had seen the emotion of those who were the most impacted by this coming war, so I thought it was okay to do this. My seasoned Press Secretary, Brian Walsh, sent out a mass release to the press.

When we walked into the Longworth Cafeteria on March 11, 2003, I was in absolute shock. That very large cafeteria was packed full of people, including media from all over—Britain, Japan, CNN, Fox News—you name it, they were there. The place was jammed!

On our way in, we saw a veteran who was about 78 or 80 years old. He was wearing his Veterans of Foreign Wars cap. He came up to Walter and me and said, "I saw that you were going to do this." He began to cry and then continued, "I've served my country. I think this is a great thing to do." We invited him to join us and I think he said a few words to the press and it got a lot of attention.

We stood there in front of the crowd and I handed the plaque to Walter, officially renaming French fries, Freedom fries. I said, "This action today is a small, but symbolic effort to show the strong displeasure many on Capitol Hill have with our so-called ally, France."

After that, it was on all the menus for the House restaurants, the snack bars, the whole food system for the House. The French Embassy in D.C. made no comment except to point out that French fries come from Belgium and not from France.

Walter Jones and I were not the first to rename French fries, Freedom fries. A few private clubs had done so. The most famous of these was Cubbies in Beaufort, North Carolina. After I did this, the number of phone calls to my Press Secretary, Brian Walsh, was beyond anything we had ever seen. We were getting more phone calls from the media than during the consideration of impeaching President Clinton. It was completely overwhelming. Freedom fries was becoming iconic, going global.

I was doing interviews with the London version of *The Today Show,* CNN, Fox News, national magazines, foreign television, and scores of other American media—you name it, I did it. Later, when I spoke at a school in the 18th Congressional District in Ohio, the kids had put up signs that said, "Only Freedom Fries Served Here." So back in my district, it was very, very popular.

It brought worldwide attention to our issue, there's no question about that. AOL did a poll, and I believe there were 600,000 responses worldwide—125,000 objected and the rest supported our efforts. It took on a life of its own—almost like those pop movies that become cult-like.

Not everyone was happy. The liberals were freaking out. Nancy Pelosi, the minority leader, even had her office research that my relatives were from Paris, which I already knew, and they put that information out! They then used the tactic that I was wasting valuable taxpayers' time, but as I said, it took just seconds to sign this thing. There was no time wasted—except for those in the House who wasted valuable time in trying to slap me around for it. Those who thought we should be in these conflicts supported it and the left went absolutely crazy.

I was weary of the Democrats and the left responding so badly and I finally called Walter Jones and said, "You came to me with this idea, so why don't you do these shows if you want to?"

Walter's a rather humble, stand up, wonderful guy, and he said, "No, I don't want to. You handle it. I don't do well with this much media."

A lot of people thought that I did this purely as a political stunt. Frankly, if it were a political stunt, I would probably have done it when Walter first came to me. I don't believe that Congressman Walter Jones was trying to pull a stunt either; he was sincere. For my part, Freedom fries stemmed from my raw emotion as I saw all those people down in Morgan County grieving as their loved ones prepared for war. It just touched something in me. When I got back to my office and saw on television that France was going crazy, I thought: *That's enough! These are our troops and whether France likes the war or not, we have to do something to stand up for them.* That's why I did it—not because I planned to have a great following from the Freedom fries publicity.

(When I resigned in 2006 and left the House Administration Committee, Vern Ehlers (R-Michigan) took my place. In a very quiet manner, he just let the menus in the House go back to French fries. By July 2006, Walter Jones had changed his mind about the war, saying that he really didn't think it had justification—and I agree with Walter on this.

When I got out of prison, I did a documentary for the Independent Film Channel. As part of that documentary I was asked [as I often am] about Freedom fries and my answer was that I'd do it again. It angered the left and it was a token of support for the troops, so I'd do it again. I've been asked as recently as 2012 if I would take it back if I had the chance and the answer is no. Had I still been Chairman of House Administration, I would have continued Freedom fries until the American troops returned from Iraq.)

Amazingly, the thing I did as Chairman of the House Administration Committee I am most famous for was the Freedom fries!

House Rule X – Organization of Committees

(j) Committee on House Administration.

(1) Appropriations from accounts for committee salaries and expenses (except for the Committee on Appropriations); House Information Resources; and allowance and expenses of Members, Delegates, the Resident Commissioner, officers, and administrative offices of the House.

(2) Auditing and settling of all accounts described in subparagraph (1).

(3) Employment of persons by the House, including staff for Members, Delegates, the Resident Commissioner, and committees; and reporters of debates, subject to rule VI.

(4) Except as provided in paragraph (q)(11), the Library of Congress, including management thereof; the House Library; statuary and pictures; acceptance or purchase of works of art for the Capitol; the Botanic Garden; and purchase of books and manuscripts.

(5) The Smithsonian Institution and the incorporation of similar institutions (except as provided in paragraph (q)(11)).

(6) Expenditure of accounts described in subparagraph (1).

(7) Franking Commission.

(8) Printing and correction of the Congressional Record.

(9) Accounts of the House generally.

(10) Assignment of office space for Members, Delegates, the Resident Commissioner, and committees.

(11) Disposition of useless executive papers.

(12) Election of the President, Vice President, Members, Senators, Delegates, or the Resident Commissioner; corrupt practices; contested elections; credentials and qualifications; and Federal elections generally.

(13) Services to the House, including the House Restaurant, parking facilities, and administration of the House Office Buildings and of the House wing of the Capitol.

(14) Travel of Members, Delegates, and the Resident Commissioner.

(15) Raising, reporting, and use of campaign contributions for candidates for office of Representative, of Delegate, and of Resident Commissioner.

(16) Compensation, retirement, and other benefits of the Members, Delegates, the Resident Commissioner, officers, and employees of Congress.

Chapter 14

MEK: TERRORISTS AMONG US

"The enemy of my enemy is my friend." (Maybe!)

—ARABIAN PROVERB

It wasn't until I was elected to Congress and settled into my new office that my previous experience of living in Iran after college and my perspective on Iranian politics became useful. As the only Congressional Member who spoke Persian (Farsi), having lived in Iran helped me to differentiate myself. Many Americans either misunderstood the revolution in Iran or were a part of those who monotonously analyzed the activity in the Persian Gulf. Although I clearly wasn't an academic in the field of Middle Eastern affairs, I was someone to consult with, and I was in a unique position to analyze the waves of change passing over Iran. For all of the emotional bitterness I experienced after I left Iran, the concerns of the Iranian middle class were something I could relate to after having spent so much time with my host family. I understood their hesitancies when it came to politics. The political rhetoric streaming from Iran when I was a freshman in Congress was similar to the anti-Western tone I had experienced in Iran in 1978. The new Islamic government's policy fostered a deep distrust of Americans that many Americans at the time reciprocated.

Despite my background, I was by no means a high-profile foreign policy figure on the Hill, and so I was very surprised when soon after I was elected, I was approached at my Congressional office by a member of a group that called themselves the "National Council of Resistance of Iran"

(NCRI) or the Mujahedin-e Khalq (MEK). At the time, the MEK was an influential group in Washington, allegedly concerned with protecting the common interests of Iranians and Americans and purporting to work toward democracy in Iran.

Nevertheless, behind their polished exterior image there was a dark, but open secret: The MEK was and remains a brutal terrorist group with American blood on their hands. The group was founded in the 1960s to overthrow the Shah's regime. Guided by fusion between Islamism and Marxism, the group was the first organization in Iran to use terrorism and violence as a political tool. While the notion that Iranians deserved better was a notion very close to my heart, I was also very aware that the MEK was a terrorist organization: one that had supporters in Congress.

Since the 1979 revolution, Iran had handicapped itself, constantly choosing to oppose and antagonize the West, while simultaneously repressing the Iranian people. There was evidence of a severe "brain drain" of intellectuals and young people from Iran, who were fleeing the suppressive new regime, and discussions of the restrictions on the civil liberties afforded to Iranians were regularly in the headlines. Additionally, human rights abuses under the Ayatollah's reign were worse than under the Shah. All of this evidence of improper governance, the widespread suppression of civil liberties, and enthusiastic anti-American campaigns made the Islamic Republic an enemy in the eyes of the United States. Ever since the hostage crisis, officials in Washington had regularly preferred dealing with virtually any Iranian opposition group to dealing with the Mullah (clerical) regime. The MEK was one such "resistance" organization. According to the simplistic and superficial analysis of the "good-versus-bad," the MEK was with us because they were committed to overthrowing the Mullah regime.

What members of Congress and other key Washington officials were ignoring, however, was the MEK's deep involvement in terroristic activities. They were directly involved in the deaths and assassinations of both Americans and Iranians in the name of their resistance against the Shah. During the 1970s, including during my stay in Shiraz, the MEK (at that time set on overthrowing the Shah) was linked to killing U.S. military personnel as well as U.S. civilians.

In 1981, under the Islamic Republic, the MEK once again turned to terror by setting off a bombing campaign in Iran. After falling out of favor with Khomeini, the group fled to Iraq and joined forces with

Saddam Hussein's brutal and bloody invasion of Iran. In the eyes of most Iranians, the Mujahedin were now traitors because they had sided with Iran's Arab enemy. Whatever one's view of the Ayatollah's regime, siding with Saddam was unforgivable. This would be like an American joining Osama Bin Laden's war of terror against America.

Within Iraq, the MEK were utilized by Saddam Hussein as an execution army. As "Saddam's most loyal troops" the MEK were sent into Kurdistan and Shi'ite strongholds to "ethnically cleanse" them, in acts which some would later call genocidal. However, in spite of their terrorist acts, the organization had the audacity to walk unapologetically into Congressional offices in Washington with gory pictures of victims tortured at the hands of the Mullah regime when they themselves had done the same. They sold themselves as the answer to the prayers of those in Congress who viewed Iran's Islamic government as a worse evil. Congressional supporters were often in tune to the inconsistencies and stretched truths of the MEK's appeals, but the perceived menace of the Mullah regime made any of their foes a friend of the United States. The Congressional tolerance for terrorism was much higher in this era—before the U.S. had itself been a target of a modern, large-scale terrorist attack on U.S. soil.

The representative that I received at my office during my first contact with the MEK carefully and gingerly described the organization's goals and listed the interest group's concerns. These included allegedly prioritizing stability in the region, claims that they were working to eliminate the suppression of media entities and reporters in Iran, and allegedly encouraging the opening of Iran to the West. At the time, the MEK had succeeded in making most of us in Congress believe that *not* supporting the MEK meant support *for* the Mullah regime. Having closely followed the crimes of the Islamic regime myself and having witnessed the Mullah regime's brutality, I was no friend of the Islamic regime. By default, I committed myself to supporting the MEK.

To this day, I'm not sure how my conscience could have supported this decision. I could write it off as freshman ignorance or the strong influence of my anger against the Islamic regime. Nevertheless, I chose to support an organization that preached violence and was responsible for the loss of American lives. Ironically, as an American in Iran in 1978, I could have been murdered by this very organization. The tragedy of history is that it is written by the winners, meaning the voices of the losers are often lost along with their lives. Those Americans who were victims of the MEK weren't alive to walk the halls of Congress distributing flyers or testifying on the floor, so choosing to minimize their experiences was easy, even if I could have been one of them. The Mullah's regime and the MEK had blood on their hands, so, when faced with a decision to support one of them, the MEK appeared the lesser evil.

After a time, my involvement in the organization's events and discussions grew, and I became one of the group's key supporters on the Hill. To that end, I was more than happy at the time to share my experiences on the edge of the Islamic revolution at lectures, and I was proud to take part in a dialogue that denounced the Islamic regime in Iran. *(In retrospect, my support of one terrorist group over another would prove to be painfully immature. Whether there's a worse terrorist regime out there is irrelevant; the U.S. has no business cherry-picking terrorist groups to support and provide them with American tax dollars to carry out their dirty work.)*

I was not alone; well over half of the U.S. Congress publicly supported the MEK. Many of us thought that these "enemies" of Iran were surely "friends" to the U.S. They brought in singers, took time to visit hundreds of offices and brought a message of peace—or so we thought.

My relationship with the MEK cooled down considerably within two years' time when an insurmountable gap emerged in my mind between the realities of the group's activities and the organization's rhetoric. This schism became blatantly obvious when a new president was elected in Iran in 1997. Mohammad Khatami was the fifth President of the Islamic Republic, and his policy focus and rhetoric was markedly different from that of his predecessor. He almost spoke a different language, suggesting that dialogue with the West was an undeniable inevitability and he called for a "dialogue of civilizations," clearly a foil to the war hawks' call for a "Clash of Civilizations."

Almost immediately after taking office, President Khatami's calls for greater openness were noticed in Washington. In a historical interview with Christiane Amanpour on January 7, 1998, Khatami made it clear that "The American civilization is worthy of respect." Khatami added that he felt an "intellectual affinity with the essence of the American civilization," with whom he called for "discourse, debate, and dialogue." In Washington, one could feel the shock and astonishment at this new leader's change in tone, as politicos rushed to dissect the interview and interpret the Iranian regime's positioning. For the first time in decades, the U.S. and Iran were poised to begin a dialogue, and I was proud to be the first individual in the House to acknowledge and welcome

Khatami's comments. This was a historic window for policy change and Khatami's invitation to turn a new page in U.S.-Iranian relations was the diplomatic chance of a lifetime to alleviate the tension, which had been repeatedly exacerbated by misunderstandings and mistrust.

Unfortunately, not everyone in Washington saw this break as an opportunity, and while I was among the first to speak out in praising this development, the MEK would be among the first to express their outrage at a possible diplomatic solution to the legacy of tensions between the U.S. and Iran. At this point, it became clear where the MEK's objectives could lead the U.S. With an army waiting across the border in Iraq and abundant funding from extremist war hawks, the MEK's true colors were on display. For their terrorist attacks against Iran, the MEK became increasingly unpopular in Iran, meaning that the MEK's last hopes of taking power in Iran relied on the United States. The MEK self-ishly wanted the U.S. to commit the same mistake we had made in installing the Shah, only this time the MEK thought they could convince the U.S. to install them as Iran's new ruling class. The idea that the State Department would attempt to reduce tensions with the Mullah regime through a dialogue was the worst nightmare of this truly malicious organization. While diplomacy could save the U.S. from greater con-frontation with Iran, the MEK were completely uninterested in dialogue or even stopping anywhere short of violent regime change. What the MEK hadn't accounted for in their vision for a future U.S. invasion of Iran was that U.S. officials might be interested in avoiding all-out war, and instead favor diplomacy to resolve tensions with Iran.

Appalled by the MEK's response and their blatant agitating for con-flict with the Khatami administration, I decided that we would need to part ways. They would no longer be welcome in my office, and I even suggested that their representatives try talking to Khatami's administra-tion themselves, if they remained convinced that their differences were truly irreconcilable. It was clear to me that I had made a grave mistake in supporting them, and I was determined to avoid ever making the mis-take of supporting such a morally compromising group in the future.

Of course, in return for voicing my support for a diplomatic resolu-tion, the MEK attempted to defame my character by releasing reports claiming that I was a lackey of the Mullah regime for favoring an approach other than war, and insultingly calling my patriotism into question. But while my relationship with the MEK became more dis-tanced, I remained positive that a U.S.-Iranian dialogue could be established. The American public was smarter than to be convinced by a small group of war-mongering hotheads to charge into battle so carelessly. I saw the MEK's inability to cope with reason, and dismissed the organization as a nuisance.

As no policymaker could have previously conceived, an abrupt and sharp change in U.S. foreign policy would soon occur, not as the result of reform but by the success of a horridly cruel act of terrorism. As it was for so many Americans in 2001, my life was dramatically affected by 9/11. I was an advocate of invading Afghanistan based on the absolute necessity of eradicating such an evil organization as the Taliban. The U.S. had been picking favorites among terrorist groups in the Middle East, Africa, and Asia for some time, and it was only because of 9/11 that a change in policy was triggered. The post-9/11 policy change was the direct result of the recognition on the part of a handful of leaders that terrorist organizations were not groups to be associating with, let alone collaborating with or funding.

Around the same time, while relations with Iran hadn't necessarily changed for the better, Iran did passively cooperate with U.S. policy in invading Afghanistan. What many Americans still aren't aware of is the important role that Iran played in coordinating throughout the Middle East to accommodate for the instability within neighboring Afghanistan. I was present during the talks in Washington with Afghanistan's President Karzai, which were sponsored by Congressman Ben Gilman and the late Tom Lantos, respective Chair and Ranking Member of the House Committee on Foreign Affairs (named the House Committee on International Relations at the time). The issue of Iran was mentioned and noted. As time would show, Iran was investing heavily in Afghanistan's stability, even accommodating Afghan refugees and preventing the drug trade from spilling over its border.

Also alluded to during these talks was the Afghan intention to avoid becoming a puppet of U.S. foreign policy ambitions. Afghan concern centered on its Cold War history as a battleground for changing dynamics between the U.S. and the Soviet Union, and the prospect of once again falling victim to the United States' ambitions was discouraging—while at the same time the Afghans appreciated the American pressure on the otherwise impossible to control militant Taliban. Interestingly, as the Afghans began questioning whether the U.S. had an exit strategy, the MEK was busy at work on the Hill attempting to channel the U.S.'s lingering post-9/11 terrorist paranoia into a full-blown war with Iran.

Obviously, discussions of an invasion of Iraq were already on the table, but the MEK had much to lose from a conflict with their sponsor—Saddam Hussein in Iraq. They instead sought to convince U.S. officials that an attack on Iran was necessary. Using the same rhetoric that the Bush Administration employed to send shivers down the spines of Americans for fear of an Iraqi nuclear missile, the MEK ingeniously applied the same rhetoric to attempt to steer U.S. military might to invade the Islamic Republic.

It was no coincidence that Saddam Hussein was among the militaristic MEK's top sponsors. There was an MEK camp in Iraq called "Camp Ashraf." By funneling money to the MEK's fast-talking Hilltop representatives, Saddam Hussein was making an investment in distracting the U.S. from human rights abuses under his government, as well as Iraqi ambitions to acquire a nuclear weapon. In Washington, the MEK's influence at such a time of panic was deeply troubling. Without having done proper background research, many in Congress were more than willing to listen to the MEK's calls for war with Iran without questioning this dangerous group's intentions or goals. Over 200 Members signed letters. Among them, unfortunately, was Robert Ney.

Additionally, many Members of Congress were unaware that the group had been on the United States' list of designated terrorist organizations since 1997.

As the temperature in Washington climbed in 2002 and 2003, there was evidence of the MEK's meddling everywhere, and the group's selfish, shortsighted militaristic ambitions became revolting as the U.S. once more prepared to send our nation's finest into danger. I considered the MEK's attempts to steer the U.S. into a completely unnecessary war with Iran criminal and treasonous. In my view, the MEK's ability to promote their own agenda by stirring up a phobia of Iran among Congress Members became worthy of an investigation. They were dangerously misinformed about the interests they were supporting. I considered the MEK a significant enough threat that I asked my staff to prepare a package of this organization's clear history of terrorism. I took this issue on, personally discussing it with my colleagues at every given opportunity. At every floor vote, I personally handed these packets to fellow Congressmen one-by-one.

Within two months, simply by discussing the matter with my colleagues and exposing the MEK's true nature, Congressional support for the organization dropped from 220 to 6 Members of Congress. Of course, ridiculous accusations ensued that I was "in the pocket of the Mullahs" or was an Iranian terrorist, but my part in exposing the MEK as a criminal organization is one of my proudest accomplishments.

Unfortunately, in recent years as the U.S. and Iran edged closer to a military confrontation, more U.S. officials have looked the other way and ignored the MEK's crimes, instead contemplating their use in a potential conflict brewing with Iran. My advice to Congress and to the President as the U.S. comes to the table with Iran for the first time in recent memory to discuss a legacy of misunderstanding, is simply to avoid being fooled by fast talkers and the attractive presentations of those in favor of conflict. It has been a very long time since the U.S. has engaged in a dialogue with Iran, and even longer since I fled Iran as one of the last Americans to visit the country before the Islamic Revolution. Anyone who discourages a dialogue by default encourages dangerous ambivalence or war—both equally devastating and unoriginal prospects.

At one point, the MEK came to my office and a woman draped in a veil told me that Trita Parsi, the foreign exchange student who lived with us at one time, was a spy. I realized the MEK were insane and the average Iranian hated them, both in Iran and in America. They have attempted to destroy Trita for years. They have been in trouble due to their terrorist designation. They have thrown money all over D.C. in an attempt to buy access.

As bad as the current Iranian regime is, let us not repeat history with the big lie that sucked us into Iraq—the Weapons of Mass Destruction ploy. Iran's history of non-dialogue since the year 1979 when our embassy was taken over and our people were taken hostage hasn't seemed to stop them.

★ ★ ★

After I wrote this chapter, the MEK was delisted by President Obama. It did not happen on its own due to merit. A lavish, expensive, lobbyist/money gluttony campaign was initiated. For President Obama, it was a chance to appear to be tough on the Iranian regime—we were recognizing their enemy, the MEK. It took away the "Obama is weak on Iran" mantra by the Republicans. The move by Obama was not something that would be disputed by Obama's opponent in the 2012 presidential race, Mitt Romney, due to the fact that MEK leader Rajavi's "cult" had successfully greased the palms of Republican and Democrat politicians, as well as former politicians, with campaign contributions and expensive honoraria for speaking engagements. Some of the bipartisan support gathered by Rajavi's regime for the Terrorist MEK delisting campaign include former FBI Director Louie Freeh; former Mayor of New York Rudy Giuliani; and former Democratic presidential candidate and Party Chair, Howard Dean.

The Guardian reports that Representative Bob Filner (D-California), who was "twice flown to address pro-MEK events in France, pushed resolutions in the House" calling for the group to be delisted. Representative Ted Poe (R-Texas) received "thousands of dollars in donations from the head of a pro-MEK group" in his state, and Representative Mike Rogers (R-Michigan), chairman of the House Intelligence committee, "has been among the strongest supporters in Congress of delisting the group."

The following are some excerpts from an article by Richard Silverstein in *The Guardian*, summing up the MEK lobby saga of utilizing campaign contributions that make Jack Abramoff look like a piker.

It [MEK] now claims it has renounced terror and devotes itself to establishing an Iranian democratic form of government that would replace the rule of the Ayatollahs. But former leaders and members of the MEK have noted the ruthlessness and duplicity of the group. They believe that the Iran it envisions would be a dictatorship rather than a democracy. These dissident former members decry the MEK's slavish worship of its leader Maryam Rajavi in a cult of personality not unlike that of North Korea and other Communist regimes . . .

The Iranian dissidents have plotted for years to be removed from the terror list. They enlisted numerous Republican and Democratic officials to lobby on its behalf. Instead of paying lobbying fees to them, it offered honoraria ranging from $10,000–$50,000 per speech to excoriate the US government for its allegedly shabby treatment of the MEK . . . Many of them profess to have little interest in the money they have collected. Instead, they claim they are sincerely moved by the group's suffering in Iraq and wish to correct an injustice. I'm sure the money doesn't hurt . . .

The US delisting of the group is a sham. The Obama administration isn't even claiming the MEK has renounced terrorism. If it did, it knows that it's likely such a statement would rebound should the MEK's activities become exposed. The chief argument offered in defense of the change of heart is that the group has agreed to relocate from Camp Ashraf, where it's been a thorn in the side of the Iraqi Shi'ite-led government, to a US facility, from which the residents would be relocated to foreign countries.

So, we're removing a terror group from the list not because it's stopped being a terror group, but because it's agreed to leave Iraq, where it had been a desta-bilizing influence. That's not a principled position. It's a position based on pure political calculation . . .

Alan Dershowitz has argued that the MEK should be removed from the treas-ury list not because it has stopped being terrorist, but because it collaborated with US covert activities inside Iran, meaning that it was serving US inter-ests. Or put more simply: the MEK may be terrorists, but they're our terrorists.

Delisting the MEK serves several goals for President Obama. He can flex his muscles in the face of both the Iranians and Republicans. To the Iranians, he's implicitly saying he will make alliance with their worst enemy as long as they resist him at the negotiating table. To Mitt Romney, he's saying he's will-ing to get tough with the Iranians. This inoculates him from campaign attacks claiming he's soft on Iran or that he's willing to let Iran get the bomb . . .

Just as President Obama's anti-terror policies, including targeted assassina-tions and drone strikes, have betrayed his previous denunciations of such vio-lations of constitutional principles, so his granting a seal of approval to the MEK marks a further erosion of his commitment to diplomacy and negotiation as the means for resolving international disputes, including the one with Iran.)

A Guardian article by Glenn Greenwald on September 23, 2012, relates to the tens of thousands of dollars received by prominent former U.S. government officials from both political parties over the last several years for giving speeches to the MEK. They have then become vocal, relentless advocates for the group, specifically for removing them from the terrorist list.

Greenwald cites the *Christian Science Monitor* in describing these for-mer high-ranking U.S. officials. In addition to those I have already listed, they include Democrats Ed Rendell, Wesley Clark, Bill Richardson, and Lee Hamilton; Republicans include Fran Townsend, Tom Ridge, Michael Mukasey, and Andrew Card.

The *Christian Science Monitor* quotes a State Department official on how the scheme works:

"Your speech agent calls, and says you get $20,000 to speak for 20 minutes. They will send a private jet, you get $25,000 more when you are done, and they will send a team to brief you on what to say. . . . The contracts can range up to $100,000 and include several appearances."

These articles clearly sum up the political influence of the neocons—war mongers who are able to entice a Democratic president to do their bidding. Dr. Trita Parsi has led the good fight to expose these terrorists and although Obama has legitimized them, and they are free to roam the hallowed halls of the Capitol, the MEK will never be a substitute for democracy in Iran. One day, hopefully, that democracy will come about.

Chapter 15

☆ ☆ ☆

AFGHANISTAN

"As the country now turns a new leaf,
our ambition is to give hope to each and every Afghan."

—Hamid Karzai, President of Afghanistan

Because I had lived in Iran, had knowledge of the Mideast, and could speak Farsi, I was contacted by Congressman Dave Hobson (U.S. Congressman from Ohio) to be part of a delegation to Afghanistan. Dave, who was to be the Chairman of the Delegation, said that it was time for Congress to see the troops and thank them for the mission. He also pointed out that since no other Congressional delegation had been there since the war began, it would be a good way to assess the situation on the ground and report our findings to other Members. There was also the ability to meet with the new Chairman, Hamid Karzai. We would be able to spend some quality time with him and see what he was about and what direction he was heading with not only his country, but also with America.

The delegation led by Chairman Hobson arrived in Tashkent, Uzbekistan, in February of 2002. We had a rather extensive meeting and dinner planned with then Interim Chairman Hamid Karzai of Afghanistan. He was selected by prominent Afghani political figures to serve a six month term as Chairman of the Interim Administration during the December 2001 International Conference on Afghanistan in Germany. Even Iran was involved in the Bonn conference that picked him. *(He was later elected for a two-year term as Interim President during the June 13, 2002,*

Loya Jirga [grand assembly] that was held in Kabul, Afghanistan. Karzai then became President in 2004, becoming the first democratically elected leader of Afghanistan.)

Our delegation had a long meeting with Karzai where we discussed just about every aspect of looking ahead to the new Afghanistan. We then attended a dinner that was almost three hours long. The evening's event was excellent, consisting of an interesting variety of fine cuisine— semi-American, Russian and Afghan. There was festive Afghani music with beautiful Afghani women dancing in belly-dance-type of costumes. I translated some songs that were in Farsi for Congressman Mike Rogers of Michigan and others at our table.

After the dinner, which was also attended by American Embassy staff and local business leaders, only the Members of Congress were invited upstairs to Karzai's private suite. It was there that he became more frank about a lot of things; the uncertainty of the situation, the regional players, and the help he needed. He stressed to us that the statement he was about to make must remain totally confidential or it could cause problems. He then conveyed his uncensored feelings about the Iranians and what he would be dealing with and what he thought of them. I think part of what he said was true and part was playing to the ear of Americans who mistrust everyone in the Iranian Government, just as the Iranians mistrust us.

When we joined the others, the American Embassy official asked what was said upstairs. We all gave a general answer, but he began to push back and lean heavily on a few of us to answer. He said, "I need to cable Washington." I found Chairman Hobson and told him what was going down. Dave walked over to the Embassy official (who was previously at the American Embassy in Israel) and told him that we were bound by a promise not to repeat what we were told. The official pressed harder until Congressman Hobson got in his face and said, "We are not telling you anything. I can call State [the State Department] and have your ass in problems. Stop asking!" With that, we moved on to our rooms and departed for Afghanistan the next day.

We flew into Bagram Air Force Base on a Hercules C-130. The flight was somewhat harrowing. This was early in the Afghanistan War— snipers and handheld ground-to-air missiles were common. As the plane was nearing the air force base, flares were expelled from the plane as a precaution in the event of a heat-seeking missile. Most of the attacks on these planes at that time came from fire below, up through the belly of the plane.

There were only four Members in CODEL (Congressional Delegation) Hobson. We were, I am told, the first four Members of Congress to do a delegation trip to Afghanistan since the war began. We were wearing flak jackets, and as the huge mouth of the Hercules opened, we were surrounded by Special Forces and were told to move quickly from the plane into the building that served as a U.S. Air Force operations center and of course we did!

At this point, Bagram Air Force Base was set up, but was really in a primitive state *(compared with when I returned to Afghanistan a year or so later)*. There were briefings about Afghanistan in general, this new war, the Taliban, Interim Chairman Karzai, the pitfalls ahead, and the mission in Afghanistan. This was particularly interesting, as the military described a mission that was not only military in nature but had our soldiers working on a number of large "civilian" projects. Farming, water irrigation, and rebuilding skills were just a few of them.

Early on in the briefing, I had the gut feeling that we may possibly, with these civilian projects in place, be here longer than we were in Vietnam. After inquiring about the heavy emphasis on civilian missions, we were told by our briefer that Afghanistan has fewer than 20,000 phones in the country; the average person dies by the age of 44; infant mortality is through the roof; there is no structure to speak of (totally destroyed by the Taliban); and that all this was comparable to living in the fifteenth century.

From Bagram we traveled to Kabul by convoy through the blown out, mined roads. There were semblances of small bridges that had been blown up. Holes abounded where missiles must have rained down. The convoy followed a narrow, winding path that had been cleared of land mines, but the markers were a warning to stay on that course. The cars we rode in were armored vehicles, retrofitted for the war zone. It was a six or seven-car convoy that finally reached its destination—Afghanistan's Capitol City of Kabul.

Kabul was miles and miles of endless rubble. It was dusty, packed with people, and chaotic. The people were everywhere—walking or riding ancient-looking bikes, and scores of them making homes amid the rubble. As we turned toward the U.S. Embassy, we could see bombed-out buses, torched cars, pieces of metal, and tires scattered here and there in no specific order. The veiled, head-to-toe burka was prominent with not one woman uncovered.

We drove past the barbed wire and the marines who were on duty and approached the front of the Embassy. Remarkably, the Embassy Seal from years back—the American Eagle and the words, "Embassy of the United States"—was still intact above the bullet-ridden, front glass doors.

We found our temporary ambassador and staff within the dingy-looking interior. Pieces of furniture were here and there and makeshift cots were set up in several of the rooms, as this is where the embassy staff was living. (*My next visit to Kabul was to the same embassy, but it was brightened up with new walls, doors, a thorough cleaning and the added touch of paint.*)

We sat down with the six people who were there and began the conversation. We were told that the number one thing we could do was talk to Karzai about his personal security. They said to "work it into the conversation" when we met with him again. The U.S. representative from the State Department who was present had been in Afghanistan for over a month at that time and he said that Karzai waded into open crowds, and that was not good.

A question arose from another delegation Member as to when we were going to "napalm the poppy fields." The State Department man said, "It is not that easy."

I chimed in, "There is no way that we will do that. A hundred thousand Afghanis are picking poppies and the warlords make the money from that. It is sold to international drug dealers and then the poison hits the streets of the world. If we stop it now, Karzai will be assassinated within ten seconds." (*I was right. As of this writing, we have virtually torched none of the poppy fields.*)

We then talked about a U.S. exit plan, which did not exist. They kept it open-ended.

Near the Embassy was a hospital that the embassy staff asked us to tour. We walked into a hospital where I seriously, in good conscience, would not have left my dog. When we went into the "breathing room" for the tuberculosis cases, although there was no equipment or medication of any type, there were about nine women and nine kids in a room that would be cramped for three. The kids looked like Holocaust survivors—skin and bones wrapped by flesh. The mother of one of the kids who was a patient said something to Congressman Hobson, and he asked me to translate. She had said in Farsi, "Welcome, thank you, please have some of my juice." The woman was offering Dave juice that was rationed for her child's benefit. The Afghani kindness and spirit in the midst of this hell was unreal. I translated what she said for Dave Hobson and his eyes welled with tears.

After viewing more rooms, more war sites, more rubble, more chaos, filth, and starving children in the streets, we headed to the "Palace." It was a far cry from the grandeur of what we imagine a palace to be.

At lunch, I turned to the Afghani next to me and made conversation. I talked about D.C. and he said, "I know D.C., I am from Baltimore. I am Hamid Karzai's brother. I have a restaurant in Maryland."

Later we learned that Karzai had asked his brother to stay at the palace while he met with foreign delegations in Europe and Tashkent for the purpose of shoring up support. The reason for his brother's stay was that the situation in Afghanistan was so precarious they were afraid of a coup—even before he became president.

We went into a tent where there were top U.S. military brass surrounded by sophisticated electronics. We watched the beginning of a major military incursion against the Taliban. Because there had been cases of friendly fire in the beginning of the war, a soldier next to the general who was running the mission would yell, "Silence." All the stations out in the Afghani terrain would then report in one-by-one so that no missiles were sent into our troops by accident.

We then returned to Bagram Air Force Base by convoy, and then on to the United States.

When we returned, a lot of attention was focused on us due to the fact that we were one of the first delegations in. I felt determined—driven—to do something to help the Afghani people. What we had observed was incredibly moving. Congressman Hobson, Congressman Rogers and I all committed to do whatever we could to get the word out to our Members about the plight of Afghanistan. I formed the Afghanistan Caucus of Members with Sheila Jackson Lee of Texas, a Democratic Member who had also been on the trip and was supportive of the issue.

A statement I made was carried in a few press reports. When asked to describe Afghanistan I commented, "The devil has touched his foot on earth in Afghanistan." When I later called the new Afghani officials to come to my office to talk about the caucus and what we could do, I started by saying, "I may have offended you by my statement about the devil. I did not mean to say that your country is bad; I just wanted to draw attention to the terrible plight that you have."

The official responded, "Congressman, we were happy when we saw it. The world has to understand how bad and how serious this is."

I returned to Afghanistan one more time within the next year and a half. My Chief of Staff, Will Heaton, and George Shevlin (Chief of Staff for Ranking Member of House Administration Committee, John Larson) went with us. We returned to the hospital and toured the orphanage. Sheila Jackson Lee and Paul Kanjorski, both Democratic Members of the House also came on CODEL Ney, as I had arranged it this time and it was my delegation.

On the day we were to leave Afghanistan, we had a meeting with Ambassador Zalmay Khalilzad, a longtime political ally of President Bush. When he was arranging our passage back to the U.S., one of his people got on a cell phone and I heard him say in Farsi, "A Congressional delegation from the United States will be going back to Bagram by convoy tonight."

We went to the Palace for dinner that evening, and were to meet with President Karzai, but he was running late. When he arrived, he wanted us to stay longer, but the convoy needed to leave. Not wanting to offend President Karzai, and after conferring with Kanjorski and Sheila, we asked the military with us if the convoy could please be held. They responded that it could not, but they could arrange Black Hawk helicopters for a night run. We opted for that.

In the Afghani night, lights out, flying low, we headed to the base in two Black Hawks to depart from there for Doha, Qatar, to view our intelligence center and to discuss Iraq.

We discovered through a conversation with the military that the State Department, due to some funding situation or some other bizarre reason, did not use encrypted phones. Thus, the telephoned "Congressional request" from the person at the embassy earlier that day was like putting it on Kabul Radio. That evening we arrived safely at the base, but the convoy was attacked. Paul Kanjorski, Sheila, and I all believe that we were the designated targets, but a president who was late for dinner and our diplomatic courtesy of not wanting to leave early spared us from the bombing.

Chapter 16

☆ ☆ ☆

PRESIDENTS

"In our brief national history we have shot four of our presidents, worried five of them to death, impeached one and hounded another out of office. And when all else fails, we hold an election and assassinate their character."

—P.J. O'ROURKE

My political career has afforded me the opportunity to meet seven presidents at various times along the way.

I met President Nixon when he did a fundraiser for the Ohio State Senate races. It was the first after his resignation, and had been arranged by Senator Tom Van Meter. Although controversial, it raised money.

As I related before, I met President Ford when I was the third youngest delegate at the 1976 Kansas City Republican Convention and was invited to dinner at the White House to "firm up" my vote for Ford.

President Carter and I met in passing at a conference years later, after he was president. A few years later he called me to congratulate me on passing my legacy bill, HAVA (Help America Vote Act), as did Gerald Ford, right after Carter called. They both had served on the Ford Commission, and I incorporated suggestions from that commission into HAVA.

I campaigned for former President George H.W. Bush (41) when he was vice president, running for president. I was on a boat on the Ohio River with Vice President Bush, Nancy Hollister who was then Mayor of Marietta, Ohio, and Ohio State Representative Tom Johnson from New Concord, Ohio. It was a campaign event. We were to head into shore,

Bush was to disembark and then shake hands with the people. During the security check on shore, we were alone with the vice president for twenty minutes, which is a gift in presidential candidate time at a fundraiser. He was kind and charming. I, of course, being the "hoopie" (Appalachian slang for hillbilly) that I am, asked to see his driver's license, which he produced for me to inspect. I then asked if he had a personal card, and he said yes. I asked if he could sign the card to my only child at the time, my son, Bobby. He pulled out a white business card, signed the back "To Bobby," and handed it to me. When I turned it over, the only words printed on it were, "The Vice President" and nothing else. He laughed and pointed out, "People know my address and who I am."

The first time I saw Bill Clinton he wasn't President Clinton. I was walking through the rotunda of the Ohio Statehouse. Ohio State Senator Gene Branstool motioned me over. Gene was a nice guy who eventually, for a period of time, became Chair of the Ohio Democratic Party. Gene came off as a good-old-boy farmer, but he was quite street-savvy about politics. Gene said, "Bob, come here, there's someone I want you to meet."

As I walked toward Gene, I saw a tall man in a nice suit looking up at the ceiling of the rotunda. As Gene introduced him, the man simultaneously smiled a large bright smile and clasped my hand with his other hand over mine. Gene said, "Senator Ney, meet Governor Clinton, the next President of the United States." We both exchanged pleasantries, I welcomed him to Ohio and Gene indicated to Governor Clinton that I was one of the "good" Republicans.

Clinton then, as only he could I would later discover in my time around him, proceeded to engage in and dominate the conversation, leaving me with the feeling that I was initiating the discourse. In that unmistakable "I feel your paaain" accent he said, "I've known quite a few good Republicans and Gene is a good guy. If you are complimented by him, then you have to be a good guy too."

He then talked about the beautiful Statehouse, asked where I was from, and spoke about everything else except running for president. I walked away thinking that he was charismatic and a great guy, but just from way too small a state to be president; however, he might make a good secretary of state(!)

After Clinton, I spent a lot of time with George W. Bush (43).

I met President Obama when he was a U.S. Senator. I remember that night well. We were in the Mansfield room off the Senate floor for some reception, which I think was sponsored by labor. In walks the new Senator from Illinois. He had a big-time media/paparazzi following as soon as he arrived. I was there with Will Heaton, my Chief of Staff. I recall overhearing some comments from the "old bulls" (old guard Democratic Senators) who were looking at him. One of them quietly said, "He thinks he is a big deal. He will learn the pecking order in the Senate."

Obama bypassed that pecking order in two years, to advance further than that Senator who commented! As we say in the House, "Every morning, every Senator awakens and stares in the mirror at the future President of the United States"—or at least in his or her own mind.

Of the seven presidents I have met, President Clinton made the biggest impression on me. Before I go into the details, let me give you some background on my pro-union position, which impacted my first meeting with Bill Clinton.

(As I campaigned for office in 1994, one thing was certain. I hated free trade agreements. Bellaire, Ohio, where I was raised, was culturally a pro-union, save-American-jobs atmosphere and demographically, largely made up of immigrants. The people of Bellaire were opposed to "foreign job killers" like China, Japan, Mexico and Canada. Therefore, I was raised to dislike foreign trade. The North American Free Trade Agreement (NAFTA) had been passed under President Bill Clinton and the unions were angry—not angry enough to vote against him in the next election, but angry in general. The anger was directed more at Congress. In my largely Democratic area of the State of Ohio, NAFTA was more likely blamed on the Republicans (although the Democrats controlled all three branches of government). I seized the opportunity to bash the "Congress" in general as anti-worker, which in my opinion was 100 percent true.

The tough election against my most difficult opponent ever, Greg DiDonato, went as expected. It was a win, but not in the blow it out category. Senator DiDonato was seasoned, paid attention to his constituents, was a relentless campaigner, and came off as very genuine to those who met him.

It was then on to D.C. as part of Newt Gingrich's, Contract with America. One of the issues that came up in the first 100 days, besides the implementation of the "Contract," was the issue of MFN (Most Favored Nation) status for China. This is an exclusive status that is not full-blown free trade, but would make China a favored nation of ours, allowing for easier trade. After NAFTA, this was an issue I campaigned against. I railed (and still do) against the "Commie Red Chinese Dictator Government." I like the Chinese people, but cannot tolerate their dictatorial, anti-human rights, Christian-hating government. I was unbendable on this issue—or so I thought.)

I soon found myself in "Slick Willie's" hands. I do not say this with venom or spite because, frankly, the man was/is Teflon. He is charming, visionary, witty, persuasive and comes off as one who can bring people together while he is picking their pockets. Perhaps he is sincere; some doubt it, but who knows. President Clinton was good at his craft.

In mid-1995, I sat in a meeting at the Executive Office Building with a few other entrenched pro-labor, anti-trade Representatives. It was approximately 10:30 in the morning. President Clinton arrived, gladhanded, complimented and small chatted—all the things that make him Clinton. We then proceeded to discuss Most Favored Nation Status for China. The president gave us his articulate and comprehensive view of why we needed it. He reminded us that he and Newt Gingrich were working together on this, which reminded *me* that I had firmly told Newt the day before, after his inquiry about my possibly supporting the MFN vote, "Absolutely not, no way, don't ask, don't bother—"ain't gonna happen." I felt that although I was a "no," this was, after all, the president. I owed it to the office to hear what he had to say before I said no to him. Plus, I got to sit with the president. (Later in my life, chatting with POTUS –President of the United States, became routine.)

Clinton finished his rationale for the MFN vote and he knew what we knew—the vote would be tight. The combination of Conservatives who don't like to lose sovereignty with these deals, moderate labor Republicans, and liberal Democrats make the trade deals a tough climb for the leaders. We responded to the Clinton/Gingrich MFN vote as expected. I talked about losing American jobs and the unions. Other Members at the meeting raised the issue of human rights, recalling that Congresswoman Nancy Pelosi once unfurled a pro-democracy banner in Tiananmen Square to prove a point. That made worldwide news and pissed off the Communist Red Chinese Government for sure.

Clinton responded on the human rights issue. He said, "I agree. They have a long way to go." He then related a recent conversation he had had with Jiang Zemin, the premiere of China, as if it were a conversation with a next-door neighbor. The way Clinton told it really opened my eyes to the fact that world leaders converse like regular people— they joke, and sometimes cuss. I experienced this same thing when talking with constituents. They would say things such as, "Wow! We're talking like regular people." It always amazed me when they said that, and in the meeting that day, it amazed me that I had the same thought relating to world leaders.

Clinton continued, "I called Jiang the other day and said, 'Jiang, you've just got too many people in prison,' and he responded, 'So do you.' I said, 'We are trying to change that and you need to also.'"

Of course, Jiang Zemin (General Secretary of the Communist Party of China at that time) was referring to the fact that we are an incarceration-happy country, and Clinton was referring to something different—political prisoners. After Clinton related this "trite" conversation, he somehow, like Svengali, wrapped it into a discourse of how he was going to change their behavior, improve human rights, open it up to a democratic form of thinking, empower its people—all the same arguments Newt made. The president also made the strong argument that under the agreement we would be able to sell our goods and products to China and create jobs here at home.

He then turned, looked me in the eye, leaned forward slightly, gently bit that lower lip and delivered the punch line for the vote—the same sort of strong punch line that Newt had given me in convincing me to run for U.S. Congress: "Your President needs the power to change their behavior. Your President needs just a couple more years to push the Chinese, and legislation will do it. Your President needs your vote to help me accomplish this."

I said, "That sounds convincing, but I have committed a 'no' vote, have announced it, and I have a big-time Democratic district that will counter this vote like a kitchen sink crashing over my head."

He then said, "I will personally defend you on this needed vote. Your President will support you against anyone on this vote."

I swear, having been hypnotized or politically drugged, I then committed a "yes" vote for the MFN. Of course I met with Newt right away. I did the vote for Clinton, but being a bit "politically disingenuous," as people are, I let Newt believe that I was giving the "yes" vote to him, thus letting him think that he would owe me a favor down the road. Yes, it may be shocking to you, but in D.C. we may give the credit to many for one vote.

Although it was tight, the vote passed—and as I had predicted, in my 1996 campaign my opponent, Senator Burch, stuck the vote as far up my ass as possible. When I called the White House to ask for a statement of support from "My President," there seemed to be amnesia concerning that commitment. I barely hung on in that election. As I stated earlier, it was only a 5,000 district-wide vote difference. I never again supported a trade measure for China.

My next major encounter concerning President Clinton was during his impeachment, when I was thrown into the middle of the national media. The Republicans were about six seats short of enough votes to impeach him. Congressman Tony Hall, who was a fervent, moral Christian and a leader in the movement to stop hunger, at one point asked me if I was close to deciding. We were on the floor of the House, and it was a strange conversation as I sensed that he was asking for some reason beyond curiosity. (I later discovered that President Clinton had called him from Israel and asked him, since Congressman Hall was a friend of mine, to see where I stood.)

I received an intense call from President Clinton's attorney after I did the national show, *Meet the Press*, about my undecided status. My high profile was not politically helpful to me in my overwhelmingly Democratic District. The president's attorney, the late Charles Ruff, said, "I want to invite you into a private, one-on-one, un-taped conversation with the president, where you can ask him anything—and I mean, anything." He added that Congressman Chris Shays of Connecticut had taken the president up on the same offer.

I responded, "I don't really want to do that, as I would ask him one, and only one, question, 'Did you perjure yourself?' I couldn't care less whether he had oral sex."

Ruff then said, "Let me make this clear, I am the president's attorney so I have confidentiality, but let's assume hypothetically, and I mean TOTALLY HYPOTHETICALLY [he emphasized this] that he, Clinton, is guilty as hell of having had oral sex and perjuring himself—totally perjuring himself. My question to you is, does that rise to the level of impeachment?"

I then said, "I am declining the meeting, but I can tell you that if the president 'hypothetically' did perjure himself and admits to it on television, I would say that will be enough for me to vote no on impeachment, and he can suffer the legal consequences after his presidency ends." I knew that others felt this way also. I later found out from a friend of Clinton's that the White House knew that other Members on the Republican side thought as I did. He also told me a debate ensued with some of President Clinton's staff wanting to take "us" up on our offer

The other side won, which was for the president to go on television and stop short of admitting perjury. I then decided to impeach. I made the announcement during the *WWVA Dimitri Vassilaros* radio show, which at that time was broadcast out of Wheeling West Virginia, and the networks went crazy. The opening of the *Donny and Marie Show* was interrupted for a special bulletin, and it carried me live from Wheeling, West Virginia (across the river from Ohio), to announce my decision. I started to receive in-depth questions from the national media about my important decision, as it was speculated that some others would follow suit and the impeachment would go through.

My time of indecision was over, and many people in the District were furious.

Chapter 17

☆ ☆ ☆

POLITICAL
STRONG-ARMING

*"Coercion, after all, merely captures man.
Freedom captivates him."*

—RONALD REAGAN

I had a major blowout over the Head Start program with Andy Card, President George W. Bush's Chief of Staff. The first of the legislation debates centered on Head Start. John Boehner was doing his best to acquire votes to hurt the program. I had supported Head Start for years as an Ohio State Senator and again as a U.S. Congressman. When George Bush became president, every issue, including this one, was treated as though, if lost, it would be the end of the world—as if "winning" were vital to saving the presidency.

Speaker Hastert became a lap dog for President Bush. It didn't matter whether it was overspending, crushing unions, or ripping the legs out from under Head Start, Hastert acted like the President ran the House instead of the other way around.

I found myself under immense pressure to vote against Head Start. I was bombarded by all sides—Tom DeLay, Hastert's staff, and the Chairman of the Education Committee, which at the time was John Boehner. I found it amazing that a sitting president would make a *do or die* issue over taking money away from poor children who needed a jump on school—a head start. Anyone in the field of education knew that Head Start had a rocky beginning, but it had proven to be statistically and socially a very fine program and I had always supported it.

I had a private "hideaway" (an office the Speaker gives to leaders and long term, older Members of Congress) that very few people knew about. Even Brian Walsh, my Press Secretary, was unaware until one day I had to have an emergency call placed between a few Ohio Members and Governor Taft. My hideaway was the only place to make the call. Brian walked in, looked around, looked at Chris Krueger, my Executive Assistant, and said, "Did you know about this?" Chris just grinned and knew he would later be getting an ass chewing from Brian for not telling him.

On this particular evening, I was in that Capitol hideaway, one floor directly below the Chamber. I was sick and tired of being lobbied and bullied on this vote. I had to escape the *arm-twisting*. I used to say it was so bad that you could hear the bones snap on the floor of the House. My private phone in the hideaway was ringing, so I knew that only Ted Van Der Meid of the Speaker's office could have given it out. Chris Krueger, my Executive Assistant, answered it and signaled me that it was Andy Card (White House Chief of Staff).

Andy said, "We need this Head Start vote—it is critical to the Bush Administration's future." I was stunned at this. The entire future of Bush's Administration was predicated on beating up on little unfortunate kids by taking their Head Start funding away? I thought this was idiocy and stupid politics.

I said, "I have always supported Head Start over my entire career. I don't like this vote, and I just cannot help you."

Card blew up and responded with, "Let me make this clear. Boehner said you were a vote 'for us' and we are holding you to that."

"I don't know where Boehner got that from," I said. "I can rethink this, but I don't like it and I'm sure I will not change my mind."

Andy then said, "You are a fucking liar!"

I said, "Fuck you, Andy, and your idiotic Administration," and I hung up on him. I then went to the floor of the House where Boehner confronted me. I told him that "Andy is disrespectful, way out in left field on this, can kiss my ass, and fuck him—period."

Boehner continued to strong-arm me. They were one vote short. It boiled down to the fact that this vote was so hideous, so wrong, that they simply could not get the votes. One of my best friends in Congress, Steve LaTourette, took a *bullet* for me on this to move the bill along. He told them to back off of me and he would help them through this process in the House, but not necessarily if or when the vote came back from the Senate.

The second time Andy Card ran afoul of Congress he had to confront Congressman Steve LaTourette. Steve is one of the finest members of Congress; very brave in his positions, an independent thinker, good at politics, and is no wallflower. He is conservative on some issues, but he cares deep down about working people and how they survive in America. (*At this writing Steve has left Congress, frustrated with the lack of acceptance of moderates within the Republican Party.*) Andy decided that he wanted to remove Davis-Bacon (a federal law that requires payment of prevailing wages to workers on public works projects) from the Transportation Appropriation bill. Don Young was a strong Transportation Chairman and let LaTourette take the lead on this issue.

I dug into Andy's history and found some interesting things: He had been a Massachusetts State Representative; he had worked for President Bush's father, Bush 41; when Bush 41 lost to Clinton, Andy felt that the Transportation Bill had done the president no good; and, he disliked organized labor and unions.

We all kept up a tough front. The Transportation Unions' lobbyists for the building trades, like Tim James, were very effective and helped the "labor Republicans" push back. Bush 43 kept putting up roadblocks at every step. He simply did not want a Transportation bill. John Mica, Transportation Subcommittee Chair, during a private Republican caucus meeting made the best statement of the day. John said, "Hell, the president doesn't think we need a bill. As he travels in cities by car, they stop all the traffic for his motorcade. He thinks that there are no traffic problems—the streets are deserted." We all howled. As one Republican Member from a farm state said, "It's funny because of how John said it, and it's funny because Bush is a dumbass and is dumber than a hoe handle." We eventually passed a bill and working wages were protected.

Sometime later, I received a call from the White House asking me to come over to talk about CAFTA (Central American Free Trade Agreement).

When I arrived, the other two Members who had been invited, one of whom was a newer Member, and I were taken into the Oval Office, versus the conference room outside the Oval Office. This was the first Oval Office visit for the newer Congressman. He was amazed and talked about the greatness of the office, its feel, and all the history in this room.

In walked Dick Cheney, Karl Rove, Rob Portman (former U.S. Congressional Member from Ohio, later U.S. Senator, but at this time Trade Rep for President Bush) and Andy Card. I was placed next to Andy Card, and neither of us acknowledged that the other one existed.

President Bush leaned forward as he often did, with his head lowered and his shoulders going up and down as though he were chuckling and said, "You're in the Oval Office—the most powerful office on earth; that is how important this vote is for me." I think one of the Members was impressed; however, I thought, *Who gives a shit about where we are sitting?* He repeated his statement. Later, I figured that was because he didn't know what else to say, as he most likely didn't understand how the CAFTA legislation worked.

He then launched into a seemingly endless tirade about Hugo Chávez and how this bill will stop Chávez and communism by building up the region and showing people in Chávez's country that surrounding countries have better lives with free trade by being a democracy. If I had not been in the Oval Office I would have spit my coffee out—it was seriously something out of *Saturday Night Live.* No one disagreed, although it was ridiculous. Then when no Member seemed to bite on that, the president said this would help farmers.

I spoke up and said, "I have studied the bill and the gains are small. Ohio farmers may make some money but it will take years, so it is ineffective. Look at China. We got raped by them after the [China] Trade Bill. This just will not significantly help farmers."

The president disagreed, went back to Chávez and the communists and how this would end them. As we walked out the president looked at me and said, "I need your vote."

I looked at him and said, "I should vote for this as a thank-you for appointing Portman and taking him out of the House so we don't have to put up with him." Rob laughed and the president lightly slapped the left side of my face, meaning, *wiseass.*

Later that week, thirty minutes before the vote on CAFTA, the private line on my desk rang. Two staffers and Will Heaton, my Chief of Staff at the time, were sitting in my office. It was the vice president. He said, "Hello, Bob, Dick Cheney here. I want to talk to you about CAFTA."

Just being ornery, I didn't indicate to the staffers that it was the vice president by saying, *Hello Mr. Vice President.* I simply said, "Sure." He asked me if I could support this bill and I asked why.

He said, "This stops communism." I told him that it would not make a bit of difference to stop Chávez. He then said, "This is good for farmers."

I said, "By the time this works for farmers they will have to learn Mandarin Chinese, as these trade bills are ruining us."

Having exhausted the issues he said, "Can you do this—the team, the president, needs it for a win."

I then said, "Look, I have an overwhelmingly Democratic district, I supported you and the president publicly at events, and I was good to your campaign." The staffers looked up at this time, realizing that it was the V.P. "I just cannot help you."

Cheney said, "Okay, thanks" and the conversation ended. The staffers remarked how I shocked them; they thought it was someone else on the phone. I told them that the administration was obsessed with Chávez and that Chávez would still be head of his country after Bush was out of the Oval Office. At the time of this writing, Chávez remains the head of his country.

☆ ☆ ☆

ENCOUNTERS OF THE BEST KIND

"I don't believe in accidents. There are only encounters in history. There are no accidents."

—PABLO PICASSO

During the nearly three decades of my political career, I was privileged to have had encounters with many interesting, wonderful people. Many of the individuals I met were unknown, regular citizens who were famous in my eyes for their wealth of knowledge and insight. Although I would like to, it is impractical to write of all those experiences in this book. I am focusing on some more "well-known" personalities in this chapter and I have chosen four whom I would like you to encounter also.

POPE JOHN PAUL II

"Radical changes in world politics leave America with a heightened responsibility to be, for the world, an example of a genuinely free, democratic, just and humane society."

—POPE JOHN PAUL II

I was raised Catholic, and there having been only a few popes in my lifetime, Pope John Paul II was surely the most popular. In 2000, on a trip to Italy for a conservative conference, my children, Bobby and Kayla, and I had the good fortune to attend a Papal Mass. Bobby was sixteen and Kayla was eleven. These trips were approved by the Ethics Committee and paid for by groups that advocate issues such as Conservative and Liberal platforms. Children of the Members could go on the trips if the Members personally paid for their airfare.

The Congressional delegation was to the left of the altar about 150 feet from where the pope would be saying mass, outside St Peter's Basilica. The altar was prepared, draped with a white cloth, ready for the pontiff. After being seated, we were informed that the wait would be about fifteen minutes. The sky darkened as we were led to our seats, but then it started to rain. The rain certainly didn't seem to dampen the spirits of the throng of people to our left who were amassed in St. Peter's Square, waiting to see a glimpse of one of the most popular popes in modern history. The pope was running late, it rained harder, and without umbrellas or any form of cover were becoming drenched. My children were getting fidgety. They suggested that we might want to leave. Because of the rain and lightning, I considered it. But as I pointed out to the children, the pope was in frail health and I thought he might not be around very much longer. I wanted Bobby and Kayla to have the opportunity to see him.

As the rain poured, the Pope arrived in the archway, assisted by priests on both sides. The pontiff was moving ever so slowly, hesitantly placing his foot toward the bottom step that would place him outside, moving toward the altar. Then, as he was about to come out from under the shelter of the archway, the rain suddenly stopped. Congressman Boehner, who was sitting next to us looked at me, puffed on his cigarette and said, "Neat trick."

I never thought Pope John Paul II would live six more years, and the next time I saw him was in Rome, April of 2005, at the time of his death. I had pushed hard to be included in the official U.S. delegation. We were told only twenty-four people from the Senate and House would be allowed to go. Luckily, I was among those twenty-four. It was a high-powered delegation: Speaker of the House Dennis Hastert and his Chief of Staff Scott Palmer, Tom DeLay, Hillary Clinton, John Kerry, Chris Dodd, Mike DeWine, Rick Santorum, Phil English, and other fortunate Members. We flew over on government jets; one for the House and one for the Senate Members. Accommodations were tight, security intense, and space limited.

Upon our arrival on April 7, we went inside the church and waited until President Bush and former President Clinton finished paying their respects. George Shevlin, Staff Director for John Larson, Democratic Ranking Member of the House administration committee, took a picture of the two presidents kneeling and viewing the body of Pope John Paul II. We each then took our turn to kneel. It was a moving moment, especially for a Catholic.

That evening I went to dinner with Sheila Jackson Lee, U.S. Representative from Texas. The next morning at the Holiday Inn Rome, we all gathered downstairs. It was the morning of the funeral and the Congressional delegation was in the hotel dining area preparing to eat breakfast. Ironically, I sat with Tom DeLay. We shook our heads about the Abramoff brouhaha and both agreed that it was made into a media circus and that it should blow over. However, the conversation on Tom's side seemed extremely guarded. We wished each other well. From the first days of the scandal through to its conclusion, it was one of the few times we would speak to each other until Tom resigned.

Members of the Congress were under tight security, as always when gathered in groups. The public was not allowed in our eating area, just Members and a limited number of staffers. Some of us noticed a well-dressed, impressive-looking man whom no one knew, yet he seemed familiar. We wondered who he was and how he got into a secured area with us. Someone then said he was James Caviezel, the actor who played Jesus in *The Passion of Christ*. Senator Rick Santorum had seen him sitting alone at a restaurant the night before and invited him to his table. They both, I was told, were devout Catholics and had a long conversation about Catholicism and the Church. Senator Santorum invited him, inappropriately, to be part of our delegation. Although an infraction of protocol, Jim Caviezel was interesting. It happens that I sat next to him at the funeral, behind Senator and Mrs. Santorum. During the service, the three of them knew all the Latin in the mass and all of the details on the rituals—far more than I had ever learned.

The funeral was held outdoors on April 8, 2005. Delegations from many countries were seated outside St. Peter's Basilica in sections, per country represented. Seeing the world's leaders of all countries and religions on one stage was amazing. We faced the altar, behind us was a small, makeshift wall, and behind that wall was an estimated four million people. We then heard a rumbling sound. At first we were bewildered and somewhat frightened at the intensity of it, thinking it might be a riot. We then realized that the crowd was chanting, "St. John Paul" (advocating sainthood for the pope).The chanting of those millions of voices caused the area to vibrate intensely.

After the funeral, the simple, wooden coffin of Pope John Paul II was lifted and carried toward the arch of the entrance to St. Peter's Basilica. Then suddenly the pallbearers stopped and switched hands, grasped the coffin with the opposite hand, turned and faced the crowd. They then tilted the coffin forward, almost straight up as if to give a good-bye nod from Pope John. The crowd erupted in cheering, applause and tears. The pallbearers then turned again and the "Shoes of the Fisherman" was carried reverently inside to be laid to eternal rest. The bells at St. Peter's rang non-stop. I called my wife with my cell phone so she could hear it live as she was watching from home in Ohio. It was a very emotional moment for all.

A couple of incidental moments stood out on that trip. Before the service, Senator John Kerry was standing in a group of people tossing his perfectly coiffed hair from side to side and speaking French like a star. Congressman Phil English (R-Pennsylvania), a nice, down to earth guy who has a very distinctive, slightly rough voice, and a dry sense of humor, looked at Kerry and said, "That's why he's not president."

Scott Palmer, Speaker of the House Dennis Hastert's Chief of Staff, engaged me in a conversation and told me that "Denny" had a medal on his desk from the Pope whom he had personally met with a few years before. Scott, in this weird face that he always made, one that reminded many people of Lurch on *The Adams Family*, said with total seriousness that the medal on the Speaker's desk is what possibly saved the Capitol from being hit by the airplane on its way from Pennsylvania on September 11, 2001. I looked at Scott; he tilted his head to the left, raised his left eyebrow, said no more, and moved away.

People approached Jim Caviezel for autographs after the funeral, overwhelmed that he had played Christ. Senator Santorum went into a discussion of abortion with Jim and then the subject of doing fundraisers and appearances came up.

(*Two years later I was in prison and George Shevlin, who had also been on this trip as Congressman John Larson's [D-Connecticut] Staff Director, and wrote to me frequently while I was in prison, sent me a card with a picture of President Bush looking at the body of Pope John Paul II. The cartoon speech bubble had the president saying, "Santa Claus died?" I looked at the picture of the Pope dressed in a red robe, the look on President Bush's face, and the inscription from George: "Remember when this was taken?" I simply smiled.*)

MOTHER TERESA

"Let us more and more insist on raising funds of love, of kindness, of understanding, of peace. Money will come if we seek first the Kingdom of God—the rest will be given."

—MOTHER TERESA

It was 1997 and I was Vice Chairman of the House Administration Committee under the firm-handed chairmanship of William Thomas (R-California). Any time the Rotunda (center point of the Capitol) is used for an event, which isn't often, a formal resolution has to be passed by House Administration and carried on to the floor of the House of Representatives, and agreed to by the Senate, for consensus or a vote. It is a consensus about 99 percent of the time. The motion is moved for passage, no one objects and no vote is called. I was selected to manage the resolution on the floor of the U.S. House allowing use of the Rotunda for honoring Mother Teresa with the Congressional Gold Medal, the highest civilian honor bestowed by the United States Congress. I, like millions of people, revered Mother Teresa. My son, Bobby, had been absolutely fascinated with Mother Teresa and everything about her ever since he was a little boy.

I carried the resolution to the House floor and the date of the event was set for June 2, 1997. Bobby was twelve years old at the time and was spending the week in D.C. with me. Whenever he visited me, he would hang out at the office, play around the Capitol, go underground where a tram connects the Longworth, Cannon and Rayburn office buildings to the Capitol, and he especially liked to visit Newt Gingrich's office. *(He likes Newt and invited him to his and Julie's wedding in 2011.)*

The day of the Gold Medal ceremony, Bobby took off without the cell phone pager that he usually carried. I got a call from Newt's office to come over and join a small group of people to meet Mother Teresa prior to the beginning of the ceremony. My staff and I endlessly tried to page Bobby, not realizing that he didn't have his pager with him. Unfortunately, he missed the opportunity to meet Mother Teresa—something I feel bad about even now.

I arrived at Newt's office and there, incredibly, sat this small, frail woman wearing her familiar white robe and head covering that bore blue stripes. She looked so tiny, sitting in a big leather chair in the

Speaker's office. Newt was there with just a few Democratic and Republican top leaders and the Cardinal of the Catholic Church for the District of Columbia. Newt introduced me to Mother Teresa as the man who carried the resolution to do this ceremony in the Rotunda. She nodded, smiled, simply said, "Hello" and extended her hand. I didn't shake it, but gently held her hand in mine, and lightly pressed my hand around hers. It was a personal moment for me to actually be able to make contact with this incredible, living saint of a person (in my opinion) and feel such a connection—a closeness—to one of the most remarkable persons to have walked this planet.

Newt explained the process very slowly and deliberately: "Mother Teresa, we are so glad to have you here. Soon we will go to the Rotunda and I will say something, then the leader of the Senate, the two Minority Leaders of the House and Senate and President Clinton will each say a few words. You will then receive the Congressional Gold Medal of Honor and can address the people who are present."

Then Mother Teresa calmly, with a pleasant look on her face, said in her beautiful accent, "I thank you for this of which I am not deserving. I will accept this medal and then sell it and give the money to the poor. Thank You." With that, and a nice smile, she stopped talking.

Having been around Newt long enough, I could sense when he was nervous. He has a *tell* at those rare times when he is at a loss for words. The *tell* was now apparent. Newt looked at Mother Teresa with a nervous smile on his face, tilted his head to the left, slightly dipped it toward his shoulder and said nothing, looking as if his mind were a computer surfing for the response. I could see Newt's dilemma. He couldn't just say, *"The hell you will!"* or *"No way!"* This was Mother Teresa!

Now keep in mind, space is limited for these events. Media from all over the world is present and this event was carried live by many major television news channels. I had this humorous vision, as probably others in the room did also, of Mother Teresa in the Rotunda, in front of the world, saying, "Thank you," then holding up the medal and starting an auction. Of course I knew that she would be proper and merely say that she was going to sell it for the poor—but how does one deal with that?

Before anyone could speak, argue, or plead, the Cardinal of the Diocese of Washington D.C. very calmly looked at Mother Teresa and said, "Thank you, Mother Teresa. You can accept the medal. The Church will give you the money for the medal, which you can give to charity [gold worth approximately $38,000], and we will keep it for you in a beautiful display case within the Church." She smiled, nodded, and then we all made our way to the Rotunda.

It was an amazing example of humility on her part, and an amazing spectacle of some of the most powerful men on earth who were made speechless by a little nun.

In a side note, two days after the ceremony, for whatever reason, the Capitol clean-up crews had not removed the chairs and other things set up for the ceremony from the Rotunda, or the Styrofoam cups outside that had been used by the people who were in attendance. I was radical about things being kept in order in the Capitol, even before I became Chairman of House Administration, so I complained to Chairman Thomas. He did have a great sense of humor, and in a bit of a high-pitched tone he used to emphasize his points he said, "Maybe we should have had the nuns use their long robes to sweep the cups up under them and clean up the property. Why don't you suggest that next time?"

JOHN TRAVOLTA

> *"I have no longer any desire for fame and fortune.*
> *My one ambition and my daily prayer is that I may live*
> *long enough to make beautiful the Capitol of the one*
> *country on earth in which there is liberty."*
>
> —CONSTANTINO BRUMIDI 1805–1880

The year was 1997, before I was Chairman of the House Administration Committee. A lobbyist who represented some actors and, as it later turned out, the controversial Church of Scientology, approached me and asked if I would like to meet Ann Archer, the actress, and Chick Corea, the famous jazz pianist. Of course, I said yes. I had followed the career of the beautiful and talented Ann Archer for quite a few years. Although I didn't know of Chick Corea at the time, I came to appreciate what a tremendous jazz musician he is. They arrived at our office where we had a nice chat and then headed to the Senate dining room. We didn't have a lot of time and the Senate had a buffet, so it was faster than eating in the House dining room.

Chick Corea seemed uncomfortable, and I asked him if he was okay. He said, "I am a bit nervous being around all of these high-powered political figures."

With a smile and a laugh I responded, "They will be nervous being around you."

A couple of other Members arrived and while we were eating, we discussed the issue of the discrimination in Germany against American Actors who were Scientologists. Let me frame this issue with how I firmly felt then and continue to feel: America is a country that was founded on faith and the freedom of that faith for everyone. As a Christian, I grow weary of some people today who think that America is only for Christians. There is the belief that it is strictly a "Christian nation"—as though the other faiths in America don't matter. The basis of freedom of religion, not just the one each of us prefer, is a fundamental, basic, long-standing ideal and belief inherent in the foundation of our great country. Based on that, I felt that the discrimination suffered by American actors in Germany, solely because they were Scientologists, was wrong and we as Americans should support freedom of religion for Americans here or abroad.

A growing number of Members began to feel that way. Anne and Chick's brief visit and a follow-up visit helped to gather Members' support, as "celebrity lobbying" always does. By the way, the lobbyist representing them was Jewish, not a Scientologist.

Dave, the lobbyist, asked if I would help a friend of Anne's who was coming to D.C. to testify for the Senate hearing before Arlen Spector's judiciary committee. I said, "Sure, who is her friend?"

"John Travolta."

I have seen kings, queens, presidents, actors, celebrities, famous activists, and others grace the halls of the Capitol, but never have I seen such a reaction as the one when John Travolta glided into D.C., flying his own jet.

My family found out that John Travolta was coming to my office and that I would be helping him with what he could expect from the hearing. I say with the utmost love, what started out to be fulfilling a long-time desire of my sister's to meet John Travolta, turned into a "family affair with friends."

I had to laugh. Nearly all of my immediate family (my daughter, Kayla, couldn't make it) and friends of family—about twenty in all, made the trek to D.C. I soon learned that they weren't the only ones who were fans—the Longworth building was abuzz with excitement. When we were notified by the Capitol Hill Police that John Travolta's car had pulled into the area, my Chief of Staff, Dave Distefano, went out into the hallway and literally had to wave his arms in a "get back" motion as house staffers who had heard the word jammed the hallways. This was going to create a problem for Travolta to walk down to our office, so with the assistance of the Hill police, we went down and escorted John past the security machines and up to our office. We exchanged pleasantries all the way up the hallway.

Travolta walked into our office to find family, friends, staff, and significant others of our staff who were all crowded into every square inch of our office. I explained to him, "If I didn't include all these people, I wouldn't have to worry about the next election, as I would be finished off by my family and friends before the opponent could."

He laughed and said, "I get it, no problem, let's say hello."

John wore a neatly tailored suit, and had a distinguished yet youthful look about him. He seemed relaxed, and his broad smile, easy-going nature, and casual manner put everyone at ease. He spoke with sincerity and was extremely personable, taking the time to engage everyone he met. At no point in time did he show any sign of displeasure or stress at the crowds who were incredibly excited in his presence

Eventually we went into my office and only Bobby, my son, came in. John smiled, motioned to Bobby to come over near him and Bobby sat on his knee. Then everyone left and we got down to the discussion of Scientology, how the Congress works, and what happened to John, Anne, Chick and other Scientologists in Germany.

John explained that when they would perform or make commercials in Germany (in Anne Archer's case, Revlon), extreme pressure was leveraged against them and in some cases contracts were actually cancelled only because they were Scientologists.

We went upstairs to the House Administration hearing room where we could privately rehearse John's appearance before the Senate Committee. With John was Tom Davis, Anne Archer's son. He was an official who was high up the food chain with the Scientology Center in California. He was a very pleasant young man, but did get a bit agitated with me when the role-play began.

I sat in the Chairman's seat and John sat at the witness table. I said, "Now, Mr. Travolta, what about the claims that Scientology is a cult?"

Tom interrupted and said, "He cannot be asked that!" John motioned to Tom that it was okay.

I then explained to Tom that Members can and will ask anything, especially because this is an issue dealing with a friendly country—

Germany. I said, "Don't think that the German Embassy here will not quietly talk to some Members to get them to ask pointed questions, without implicating the German Embassy in any way. In politics, this is commonly called "leaving no fingerprints."

After we finished rehearsing, we made the rounds. First stop was the House Cloak Room. In the back of the floor of the House on each side are two rooms not seen by C-SPAN cameras or by the public at large. One room is designated for the Republicans, and the other is an identical room for Democrats. There is a TV with C-SPAN on, and a small counter where a private citizen who has been approved by the House sells sandwiches, ice cream, soda, and so forth to Members. There are some couches, and many times Members lie down and take naps. The pages wake them up if there is a vote. There are about six phone booths where a Member can call anywhere at no charge.

Peggy Sampson, the head of the Republican page program at that time, is not only a class act and a caring person, but she also has a great sense of humor. When John came in the room and the pages packed around him, I made sure that Peggy was introduced to him—and she began fanning herself!

Next, we walked into the glorious Capitol Rotunda, where the amazing fresco of George Washington by the artist Constantino Brumidi appears in the Capitol dome. (*I still get the same chill as when I walked through it the first time as a young child.*) I had been talking to John and then realized that he had stopped and was about ten feet behind me. I walked back and saw that he was staring, transfixed. I said, "You've never been here before, have you?" He replied, "No, not even as a child, and I am taken aback. This entire place gives you such a feeling of awe, and also a great sense of politics and public policy. I think I could catch the political bug quickly."

I said, "Let's run you for something—say Governor."

John said, "Which state?"

I responded quickly, "Whichever one you want."

We went into Dick Armey's office and Dick said he liked John's movie *Faceoff*. In that movie, John does a cigarette trick where he rapidly moves a cigarette through each finger starting with the pinky finger to the thumb, and then it ends up in his mouth. Dick, as only he could, asked John to teach him that trick. John did, and Dick, who was a smoker, tried it with a lit cigarette and just about burned his face!

John asked that there be no pictures with the cigarette. I think he didn't want to appear to be promoting smoking in the Capitol. He told Dick Armey about his issue, pointing out that it was about religious freedom and the right to practice it without being penalized in his profession by German authorities—not about debating Scientology. In telling Dick Armey about the German authorities making it impossible for Anne Archer to do Revlon advertisements in Germany, he made it clear that it wasn't about money, but about rights of American citizens overseas. We then moved on to Speaker Newt Gingrich's office.

We all sat in chairs on the historic Speaker's balcony, which faces the Washington Monument and the Lincoln Memorial. Many times during the course of the civil war, Lincoln and his Generals would look out from the Capitol, see the White House, and contemplate the future of America. John sat between us, with Newt on his right and I on his left.

Newt said to John, "You have to stay because my wife, Marianne, is on her way and she would absolutely kill me if she didn't get to see you." I found this amusing because Newt and Marianne, like I, had met many famous people, yet the popularity of Travolta was undeniable.

The sun was setting on a beautiful Washington evening. We were sitting in the exact spot where Lincoln and his generals sat with the Congressional leaders to contemplate the future of America and how she may end up. John looked straight ahead and said, "I feel . . . I feel . . . I feel so . . ."

Newt offered, "American." Then like a Hollywood scene, but for real, John said in a low, calm voice, still looking straight ahead, "Yes, so American."

We talked about one of my favorite Travolta flicks, Quentin Tarantino's *Pulp Fiction*. John let me in on some of the hidden meanings in the movie, which I later shared with friends. (When I saw the movie, I had no idea that the briefcase Travolta's character opened had a combination lock of 666, and that the "glow" when the suitcase was opened was the character Marcellus Wallace's soul. Travolta's character was retrieving his soul. Marcellus also had an unexplained bandage on his neck. According to ancient folklore, that is the place from where the soul is stolen. The men in the apartment whom Travolta visited were the helpers of the devil and they had Marcellus's soul. When they shot at Travolta and missed, it was because God intervened.)

We spoke about his son Jett, who has since passed away, and our families. John showed me his watch, which had "Jett" on it.

He said that one of the absolute greatest moments of his life, besides with his wife and family, was the time he danced with Lady Di in the famous photograph taken at the White House. He spoke genuinely about it, with barely detectable tears in his eyes.

When we left Newt, John offered to fly me back to Pittsburgh. (This is where I would leave my car when I flew to D.C. It was only an hour from the airport to my home in Ohio.) I declined and it was time for them to leave. They had had their visit, had given testimony in the Senate and did a great job of lobbying for the issue.

In a few weeks, Democratic Representative Don Payne (now deceased) and I co-authored a resolution, which doesn't carry the same weight as a law, calling upon Germany to stop their discrimination.

While on an official trip to Germany with some other Members for general discussions, I raised the issue of Scientology, and one of the Ministers just became unglued—called the Scientologists cockroaches. Packages of condoms were given out on the streets in Germany displaying the word "Scientologist/cockroach" with a circle around it and a line drawn through it—the obnoxious message was birth control to prevent more Scientologists.

Upon returning to the United States with no resolve from the Germans, Congressman Payne and I pushed the resolution. The lobbyist offered to arrange a fundraiser by Travolta and some other actors if we desired, but we both declined. However, one Member whose support we needed insisted that (to make the Member look good with his kid) Travolta call his child to say goodnight. John did this, and I later apologized to him for his having to do that. He was gracious about it, and we got that Member's support, so I was pleased. The things that are done for votes!

After continued pressure by Don Payne and me, the resolution was brought up begrudgingly by Newt Gingrich and Tom DeLay. They were afraid of insulting German friends so we cut a deal; no one would ask for a vote and it would pass on voice. This would be less offensive to the Germans as we actually did not vote on it. One Member made a mistake and called for a vote. It wasn't part of the game plan and the resolution failed.

I received some terrible letters from people about my abandonment of my faith, and so on. Some said I was supporting Satan. I responded in a letter, "I am a Christian but my issue is not Scientology, it is the basic principle of religious freedom." Some of the language in the responses shocked me.

I was invited to the premier of one of John's new movies a year later, but had a commitment in the district. I didn't see John again—only on the big screen. It was a pleasure to work with him.

SONNY BONO

"I feel kind of like the black sheep in Congress,
but here I am."

—SONNY BONO

I first met Sonny Bono in 1976 at a Republican National Convention when I was nineteen years old. I was one of the youngest Ohio Delegates to the convention. Sonny was one of the entertainers who volunteered to "woo" the delegates, most likely for candidate Ronald Reagan rather than Gerald Ford. I was "morally" committed to Ford, but not legally under the Republican rules. (When I was selected to be a delegate by the party hierarchy, I said privately that I would vote for Ford, but could have changed my mind at the convention in Kansas City. In some states, if you ran as a delegate for Ford or for Reagan, you had to vote that way on the floor of the convention. We from Ohio did not, and many other states are the same, so, a lot of delegates in a tight race like that one, were up for grabs and were "courted" at the convention.) Therefore, the convention in Kansas City was still considered to be "open," "up for grabs," "wild, wild West."

I saw him as he walked down a hallway and I remember thinking, *Wow! It's Sonny Bono!* He was in a hurry and he was cursing—"dammit" something.

The next time I saw Sonny we were both new to Congress. He, too, was part of Newt Gingrich's Contract with America class. We were both members of the Banking Committee and my seat was next to his. I was star-struck. There I was, sitting next to Sonny Bono who had been married to Cher. After about three months of sitting next to him, I finally asked, "What was it like to be married to Cher?"

His comments about Cher were not flattering. (Nor were Cher's about Sonny. She had made the comment that Sonny was where he belonged—in a circus like a clown, or something to that effect.) I could sense that there still were some feelings there for Cher but the words and bitterness between the two were preventing reconciliation. However, Mary,

Sonny's wife at this time, got along quite well with Cher. This was a good thing for Sonny and Cher's daughter and his two children with Mary.

I recall a funny incident on the opening day of Congress and the convening of Committees for organizational purposes. This took place during the introduction of the new Members of the Banking Committee that was broadcast live on C-SPAN (Cable-Satellite Public Affairs Network). Congress authorized C-SPAN in 1979. It was not accepted at first, and Congress fought it for a long time on the basis of "an invasion of privacy" and just plain a bad idea politically. Members could be seen talking, laughing, sleeping, picking their noses (it has happened) and a wide variety of other no-no's.

The Committee was called to order by Chairman Leach, a Republican from Ohio. Sitting with me in my chair was my son, Bobby, who was about twelve years old. At that stage of his life, he loved to dress in a suit, and I had purchased a look-alike "Congressional pin" for him to wear on his lapel, similar to the one I was issued as a Member of the House. Members were to wear them for security reasons, one of which was for the Capitol Hill Police to identify us—especially new Members. That day C-SPAN was bringing the new Members' faces to their constituents across the Country. The C-SPAN camera panned down the row as each Member's name was called. It got to Congressman Steve LaTourette, my good friend from Ohio and a brand new Member also. Then my name was called and the camera was on me. Sonny's seat was next to mine, but he had left for a minute, so Bobby was sitting in it. Sonny's name was called, but the guy in the seat was Bobby. The room burst out in laughter, Sonny later found out and laughed about it as well. Sonny really liked Bobby, and the feeling was mutual. Bobby spent a lot of time visiting Sonny's office, as did my daughter Kayla. The staff of Congressman Bono's office was fantastic.

Sonny and I became very good friends, and when I was in the process of getting divorced in 1996, he talked to me about his divorce from Cher. Cher was eleven years younger than Sonny, and he said she felt that he had a sort of Svengali hold on her because she was young and naïve. He mentioned how mad he became when he walked into his house and saw David Geffen (record executive, film producer, theatrical producer) sitting at the dining room table with Cher, encouraging her to leave him. It caused a lot of bitter feelings. Sonny said, "I hope you don't have bitter feelings in your divorce." I didn't, but I appreciated his guidance and support. Like any emotional situation, it was traumatic for Candy and me, as well as for our families. I received a lot of advice from Sonny, plus moral support, and it was a great comfort to me.

One day when Sonny and I were sitting in the Banking Committee, Paul Kanjorski, a Democratic Congressman from Pennsylvania, walked up to the two of us and said to Sonny, "I was in Las Vegas with my wife and we saw a show where Cher was performing. She spoke really nicely about you on the stage."

Sonny told me a couple of days later that he had called Cher as a result and it was a very cordial conversation. Before Sonny passed way, he and Cher had renewed their friendship. As Sonny told me, it was due in part to the Kanjorski conversation. It was soothing to hear Sonny speak warmly about Cher and the life and career they had had together.

Sonny was a great guy. In November of 1995 I was up against the wall with the 1996 campaign coming up. People were coming after me with fangs bared to defeat me. In Congress, we were close to a vote about a shutdown. *(There was a severe budget crisis when Speaker Newt Gingrich and President Clinton quarreled over apportionments and failed to pass a continuing budget resolution to apportion temporary funds. It forced closure of most non-essential government offices for several weeks.)* Almost all events were canceled and Sonny had cancelled many of his fundraising commitments. There was to be a big fundraising event for me in St. Clairsville, Ohio. Sonny said, "We are going to do your event!" There was a very tight timeframe before we were to be present for the vote. He requisitioned a private Lear jet and Sonny, his Press Secretary, my Press Secretary (Neil Volz at that time) and I flew to Barnesville, Ohio, drove to St. Clairsville, did the event, drove back to Barnesville and flew back to D.C. immediately.

When we returned to Washington, Newt convened a meeting of the Republican Caucus. Tension was high; should we shut down the government? To add further to the problems, Senator Bob Dole, the Republican Leader of the Senate, was "blinking." He was not as steadfast as the new, "piss and vinegar" majority in the House, and we heard that Dole would not continue with a shutdown.

As tempers flew, and the meeting was steering out of control, Sonny took the microphone. He said, "You know, I remember when my career was going down the tubes and I did that show where the little person yells, 'Ze plane, ze plane.' All of a sudden, this little person called Tatu was yelling and screaming at me on the set. I thought, 'Where have I ended up that this little guy is screaming and yelling at me?' That's when I decided to get into politics. Sometimes you can't take yourself too seriously. Tonight we voted, but we also have to keep in mind that there are other lives out there and life goes on with or without us."

We then voted to call Clinton's bluff on the budget and shut down the "system."

There were those moments when Sonny really helped—such as his great sense of humor that helped us during that very tense time of the shutdown. He helped a lot of people. He was sometimes ridiculed, but he proved that he was a smart guy and a good Member of Congress.

Sonny was great to my constituents; both those on the Right and on the Left would come to see Sonny Bono in D.C. He was always great about inviting them into his office, where he would give autographs and talk with them.

We really liked him. His death took the wind out of several of us, especially Congressman LaTourette of Ohio and me.

It was January of 1998. Sonny had been encouraging me to take my children skiing, and I was planning a trip with my kids during the recess. I went home to prepare for the skiing trip when I got a phone call that Sonny Bono had died when he hit a tree while skiing at the Heavenly Ski Resort near South Lake Tahoe. I cancelled my trip. There was just no way I was going to go.

We boarded the Air Force jet formerly known as Air Force One. *(It was called that when presidents were aboard from 1962 when John F. Kennedy was president, through 1972. This plane carried JFK's coffin from Dallas to Washington, D.C.*

The plane was retired in March of 1998 with Vice President Al Gore making the last official flight and it is now on display at the Air Force Museum, Wright-Patterson Air Force Base near Dayton, Ohio.) The plane was packed full of Members flying to Palm Springs, California, where the funeral was held.

When we arrived, Newt Gingrich walked in with our Congressional delegation. Newt then privately went over to Sonny's staff who were standing together in the private courtyard behind the Church. Newt put his arms around them and they all they wept together. The Bono staff was crushed; Sonny's death drained every ounce of emotion from them. For those of us witnessing Newt and the staff, it was overwhelming.

President Ford was in the courtyard also. A group of little children who were going to be singing were standing together under the shade of a tree with their teacher. Congressman Mark Foley of Florida went over to the kids and said, "Do you know who the President of the United States is?" They answered that it was President Clinton. Congressman Foley pointed to President Ford, who was nearby and said, "That man was president too." Foley went over to President Ford and brought him over to speak to the children. It was a special moment.

When I went inside, I heard a Member of Congress talking with Chastity Bono, Sonny and Cher's daughter *(now Chaz)*. Chastity was saying that her father, who was a Conservative Republican, took the news that she was a Lesbian better than her mother, Cher, who was a Liberal.

I had previously heard the same story from Sonny, a few months back. I remember hearing Cher make light of it on TV when she said, "I wanted my daughter to get married, have kids, get a divorce—you know, all the things that American women do."

Suddenly, Cher walked in with a handkerchief in her hand and was moving toward us. It was obvious that she had been crying. It was amazing for me to see this icon walk up to us and then hear Chastity say, "Are you all right, Mom?"

Cher said, "I'm okay," and quickly the basics of life—sorrow, a person's private grief—overshadowed Cher, the "icon," Cher, the superstar. She was Cher, the mom; a grieving woman whose daughter cared if she was doing okay.

When Cher went into a private area of the church just for family and Members of Congress, some of the Members pulled out disposable cameras and took pictures of her from right in front of her. I told them that was really tacky. They smiled and snapped a few more.

We were still in the private room when several of us decided to have a seat prior to being called into the main Church where the crowd and cameras awaited. I sat down and Cher sat next to me for a moment. We exchanged hellos and a brief conversation about how great Sonny was.

Mary Bono was also in that room. She seemed numb. She was quietly grieving the loss of her husband. It was in stark contrast to something I witnessed in the courtyard earlier. There was a State Senator from California—I have no idea who he was—but some Republican Party "chief" was introducing him around to the Members of Congress as a "good replacement for our beloved Sonny." I told one of the House Staff who was there that in politics, whenever someone dies people immediately say, "Oh that's terrible. Who should replace him?" It's just the cold nature of the blood sport of politics. I always mused that my staff would say, "Bob wanted me to replace him" before the service even began.

Cher gave an amazing eulogy. The tears, laughter, memories, pain, grief, and special memories of Sonny flowed throughout the crowd. As I looked at the Church, Congress sat on one side of the Church, and Hollywood on the other.

The funeral ended and we went to the cemetery. It was a wonderful sendoff—Sonny would have probably liked it. It was broadcast live on CNN as a national event. He would have most likely said, "Can you believe this? They must have had a slow news day."

Sonny's wife, Mary, who was not sure of where her life was headed, eventually made a decision to run for office, which pleased all of us. Mary took Sonny's Congressional seat and served in Congress from January of 2003 until she was defeated in the November 2012 election. Mary has remarried, and her husband, Congressman Connie Mack of Florida, lost his election challenge for a U.S. Senate seat in 2012 as well.

Despite the public's perception of Sonny as just another actor, not too bright, who got into government, the truth prevailed in his short service in D.C. that he had something to offer. Sonny worked diligently for those who sent him to Washington.

PART III

THE SLIPPERY SLOPE OF POLITICS

"Do not look where you fell, but where you slipped."
—ASHANTI PROVERB, GHANA, AFRICA

There were many parts, aspects, facets, to the complicated puzzle of the Abramoff scandal. It took on the drama of Congressional players, Indian tribes, junkets, foreign sweat shops, overseas intrigue, and many more rumors and facts that leapt onto the front pages of the newspapers and dominated the nightly news. Although this story at first seemed mundane, the trifecta of the "gangland" hit of a Greek immigrant, casino boats, and Jack Abramoff, started to baffle even the seasoned people involved with Capitol Hill politics. Combine this with what you have yet to read, and this story takes on the semblance of an intriguing novel instead of the alarming reality that it was.

Chapter 19

☆ ☆ ☆

WHAT A TANGLED WEB
WE WEAVE

"Oh what a tangled web we weave
when first we practice to deceive."

—SIR WALTER SCOTT

I hired Dave Distefano through a weird twist of events. The Chairman of the Ohio Republican party hired my page, Gwen. It was 1988 and I was on the rise in the Ohio Senate as the Vice Chair of the Finance Committee and the Chairman of Insurance and Banking. I needed a page and my staff guy Tim Snyder came in and said that one of his friends was looking for a job. We called a couple of times and the line was busy (ah, the joy of pre-cell phone days). Within ten seconds, Dave Potts (who came to the Senate from Shadyside, Ohio, and was the brother of Joel Potts, my first Senate Campaign Manager), said he had someone.

Potts told us, "There is a guy from Shadyside who would like to have a job. His name is Dave Distefano, and his dad is union guy who works for Ormet [a large aluminum-producing company in Ohio]." This was in the 18th District, which I represented. We called, Dave Distefano answered, and he came down the next day. Tim Snyder and another staffer were working in my office at that time and they usually pre-screened applicants, but I didn't want to go through the usual process so I interviewed him myself.

I asked Distefano the routine questions and he seemed nervous, but then most people are in that type of a situation. But he presented himself as an intelligent young man and he was from the Valley—down the road from Bellaire where I hailed from. I then caught him off guard. Knowing that his dad was a union man, I asked, "Are you a Democrat or a Republican? Tell me the truth." He gulped and said, "I don't know."

I said, "I don't care, just be good to the people of the District and loyal to the office." Distefano said okay and we ended the conversation by my telling him to come to work the next day.

It was 1988, a reelection year and in the months to come Distefano worked as our page, then as a staffer in my reelection campaign for the State Senate against Dick Carter of Cambridge, Ohio. It was during this time that something bothered me about Distefano's attitude concerning money. It should have set off alarm bells, but I thought nothing more of it at the time. Some of his friends had indicated that he was "money hungry" but a lot of people can be. This incident involved a matter concerning my opponent, Dick Carter, and his ramming Distefano's vehicle.

Dick had had a string of personal setbacks and frustrations, and the weekend before the election he cracked and rammed Distefano's truck by accident in an attempt to scare our workers. Dick and I did a private deal; he paid for Distefano's truck and medical bills for another staffer who was slightly injured in this incident, and we did a gag order with the media. There were all types of rumors about guns, shots fired, and so forth, but I felt it was just one of those things that you have to work through, and it was days before the election. Therefore, this "deal" was the best for all concerned.

Distefano said to me that if there was not enough money in the "settlement" he wanted to make sure that he was fully compensated. I assured him that his red truck would be repaired. He shocked me by saying, "Can I get around this to get a new one?" My response was no. This was not the last time he acted inappropriately about money—he earned the often-repeated phrase, "It is strictly all about Distefano and money."

Distefano wanted to be my staff guy, but got upset about his future and became convinced that he had to get a master's degree. He was also upset that we could not pay him more. He felt his brief stint as a campaign staffer qualified him for a pay increase. I remember clearly the day he left and said to me, "I will never be able to make over 100,000 dollars a year without a master's degree." *(Today Dave Distefano is a millionaire and is rolling in big money as a lobbyist—still no master's degree.)*

He went on to Texas to work for Steve Maradian whom he had met through me when Steve was president of the then Belmont Technical

College in St. Clairsville, Ohio. Steve was at this time president of a small community college in Texas, and Dave lived with Steve and his family and became his Staff Assistant. *(Ironically, Steve's son later served as a page in the U.S. Congress with Will Heaton who was eventually my Chief of Staff, and they became good friends.)*

Within a year, Distefano had some type of falling out with Steve. He returned, no master's degree in hand, and contacted me, pushing aggressively for a job. I had become the chairman of the powerful Senate Finance Committee in Ohio. Distefano was a great numbers guy (he liked money and enjoyed counting it) and almost begged to be my finance man for the committee. I finally made him an offer, but it was just not enough money for him. As it was, he would be one of the best-paid staffers with the least experience and I could not pay him more. He decided to take the job with the promise that I would try, not commit, but try to get him more money.

Time went on and I ran for U.S. Congress. Early on, Dave Distefano maneuvered his way into the chief of staff position by convincing me (erroneously) that the current Chief of Staff for my State Senate Office, Dave Heil, was not up to speed on things. Dave Heil is a nice guy who was, and is, quite competent and currently serves as Chief of Staff for a member of the U.S. Congress.

After the election Distefano, a handful of staffers and I headed to D.C. to be part of a major paradigm shift and embark on new careers as we each turned to a fresh page in our lives.

It was December of 1994 and Dave Distefano, Neil Volz, a couple of other guys, and I shared a house that we leased from a lady who had gone to France for two years. We lived in the house until late in 1995, when the lady decided to return early and wanted her house back. She called Distefano and without consulting any of us, he made the decision to give her the house back for one month's rent. We were caught off guard and had to scramble to move. I suspected then and now that he pocketed some money for "his trouble" in negotiating this. No one leases their place for two years, returns early, and expects the lessees to move out for one month's rent.

Distefano continued as my Chief of Staff. He wanted to do something personnel-wise that, had I let him, I would not be writing this book—at least not one about prison and Jack Abramoff. There is no guarantee that I would not have gotten into trouble in some other way. If, however, Neil Volz had not been working for me, we surely would have taken different paths. Distefano came to me and said that Neil Volz was not conducting himself as he should be and wanted to fire him. I said, "Dave, holy hell, it's Neil, we can't fire him!" An argument ensued and I finally said, "Have a conversation with him, get him on track as you think he should be, but do not fire him." *(Even after all that Neil and I went through with the Abramoff saga, I look back on this decision and I'm still grateful for the many good things that Neil and I did while in service to the people of the 18th District.)*

As time went on, Distefano came to me and said he had an offer with the U.S. Chamber of Commerce and that he had talked to his confidant, Barry Jackson, who at the time was John Boehner's Chief of Staff. Dave wanted my blessing and I gave it to him. I told him that I appreciated all his work and that we were, and would remain, friends.

He then said, "I think with your help and what I know I can get from [Barry] Jackson, I should be able to do pretty good there." He worked under a nice guy named Lanny Taylor. Later, something happened at the Chamber and Lanny moved on, but Distefano stayed, getting some more seniority there.

Dave Distefano was friend, former coworker, and former roommate with not only Neil and me, but with one of our Legislative Staff Assistants who handled banking, which was of particular interest to Distefano. He came in one day and said he wanted to talk. We went to dinner in D.C. and Dave said, "I want to open my own lobby shop back in Columbus and lobby Ohio and D.C. What do you think?"

I told him that he was pretty new at lobbying and maybe he needed a few more years under his belt to succeed at a venture like that.

He responded, "I need your help—really need your help badly." I sent him to a few people I knew, but didn't make follow-up calls for him. One of the guys I knew, an Ohio businessman, hired him and became Distefano's "anchor client" for his new company.

Later, somehow Distefano ran into Roy Coffee in Washington. Roy is a very smart, likeable guy, who knows how to play the game and comes from a prominent political family in Austin, Texas. Distefano linked up with Roy, who was the head of then Governor George W. Bush's D.C. office.

FREDDIE MAC AND FANNIE MAE

Distefano used Roy Coffee's pull to be part of FM Watch, a group run at that time by Haley Barbour. Its backers were bankers who hated Fannie Mae (FNMA—The Federal National Mortgage Association) and Freddie Mac (FHLMC—The Federal Home Loan Mortgage Corporation), and wanted to stomp them into the ground. I was on the banking committee, became Vice-chair, and eventually Chair of the Housing Subcommittee. Distefano utilized every aspect of our friendship, which included telling potential clients that we were so close he actually lived with my family years back when his mom and dad moved to Arizona. This was true, but a cheap ploy to magnify his closeness to me.

Distefano was on board and making a decent wage with the FM Watch group. Eventually a problem arose between Distefano and Roy Coffee. I learned from a former girlfriend of Distefano's that Barry Jackson wanted him to make some moves to be on the inside of what is called GSEs (Government-sponsored Enterprises such as Fannie Mae or Freddie Mac). Distefano left Roy to lobby for the opposition to FM Watch, Freddie Mac. Dave Distefano had committed the biggest sin—stepping on the toes of the one who brought him (Roy) and without notice, going with the opponent. I could tell Roy was personally hurt and devastated by what Dave had done to him. Roy and I had some drinks and mutually agreed that money was Distefano's Achilles' heel and he always took the next buck no matter who he had to mow down.

Distefano said that while he was with FM Watch, he was contacted by another Ohio lobbyist who represented telecommunication companies and Freddie Mac. They wanted Dave because he had worked for me—if Distefano were still on the FM Watch team, they were afraid I would lean his way versus the GSEs. This was hilarious, as it was not going to happen and Distefano knew that. Yet somehow he managed to convince the other lobbyist that I may go the way of FM Watch instead of with Fannie or Freddie. I had long relationships with the banks, but they knew we parted ways when it came to Fannie and Freddie, and this was known by everyone else in D.C. as well. Therefore, in a brilliant, lucrative move, Distefano convinced the GSE, Freddie Mac, that they needed him before I bolted and supported FM Watch. His scheme was successful, although it temporarily cost him the friendship of Roy Coffee. *(They later patched things up and now do business together.)*

Fannie Mae had an audit problem that came up and Freddie Mac was under fire for practices. Fannie and Freddie simply did not want to be "done away with" as some suggested. They were too big and had too much of a portfolio to be disbanded. They also wanted to keep their Congressionally granted tax-exempt charter.

Congressman Richard Baker had the worst "political hard-on" for the GSEs I have ever witnessed on Capitol Hill. I did agree that the Office of Fair Housing and Equal Opportunity (OFHEO) that was regulating the GSEs was not doing the job. Eventually, OFHEO was done away with. In the legislative battle that ensued, Distefano came to my office and wanted me to communicate with him and him only if anyone from Freddie Mac asked to see me. He was brazen enough to want me to ignore his boss at Freddie Mac, Mitch Delk, and call him (Distefano) directly so he could say to Mitch, "Yes, Bob will meet with you." I don't think Mitch fell for it. Mitch Delk is seasoned, smart, and no one's fool. I think Mitch simply humored him.

(As a side note, in 2002 when things were heating up with Fannie Mae and Freddie Mac, I asked to see Mitch Delk. He was a couple of days late in coming to my office. When he did come, he said, "Sorry, I had to fly to Beijing and reassure the Chinese that we are okay. They have seen all this publicity." I was baffled and said, "What the hell do the Chinese have to do with Freddie [Mac]?" Mitch responded, "They have invested in huge chunks of the American housing market." I later found out that I wasn't the only "dumbass" who didn't know this. Many Members had no idea that the "red communist government" had the U.S. housing market by the short hairs—and it continues to be so.)

Distefano continued to milk Freddie Mac. My Legislative Assistant who handled banking said that Distefano was trying to take him to sports events, dinners and drinks. Pre-Abramoff, that wasn't such a problem, but my Legislative Assistant told me that Distefano was more than crossing the line with him and making him uncomfortable. Later, when Will Heaton was Chief of Staff, Distefano frustrated him to the point that Will wanted him banned from the office. I had to have a conversation about it with Distefano. He squirmed around it, denied it, said it was a misunderstanding.

I said, "Dave, look, you yourself have asked me to do shit that is way out of bounds, including not responding to your client when he directly calls me." (Freddie Mac was Distefano's client, and Mitch Delk was the person at Freddie Mac that Distefano—as the lobbyist—had to report to. In other words, Distefano was not the boss.)

I ended the conversation with, "Dave, I am willing to help, but you have to stop this shit and I am also tired of your going behind my back and trying to manipulate the staff."

He said, "Okay, I get it—don't be upset, I will handle it differently. Sorry." I think it says a lot that we considered Distefano far more aggressive and unethical than Jack Abramoff—and frankly, with some of the staff and me, he was.

HAVA/DIEBOLD

The Help America Vote Act (HAVA) was my legacy bill. Dave Distefano crossed the line in a huge way with a request that was downright illegal. It was a request that I have been accused of fulfilling by some "conspiracy theory" groups. The allegation concerned fixing the elections through the Help America Vote Act—my bill that became law. I now realize that where there is smoke, there is usually fire. Dave Distefano, Barry Jackson, the late Mike Connell, Karl Rove and John Boehner (the Speaker of the House at this writing) may have all been involved—utilizing one another to have me produce a bill that would do as they wished.

The HAVA bill was complicated, and an amazing effort conceived by Steny Hoyer (D-Maryland) to repair the lack of confidence in the American election system due to Bush vs. Gore in 2000. In the early stages of the bill, it was widely known that it would be a monumental piece of legislation—a precedent-setting law in which the feds were addressing comprehensive reform for all the states in the most significant election system overhaul in American history. The bill has done much to facilitate the fairness of elections, and to help the American people vote more easily.

I hired Chet Kalis, my friend and neighbor from Ohio, to help with this bill. Chet was brilliant, and as a Democrat with an amazing charm, he could make it happen. He worked tirelessly on it. Chet and I were also roommates on a boat we stayed on when we were in D.C. We would drive home together to St. Clairsville when session was over. Dave Distefano had been approaching Chet, and Chet let me know about it. He said, "Bob, this is a big-time bill, and your legacy; be careful of Dave [Distefano]. He's not a bad guy, just a bit too hungry, if you know what I mean." I thanked Chet, and then waited for Distefano to make his move, which he did.

Barry Jackson (Boehner's former Chief of Staff, but at this time Karl Rove's number one man) was Distefano's confidant and political sugar daddy. Through Jackson's Ohio contacts, he managed to secure a huge lobbyist contract for Distefano with Diebold, a large, international security-systems corporation located in Ohio that also deals with self-service transaction systems such as ATMs, and at that time, voting machines. Dave Distefano was not a large player in the lobbying scheme at all, and should never have had the Diebold contract. Previously, Distefano had zero Diebold connections.

I told Chet Kalis of my concerns. "Look at it—a large international company such as Diebold that is located in Ohio, and a national bill such as HAVA that deals with computers and elections. Chet, this one we have to watch closely or this entire bill sinks due to Diebold." Chet agreed. This scenario needed watching, as there had to be some other reason Barry Jackson wanted Dave Distefano in there.

Wally O'Dell was the president of Diebold. He was an extremely good backer of the Ohio Republican Party and close to Bob Bennett, at that time the longtime Ohio Chairman of the Republican Party. Diebold had been running into some controversy about their computer systems as the bill was progressing. They wanted to clear up any misconceptions, so their U.S. Congressman, Ralph Regula, a really nice guy and dean of the Ohio delegation, approached me to let me know that they were writing a *white paper* (an informative report), and that everyone involved with the bill would get a copy. I thanked Ralph, saw nothing unusual about that, and awaited the report.

Distefano called me and asked to see me ASAP. When he got there, he wanted to let me know that a *white paper* was coming from Diebold and pointblank asked me to send it personally on my letterhead to all Members. I said no. He then asked if I could send it to just the Members involved with HAVA. I again said no.

I told Dave, "You are their lobbyist, you are making the big-ass cash, you do your job and circulate it."

He said, "That's not fair."

I said, "What—doing your job or the big-ass cash?"

He responded, "I do my job. I am not asking you to do mine for me, just help me."

I had grown tired of Distefano's constant whining and begging for help. Sometimes he acted like a child. He was the baby of the family and as his sister Paula, my longtime scheduler, often said, "He is simply spoiled and expects everyone to do everything for him." She was correct. I again refused.

About a day later, Distefano called me and asked if I would do a conference call with him, Wally O'Dell and some of the other Diebold people involved in the white paper so they could explain what was going on. I agreed. We started the conference call a few hours later. They thoroughly explained what they were doing, how they were building better systems and so forth. Then Wally said, "When can you circulate this for us?"

I was floored. I said, "I cannot. You have Dave Distefano, you can come to D.C. yourself, or if your Congressman for your area, Ralph Regula, deems it appropriate, he can circulate it under his name. But as Chairman, I would be way out of bounds, and as author of the bill it would destroy all of my credibility by making me look like I was promoting Diebold." The conversation ended.

Distefano, being the lazy lobbyist that he was then, did not personally circulate it. (*Recently a good friend of mine who knows him said to me, "Dave is the luckiest man on earth. He simply does nothing for the money his clients pay him." And then he said, "You know Distefano!"*)

As we continued working on the bill, I had one more run-in with Dave Distefano, Diebold, and Bob Bennett. They were a trio this time—"dumb, dumber, and dumbest." Bob Bennett, chair of the Ohio Republican Party, was having a Wally O'Dell-sponsored event; a large fundraiser for the Republican Congressional cause, and wanted all Members to be officially listed on the invitations, along with Wally's name. I told my finance guy (this is campaign staff, separate from the federal government staff) to refuse, period. This would be the worst timing for my bill, would look way beyond inappropriate, and would create havoc.

I know what you're thinking as you read this, and I can't say that I blame you: *"Come on, Bob, ethics, standards, worries about how things look—you?"* I candidly admit that with my actions over the years, there could be conflicts, ethics discrepancies, things that look and smell not quite right. But beyond the Jack Abramoff experience, which put everything else on steroids, my staff and I raised millions of dollars, serviced tens of thousands of constituents (who caused minor problems at times by wanting to thank us with gifts), and dealt with thousands of interest groups. We kept boundaries for over two and a half decades—not perfectly, but for the most part—as did many others in politics. I can cite many examples of times we threw people out of our offices. We publicly stated that Proctor and Gamble pressured a woman on our staff to get a vote, and we often refused donations because the insinuation was that they were to be linked to favors. I wish we had used the same discretion with Jack. The "we" is "me" first, and then my staff—it was incestuous. Although Distefano wanted to be at that level of political incest with us, neither I, nor our staff of Chet Kalis, Will Heaton, and others were going to do that. We had a meeting at one time to talk about the "Distefano problem." Selective ethics? Again, it was so bad with Distefano, I was more cautious with him than anyone else I dealt with. He had an agenda pushed by big players and I could sense that.

After our campaign finance guy refused to allow my name to be listed on the invitation involving Diebold and the Republican Party, I got a call from Congressman Ralph Regula (R-Ohio) inquiring as to why I would not go on the invite. Once I explained, he agreed. Then Distefano called doing and saying all he could to persuade, beg, or "deal" me onto the invite. He said, "I really need this done. I'm looking bad."

I retorted, "Frankly, Dave, I don't care how fucking bad you look. I have done enough for you. It's time for you to get off the *tit*. I am not doing this."

He said, "You're harsh." He then asked me to hear him out, and I told him to go for it.

Distefano said that as my former finance guy, he knew this was all correct—raising money and policy are separate and Wally O'Dell told him he would not talk about the bill at the fundraiser. Dave went on to say that I needed to be a team player, I needed Chairman Bob Bennett for my future aspirations in the Congress (Speaker) and this was a great way to do it.

I listened to his arguments and said, "No Dave, this is just not in the cards. I don't care if mine is the only name missing, this will totally screw up the bill." Distefano then crossed the line as he had time after time. I usually dismissed his transgressions, but this one I had to address.

He thought he was throwing out the "catch line" when he said, "I am okayed to tell you that if you do this, I can raise a ton of money from O'Dell and on top of it, I have a commitment from Barry Jackson that Boehner will kick in, plus Barry assures me that he can involve Rove."

He threw out the R word—Rove. Also, he had Boehner in this. I then thought about all the money I could make for the campaign; how it would help not only my elections, but to be able to dish it out to Members (no bones about it, both parties function that way), and it would help in my aspiration to be Speaker. I never thought about the fact that John Boehner had the same goal; I simply thought they were offering to help because Dave Distefano had begged Barry Jackson, to help. Then reality hit me. *There is something wrong going on here beyond what I can understand. I'm a pawn in some type of game, and Distefano just wants to use me to get rich.*

I said, "Dave, no! This is the same as a bribe and this conversation is over." He was silent, most likely because I had used the word "bribe." I hung up the phone, happy that I held firm despite temptation and even more delighted that I took the option of preserving my legacy bill, HAVA, versus campaign dollars and personal aspirations.

Some detail concerning HAVA: Democratic Congressman Steny Hoyer approached me after the Bush vs. Gore debacle and said that this was an opportunity for the Congress to pass a bill to restore voter confidence and modernize our voting systems. Steny and I agreed on HAVA, the Help America Vote Act. Both sides, Republicans and Democrats, had to compromise to pass the act. Steny and I stated many times, accurately, that HAVA made it "easier to vote and harder to cheat." Both parties agreed on an election commission that would help in the election process nationally, but unlike most legislation these days, brilliantly assured that this was not an overzealous federal entity that could bypass Congress and make its own rules, thus having the force of a law. Many agencies do this repeatedly and we did not want to create a new bureaucracy.

The Republicans wanted a full-blown voter ID card. The Democrats did not. We compromised on an ID, or the last four digits of one's Social Security number, or a current utility bill or bank statement. Of course, states could implement a stricter ID law if desired.

The Democrats wanted to prevent disenfranchisement, where people were turned away from the polls and told they were not eligible to vote. The Republicans were not as concerned about that, as they felt people were turned away due to legitimate ineligibility. I agreed with Steny Hoyer and we came up with a compromise—"provisional ballots." If eligibility were in question, the person could vote "provisionally." If determined eligible, the vote counted. If not, the vote was shredded. No one was turned away from the polls. Yes, this could delay election results in a close race, but it stopped arbitrary disenfranchisement due to race, party registration or any other non-bona fide reason.

The other provision was an attestation on all federal elections where the voter signs that he or she is a citizen of the United States. The Democrats did not openly dispute this, but a group called "La Raza [the race; the people] despised this. Call me old fashioned, but I think that a person should be a citizen in order to vote.

These were some of the main components of a well-thought-out piece of legislation, signed into law by President George W. Bush and supported by a majority of both parties in the House and Senate.

(However, there was something mysterious when it came to the Help America Vote Act and the accusations of my rigging the elections. I have said many times, "If I rigged the damn 2004 elections for Bush, do you think I would have gone to his federal prison?" I do think, however, that without my knowledge, HAVA possibly had some behind-the-scenes dirt that either did happen or had the potential to happen, and it was convenient for Barry Jackson and the White House to have me put away. The benefit of this was [and is] to be able to say about me, "Look where he went. Look what he did. How can he be believed?"

Another matter of grave importance that was treated in the same off-hand manner—no credibility because I had been in prison—involved my good friend, Dr. Trita Parsi, Iran, and the Swiss Ambassador to Iran, Tim Guldimann.

In 2003, the then Ambassador to Iran, Tim Guldimann, came to my Capitol Hill office. He was excited, as he had an amazing document that detailed how, under certain conditions, Iran would allow American inspectors on the ground for their nuclear program. The document also spoke of disbanding Hezbollah as a militant organization, thus averting many problems in Lebanon, and a way for Iran to recognize Israel's right to exist. The United States had desired this from Iran for years. It was a wonderful opportunity as a starting point for discussions. I sent it to the White House, not by mail, but by a staffer as I wanted it to go directly to Karl Rove. I called Karl and told him it was coming. He called me after receiving it and said, "Is this real?"

I said, "Yes, to the best of my knowledge."

Later, Ambassador Guldimann was reprimanded by the White House for bringing the document; former Secretary of State Condoleezza Rice denied seeing it, even though she was contradicted by a National Security Agency (NSA) staffer; the late Tony Snow, then Press Secretary to President Bush, denied Karl Rove's knowledge of it; and the White House "Dick Cheney neocon warmongers" won out in dismissing this important opportunity.

I gave Dr. Parsi permission to include this in his book, Treacherous Alliance: The Secret Dealings of Israel, Iran and the United States. *When I revealed through Dr. Parsi as I entered prison that this had been sent to Karl Rove from the Iranians through me, the canned answer from the White House was, "Look where he is." I assume, as I write this book, that the response might now be, "Look where he was."*

There is an article by Tom Suddes, a long-time, respected, journalist that I

have provided a link to in Resources. I read it while I was in prison, and it gave
me a sense of vindication.)

DISTEFANO/JACKSON

The Dave Distefano/Barry Jackson saga continued. Distefano outlined a plan to me that he said would involve Neil Volz (who was at this time a lobbyist for Jack Abramoff), Barry Jackson, Karl Rove, and John Boehner. Barry worked for Boehner at one time so as a former staffer, he utilized Boehner's power and had Boehner's ear for anything he needed—it was a matter of *insider* power plays. To help you follow this convoluted plan, let me explain how things work: Distefano had his own lobbying business at this time, but in this business, they are all incestuous. One lobbyist may have no pull in one area, so he gets another lobbyist or lobbying firm to help him. At another time, the lobbyist who helped him may need help and the favor is returned. In this case, Distefano had no appropriation contacts, so he got Neil Volz (part of Team Abramoff at that time) to help him with Members of Congress on the Appropriations Committee, because as everyone knew, Abramoff did have pull with them. Dave Distefano, on the other hand, had the friendship, closeness, and ear of Barry Jackson—therefore, Dave's role was to bring more access to the White House for Neil through Barry Jackson, who was number two to Karl Rove. *(The White House later denied dealing with Abramoff, yet in a draft report by the House Government Reform Committee, of 485 contacts with White House officials over a period of three years, 345 of these were meetings or in-person contacts, and ten of those documented were with Karl Rove. Distefano was a part of this.)*

I knew Distefano had pull because of an incident that took place previously during my career in Washington. Dave Distefano, Barry Jackson (by this time, top assistant to Karl Rove) and I met at Haley Barbour's restaurant, The Caucus Room. At the meeting, which Distefano had arranged, Barry handed me an advance copy of the President Bush 43's White House energy policy and begged me to guard it. Distefano was happy, as he had asked Barry to breach the White House confidence and give it to me. Barry stressed to me that I guard it and not pre-divulge it. We all got to drinking. I left it on a chair and went to the restroom. We left after that, and I realized when we got in the cab that it was missing. I remember Barry (rightly so) having this horrified, disgusted look on his face, shaking his head from side to side saying, "For the love of

Christ." I went back in, and magically, it was on the chair. I found out later that a young lady I had asked to join us saw it, took it to look at it, and then returned it to the chair.

The Dave Distefano pursuit of power took on a different tone—one that is not pretty on the surface, but illuminates the fact that human beings are involved in politics, and therefore personal situations occur and blend with public policy. The relationship between Distefano and Barry Jackson was becoming, for many of us, nauseating. Dave made sure everyone in town knew that he was "Barry's man."

Distefano was always beyond secretive with everyone, including me. I liked to play a game by finding out things he had done, and then letting him know I was on to him. I had an extensive network of information from great sources that I faithfully kept confidential. I could find out almost anything. For example, Distefano had said that this one particular guy "made him nervous," yet I found out that he had been regularly jogging with him on the Hill because he was a staffer to a powerful Member and could help Distefano's business.

However, Distefano had begun to drop his guard a bit toward the last couple of years of our relationship and he shared some things, usually when he was blind drunk, that were shocking—first, because he was telling it on himself, and second, because of the things he indicated about Barry Jackson.

One night when several of us were hitting the bars in D.C., Distefano shared with me in confidence that he had been out in Columbus the week before and picked up Deborah Pryce's nanny. Deborah, a U.S. Representative from Ohio, had adopted a child after the tragic passing of her daughter, Caroline.

He told me, "It was really strange, banging the hell out of this young bitch right in Deborah's bed."

The story could have ended there, but within two days it got carried a bit further in a more public forum. We were all at Deborah Pryce's fundraiser at a bar up near the Capitol. It was a wine bar and the booze flowed. When Distefano arrived, Congresswoman Pryce said, "There is the man I want to see."

Distefano said, "Hello Congresswoman," and she said, "Any interesting times in Columbus recently?" He said, "Not really." She smiled like the cat that ate the canary and said with a grin, "My nanny seems to be 'impressed' with you!" Dave said, "I was impressed with your interior decorations." Deborah laughed and said, "I bet you were."

Distefano then checked the situation out, asking if apologies were in order. Deborah answered, "No, it is 'mutual assured destruction,' but you *will* be raising some money."

Distefano told me the next day that he was going to be delivering some client money to her. Letting his guard down and the brazen nature of their conversation in front of people indicated to me that Dave was beginning to feel that he had some type of backing or had reached some level of *Teflon*.

The next gaffe stunned me. It was made in front of several staffers at Jack Abramoff's restaurant, Signatures. One of our District staffers had come to D.C., and after a couple of hours, the conversation led to all of Distefano's new clients, his new home purchase in Columbus, the speculation that he had also bought a house in Arizona, his new car, new suits and so on. Our District staffer said, "I hear you have a political sugar daddy. Anyone we know?"

Distefano, loaded as hell, said, "He is a pretty big deal. You would like to have him back you, but you don't have the pull and power over him that little Di has." (*We often called Distefano, "Dave Di" or just "Di," pronounced like the letter D.*)

We all laughed about his bragging and some crude, blatant comments were made about owning people and getting what you want.

I thought that either the *locker-room talk* had a ring of truth to it, or he was taking one big chance of pissing off one of the most powerful men in the country. There were too many people around for that story not to get back to the White House and to Barry. The fact that there was no retaliation told me that "mutual assured destruction" must have counted not only for the Pryce nanny deal, but counted protection-wise for Distefano in regard to his comments about Barry Jackson.

(Toward the end of my time when things were getting bad, my Executive Assistant, Chris Krueger, and I were at the Ugly Mug sports bar. It was one of those nights when I was avoiding regular Capitol Hill haunts like the Capital Grille or the Oceanaire. The Ugly Mug is near the Hill, but not frequented by a lot of Members. It's nothing special—regular fried food, loud music, but no dance floor. Chris was good about trying to keep my morale up. I felt there were few those days who wanted to be around me.

I saw Barry Jackson and Dave Distefano watching the TV at the bar. It surprised me with all the lobbyist witch-hunting going on that Barry would be out with Distefano, and on top of that, they were both damn near falling-down drunk.

They were loud, talking about a trip the two were going to take to Florida to watch, I believe they said, some spring training by a baseball team. Distefano winked and said, "Of course it is all legal," and they both laughed their asses off. When the tab came, Distefano said, "Christ, I don't want to buy the place." Obviously the two had racked up a big tab, but Distefano pulled out his credit card and paid for it—a clear violation of the ethics law, especially for the internal policy of the White House, since Dave Distefano was a lobbyist and Barry was working for Karl Rove.

No doubt, I was late in getting on the ethics watch, but by then even I was cautious not to have any more grief than I already had. Distefano simply seemed not to care.

Dave Distefano never had one day of trouble with the Justice Department, although his dealings, in my opinion, were so much more corrupt and geared toward out and out bribery than Jack Abramoff's ever were with us. I could see that, for his own protection, he had someone higher up as his guardian angel, and that must have been Barry Jackson. Anyone as out front as Distefano was, had to have been reassured that he was not a target of the Justice Department.

In addition, his sister, Paula Sievertson, was my scheduler. She had monitored enough of my daily moves to help the FBI put the final nail in my coffin. Dave Distefano had his bases covered all the way around—and he is still a lobbyist in Ohio and D.C., making a lot of money.)

Chapter 20

"LET'S GO TO LONDON, BOB!"

*"The safest way to double your money
is to fold it over once and put it in your pocket."*

—KIN HUBBARD (1868–1930)

I received a call from Dave Distefano in January of 2003. He said, "I know, of course, of your interest in American/Iranian relationships and their possibilities, so I have something I want to run by you."

I said, "Sure, come by today." When Distefano came to my office he told me of his idea to take a trip to London to meet a man named Fouad Al Zayat, someone I had never heard of. He said the purpose of the trip would be to discuss Boeing interests. Of course, Boeing is an American company. He said, "For you, this is interesting because this man Fouad is close to the pulse of the Iranians and may be able to do some helpful things to make communication between the two countries possible."

This intrigued me. Both during the Clinton Administration and at this time, Bush's, I had been asked to be involved (or sometimes initiated my involvement) with issues of rapprochement (reestablishing cordial relations) with Iran. Distefano told me that he and a business partner had previously traveled to meet Fouad and his business partner, Nigel Winfield. They thought he was a "good man" and they had a blast with him, traveling to the casino and eating some good food. Distefano said the trip was totally legit, had a purpose and Dave's lobbying firm was allowed to pay for it. Later, through all my legal wrangling, this proved to be true. The government never tried to go after me for improper filings or anything in that direction, although the trip itself and the eventual gambling proved to be problematic.

We set off for London in February of 2003. Our traveling group consisted of Chris Otillio (my legislative director who handled Iranian issues, among other things), Dave Distefano, Roy Coffee (lobbyist and now Dave's business partner) and me.

When I met Fouad al Zayat, he was an entity with which I was totally comfortable. He was a Syrian Christian, and an Arab. He was quite hospitable in the Arab sense. He was a kind man—not a man impressed with meeting Congressmen, or people who were powerful or rich. On his own, he had met many famous people and financially proved to be a self-made man with a great personal story to tell. He had a look of innocence about him, and was a man who had a zest for life and loved to laugh.

Our first meeting involved Chris Otillio, Dave Distefano, Roy Coffee, and Fouad Al Zayat. We met in Fouad's office in London. It was a nice office, clean, but not too opulent or too plain. We discussed Boeing and Fouad's involvement with the Iranians. He had an aviation company and simply sold airplanes. We really didn't get into the heart of business, or about what I had come for, which was to find out more about what the Iranians were thinking concerning rapprochement. Instead, we talked about families, the Mideast/American issues, life. We laughed, had serious discussions then moved on to the topic of soccer. There was a game that night and Fouad had, I assume, some type of financial interest in Manchester United, the famous, premier soccer team of the U.K. I didn't want to go to the game. I had been around soccer in the Middle East when I lived in Iran and Saudi Arabia, but never developed a big interest in it. Chris Otillio jumped at the chance for tickets and made plans to go that night. Chris was a "Cajun" from Louisiana. He was a new attorney, a bit adrift, didn't settle into the legal world and instead, not unlike what new attorneys sometimes do, came to the Hill to take a low-level entry Legislative Assistant position. Chris handled several issues for me, including foreign affairs—specifically Iran.

After leaving Fouad's office, I met with the Boeing representative, who told me his interests were to sell Boeing parts to Iran, and he wanted to know my thoughts on whether the U.S. would eventually do that on humanitarian grounds. He said, "I am after this angle strictly for humanitarian purposes, as planes will crash and people will die if this does not happen."

I said, "I understand that, but also realize that if the Iranians cannot get spare parts from the U.S. for domestic airline use, they could eventually make the decision to abandon using the American Boeing planes and buy new French Airbus planes, thus bypassing the American business totally. I was sure that in some of that *smoke* was the fact that Boeing, being Boeing, hoped that years or so down the road, the two countries would eventually speak and business would resume as it had been prior to 1979. I added, "My interests are clear. Although I personally believe that foreign parts should be sold for domestic airplanes to avoid loss of innocent civilians' lives, I am searching for any thoughts or personal experience with the Iranians that can tell me what they are thinking about concerning talks with America."

He nodded and said that he would be happy to give his perspective on that. After listening to him, I concluded that he had nothing new to offer about the Iranian thought. The conversation became mundane, and I looked ahead to dinner later that night at the Ambassador's club with Fouad and Nigel Winfield, his business partner.

When I arrived at the Ambassador Club dining room, I could see that it was the hub of a lot of prominent people in the London or international community. It was a private club for members and their guests only. I have seen clubs that were more elegant, but it was tastefully done. We ate Arab food in a large, private dining room in the back. The doorway to the main dining room was large and we could see out into the room and view the guests. As we spoke about American/Iranian, American/Mideast issues, Fouad turned to me and said something that is burned into my brain. He pointed to two men who were sitting at a table, involved in an intense conversation and said, "Do you see those two men?" I said that I did.

He said, "Do you recognize them?" I realized that somehow, someway, I knew one of them, and it took a few moments until I remembered.

I said, "I know one of them. The man to the left is King Hussein of Jordan's brother, the crown prince, but I do not know the other man." In 1998, I had met the crown prince on a trip to Jordan with John Boehner.

Fouad replied in a very calm but firm tone: "This man will lie to your country; this man will catch the ear of your president; this man is a wanted criminal in Jordan, yet he sits with the King's brother; this man is here in London carrying out one of the biggest schemes in modern history and this man will soon take your country into war in Iraq. His name is Ahmed Chalabi."

Those words were so true—so prophetic. This was just before the Iraq war began, but here I was in London as a sitting Congressman, not knowing who Ahmed Chalabi was. Yet he was known to the White House and was part of one of the largest lies in history—weapons of mass destruction. In one month's time from my conversation with Fouad, we were at war with Iraq. It would take the lives of our brightest and best; it would economically, politically, and strategically bankrupt the United States.

Fouad went on to explain how Saddam Hussein could be dealt with through money and international pressure. It seemed more logical than the alternative—war. But then again, I really did not know Fouad and did not necessarily buy into his prediction that night.

The dinner continued with very little business. Fouad was not one to ask for anything or pressure anyone. There was something about his business partner at the dinner meeting that I could not put my finger on. Nigel Winfield had a British accent, but had lived in America for years, and was in business with Fouad in the aviation company. Nevertheless, it seemed to me that he was a guy who had some other motivation. Distefano had said that both men were reliable and were okay.

We went on for several hours with tremendously tasty Arab food that, due to my background, made me quite happy. I liked a variety of alcohol, but my taste for wine kicked in that night. My usual Bud Light may have been a bit too *blue collar* for the place. As I ate, drank, and talked, I felt very at ease with Fouad, but wondered in the back of my mind how much money Distefano was making off my visit. With Dave Distefano, it always seemed to be about money.

After dinner Distefano asked, "Shall we go to the casino?" Fouad responded "Of course," and off we went to the lower level of the building—to the casino.

The upscale casino was small. There weren't many people—some men in suits, some in tuxedos, and stylish ladies wearing long dresses. We began to play a game: London-style Baccarat. As Fouad got chips for everyone to start, I asked Distefano, "Can I buy chips myself?" He said no. I said, "I will need to buy them." Without saying anything, he waved his hand side to side, shook his head no, and proceeded to play. By that time I was not inebriated, but well on my way. We all drank and played, drank and played throughout the night.

In the sedan on the way to the airport the next morning, Otillio said he was going to claim his winnings on the customs form. I felt that I didn't have that much to claim, either on the customs form or, subsequently, with the House Ethics Committee. (In retrospect, I should have!)

Almost angrily, Chris Otillio said, "I don't care what you guys do, I am claiming them." Distefano said he never did before and was not going to now, and that he did not win that much this time anyway. I had some Cuban cigars and was definitely uncomfortable about taking them back into the U.S., so I split them among Dave Distefano, Chris, and Dave's business partner.

When I arrived at Dulles, Will Heaton picked me up. I told him about the trip; I had gambled, as had Chris, it was fun, I learned a lot, and felt the trip was productive. Will said he would like to go on the next trip for sure and he drove me back to the office.

(Contrary to later statements by the Justice Department and leaks by them to the press, I never had any conversation with Colin Powell about airplane parts or the meeting I attended in London. My conversations later were about a secret meeting in Stockholm that was on a much higher level than airplane parts. I believe that the Bush Justice Department intentionally threw in the airplane lobby story to pressure me later for a plea, insinuating that if I did not, they would pursue me for the casino nights and possibly a "William Jefferson-style" charge. [The former Democratic Congressman from Louisiana pursued for foreign violations acts.] I continue to believe that the pro-war, neocon, Dick Cheney followers utilized the "Colin Powell" lobbying to attempt to put a link between me and Iran for business purposes. Anytime something positive arose between Iran and America in the form of talks, a highly placed neocon was there to make sure it all went south.)

I was never charged for anything dealing with that first trip to London (and Dave Distefano certainly wasn't, possibly due to his "Barry Jackson friendship"), but the second trip was utilized to achieve what the Justice Department would find impossible to do on its own with the Abramoff affair. *(It was used to pressure me for a plea on the Abramoff case. It was becoming more and more difficult to prosecute me on the Abramoff issues alone, so this trip to London was an "outside nugget" that they threatened to use against me. I was worn down by that time and this was just one more nail in the coffin.)*

In August of 2003, I was off to London again, by way of Stockholm, Sweden. This time Chris Otillio and Will Heaton were with me. Will liked to drink and definitely wanted to hit the casino, neither of which I objected to.

This second trip was not paid for by Fouad, but rather organized by the military after I told them that I would be headed to Stockholm for a meeting. This was a high-level meeting between an American delegation that included a representative for then Senator Joe Biden and Iranians who came from Teheran to discuss every issue conceivable concerning America and Iran. We were hoping for a breakthrough due to Iran's moderate president, Khatami.

I didn't tell Dave Distefano the nature of the meeting—it was a secret, classified type of meeting. Only Chris Otillio and Will Heaton were aware that I was going, but did not know the nature of the meeting. I did tell Distefano that I would be headed to London, which is a stopping point for most Congressional trips.

After leaving Sweden and arriving in London, I made an impromptu call to Fouad to see if he was available to eat. His office said he would meet me that night at the Ambassador's Club. Will Heaton, Chris Otillio, and I left the rest of the people in the delegation to Sweden and met Fouad at the Ambassador's club. We had a very cordial, enjoyable dinner and talked about a lot of general subjects such as world politics, family, personal interests and viewpoints, but nothing pertaining to the airplanes.

Here is the part that two years later becomes exceedingly overblown by a "hungry" Justice Department after information from Otillio was *downloaded* (told to them by Otillio and Heaton). Based on my inquiry about Fouad's family, he mentioned that he had a daughter in the United States and that for some reason he was turned down for a visa to go see her and her husband. It was strictly a casual mention.

I then asked, "Why would they turn you down? You have no reason to try to stay there since you have property, business and money abroad."

He answered, "There may be some other reason—one never knows—of someone who has blacklisted me with the State Department."

I responded, totally unsolicited, "I have the ability to check out why you would be turned down for a simple tourist visa and will do that when I return."

He said, "Thank you."

(The Bush Justice Department tried to take this "tidbit" from Chris Otillio and Will Heaton and turn it into a bribery case: A night on the town gambling, money fed to me in the form of winnings by Fouad for the exchange of a visa— there was zero truth about a quid pro quo for a visa.)

It is amazing the lengths that the Justice Department would go to get what they wanted. However, if Alberto Gonzales would twist the constitution as he pleased to rationalize torture at Guantanamo Bay and would make a late-night visit to hospitalized and heavily medicated Attorney General John Ashcroft to get his signature on a certification authorizing a government surveillance program that both Ashcroft and the Justice Department at the time had concluded was of questionable legality, making up a story about an "arms dealer" exchanging a fake gambling win for a visa was child's play.

When I returned to the United States, I utilized contacts within the State Department and the CIA to find out if Fouad was on a blacklist. I was told by the highest ranking people I knew that there was no problem; most likely it was some bureaucrat in an Embassy that, for whatever reason, made a decision to keep him out. This happens frequently over all parts of the world.

Fouad again bought the chips and the more we gambled, the more I drank. We continued playing until about four in the morning. One of the last hands was a three-card poker game. By this point I was fairly drunk and tired. I started with one hundred dollars, and after a few hands it had grown to one thousand. I placed the entire thousand on the high stakes mark, which paid 34 to 1 odds. The dealer turned up a jack to qualify a win. (In a high stakes bet, if the dealer does not have a jack or higher in one of the three cards turned up, the player cannot win, regardless of having a winning hand.) I beat her hand with a flush—three spades. I was in shock.

When I went to collect the money I was asked, "Do you want a check or cash?" I said, "Cash." I was handed a small, pretty bag that contained the equivalent of 34,000 dollars in British pounds. It really was smaller than I thought it would be. I handed it to Fouad and said, "Here, you take this. It is difficult for me to deal with and it can cause me problems in the U.S."

He said, "It is your money, you won it, take it. No problem." I made a half-hearted offer to give it to him. We left the casino and I went back to the hotel. I woke up the next morning with a hangover and cash spread all over my bed. It looked like a scene out of a Vegas movie.

At Heathrow Airport before leaving London, I went to the exchange window. There was a man of Indian origin at the American Express window wearing a turban. I said, "I would like to convert pounds to dollars." He gave me the forms, which I filled out and put gambling winnings on them. He said, in a heavy Hindi accent, "This is an incredible amount of money. How did you acquire such a large amount?"

I answered, "Just as I have marked on the form, gambling winnings."

He repeated, "I must know how you acquired such an amount."

I said, "I have provided you my passport, I have filled out and signed that I won this gambling. Let me ask you something. Have you not seen this amount of money before?"

He said, "No, under the Patriot Act we monitor money."

This made me chuckle as I, one of three Republicans, voted against the Patriot Act. I retorted, "Wow, the Patriot act is really working. The only one that turns in their money is an American Congressman and if you have not seen this large of an amount of money before, then obviously the terrorists are not coming through this exchange and the Patriot Act is not working."

He looked confused at my sarcastic response, and proceeded to issue me 34,000 American dollars in neatly wrapped bundles.

Otillio was close to the vest about his winnings. Heaton won about nine thousand dollars; I knew this because when we got back to the States, Will put his undeclared winnings in the safe in my Congressional office.

(Heaton later played down the money he got in London, but on a trip to the Congressional District in Ohio, he wanted to buy a ring for his fiancée, Katie, with the cash. He did, eventually, but not in Steubenville. He said, "Katie is hard enough to satisfy. I'm going to spend a large chunk of change on the ring, but luckily, it is tax-free dollars from London.")

When I got back through customs in the U.S., I claimed the money, called my accountant the next day, put aside an estimation of my tax and put it in my savings account. I then properly filed it on my financial disclosure forms when they were due. What I did not do was declare all of the money I had won. This was a huge mistake on my part. If I declared some of it, why not all of it? I was a "functional" alcoholic who was hurting myself—using bad judgment and not thinking clearly. This gave the department the leverage they needed to pressure me on the Abramoff case, which had nothing to do with the London trip.

Later, Jack Torry, a *Columbus Dispatch* reporter, twisted all this into a "100-dollar-bet turned into a 34,000-dollar-win" article.

Jack Torry was actually a friend of one of my lawyers. Jack was a gregarious type of guy, always seemed nervous, giggled constantly and loved controversial stories. He would call our office and others over the years and ask for "off the record" information. As time went on, Torry became involved in fostering rumors all over the Capitol concerning my case. In addition to being the "100-dollar-bet turned into a 34,000-dollar-win" guy, he also started rumors through inquiries with other Members, that the Shah of Iran's daughter bought me a boat.

After London and this article of Jack Torry's, I just could not shake the publicity of winning the money—although it was not rigged, and I reported it, Torry made the story read like I was hand-fed the money. There is no way that the prominent, high-profile London casino would risk their license and business to "let" someone win 34,000 dollars! I made a high stakes bet and won—it happens.

To further complicate matters, when I got into trouble with the Justice Department, it was dredged up that I was "doing business" with a guy who defrauded Elvis and caught some felonies and did time. (*Nigel Winfield, Fouad's business partner, had defrauded Elvis Presley on an airplane sale thirty-two years prior. I would have been twenty-two at the time, but the Bush/Gonzales Justice Department seemed to think I should have known about that.*)

Fouad Al Zayat was made to look like a big-time arms dealer. The government had to make him look as bad as they could to drag me further down. He was actually a kind man who asked for nothing. Fouad mentioned the situation on his Web site through a publicist. He spoke kindly of me, but hit the nail on the head about the lobbyist who was with me, alluding to Dave Distefano and his motivations. Distefano loved being around Fouad, gambled with the money Fouad gave him, and tried everything he could to get a lucrative contract from him.

Something still puzzles me. At the dinner we had with Fouad in London on the first trip, Dave Distefano had a big-time Bush White House contributor show up. I wish I could remember his name, but he was a Pakistani American who had a lot of personal exposure with President Bush and was a heavy contributor. His being at the table with us makes me wonder if Distefano (who received zero problems from the Justice Department, was never charged with any misconduct for the London trip, and was never investigated for the cash money he never reported) was significantly aided, sheltered and shielded by the Friends of Bush.

Eventually I was told that Dave Distefano had a part in planning the trip to London to stir up controversy and to have something over me when it came to the Iranians. I did discover later that Distefano's client, Nigel Winfield, an associate/friend of Fouad's at the time, was passed to Dave via Jack Abramoff. I still wonder how Distefano dodged all of this with the Justice Department. Even though they got Jack, I would think that they would want more than one lobbyist *trophy*.

Chapter 21

☆ ☆ ☆

"FORE!"

"I'm not saying my golf game went bad,
but if I grew tomatoes, they'd come up sliced."

—Attributed to both Miller Barber and Lee Trevino

"Wanna go to Scotland?" I was at home in Heath, Ohio, on a weekend in 2002 when I received this e-mail from Will Heaton. The trip was to occur in August of that same year. My e-mailed reply said, "Will talk to you the beginning of the week about it." Myths of the entire Abramoff affair abound, but the most laughable, egregious one is that I would ask someone to take me on a golf junket. That one is not believable to one single person who knows me. Now, if someone said that I went on a drinking junket, a fun junket, a junket to the Middle East, yes—that would be believable. My friends howled at the thought of my requesting a golf trip when it hit the press.

Essentially, the extent of my golfing was in high school, and then only once in a while on a par three course at Oglebay Park with my high school friend, David Busack from Bellaire, Ohio. On rare occasions over the years I attempted to golf, but completely abandoned the idea.

In the Ohio Senate days, I traveled with ALEC (American Legislative Exchange Council) and NCSL (National Conference of State Legislatures). Like many members of the legislature, I traveled to conferences that were held at some of the best golf resorts in America. So in addition to the meetings, a lot of golf was played. I would open my balcony doors to view the impressive greens, but simply never played. I did rent

153

golf carts to accompany friends, drinking, smoking cigars, laughing with them, enjoying their company, and somewhere along the 18 holes I would possibly take one swing.

The Ohio Legislature is no different from the U.S. House in the sense that you have to raise money to achieve and excel, and then help other Members achieve and excel, so you can better help your district, in a never-ending cycle. I was convinced by my campaign advisors that I should start having golf fundraisers. My invitation the first year read: "I don't golf, but you can." In subsequent years the invitations read: "I still don't golf, but you can." It became the standard joke.

As a U.S. Representative, there was one time when I really regretted not being a golfer. I was asked to be in a foursome with President Clinton. I told the White House that I did not golf. The reply was, "You don't have to play well."

I said, "You don't understand, I simply do not golf at all. I would do better to throw the ball around the course."

The second weird factor of the infamous Scotland trip has to do with foreign travel. I lived in two countries, Iran and Saudi Arabia, as an expatriate. I have traveled to over fifty countries. As Chairman of the House Administration Committee I could snap my fingers and commission a delegation trip to anywhere I wanted, and did. I could have gone to Scotland at any time on the State Department's dime and most important, at that time under House rules, could have spent three to four more personal days doing as I pleased—drinking, golfing, touring—and it was all legal. I simply did not need Abramoff to go to Scotland, period; end of the myth.

These are the facts of that ridiculous disaster:

When I returned to D.C. after my weekend at home, Will Heaton said that Tony Rudy, a former Tom DeLay associate and current Team Abramoff man, had invited me to go Scotland. I said, "Does this involve golf?"

Will replied, "Yes, at St. Andrews, the greatest course in the world, but it involves a lot of other stuff."

I responded with, "Will, you know I despise golf, I do not golf, I do not want to go on a trip involving golf." Matt Parker, my Executive Assistant at the time, witnessed either this conversation or a similar one after that.

The trip didn't take place until August, but Will approached me about going at least two months before then. When I eventually agreed to go and Will asked if he and another staffer could go also I said, "Sure, I don't care. If they approve you, it's okay with me." What I did not know until I read Neil Volz's book, *Into the Sun*, and his point of view, was that Will Heaton called Neil and said, "Bob wants me to go to Scotland." Because of this, Neil believed that I put Will up to it. The reality of the matter was that Will wanted to go to Scotland, so he told Neil that I wanted him to go. I never did have a problem with Will going on the trip, and I supported his participation. Will simply applied some "pressure" to Neil.

Neil was a lobbyist by this time, and worked for Jack Abramoff. Now, does anyone really think (despite my lack of judgment and bad behavior) that I would risk all by forcing a lobbyist to take two staffers? Pure and simple, Will and the other staffer in our office were salivating like dogs to golf. They liked golf, were into it and wanted to play the golfer's *wet dream*—St. Andrews. I personally didn't care if I ever hit a ball across the "gorse," as the weeds are called.

Will then said that I could invite another Member. He specifically named one I thought would be a good one to go on the trip. I agreed that if the other Member went, I would go. Fortunately, the other Member declined or would have had to endure some *heartburn* over it, although he would not have been sent to prison. Only I would be given that distinction. (Tom DeLay and Tom Feeney, two other Members who had been on a similar trip to Scotland, were untouched despite disclosure filings by them that smelled from St. Andrews to Washington, D.C. None of the Abramoff Scotland junket Members were questioned on the costs filed for the trip and only I was mentioned in McCain's hearings in regard to Scotland. *I'm not complaining here; at this point in my life, I'm just throwing out some interesting facts to ponder.*

After the Member declined the trip, I said it was a no-go. Will brought Paul Vinovich, an attorney and my House Administration Staff director, to my office and they both did their best to convince me to go. They said the following and it is indelibly burned into my brain as I repeated it time after time to the federal prosecutors: "This type of trip was previously taken by DeLay, it is approved by the Ethics Committee, it will be a fundraiser to benefit unfortunate kids in Scotland, we will be visiting members of parliament, it is a great opportunity to get to know Jack [Abramoff] who we will need help from for leadership, and it will be fun." This was said several times.

I have learned through rehab, through behavior change, from self-help books, and from experts in the psychological sciences that no one can *make you* do anything. Just as "Altar Boy" Will's defense: "The devil (Bob Ney) made me do it" and Neil Volz's attribution in a *Columbus Dispatch* article: "I was young and naïve," I did not make them do anything they did not want to do, and Will did not make me go to Scotland.

★ ★ ★

The group flew to Scotland on a private jet. The same type, I was told, that DeLay and Feeney had flown on when they went to Scotland. When I boarded it with Will Heaton, Paul Vinovich, Neil and Jack, I saw that Ralph Reed (former executive director for the Christian Coalition) was aboard, and thought that was strange. My second thought was that I had better watch my mouth and my drinking. I happened to be on the phone with Neil Clark, a Columbus lobbyist, while I was on the plane and had even remarked to him that Ralph Reed was on the trip and it was a surprise to me.

I despised small private jets, and at one point in my career refused to ride in them. This particular model seated about eight or so people. It looked relatively new with nice wood trim, and that day's newspapers were on the pullout table. Fresh fruit, snacks, sushi, and of course, booze was readily available. When the jet took off and Ralph hit the booze and threw out a "God damn" in relation to golfing, I was not only surprised at the language from the former head of the Christian Coalition, but I quickly realized that the good behavior button had been disabled for this trip. There was a lot of small talk about life, politics, families, and the president, but absolutely no deal cutting or "shop talk" was to be heard.

We arrived in Scotland, and although I was nervous about the golfing, we did sip some 100-dollar or so per bottle Scotch (obviously aged, at that price). In Saudi Arabia in 1983, the only alcohol available was Scotch. I absolutely despised it, but managed to get this pure *Scottish* Scotch down. It was Scotland and the glass was expensive. Why waste it?

The trip got weirder by the day. Here is where my recollection and that of others may vary—but regardless, the trip was a sham. It had not been presented that way, but it was quickly evident that something was amiss. We had done a round of golf at Kingsbarns, then the biggie—St. Andrews. (When a caddie who depends on golfers for good tips tells you that you are the worst golfer he has ever seen, you are bad!) I also, for whatever reason, didn't wear sunscreen. I was terribly sunburned and golfed horribly, but talked with Jack, and made friends with David Safavian, who was an exceptionally nice man. He was half-Iranian, although he spoke zero Farsi. We had spoken on the plane about Iran, as he had never been there. We had brief, personal conversations about family, life, and D.C. in general, but not about any business issues. At that time he was Chief of Staff of the United States General Services Administration (GSA), and a long-time friend of Jack Abramoff's.

After a couple of days, I simply quit golfing. Everyone understood. I spent my days at the local pub that was attached to the place where we were staying, and ran up a large cell phone bill calling in for work and calling places for constituents. I called Lynne Crow, who was on the House Administration Staff, and confided in her that this trip was strange and not coming down as planned.

We gathered one evening when the parliamentarians were to meet with us. I remember Jack's receiving a phone call. His cell rang and he said something to the effect of "Oh, okay, maybe we can reschedule." When he got off the phone, he said the parliamentarians had to cancel. We ate and drank.

I did actually believe that the golf was raising money for underprivileged kids in Scotland. The Justice Department later found this impossible to believe, but I knew of past situations where people donated money if Members or celebrities played golf. Although I saw no banners, I thought something might have been privately arranged. Why would anyone make that up? (The Justice Department later quizzed me, "Where were the banners that said 'charity event,' Congressman?")

I mentioned to Neil and stressed to Will that I was getting nervous about not meeting with someone from the parliament. This was one of the purposes of the trip that made it legitimate. I couldn't arrange it myself—who would I call? I was in Scotland! This was to have been done by Jack or his scheduler for the trip. I could not find Jack. He literally vanished with his eleven-year-old son, who had come over on the jet with us. It was like a secret or a mystery as to where he was. We all spoke about it and wondered what was up. We didn't see him for a day or so. Even Neil didn't know where he went.

When Jack did return, I mentioned to him that we needed to meet with the parliamentarians. I tried for two days to get him to organize a meeting with them. He indicated he would either talk with Neil or arrange it himself. Here is the strangest part of this scheme: I had a note at the front desk the next morning telling me to go to the main clubhouse and I would meet some Scottish staffers. I thought this was better than nothing. (It turns out that I later saw a picture of one of the men I met with, and he was not a staffer—he was a tour arranger or something to that effect, although he never really indicated when we met that he was or was not a Scottish staffer.) There was also one man and one woman who indicated that they were involved with the "political system." We ate a brief lunch and I left somewhat satisfied that two of the conditions were met; the kids' charity (the golf) and a meeting with whom I thought were parliament staff, or at least someone connected to them. The rest was nothing as had been described to me.

We departed Scotland and flew on the private jet to London. One thing struck me as we got off the plane and into cars at the airport in London—we did not leave Scotland with an exit stamp of any type; no check-in with immigration—and, we were entering London with no immigration stamp. I asked Jack about this because Will Heaton and I were going to be returning to the U.S. on British Airways, not on the private jet, and I was concerned about how we would leave England. He said, "No problem, just tell immigration you came on a private plane." (It actually worked.)

London turned out to be a bust. Heaton and I were practically going door to door in the parliament, looking for someone to talk with. In my mind, I needed somehow to meet someone to make this weird trip legitimate. By this time I knew the trip smelled, was not good, lacked substance, and was just some vacation that Jack planned and used me to pay for through this *charity*, which I now know did not exist and was an out and out lie.

After returning from the trip, I remember walking across the street with Will Heaton and Paul Vinovich from the Capitol as we headed toward the Longworth Building where House Administration was located. We hadn't been talking about the trip, but I said, "Was that not the weirdest fucking trip you have ever been on?" Paul said, "Yeah" and laughed slightly. Then Will said, "If ever questioned, after all, it was Ethics approved."

I had a bad feeling in my gut that I should follow up on this—that something just wasn't right. It would have been so easy at that moment, so right, so smart to have just written a check for the trip and possibly been spared the loss of a good salary and all that I owned, the humiliation of the story, and running afoul of the law. But I didn't. (*Looking back on it today, it would have been that "right thing to do when no one is looking," although inevitably it would not have spared me. It did not spare David Safa-vian, whom I met on the trip, but it took them two trials to get him. They would still need someone—something else would have been dredged to the surface; someone else's buttons beyond Will and Neil would have been pushed. One way or the other, I was going down.)*

Even when things are the darkest, there can be a light moment. One day I was talking with my attorneys, who had been formal federal prosecutors at one time. They knew that I had problems, but they questioned whether it constituted charges and/or imprisonment—similar to my thoughts concerning Clinton during his impeachment.

When they expressed that it did not reach the level of a mountain of evidence, I said, "I'm going down. In a sense, I'm comparable to Kennedy that day in Dallas." They looked puzzled. "That day in Dallas, had Lee Harvey Oswald suffered a heart attack five minutes before the president's motorcade came past Dealey Plaza, Kennedy was not going to leave Dallas alive. Had the backup man been caught, Kennedy was still not coming out alive. One way or the other, President Kennedy was going to die that day in Dallas. One way or the other, I am going to prison."

They didn't respond to my statement, but they did ask, "So what do you know about the assassination?"

It's common knowledge in political circles that Members sometimes know secrets. Something can be said in such a way to make others think you know something you don't. I had no inside knowledge of the Kennedy assassination, so I was just leading them on; but I was totally serious about my going to prison.

Chapter 22

SUNCRUZ: A *CRUISE* DOWN THE RAPIDS

"There is no gambling like politics."

—BENJAMIN DISRAELI

For those of you who are not familiar with the various dealings (and subsequent charges against) Jack Abramoff, the following is a synopsis of one of them—SunCruz:

In 1999, a prominent South Florida businessman, Konstantinos "Gus" Boulis, began negotiations with the U.S. Justice Department over the future of his SunCruz Casinos gambling cruise line. The government said Boulis couldn't own the company because he wasn't a U.S. citizen. Boulis reached a secret agreement with the Justice Department allowing him to sell Sun-Cruz within 36 months.

Attorneys for Boulis approached "prominent Washington lawyer and lobbyist Jack Abramoff" about finding a buyer for SunCruz. Abramoff contacted an old friend, Adam Kidan, who suggested they go into the deal 50-50 and negotiations began in 2000. An agreement was reached for the $147.5 million sale of SunCruz, with Abramoff and Kidan required to contribute $23 million of their own money in return for $60 million in financing from Foothill Capital Corp. and Citadel Equity Fund. Boulis was to keep a 10 percent share of the company.

Kidan, Boulis and Abramoff quarreled over the operation of SunCruz. Kidan claimed that Boulis physically attacked him at a meeting in Dania

Beach, Florida. Boulis sued in state court, seeking to prevent Kidan from operating the company.

Boulis was shot to death in February of 2001 by unknown assailants while driving near his Fort Lauderdale office. Abramoff and Kidan said they knew nothing about Boulis' death. (Three men, one with ties to New York organized crime, were arrested in September 2005 for the murder.)

Abramoff and Kidan filed for bankruptcy on behalf of SunCruz. Foothill Capital and Citadel Equity sued Abramoff, Kidan and others for their $60 million, claiming Abramoff and Kidan misled them about their $23 million contribution, Abramoff and Kidan were indicted on federal conspiracy, wire fraud and mail fraud charges. Prosecutors said the pair faked a wire transfer to make it appear they had contributed $23 million toward the SunCruz purchase.

Abramoff pled guilty on January 4, 2006, to conspiracy and wire fraud charges.

I went to the premiers of documentary filmmaker Alex Gibney's *Casino Jack and the United States of Money*, the movie about Jack Abramoff. The first premiere was at Sundance, then New York City, and finally Washington, D.C. Neil Volz attended all of them as well. With me at Sundance was my college roommate Tim Ritter; at the New York premiere, my cousins, Amanita and Chad Heird, and in D.C. some wonderful friends showed up whom I had not seen in a while.

The recurring questions from friends who viewed the premiers were, "How did the rest of the politicos escape the mess of Abramoff?" and "What was SunCruz about, and why in the hell were you involved with that?" I have asked myself that same question—not how I got involved, but what the hell was that all about?

Neil and I were on stage during the question and answer period after the New York premier with Adam Kidan, former owner of SunCruz Casinos. In front of the audience, he turned to me and asked me a question that shocked me. "Bob, did you ever know why you were 'targeted' by Jack to be involved with SunCruz?"

I looked at Adam and with all sincerity said, "No, why?" My curiosity antennae were on full alert.

He said, "Because Jack was too close to Tom DeLay, and that's who they [Abramoff and Mike Scanlon] really wanted to use [for their purposes]."

I was taken aback—all this time I had been portrayed as doing the "deed" on SunCruz because I was Jack's baby, his confidante, his friend. I later said to Adam as he was leaving the theater, "Now you tell me, why you didn't you mention that to the Justice Department?"

He looked at me and said candidly, "I did. They didn't care."

What Adam told me later, and had alluded to in front of the crowd, was that Jack Abramoff was so close to DeLay that he wanted someone with some distance—someone who wasn't so closely tied to him. My name came up in that category. I knew Jack, but was not at his beck and call as DeLay and his staff were.

As stated above, SunCruz was a line of casinos that were boat-based and operated out of Florida. They were owned by a hardworking, proud, tough-fisted Greek immigrant, Gus Boulis. How I came to be part of Boulis's life, but certainly not involved in his mafia-style death, is a karmic chain of events that can happen in politics just as it does in life.

Corey Lewandowski was my Deputy Chief of Staff. He and I met Mike Scanlon at a Republican retreat. Mike Scanlon was a smiling, charismatic, top-notch bull shitter—he was perfect for Washington. Mike was Tom DeLay's deputy communications man, but to hear it from Mike, he was DeLay's inside, go-to, right-hand man. He did seem to have connections—or at least could foster them—with DeLay.

I introduced Mike Scanlon to my Chief of Staff, Neil Volz, when Corey and I returned from the retreat. I thought Neil and our office should get to know him, thinking that he would be helpful. Because Scanlon was so *out front* and convincing about his power with DeLay—that he had DeLay's *ear* and total run of his office, I felt that we needed to get to know this guy for my future. I wanted to be able to bring DeLay "to the table" for me as I tried to advance through the House of Representatives. DeLay was referred to as "the hammer" and wielded incredible power and influence among the Republican Members and right-wing advocacy groups.

Mike Scanlon moved on to lobbying and became a part of Team Abramoff. In March of 1999, Scanlon approached Neil Volz. His request was simple, but a bit strange in the sense that it went after one person, Gus Boulis, in a personal way. In his book, *Into the Sun*, Neil Volz best summarizes how the SunCruz involvement went down. Neil has graciously given me permission to use that passage here:

The *Congressional Record* is the official record of the United States Congress. The record is printed every day and includes a transcript of the day's floor debates, committee activity and what are called, "Extension of Remarks." These remarks are found in the back of the record, after the day's summary of speeches and debate. Extension of Remarks include everything from local congratulatory tributes to random political statements that Members of Congress want to submit for whatever reason.

Since as far back as his days in the state legislature, Bob used such remarks in the record to congratulate local 4-H students, area churches and winning football teams. He also used them to express his personal views on certain topics.

The topic of [Mike] Scanlon's submission request was a set of boat-based casinos in Florida called SunCruz Casinos. It was his second SunCruz-related *Congressional Record* request. Six months earlier, Bob and I placed a similar statement into the Record on behalf of Congressman DeLay's former spokesman [Mike Scanlon]. As such, when Scanlon approached me to see if Ney would be willing to submit another statement on SunCruz into the *Congressional Record*, the concept and topic wasn't new. But time was tight.

In March, when we received Scanlon's first request, Bob and I knew he was asking us to help one of his gambling-related clients. Which one, I didn't know. Nor did I really care, After Bob said he was cool with helping Scanlon, the specifics of why our friend was asking didn't matter to me nearly as much as what was in the statement. From my perspective, the statement needed to make sense from Bob's point of view. And from the point of view of a potential inquiring reporter or political opponent. *It was like a powerful constituent asking us to submit a statement of celebrating his daughter's science project award,* I told myself. *As long as the science project wasn't an analysis of how to end coal production, we would just do it.*

Therefore, I told Scanlon to write something up so the Congressman could see it. "Whatever you give me needs to include what you want in the submission," I told Mike. "It also needs to include a reference to Bob's district and Bob's agnostic view on gaming. We need something to hang our hat on in case a reporter asks us why Bob submitted the statement," I continued.

Scanlon got to work and gave me his proposal a couple of days later. The gist of his request was for Bob to question the actions of the owner and operator of SunCruz Casinos, a man named Gus Boulis. To bolster his case, Scanlon brought over some articles from the Florida newspapers outlining how and why the Florida Attorney General was investigating the cruise line.

I looked it over, and then passed it on to Bob and our Deputy Chief of Staff in the district. They also looked through the material. From my point of view, I was content, knowing that the submission included Bob's view on gaming, a mention of his home state and some sort of verifiable information. Ultimately, only one opinion mattered in Ney World, and that was Bob's. His only concern was specifically mentioning Boulis by name.

"Ask Scanlon if he really wants that," Bob told me. So I did.

"I will take whatever you give us," Mike said, before telling me he very much was hoping that the Congressman would keep the name Gus Boulis in the document.

Bob agreed to do so. "It's Scanlon," we both said.

In the back of that day's *Congressional Record,* the Congressman [Bob Ney] ripped into our friend's target. "Mr. Speaker, how SunCruz Casinos and Gus Boulis conduct themselves with regard to Florida laws is very unnerving. Florida authorities have repeatedly reprimanded SunCruz Casinos and its owner Gus Boulis for taking illegal bets, for not paying their customers properly and had to take steps to prevent SunCruz from conducting operations altogether."

Boulis called the office the next day. Bob said he wasn't surprised. When Boulis asked for the Congressman, Ney told me to call the casino owner back. I did. The casino owner was appalled and confused as to why an Ohio Congressman would be so interested in his cruise line. Boulis was nervous, and said he was working on improving their operation. He also asked me where we had heard about SunCruz. I told him we read about it in the paper, and pulled out the newspapers Scanlon had dropped off at the office. Telling somebody I didn't know that we were really just helping a lobbyist friend wasn't something I was going to say. That kind of comment would make Bob look horrible in the papers and get me in trouble with my boss.

The first Boulis *Congressional Record* statement ran in March. Seven months later, Scanlon was back for more. This time he was hoping we would submit a statement in the *Congressional Record* praising the new owner of SunCruz Casinos, a man named Adam Kidan. No one in Ney World knew Kidan from a hole in the wall, though by that point he had attended a fundraiser for Bob in one of Jack Abramoff's spots suites. The Congressman and I undoubtedly met and talked with Kidan at the event. But we did make a lot of events and made small talk with a lot of people. As far as Bob and I were concerned, Kidan was just part of "Scanlon's event." That isn't to diminish Kidan, nor suggest that I should have remembered him. Who he was didn't even register. Scanlon was the face of the project. And by that point, a good friend.

I agree with what Neil said in his book, and my rationale—D.C.-skewed as it may have been—seemed to make sense to me. Neil's analogy of a powerful constituent having me enter into the record his daughter's science project and how, unless its analysis ended coal production (my district had high coal production), we were for it, is how we looked at Scanlon's request. It was from someone powerful and it did not affect my district or anyone in it.

I was used to making Congressional Record remarks ever since my Ohio Legislature days in regard to everything under the sun. However, this Congressional Record statement, unlike harmless statements made before, such as 4-H news and the weddings of my constituents' children, involved a man (Gus Boulis) who was later gunned down in his car; this Congressional Record statement involved, contrary to the seemingly innocent Scanlon request, high powered lobbyists like Abramoff who were using my name and the pressure of my position to pull off deals conning millions of dollars to buy gambling boats.

I was helping to raise over a million dollars for the party by working on "galas" for the House Republican Congressional Committee where we would raise millions of dollars to be used in Republican campaigns for U.S. Representatives. It was a very structured process by the House Congressional Campaign Committee to have all Members raise contributions. I was actively involved to show I could be a player, thus enhancing my status to climb up the ladder. Both parties still do it and, to some extent, then as well as now, Members "buy" future Chairmanships and leadership positions. For the most part, you do not play, you do not reap positions.

At the time of the second Congressional Record request by Scanlon for a statement about Adam Kidan becoming the new owner of Sun Cruz, Scanlon did a conference call with Neil and me. I didn't understand the need for a second statement and became uneasy about it. Although the backing for Boulis-the-bad-guy to be out and the backing for Kidan-the-good-guy to be in seemed to be justifiable, I had an uneasy feeling in my gut. *(These days when my stomach rumbles, I listen to it—intensely.)*

I didn't follow my instincts, and after the conference call, although there was no *tit for tat* (you do this for us and we will do this for you), and although I had met my money goal, Scanlon wanted to write a check to the "Republican Party" and that seemed acceptable.

In February of 2001, I received a call from the *Boston Globe*. Gus Boulis was gunned down in his car "gangland-style" in Florida. And I said to myself *Houston, we have a problem.*

Chapter 23

☆ ☆ ☆

FOXCOM

"No good deed goes unpunished."

—OSCAR WILDE

Foxcom Wireless was a client of Abramoff's lobbying firm that was awarded a lucrative contract to install a cellular network in Congress when I was House Administration Chair. Google "Foxcom Abramoff" and invariably my name will come up. None of those accounts relate the whole story—the truth.

I became Chairman of the House Administration Committee in 2001. The chairmanship is an appointment by the Speaker of the House only, and does not have to be approved by the Republican Caucus. It brings a lot of power with it, and coordinates with the Speaker's office on running the House.

There was one leftover decision that I inherited from Bill Thomas, the previous Chairman: There were two companies that wanted to be awarded a House contract to improve cellular access for the Capitol.

This could not be done "in house" by our own staff; it needed to be done by a wireless service provider. The individual cellular companies could not do this on their own—each putting in a separate system—it would not have worked technically or cost-wise.

I soon discovered that Chairman Thomas's lack of a decision to award the contract stemmed from the fact that two Members of Congress were fighting territorially for "their" companies in "their" districts. One company was LGC Wireless and the other was Foxcom Wireless. The Members' battle, of course, turned into a lobbyists' battle. Each company hired some "guns." Foxcom hired Jack Abramoff and LGC hired Haley Barbour. (Haley was the top dog helping to organize and maintain the Republican takeover of Congress and he became a very successful lobbyist. Later, he became Governor of Mississippi.)

However, the two people most aggressively seeking the contracts were the two Members of Congress with district interests, involving jobs in their states. They also had a very powerful force behind them—the rest of the U.S. House of Representatives—and this is why: If there is one thing that Members of Congress value more than campaign contributions, it's time. When votes are called, it takes a Member an average of ten minutes to walk, often underground, to the Capitol. (After 9/11, Members were asked by the Sergeant of Arms and the Hill Police authorities to utilize the underground walkways and the "subway" to lessen their exposure.)

Members, including me, wanted to use that time (ten minutes over and ten minutes back, plus the floor time for voting, which was sometimes thirty to forty minutes) to use our cell phones. Cellular access in the underground areas was a real problem.

I was hounded so much about it that I asked our staff to do the initial inquiries with our "big three"—the Sergeant of Arms, Bill Livingood; the Clerk of the House, Jeff Trandahl; and the CAO (Chief Administrative Officer) of the House, Jay Eagan. Each had some aspect of the system under their jurisdiction, but the most likely to be affected seemed to be the Sergeant of Arms, Bill Livingood. He knew that the former Chairman, Bill Thomas, had not proceeded because he did not want to get between the two Members vying for the contract to go to their respective districts. Bill Livingood was happy that it hadn't been acted upon because he saw this wireless company issue as a potential (and legitimate, I must add) breach of security.

Bill Livingood came to me and expressed his concern. I yielded to him and put the entire idea on ice. Bill was a fine man and was a pleasure to work with. He oversaw the Capitol Hill Police and had vast law enforcement experience, including Secret Service. His concern about security was so great that I really thought this matter was dead and buried.

Four things happened:

1. First, Members were growing more and more frustrated. In the hun-

dreds of requests I received each month as House Administration Chairman, this one was topping the charts.

2. The second was that lobbyists Jack Abramoff and Haley Barbour got into the action, which is par for the course and happens constantly in Washington.

3. The third factor, which was the crux of the issue, was that various cellular companies, AT&T, Sprint, Verizon, et al, wanted this. Members would talk to each other and say, "Oh, so your phone is working underground?" They would then switch to whatever company provided the best underground service. The switches were constant. The phone companies saw this as an opportunity to retain the Members as customers. Members make a lot—and I mean a lot—of phone calls and they have an average of eighteen people on staff. Whatever phone service provider the Member likes is usually the one utilized by all the staff. We are talking targeted dollars here!

4. The fourth was that Neil Volz went from a staffer *involved* in this, into a firm that *lobbied* this. I am not saying that Neil was pursuing me on this contract; I just felt personally that I could make him look good. It seemed to be a trifecta winner: Make the Members happy, make the cellular people happy, and make Neil look good.

Due to the pressure from Members wanting service, I met with the National Security Agency (NSA) in my office. Bill Livingood and other representatives of the Sgt. of Arms office were present. I asked them to look at LGC and Foxcom, the two cellular companies. Because Foxcom was not an American company (it was an Israeli company that had an office in the U.S.), I asked them to check it out in particular. It could pose a security issue depending on the facility where the components are made. Listening devices could possibly be built in at a manufacturing facility.

The NSA went about its task, which took a long time. Eventually I received a phone call and Sgt. of Arms Bill Livingood, my IT man and I met with the NSA in an SCIF room (Sensitive Compartmented Information Facility) "on site" in the Capitol Complex. I will not divulge anything that compromises the Capitol security, but will tell you that these rooms allow nothing of an electronic nature in or out, and nothing to do with security can be transmitted or recorded. This was a safe place to talk about the security of the Capitol. Prior to this meeting I made an agreement with the Sgt. of Arms office that if this was not approved by the NSA, I would personally kill any possibility of anyone getting this contract.

After extensive conversations, both in the first meeting with NSA and the second one in the SCIF room, the nod was given to proceed. A preference of a company was not given.

The actual idea of how to award the contract was conceived by my IT staffer and the Chief Administrative Officer's staff: Let the wireless providers (Cingular, Nextel, Sprint, Verizon Wireless, AT&T Wireless and Voicestream) decide who would receive the contract by written ballot.

However, LGC didn't like this plan. Prior to my becoming Chairman of the House Administration Committee, someone promised LGC that this was all a "done deal." Most likely they were told to wait until the new Chair came in, as the existing staff would already have it in motion. After Bill Thomas was out of the crossfire between the two Members of Congress who were competing for the contract, the Administration Staff was proceeding forward and about to implement the deal when I took the Chairmanship. Without malice, I ingenuously put a halt to the contract due to the security concerns expressed by our security people.

The cellular companies picked Foxcom, LGC, or remained neutral. The major point here is that there were no taxpayers' dollars in this. The cellular providers were paying for the service, so the decision to let them pick could have easily ended with the award going to LGC.

This is pretty simple. The rest was blown out of proportion by the Justice Department and hungry reporters.

(The Justice Department's allegation that I and I alone decided to compromise the security of the Capitol—they argued that it would provide the means to listen in on Members' telephone conversations—was absolute nonsense. These were false allegations by Attorney General Alberto Gonzales and Assistant Attorney General Alice Fisher to railroad me further into submission. This and their saying that I was lobbying for Iran to get airplane parts are the most disgusting things these two did. The rest of my behavior is fair game, but this was unconscionable. It is tantamount to saying that the National Security Agency intentionally yielded to me so that I could compromise the Capitol.)

I had conversations with Neil about Foxcom, both when he was my Staff Director and later as a lobbyist. I believe Neil was told by Jack that the lawyers in the lobbyist firm said that Neil could "inquire" from me as to the status—that it was proper. Knowing now how Jack operated, he most likely never asked the lawyers what they thought. I believe that Jack lived in a world where he created all the rules and convinced others that they existed. He was everything to everyone—he was whatever you wanted him to be

The gist of the story involves Neil Volz—not as a lobbyist, but as Staff Director for the House Administration Committee. Haley Barbour, the lobbyist for LGC, called Neil. He had an air of, "Hey, it's Haley, need this one." Neil told me at that at one point Haley said something to the effect that he was fairly busy and "have Bob, call me on this sometime."

However, the real problem stemmed from something LGC's lobbyist said not only to us but also to others involved. He referred to Foxcom as the "Jews," and could not understand why I would want to give a contract to a foreign "Jew" company. As alluded to before, Foxcom originated in Jerusalem, Israel, and had an office in Virginia, in the United States.

I have been around many Jewish people and have been to Israel often enough to know that Jewish people refer to themselves as "Jews," but to have a lobbyist use the term "Jew" company, is not the same thing. I was shocked at this hardball tactic by LGC's lobbyist—but I believe that Jack Abramoff saw it as an opportunity.

Jack called me and said that he wanted to see me and bring the executives from Foxcom over. I had never met with Foxcom and Jack played this one beautifully. He had heard about the "Jew" comments and told me that I was being portrayed by the American Israel Affairs Committee (AIPAC) and others as "anti-Jewish; anti-Semitic." He said that he did not care one bit about this contract, but for the sake of my political future, he wanted to clear this up. He also told me that Foxcom was not happy about it either. When he brought them over and put the executives in my conference room, Jack and I took a minute together and we talked about it. Jack was so convincing about his concern for me that he truly deserved an Oscar.

I met with the executives, assured them that I was not anti-Jewish and that if the process proceeded, they would have a fair shake. I told them there were security questions concerning both companies.

(Looking back, I think that Jack heard about and capitalized on the "Jew" comments. He utilized it to get his people before me and I must say that it did give him an advantage. I didn't want to look anti-Jewish, which in American Politics is a death sentence. It all worked out for Foxcom and Jack. However, the House later suspended the contract—possibly due to all the controversy, and the Democrats wanted to look "clean").

In dealing with Jack Abramoff, I crossed the line. It was not direct bribery and we could not be charged with that, but it surely was not good, nor was it legal. I ate and drank free at his expense, traveled with him to Scotland, and threw the ethics laws to the wind. In rationalizing my bad behavior, I can "justify" all that by thinking that I helped a friend look good in Jack's eyes, or that I needed to help Jack go further up the ladder so I could better help my constituents. Nevertheless, whichever way I look at it, it was wrong, illegal, unethical, and immoral. Even though some of the stories were "enhanced" due to the Department of Justice, the media, or just plain human perceptions, the fact remains that all of these dealings—the trip, SunCruz, the Foxcom contract—were events that I am absolutely responsible for and could have stopped in a "New York minute" with the snap of a finger.

I am the one to blame—not Jack Abramoff, not Neil Volz, not Will Heaton. A person cannot be made angry by someone; a person cannot be manipulated by someone; a person cannot be corrupted by someone. I was the one who allowed it to happen.

Chapter 24

☆ ☆ ☆

A CONTRACT,
A CONTROVERSY,
AND A COVER-UP?

"By the pricking of my thumbs,
Something wicked this way comes."

—WILLIAM SHAKESPEARE, *MACBETH*

Once you are in a controversy, you become the poster child for blog-gers, the media, conspiracy theory nuts, and any other crackpots. *"Oh, he must have done it!"* According to these theorists, I suppose I should confess that I also fixed the Obama primary from prison because I was angry at Hillary; I arranged for Mitt Romney to win the Republi-can nomination; and at the age of eight, I personally covered up the JFK assassination. Glad I got that off my chest.

Let me shed some light on a to-date never revealed theory on a House Administration contract containing my signature that enabled an Ohio guy named Mike Connell to make millions—the start of an ongoing con-troversy and mystery. The principals in this chapter include the late Mike Connell, Karl Rove, John Boehner, Barry Jackson, Dave Distefano, for-mer Ohio Secretary of State Ken Blackwell and, of course, me.

Mike Connell was a whiz kid—a successful, highly placed Republi-can consultant who was from Illinois but lived in Akron, Ohio. Among his myriad talents, he was a Web site designer and an IT professional. He was known by many as the IT "Guru." By the age of 37, Connell was President, Chief Political Strategist and CEO of New Media Com-munications, Inc. and its spin-off (to handle its growing list of federal government clients), GovTech Solutions. One of Connell's various businesses maintained the Web site of the Swift Boat Veterans for Truth, which was a very successful 527 group (a tax-exempt political funding organization created to influence the election or appointment of officials) that went after John Kerry and successfully muddled his veteran's record during the Bush/Kerry election in 2004. By this time, GovTech's client list included more than 20 members of the U.S. House of Representatives, the Web site of the House Republican Conference, plus the House Intelligence, Judiciary, Financial Services, Ways and Means, and House Administration committees. (That last item might seem familiar to you—and yes, it was acquired while I was Chairman of the House Administration Committee.) In addition, he created a Web site for Ohio Secretary of State Ken Blackwell that presented the results of the 2004 election in real time as they were tabulated. At the time, Blackwell was also chairman of the Bush-Cheney 2004 reelection effort in Ohio . . . the plot thickens.

THE CONTRACT

At the risk of sounding like former President Richard Nixon, here are the facts of the Connell contracts with the House Administration Committee to the best of my knowledge:

In 2001, within the first two months or so of my chairmanship of House Administration,

Mike Connell received a contract signed by me to place his company's servers behind the House of Representatives firewall . . . and it has been a pain in my side ever since. The following in an article by attorney/ reporter (and political gadfly) Bob Fitrakis is just one of many reasons why:

GOP COMPUTER GURU CONTROLS KEY CONGRESSIONAL WEBSITES

Bush loyalist Mike Connell controls Congressional secrets as his firm serves Karl Rove.

July 30, 2008

In 2001, Michael L. Connell of GovTech Solutions, L.L.C., a notoriously partisan GOP operative and Bush family confidant, was selected to re-organize the Capitol Hill IT network.

Under the guise of selecting a female-owned IT company (Connell's wife, Heather, is listed as the owner), former Ohio Republican Congressman and convicted felon Bob Ney reportedly arranged for Connell to be the man behind the firewall for the U.S. House of Representatives.

Connell's role and activities need to be investigated by putting Connell under oath and examining how arguably one of the country's most zealously partisan IT specialists managed to land the contract and be allowed access to this electronic communication system.

Let me explain something here—in my first six months as the new Chairman of the House Administration Committee, I was clueless when it came to technology. Our tech guys guided me in the process. Eagan, our chief administrative officer (CAO), was the man who initiated the contracts unless the people employed by me for the Committee had an idea for a vendor. A contract would have come from the House information services to Eagan the CAO, then to our tech people, then to me. I would have signed anything in those early days. (Sorry, but this is how Congress works sometimes. I later became much more adept.) Therefore, the most opportune time to get me to sign something pertaining to technology without my checking it out was early in my chairmanship.

Fast-forward ten years to the fall of 2011. I received a phone call from a top-notch investigative writer who was doing a freelance story on Karl Rove, Mike Connell, et al. I almost didn't speak to him. However, we talked because he said, "Congressman, I know you have nothing to hide. You went to prison—'they' wanted you discredited—I know that." He continued, "You did sign the Connell contract early on for the House and I also know you did not have any earthly idea that you signed it."

He was correct. We spoke, I shared information that he did not have, and I received information that I did not have. The entire interview made me wrack my brain to piece this all together. If it looks suspicious and it smells suspicious, it is suspicious. I did sign the damn thing, but I did not know Connell. I truly would not have been able to identify him under any circumstances. I struggled to recall if there had been anything out of the ordinary with our tech guy, but he was a straight shooter, so I didn't believe so. I gave the investigative reporter his name and the names of other staff people, hoping he could find something.

Then, it struck me. I succeeded Bill Thomas as Chairman of the House Administration Committee, and in January of 2001 when I took over as Chairman, the holdover staff were terrified that I was going to clean them out. One of the reasons for that was an order I received from Speaker of the House Dennis Hastert's office. Hastert's Chief of Staff, Scott Palmer, had his assistant, Ted Van Der Meid, inform me that in order for me to cinch the deal of my being the Chairman of House

Administration, I had to fire former chairman Bill Thomas's top staff guy or the Chairmanship was a no-go. Why the powerful Speaker and his powerful right-hand man could not fire this staff guy was beyond me. Someone must have had pictures. Neil Volz had to do the dirty work. (New Chairmen don't do that sort of thing—or at least they don't get blamed for it.) As Neil told me, "A good man got fired today."

Within a day, our main tech guy came to me privately and said, "I don't know who's who, or who is important to you." He went on to say that several of our new staffers had come to the Committee from my personal office and had been with me before. He delicately related the fact that one or two of them said they "had my ear" and he did not want to step on toes. I assured him that he would remain; he was needed and I would work with him. He then said that he had been contacted by one of my former top staffers who wanted to put in a word for "things" that he needed. That "top staffer" was Dave Distefano.

I said, "Dave is a friend, but I can't imagine what he would want out of the committee." I had no idea that Barry Jackson, who had strong ties to John Boehner and Karl Rove, was leaning on Distefano to get our tech guy to cooperate. Why wouldn't Barry just do it himself? Something I had no idea about at that time was that Mike Connell's roommate had been none other than Barry Jackson. Using Distefano allowed Barry Jackson to distance himself from the situation. This tie between Mike Connell and Barry Jackson was news to me and I only learned of it when I left prison.

In politics, one cannot have, as we say, "fingerprints" on things. Barry Jackson, on behalf of Karl Rove, could not brazenly and directly contact my tech staffer. That would leave major "fingerprints" that could lead to Barry and his former boss, John Boehner. Therefore, the perfect go-between became Dave Distefano—friend to Barry Jackson and former employee of mine, who also had access to my House Staff.

I thought back to 2010 when I went to a charity fundraiser in Akron, Ohio, with Ellen Ratner and bumped into a guy who, in casual conversation without knowing who I was, said that he used to work with Mike Connell. He said that when Mike died, he (the guy) was totally cut out of the picture and it was made clear that he was not doing any more business with the Republican Campaign Congressional Committee. In further conversation with him, we got around to the people he knew, and it was clear that he knew Barry Jackson (he said that Barry was a key figure for the company he worked for), and the lobbyist, Dave Distefano, whom Barry had told him to meet a few years prior to this time.

I began putting the pieces of the puzzle together. When I got into Congress, who was the Vice Chairman of the House Administration Committee? John Boehner. John hated the committee, as he told me many times, and actually tried to do away with it, yet he had been on that committee. Why would he want to do away with it? Could it be because that particular committee has its hands on ALL house contracts for technology, acquisitions, and invoices? If there is no committee, it all goes under the authority of the Speaker of the House. As one of the four leaders of Congress, John Boehner had influence with the Speaker's office—*and* he wanted eventually to be Speaker himself. Doing away with the committee would be much more convenient for him than having to deal with a chairman whose cooperation he would have to solicit (or go around) to get what he wanted.

ALLEGED VOTE TAMPERING

In 2008, Mike Connell was subpoenaed as a witness in Ohio in a case alleging that vote tampering during the 2004 presidential election resulted in civil rights violations in the King Lincoln Bronzeville Neighborhood Association v. Blackwell case.

Connell had created a Web site for Ohio Secretary of State Kenneth Blackwell that presented the results of the 2004 Presidential Election in real time, as the votes were being tabulated. Blackwell also served as chair of the Bush-Cheney reelection effort in Ohio. The legal case was filed on Aug. 31, 2006 by Clifford Arnebeck and other Columbus, Ohio, attorneys who charged Blackwell with racially discriminatory practices that included selective purging of voters from the election rolls and the unequal allocation of voting machines to various districts.

According to conspiracy theorists Cliff Arnebeck, and Bob Fitrakis, I was somehow intricately involved. This is the story:

Ken Blackwell had initiated a voting policy that, per a lawsuit by the Democratic Party, "intended to disenfranchise minority voters," and was in violation of the federal election law—specifically a section of the Help America Vote Act (HAVA).

Two members of the Black Congressional Caucus wanted me to get Blackwell to D.C. to testify about the above. When he refused, I agreed to take the hearing to Ohio to force him to come over. Here is where the mistaken zealots on the Left, the advocacy groups, the moveon.orgs of the world, the Fitrakis (freepress.org) conspiracy groups, think I organized the hearing to help the Bush effort. My purpose was to force a confrontation with Blackwell. We were standing in the back of the room, waiting for the hearing to begin when he walked through the area. He was very angry, very cold and became combative with my two Congressional colleagues from the Black Caucus. Sadly, both Stephanie Tubbs Jones (D-Ohio) and Juanita Millender McDonald (D-California) are now deceased. They were the ones requesting the hearing, not I, although the Left believes I requested the hearing.

The problem with Cliff Arnebeck and Bob Fitrakis is they came off looking like they were *way out there*, because they had more regard for sensationalism than for the truth. I think someone may have deliberately sent them down a rat hole by feeding them *facts* about me and convincing them that I was the key.

Cliff tried to involve me in lawsuits, stated conspiracy theories about me all over the place and pursued everything regarding me in the wrong manner. He was barking up the wrong tree. The day I was released from Alvis House (halfway house), Cliff called the halfway house and left a message for me to call him. I was still under federal probation—still under the Bush holdovers (many of the people involved in my prosecution were not dismissed when Obama became president, and some remain as of this writing with Attorney General Eric Holder's Justice Department); and there was absolutely no way I was talking to a man who thought I was in the middle of a conspiracy to fix an election when the man I supposedly "fixed" it for had his top henchman, Gonzales, put me in prison!

I had known Cliff Arnebeck quite well during my Ohio Senate days. I liked Cliff, and thought he was bright. He should have been smarter about this. I think he was on to something and we could have shared notes, but not under those circumstances. Cooperating with him could have had federal probation right up my ass.

A COVER-UP?

Mike Connell refused to testify or to produce documents relating to the system used in the 2004 and 2006 elections. He quashed the subpoena. However, he was ordered to appear for a two-hour, closed-door deposition on November 3, 2008, just eighteen hours before the 2008 national election. Although Connell had expressed his willingness to testify, he was reluctant to do so after receiving [alleged] threats from Karl Rove.

Cliff Arnebeck, the lead attorney, sent a letter to U.S. Attorney General Michael Mukasey seeking protection for Connell as a witness in the case, saying he had been threatened:

Dear Attorney General Mukasey:

We have been confidentially informed by a source we believe to be credible that Karl Rove has threatened Michael Connell, a principal witness we have identified in our King Lincoln case in federal court in Columbus, Ohio, that if he does not agree to "take the fall" for election fraud in Ohio, his wife Heather will be prosecuted for supposed lobby law violations. This appears to be in response to our designation of Rove as the principal perpetrator in the Ohio Corrupt Practices Act/RICO claim with respect to which we issued document hold notices last Thursday to you and to the US Chamber of Commerce Institute for Legal Reform.

I have informed court chambers and am in the process of informing the Ohio Attorney General and US Attorney's offices in Columbus for the purpose, among other things, of seeking protection for Mr. Connell and his family from this reported attempt to intimidate a witness.

Concurrently herewith, I am informing Mr. Conyers and Mr. Kucinich in connection with their Congressional oversight responsibilities related to these matters.

Because of the serious engagement in this matter that began in 2000 of the Ohio Statehouse Press Corps, 60 Minutes, the New York Times, Wall Street Journal, C-Span and Jim VandeHei, and the public's right to know of gross attempts to subvert the rule of law, I am forwarding this information to them, as well.

Cliff Arnebeck, Attorney

Despite Connell's elite status as a top-rung Republican consultant for years, witness protection requests went unheeded.

On December 19, 2008, Mike Connell was killed at the age of 45 when the Piper Saratoga he was flying crashed approximately three miles from the runway near Akron, Ohio. Connell was an experienced pilot. His plane had been recently serviced. He was returning from D.C. that evening. There was no one else in the plane. His cell phone was never found.

Chapter 25

☆ ☆ ☆

THE CASE OF THE NON-AMENDMENT

"We don't see things as they are, we see things as we are."

—ANAÏS NIN

The second biggest lie by Alberto Gonzales/Alice Fisher of the Justice Department, the first being that I asked for the Scotland golf trip, was that I "placed" an amendment in my legacy bill, the Help America Vote Act (HAVA), in exchange for the favor of the Tigua Indians paying for the trip. That simply, unequivocally, never happened. I know the Justice Department *said* that I did an amendment; they put it in *print* that I did an amendment; and they may have actually *believed* that I did an amendment, but an amendment was never submitted, put into a bill, put into a conference report, or put on the table. Of the thirty or so staffers and the members of the conference committee, none of them can say it ever happened. This simply was made up by the government because they had no case. (*On a November 7, 2011 edition of 60 Minutes, Jack Abramoff explained how he attempted to get his own bill tacked on to the HAVA reform bill. "So what we did was we crafted language that was so obscure, so confusing, so uninformative, but so precise to change the U.S. code . . . Members don't read the bills." It was an insidious technique that Abramoff perfected. The link to this is listed in the Resources section of this book. It would be worth your time to watch it for yourself.*)

Had I gone to trial, this plus the fact that the travel form was, and still is, in Will Heaton's handwriting (it was signed by me after he filled it in—this is the way all forms are handled), my lawyers and I would have had a chance before a jury to win this issue at least. Some of the others may not have been so easy.

Through leaks, the Government of the United States knowingly fabricated and made overblown statements about not all, but some of the facts of the case. In order to bring this to an end, I made a plea—fully aware that the leaks were at times overblown and untrue. The plea was accurate, but the department's methods were "win at all cost."

It is not true that I asked Jack for a trip and in exchange did favors for the Tigua Tribe. This was the "guts" of the Justice Department's case and in my opinion it was as fake and flawed as Alberto Gonzales's defense before the Senate about the massive firings of the federal employees under his wing; it was as false as the Bush weapons of mass destruction; but it was as effective as Dick Cheney's manipulating the Oval Office for his neocon desires of making Halliburton rich by creating wars.

I made the statement when this blew up that, "I want to be absolutely clear that at no point, ever, was I made even remotely aware that any Indian tribe played any role in this trip."

Contradicting this statement was Tigua "consultant" Mark Schwartz. Schwartz was so far up Jack Abramoff's ass that at one point in time, if Jack coughed, Schwartz's head would have popped out of Jack's mouth. Schwartz, who was making money from the tribe, was on a save-his-ass mission. *(I found it ironic that again and again in McCain's hearings regarding the Scotland trip, only the people who brought up my name were asked to testify.)* Schwartz contradicted my statement (my comments in brackets and Italics) by saying at the Senate hearings, "In August of 2002, a month after Ney's reported conversation with Dodd about the 'Tigua' amendment [*that was not submitted into the bill*] and around [*before*] the time of the Scotland trip, Abramoff arranged for Ney to meet with Tigua representatives in his office. Before the meeting in an e-mail to me, Abramoff mentioned that Congressman Ney did not want his trip to Scotland brought up, as he would show his appreciation to the tribe later."

There is a good reason why Jack did not want anyone mentioning the trip to me. First, I did not ask for it. Second, Jack was using the Tigua's to pay for the trip by invoking my name as the requester and then later told us through Team Abramoff that a charity was paying for it. I would have absolutely canceled the trip had it been mentioned in the meeting with the Tigua representatives. It would be unheard of for a lobbyist to go this far behind a Member's back, obviously lying, and it would have thrown a huge red flag in front of me, the one who was not enthused about the trip anyway. Of course Jack did not want it mentioned! Neither I, nor Will Heaton nor Paul Vinovich had any knowledge that the Tigua Tribe paid for it. Jack played both of us—me *and* the tribe.

The Justice Department prosecutors then said that the meeting lasted ninety minutes. Members of Congress do not do ninety-minute meetings, even with a president! There is nothing to talk about for ninety minutes that is not said in the first fifteen minutes.

The HAVA amendment/non-amendment saga started with a personal visit from Jack Abramoff after the bill was introduced. Jack asked to come see me at my office in the House Administration complex. I thought it was interesting that he was coming himself. Neil and I talked and Neil said he didn't know what it was about. I believe Neil because after Jack left, I wasn't sure either, and throughout the process we were never sure what it was about. When Jack finally produced something in writing during that meeting (at our request), Paul Vinovich, a lawyer as well as my Staff Director for House Administration, said, "What the fuck is this?"

(This is where Jack says I am re-writing history and this is where I say that Jack likes to write and twist his own version of history. I am skeptical today as to whether Jack Abramoff has learned his lesson or if he is "back" and after the mighty dollar rather than redemption. Watching the aforementioned *60 Minutes* segment might help you come to your own conclusion.)

Jack says he spelled out in detail what was going on with the amendment in my House Administration office that day (the amendment that he has since admitted on national television was intentionally confusing and deceptive). I do remember his smiling and laughing about some insidious plot to open and close casinos. Jack said clearly (and this I took in like a vacuum cleaner), that Senator Chris Dodd (D-Connecticut) wanted this amendment and would approve this amendment. This was significant—this was key. I could not pass my legacy bill, HAVA, without two people. One was Representative Steny Hoyer, (D-Maryland) whose idea it was to do a bill and we communicated and agreed on most items, but the second and main one in the Senate was Chris Dodd. I absolutely could not pass the bill when it went from the House to the Senate without Senator Dodd.

We had feverishly worked on the HAVA bill. I had a great team with Vinovich and Roman Buhler. Roman had been around the House Administration Office forever. He was a Bill Thomas holdover. I succeeded Bill

Thomas as Chairman of the House Administration Committee, and I kept Roman. He was fascinating—always carried a box of files with him and had amazing knowledge of the history of the Committee. He is a real expert in election law and election legislation, and had worked tirelessly on the bill. We did not clue Roman in on the amendment. He knew nothing of it, because this did not rise to the level of "Oh my Lord, we have to pass this amendment!" I made the game plan clear to Vinovich. We would explore this since Jack said Dodd wanted it, but we would not make it a priority for us. Our attitude was, if it gets in, it gets in; if it doesn't, it doesn't, and if it would kill the HAVA bill, no way that we will do it. Vinovich carried this game plan out to a "T," and this is exactly what I told Jack that day.

(In the meetings with the Justice Department, an FBI agent sat in on the meetings who had been a former inspector at power plants and was as dumb as a hoe handle. He asked me repeatedly, "Why would Dodd be significant? Why is a Conference Committee important?" After I gave him a government lesson at the hourly rate I was paying my attorneys, he still did not get it. I thought that perhaps he was the same type of agent as those who ignored the intelligence signs leading to 9/11. I told the agent, just as I had told Paul Vinovich, this "amendment" did not rise to the level of importance, but if Chris Dodd wanted it, we would try.)

I went to Dodd for the purpose of finalizing the last in a series of prickly items we had to settle to get a bill. Paul Vinovich had made a list of the six or so items, and the last one was the "gaming amendment." Paul told me to bring that up last since Chris Dodd wanted it. I met with Chris—just the two of us. *(We had a wonderful friendship that was eventually wrecked by all of this. Chris thought I was trying to throw him under the bus when the Abramoff scandal broke, which I was not.)* I brought out my list. We discussed the items one by one. Then at the end, as a side note, I said, "I have this gaming amendment that I am told you are interested in. It deals with some casino in Connecticut."

This is what I thought Jack Abramoff was referring to that day in my office. I possibly did not understand him, as this was all cloak and dagger secretive and confusing—possibly on purpose. I assumed it had some tie-in to Jack's clients, but also to something in Dodd's district. Otherwise, why would the senator want it?

Senator Dodd looked at me with a puzzled, even clueless expression on his face. He said, "I have no idea what it is. I stay the hell away from gaming in Connecticut, as it is a hot button."

I did not mention Abramoff; I did not mention lobbyists, tribes, or anything else. He clearly was not as "wired" (set to move on this) as Jack had claimed. I said, "Okay, thanks." We shook hands had some idle family talk and I left.

Paul Vinovich was waiting on me. We talked about the list, all the items we had to settle, all the important pieces of the HAVA puzzle, and then we had an "Oh yeah, by the way . . ." conversation about Jack's yet-to-be-seen amendment. I told Paul what happened when I mentioned the amendment to Dodd, he shrugged his shoulders and we went about our day.

I was irritated that I was made to look strange in front of Dodd. I related to Jack what had happened. He was visibly angry and upset. I said that whoever told him that Dodd was on board with this lied to him. Jack did, I recall, say the name "Lottie," and not in a loving way.

This happens all the time in D.C.; people lie to one another, especially within the lobby community, hoping it will all work out. Members and staff are blamed by the lobbyists when they lose. The lobbyists certainly aren't going to tell a client that they couldn't get the job done. No, they will say, "That damn Member [or staffer] killed it for . . . [this reason or that reason]." So, to paraphrase Clark Gable who was born in Cadiz, Ohio, Harrison County, right up the path from me in St. Clairsville— "Frankly, Jack, I don't give a damn."

Even though Neil Volz was curious about what was going on, Jack had told me to keep it a secret from him. I had no problem with that because I was not sure what the hell—and did not care what the hell— it was about. Dodd didn't want it, and that was good enough for me. Case closed. Move on. However, by this time, Neil and I were discussing it.

Jack started to press. He had one of his men, Tony Rudy, a former DeLay associate, contact our staff. Eventually Paul Vinovich came to me and said he needed to see something in writing, which we received and then could not understand. Both Paul and I were suspicious of this thing, Since Dodd didn't know what it was, we tried one more time, not Member to Member (Ney to Dodd), but staffer to staffer (Senator Dodd's staffer and Paul Vinovich, my staffer). Many times members delegate staff to sort through some things that are either not important to the Member, such as this was (it became annoying after the meeting I had with Senator Dodd—I was soured on it) or the staff can sort it out staff-to-staff by communicating with each other versus members having to

get involved. This happens especially when something becomes confused, like this thing. But it also indicates that by this time I really did
not give a damn about it—I delegated it to staff.

Senator Dodd's staffer still didn't know what it was and later said,
"No, no go, don't know what it is and don't want it." That was the end.
Somebody was playing a game. I was becoming pissed and irritated over
it, and let Jack and Neil know it.

On a conference call to the tribes that I agreed to do, I overdramatized
the situation for a reason—and not one I am proud of. The one mistake
I made on that call, besides trying to save Jack's ass, was to insinuate
that I was not sure why Dodd "lied." This is something I deeply regret
and continue to feel badly about—Senator Dodd deserved better from
me. I was caught up in the moment and went out on a limb, out of my
way, to protect Team Abramoff. I overdid it. I absolutely do not know
why I lacked such judgment in this. Call it loyalty, lack of thinking, or
just plain stupidity. One thing is certain—Jack did not help me that much
to warrant all that I did for him.

Neil Volz and I talked before the call. Neil made it clear that Jack was
in trouble with this client and that I needed to be a "cheerleader." I
thought, *No problem. I bail Jack out, he looks good; Neil looks good for getting
me into the spin of it; I am in the clear because I tried; Senator Dodd "lied"
and we all live to fight another day.* This was not ethical, this was not moral,
this was not legal. I thought I could help Jack out and make Neil look
good. After all, Neil was a friend, and I needed Jack—he was a player,
he was close to Tom DeLay, he could raise money and he could have
influence in my future bid to be Speaker of the House. I reasoned that
it helped "all" of us.

Over the years I, as many do, had bailed a lobbyist out or made one
look like a million dollars in front of their clients. There were many times
in my Ohio Legislature days when a lobbyist would bring a client in
and in the course of the discussion I would say good things about the
lobbyist, including what a great job they were doing. Later, the lobbyist
(who in some cases had been a former staffer) would come back to the
office or would call to thank me for making them look good. It is a common courtesy practice in many levels of government—both state and
national.

*(I remember a time when I was in the Ohio Senate when my good friend and
lobbyist, Ricky Ayish, had a client who was in a pissing match with someone
else's client. We were not sure who was going to win, and it was a big deal.*

My secretary, Charlene Molli, told me that Ricky was there to see me. When the door opened, he was on his knees holding a picture of his adorable little girl, Kerra, in his hands. I laughed for a long time. This was one of the lighter moments. There were many times when people truly begged, pleaded, cried and, unlike Ricky, were in serious trouble with clients.)

This case was different: I did not know how much was at stake for Jack, and I did not know that Jack was *raping* these tribes, money-wise. Jack Abramoff had been successful for the tribes and charged a lot, as all lobbyists do, but this was a case where I was an uninformed, yet willing tool to help him keep his money and power with the tribes—who were most likely ready to dump him. My participation in this allowed Jack to take this tribe to the cleaners. I feel terrible and have apologized to the tribes for this. Jack, the man of religion; Jack, the man with a "compassionate, conservative" heart; Jack, the humanitarian who (according to him) gave away most of his money; Jack, the man who "really wanted nothing in return," had referred to these wonderful native Americans as "troglodytes"(prehistoric cave dwellers), insulted them, used them, and took their money. He should have worn a mask and a gun. There would be no future amendment. Jack knew that, I knew that, and the only ones who did not know that were the tribes.

I later made a statement that has been twisted many, many times. Jack effectively did it then and continues to do so today. I said I was angry at Abramoff and Mike Scanlon (formerly Tom DeLay's deputy communications guy and now a member of Team Abramoff) for misleading me about Chris Dodd's wanting the amendment. In regard to the Tigua Tribe, I called the Abramoff/Scanlon activities "nefarious." Abramoff hit back at me by saying: "It's crazy for Ney to say he was duped; he was on the phone for an hour and a half." I was not on the phone for that length of time, but most important, I *was* duped as to who paid for that trip. Jack never told me he sought money from the Tigua tribe; he did it behind my back. He initially told the tribe that I wanted the money from them to pay for the trip, and later told them not to mention the money to "the Congressman," He then told Will Heaton (through Neil, who was also in the dark) that another legitimate group paid for the trip. Nefarious *and* duplicitous!

Did Jack ever spell out to the tribe that he had a secret, intricate plan involving Ralph Reed (former head of the Christian Coalition) secretly trying to close the casino on one end, and Jack and his secret partner Mike Scanlon doing activity on the other end? Of course not. At the time,

I didn't know of this cloak and dagger stuff that involved Reed, Scanlon, and Jack. To the best of my knowledge, Neil didn't know either.

If I had known of this 83 million-dollar scheme, would I have risked my career, my life, my freedom, everything I worked for so that Reed, Abramoff and Scanlon could make millions and I could take a lousy golf trip? Please! Yes, I was duped on all the intricate secret plans. I was not duped, however, to go above the call of *duty* to protect Jack and Team Abramoff—that was my own idiocy.

Chapter 26

☆ ☆ ☆

THE PRESS
Á LA ABRAMOFF

"The media's the most powerful entity on earth.
They have the power to make the innocent guilty
and to make the guilty innocent, and that's power.
Because they control the minds of the masses."

—MALCOLM X

One of the most startling "open secrets" about the Abramoff affair was the brazen collusion between Jack Abramoff and some persons in the media for the purpose of carrying out his wishes. The complete story was not revealed in either Jack Abramoff's book or Neil Volz's book. Both men could have written about the involvement with the reporters, but I assume fear of retaliation from the press prevented that.

Intricately woven into the DeLay office was, above all others, a reporter named John Bresnahan, who worked for *Roll Call*, a Capitol Hill newspaper. He received constant inside information from DeLay's then Assistant Press Secretary (and ladder climber) Mike Scanlon. Scanlon was not only a pipeline to Bresnahan, but he was a friend who socialized, drank, and gambled with him.

Tom DeLay was a very conservative Member who had owned a small pest control service in Texas. He was feisty and worked his way up the ladder by becoming a member of the Texas House of Representatives. Upon winning a seat in the U.S. Congress, he put his aggressive fundraising style and conservative agenda into action. He began raising money for candidates and campaigned for them in their districts. When the successful (for Republican Representatives) 1994 election ended, DeLay was able to parlay his support for candidates into a personal win for the coveted Majority Whip's position in the Republican-controlled House. The Whip's leadership skills are essential for the "vote counting" on important legislation. It was the job of the Whip to "whip" people into line if they weren't voting on the side of the Republican Conference on key issues. If a bill were to fail on the Floor of the House, it would be blamed on the Whip for either not counting correctly, or not *whipping* Members into a successful vote for the legislation. Tom and I started out on good terms, but as my career progressed, we disagreed tremendously on union issues. I was pro labor, and he was not.

Even Barry Jackson's use of a different set of reporters to discredit Tom DeLay in his attempt to promote his boss, John Boehner, paled in comparison to the lines crossed—especially by John Bresnahan. The only way to describe Bresnahan is to utilize the name given to him behind his back and widely used by staff, even by friendly staff, and that was "troll." He is a muckraking reporter, and it was said that he would only attempt a positive story if forced to as a means of getting to the mud. Bresnahan had no limits and no problem with threatening or destroying anyone in his path. He was considered a "bottom feeder" who eventually ended up at Politico, a political journalism organization.

Bresnahan was involved in some high-payout poker games with Tony Rudy, Mike Scanlon, House staffers, and lobbyists. It was speculated that the lobbyists purposely lost some good hands in the games in order to feed money to Bresnahan. In 2005 I personally took a dive on a hand, not wanting John to lose and be pissed off at me—I knew he could do some real damage to me in the press. It was around 200 dollars and he came by my Congressional office to be paid. Yet my payout was pale compared with the up to four thousand dollar pots in these games that went on in the Capitol for several years in various members' offices, including Tom DeLay's.

The Abramoff plan was to buy *Roll Call*, a newspaper published in D.C. that tracks the political and legislative action on Capitol Hill. One reporter from *Roll Call* had me over to the offices to meet his editor. He showed me a desk and said, "Guess whose desk this is? We call it the pig pen—it's Bresh's." I simply laughed.

I don't believe that *Roll Call* was aware of the alleged conspiracy behind Abramoff's plan to buy the newspaper and make Bresnahan the editor. This would make Jack extremely powerful and anyone who got in his way would receive a *J. Edgar Hoover–style* newspaper hit with no traceable fingerprints. Jack could rig the lobby system for any of his top clients by pounding the opposition into the ground. I, as well as others at the time, feared the vicious, corrupt Bresnahan.

Eventually they made a public mistake when Scanlon spoke about the fact that John Bresnahan was going to be best man at his upcoming wedding to Emily Miller. John was with some of us at the now infamous Scanlon bachelor party, which began at the Irish Times Pub and went on from there.

The wedding was eventually called off, as was the role that John would have played. This was how close John was to "Team Abramoff," whether it was through gambling, friendships, weddings, newspaper acquisitions, or John's attacking Jack's foes.

Bresnahan was not only reported to be the best man at Scanlon's wedding and a reporter who played cards with Team Abramoff, he was part of a plot to buy a newspaper that he would run for Abramoff. As a reporter, he was in way too deep—he lost his direction and saw dollar signs; he also had never made it to the "big leagues." He yearned for power beyond his capabilities.

I was on the receiving end of John Bresnahan's wrath throughout my turmoil, and it cost me dearly. I believe John was a conduit who leaked information about me and created a storm with other media outlets. Here is an accurate account of how the scheme went down, because it came straight from "Team Abramoff'" to me:

Jack became furious with me as he got into trouble. I said I was duped, which I felt I had been. The "duped" part was not from all my dealings with Jack, but specifically the fact that I did not ask for the Scotland trip. Will Heaton sent me an e-mail that I still have in my possession: "Want to go to Scotland?" Tony Rudy, on behalf of Jack, had called Will. Therefore, never—despite the Alice Fisher/Alberto Gonzales "leaks" to the press about my "asking for the trip," did I ever ask for it. Also, I was told by Will Heaton that Neil Volz said it was the same trip DeLay had taken, and it was ethics approved. I felt that Jack duped Neil or duped us to believe that a nonprofit was paying for the trip when in fact a tribe was hit up for it.

My Press Secretary Brian Walsh became privy to the fact that Jack Abramoff was furious with me, and that he fed any information, including what he was giving to the Justice Department, to Bresnahan. In addition, Jack had said that DeLay was sticking by him and he (Jack) would "give him a pass"—meaning that Jack was not going to leak information about Tom DeLay and his dealings with Jack to Bresnahan or any other media outlets. I also assumed this might mean (and these were my thoughts only) that Jack was not going after Tom's *jugular* when Jack sat down with the Justice Department.

To ice the cake, Bresnahan e-mailed Brian Walsh, my Press Secretary at the time, and said that we had failed to give him a big tip about our legal fund or the names of some attorneys we had hired and that he was going to "fuck Mr. Ney." I asked Brian for the e-mail that contained this information. I believe Bresnahan was quite upset that he had put it into writing. I think Brian, due to the nature of the unbelievably crass e-mail, was a bit hesitant to send it to me. I understood this, but demanded that he give it to me and he did.

This sent chills down my spine: I had a reporter who was best friends with Mike Scanlon; who was playing poker for money with Team Abramoff at card games; who was doing Abramoff's bidding against me; and he was personally angry and going to "fuck" me. This no-win situation led to story after story—as much as John could get out there.

At one point I knew of someone who flushed him out a bit by writing an obscure blog that John was to be best man at Scanlon's wedding. He instantly threatened to sue the blog site if they did not take the posting down. I thought it a bit over reactive, but it had obviously hit a nerve.

So now I had Jack Abramoff displeased with me and out to get me, and then there was Bresnahan who was mad about a scoop and told my Press Secretary that he was not happy—that (again) he would "fuck" me. Just not a good day!

(*In an interesting footnote, in 2011 when Neil Volz and I were taping* 60 Minutes *with Leslie Stahl a short time before Jack was to tape, Leslie informed us that Jack did not know we were taping—Jack had not been informed that Neil and I were involved in the segment. Our parts were taped first, and then Jack was taped immediately after. We were requested by* 60 Minutes *to keep the show quiet for a few weeks. During a break in our taping, I showed Leslie a Blackberry alert that Jack was doing* 60 Minutes. *It came from* Politico, *the news entity that John Bresnahan works for. The Jack Abramoff/John Bresnahan leaks live on.*)

There is no doubt that the calculated hits on me by Bresnahan in order to steer the media away from DeLay and do Jack's bidding were an effective part of greasing the skids for my slide.

Tom Rodgers, the Native American whistle blower, confronted Jack about the card games and the press issue at the National Press Club where Jack had joined a panel on campaign finance reform. Jack avoided the issue, stating something to the effect that he "did not recall."

Jack also continues to state that he had one hundred Members in his pocket and spent over a million dollars on them, but will not name Members based on not wanting to put anyone through what he went through (prison) . . . except for me, that is. Jack knew that once I went away, his friends like DeLay and others would be spared. DeLay's legal woes are in the state of Texas and had nothing to do with Abramoff. The Justice Department totally dropped it. You can bet that these Members "owe" Jack and may possibly be an influential part of his new quest for making money to pay off the millions in restitution that he owes. Only time will tell.

Chapter 27

☆ ☆ ☆

PRETTY ALICE

"I wonder if I've been changed in the night? Let me think.
Was I the same when I got up this morning? I almost think
I can remember feeling a little different. But if I'm not
the same, the next question is 'Who in the world am I?'
Ah, that's the great puzzle!"

—ALICE, *ALICE IN WONDERLAND*

One of the continuing inside jokes during my fall concerned the way Assistant Attorney General Alice S. Fisher would get perfectly dolled up, almost as if she were on stage, and should have been nominated for an Oscar when she talked about corruption. I nicknamed her "Pretty Alice" due to the staged, Hollywood-esque press conference when she announced my plea. You see, someone (just one) had to go away. Someone had to be quickly brought to his knees. Alice Fisher, Attorney General Alberto Gonzales, and the entire White House had grand plans, and placing Alice in the Justice Department was part of the chess game—but it was not easy.

Why the need to place her in the Justice Department? Was it her competence? Hardly, as she had very little trial experience and had never prosecuted a case. In addition, she was extremely controversial. So why not go with someone else? A friend of mine who was in the CIA speculated that Alice going to the Justice Department, despite her not being qualified to be there in many ways, was because Alice not only had Alberto doing her bidding (it was hard to tell at times which one was the Attorney General, and which was the assistant), but she had a lot of political clout as well.

Karl Rove needed someone to go into the Justice Department, act swiftly to protect all of his friends, his White House staff, his number two man, Barry Jackson, and Barry's friend, Dave Distefano.

Concerning Alice Fisher's confirmation as Assistant Attorney General for the Criminal Division of the U.S. Department of Justice, it was best said in a speech U.S. Senator Carl Levin of Michigan gave on the floor of the Senate in September 2006:

"The issue of detainee abuse at Guantanamo Bay is very much on our minds and in the headlines as we debate how we will treat detainees in the future. In this context, the nomination of Ms. Alice Fisher for the position of Assistant Attorney General for the Criminal Division at the Department of Justice is not just a routine appointment. Alice Fisher was the Deputy at the Criminal Division while the abuse at Guantanamo was occurring and while concerns about interrogation tactics were being raised within the Criminal Division at that same time. We are being asked to confirm Ms. Fisher today with unanswered relevant questions about any knowledge she may have had or actions she might have taken relative to those interrogation tactics . . .

"The information I have sought relates to what Ms. Fisher knew about aggressive and abusive interrogation techniques in use at Guantanamo Bay, Cuba, during the time that Ms. Fisher served as deputy head of the Criminal Division in the Justice Department from July 2001 to July 2003. From publicly-released FBI documents, we have learned that FBI personnel raised serious concerns about these DoD [Department of Defense] interrogation tactics at weekly meetings between FBI and Department of Justice Criminal Division officials. I have sought to find out what Ms. Fisher knew about these FBI concerns over aggressive DoD methods; what, if anything, was reported to Ms. Fisher; and what steps, if any, she took in response.

"If Ms. Fisher knew of aggressive interrogation techniques at Guantanamo and did nothing about it, or she knew about them but has denied knowing, then I would be deeply troubled. The Administration has repeatedly obstructed efforts to get this information, information which is, in my judgment, relevant to Ms. Fisher's suitability for the position to which she is nominated . . ."

Alice Fisher was the long-time, ruthless Deputy of former Homeland Security Secretary Michael Chertoff, and played a huge part in the infamous Guantanamo Bay matter. This is where she made her mark. Alice was an attorney, of course, and politically, she was deeply involved with the Republican party; but her close association with Chertoff and the inside maneuverings while she worked for him, her ties to the White House, and her suppression of "interrogation tactics" at Guantanamo Bay made her a valuable political instrument for Bush. I would say that Alice S. Fisher was undoubtedly the most covert, manipulative, cunning, stealth, vicious, cold-hearted instrument of evil that Karl Rove and the Bush Administration had.

Among others, Alice Fisher is responsible for covering up the Guantanamo Bay atrocity. This was not some small oversight; this was not a trite story made up to sensationalize a molehill; this was one our country's largest controversies, and it involved Michael Chertoff, Alberto Gonzales, Karl Rove, President George W. Bush and, yes, Pretty Alice Fisher.

The following is a story concerning Alice's background from *Lone Star Project*. It demonstrates why she was perfect for the Department of Justice, that she was a political pawn for Bush/Cheney and why she needed to put me away and no one else:

"Alice Fisher is the ideal Republican 'imbedded partisan' for the Department of Justice. She is well educated and has an impressive résumé. At the same time, she has a long history of overt partisanship and loyalty to the Republican Party, but according to Senator Patrick Leahy, 'Ms. Fisher is nominated for one of the most visible prosecutorial positions in the country **without ever having prosecuted a case.***' (Source: Senator Patrick Leahy, May 12, 2005)*

Fisher's Republican credentials include:

• *Deputy Special Counsel to the Whitewater investigation*

• *National Steering Committee, Women for Bush/Cheney 2004*

• *Virginia Lawyers for Bush/Cheney, Co-director 2004*

• *Member of the Federalist Society and speaker at Federalist Society Conference*

• *Contributed to both the 2000 and 2004 Bush/Cheney Campaigns*

• *Was a partner in, Latham & Watkins, a GOP friendly law firm that was paid $100,000 to submit an amicus brief to the US Supreme Court in support of Tom DeLay's mid-decade redistricting plan*

• *Co-Counsel for the health care firm founded by former Republican Senate Leader Bill Frist's family*

(Source: Senator Patrick Leahy, May 12, 2005; Federal Elections Commission, Amicus Brief to the Supreme Court by Henry Bonilla; Legal Times, January 6, 2003, Fisher Biography submitted to Senate Judiciary Committee)

Apart from Guantanamo Bay, Alice had two other problems. One, she was close to the Tom DeLay defense team and would not pursue him. Of course, she couldn't. The White House could not afford to go after DeLay. If they had, conservative advocacy/lobby groups would have stormed the White House.

In addition, Alice wanted to shield Tom DeLay and cooperate with his defense team, but she needed the appointment and was about to lose her chance. Bush was so desperate in 2006, the appointment was going to be made when Congress was in recess; but that would have been too *hardball*, even for Bush. Why would a sitting president continue to endure the wrath of Senator Levin over someone like Alice Fisher?

The other problem was that she was doing nothing about the Abramoff saga. The Abramoff affair was getting too close to the president himself. President Bush had said (about Jack Abramoff), "I don't think I ever met the man." There were tons of photos, White House meetings, and his sitting with Jack on the platform in front of me and 5,000 people one night at a Republican gala, but other than that, Bush did not know him.

Alice had been nominated for Assistant Attorney General for the Criminal Division of the U.S. Department of Justice on March 29, 2005. She received a controversial recess appointment to that position by President George W. Bush on August 31, 2005 and had been serving in that capacity from that time. Because of the problems stated above, things were not looking good for her confirmation-wise. I was aware that she was going to have to make her move and she did. I was offered up as the cure-all—as though I were the only Member of Congress with ties to Jack.

• My plea was negotiated with the Justice Department mid-September, 2006.

• After the plea was negotiated, Alice Fisher was finally confirmed as Assistant Attorney General on September 19, 2006.

• On October 13, 2006, I formally entered a plea of guilty to federal corruption charges.

- On November 3, 2006, I resigned from the House of Representatives

- On January 19, 2007, I was sentenced to thirty months in prison.

The dates all add up; it cannot be a coincidence—Alice Fisher received her confirmation on my back.

The left thought, *Bob Ney first, then Tom DeLay surely goes,* but that was not in Alice's plan. She knew that she could deliver me close to the time for the election and that would help Alberto in his Senate hearings to defend the unprecedented firing of a "group" of U.S. Attorneys. At the Senate hearing, in insisting that politics has played no part in the Justice Department's decisions about whom to prosecute and when, Alberto took credit (dramatically, I might add), for my pleading guilty "six weeks before last November's elections." (See the link to the actual film on YouTube as well as the *New York Times* article in the Resources section for this chapter.)

Alice also knew that there would be elections and a new president. She would do her work and move out of the Department, but not until it was guaranteed her dirty work would be carried out, thus ensuring that no other member of Congress had any problems with the Justice Department.

Alice effectively closed the Abramoff case, protected those close to the President, including Barry Jackson, and kept a death grip on the reigns of the Department of Justice.

In a *Down With Tyranny* online article, it was pointed out that "... *in nearly three years at the helm of DoJ's Criminal Division, responsible for overseeing the fight against public corruption and corporate fraud . . . our Alice [Fisher] pretty much brought whatever work was being done in these areas to a screeching halt."*

After I was safely *put away,* yet another event was uncovered and glazed over: Alice S. Fisher's Criminal Division of the Department of Justice subordinate, Deputy Chief of Staff Robert E. Coughlin II, on April 26, 2008, entered a guilty plea—yes, a guilty plea—to a felony conflict for favors with Team Abramoff. Coughlin's position in the Department of Justice placed him high in the chain of supervision of the staff investigating the Abramoff Indian lobbying scandal! In exchange for some gifts totaling a little over $6,000, Coughlin helped Jack Abramoff and Kevin Ring, a lobbyist working with Jack, get a $16.3 million grant from the Justice Department to build a jail for Abramoff's client, the Mississippi Band of Choctaw Indians. In November 2009, he was sentenced to a month in a halfway house, three years of probation and a $2,000 fine. There was not a peep—it came and went. No one connected the dots and no one called for an investigation of the Department of Justice. The subordinate of Alice Fisher (you remember her, the very person who was to rid the country of the corrupt Abramoff and his only partner in crime—me), was in bed with Team Abramoff.

The corruption went straight to Alice. Coughlin knew it, and Alice had to have known it because Abramoff knew it. Coughlin was her number one man. He worked in the corruption section but here he was, linked with the corrupt Jack Abramoff. Alice had to have known this. It would be quite embarrassing—which was the least of her problems—to have one of her own involved in this. Coughlin kept his mouth shut about Alice having knowledge of his involvement with Jack, got a *slap on the wrist* for his silence and saved himself at the same time.

Coughlin did an about-face from pleading guilty and full disclosure, to claiming unfair prosecution. FireDogLake's Christy Hardin Smith, who calls herself a recovering attorney, writes of this as well as the fact that other officials were mentioned, but nothing was ever done, in her blog, "Has Anyone Asked Alice?" (Check the link in Resources for the complete story.) The following is an excerpt of that blog:

> *"Coughlin's current whining about unfair prosecution is a bizarre deviation from what he had previously said. Under oath and as the basis for his plea of guilty, mind you.*
>
> *"And to do so right before trial? I smell something nasty in the works.*
> *"Where's Alice Fisher in all of this? Especially given all of her conflicts of interest questions with Jack Abramoff, Tom DeLay, Barbara Comstock and others? Good question. Since not nearly enough of the internal decision-making on why so many others were NOT charged has yet to come out publicly.*

With Alberto Gonzales at the helm and his Pretty Alice in jeopardy, the truth about Coughlin, was simply erased, discarded, sheltered and ignored.

Alice was in trouble and had to act quickly. She left the Department of Justice in May of 2008, therefore closing the books forever on Abramoff with just Jack and me going away as the main components of the "culture of corruption." After wreaking havoc with the American

Government's justice system, she simply picked up where she left off and went back to her former law firm, Latham and Watkins where she is now Managing Partner in the D.C. office.

Alice fisher, "Pretty Alice," is an example of what really makes the government ugly. She, along with Alberto Gonzales, Andy Card, Karl Rove and President Bush, *shredded* the Constitution of the United States and did as they pleased.

The purpose of this chapter is not as important in pointing out my personal woes as it is to shed more light on the individuals who were part of the ugliest, dirtiest, most disgusting chapters in American history, from the WMD (Weapons of Mass Destruction) lies to the torture that was allowed and perpetrated at Guantanamo Bay.

Pretty Alice was actually pretty ugly in terms of her disrespect for civil rights, liberty, and all that should be held sacred in America. I have paid my price and today I can look at myself in the mirror without shame. Can Alice Fisher do the same?

Chapter 28

☆ ☆ ☆

BOEHNER— THE REST OF THE STORY

"Our prime purpose in this life is to help others.
And if you can't help them, at least don't hurt them."

—DALAI LAMA

In 2006 we were in a battle as no other. Attorney General Alberto Gonzales had his White-House-selected, right-hand hit lady, Alice S. Fisher, pursuing my case.

I had a relatively unknown opponent in the primary, James Brodbelt Harris. He was a young man, somewhat involved in the Republican party of Franklin County, Columbus, Ohio. He had done some work as a financial planner. James was big on relating that in the 1900s his grandfather had been governor of Ohio and that his family had a continuous "generation farm." He was conservative on issues. Although he was naïve politically, he thought (and I don't blame him) that he would automatically knock me off. With the shit-storm I was in, that would most likely have been true. My redeeming links were that I had been in office a long time with a relatively good reputation in the district; I had an awesome, focused, political genius in Matt Parker, who was also a loyal friend; and I had hired David Popp who added some needed glue to a crumbling office. David was a lifeline both in the office and personally for me. Our field reps in the district and the caseworkers in the office in Ohio, plus the office management with Bob Wallace, a seasoned retired Police Chief, gave us stability—all in our District Office in Ohio. However, things were different in D.C.—members of that staff were resigning in droves. Most of our conversations were brief; their saying they felt bad and my saying how bad I felt for them and the entire situation.

Things were coming apart at the seams in Washington. It is said that all politics is local, and this primary would test that. In December of 2005, I had signed an extension of the statute of limitations to investigate my involvement in the SunCruz situation. The clock was running out on that statute of limitations, but I gladly signed my rights over to give Justice an extension to look into it. A week before the primary in June of 2006 the Justice Department contacted my lawyers and wanted another extension, which was absurd. They had had all of 2005, and a six-month extension already. I had written two statements for the Congressional Record, they had Jack Abramoff nailed to the wall, singing about every breath I took, and they wanted an extension? Not only did they want more time, but also they posed a veiled threat.

Justice told my lawyers, "If we do not get an extension, we can indict a week before the primary." This in itself is outrageous. There is a rule that the Department of Justice must abide by, and you should pray that no matter what you think of me, this rule will always be upheld. The rule is that the Justice Department cannot interfere with an election. If we start down that path, any administration, at any time, can come close to a police state by deciding who serves and who does not. I understand that most people don't care about the individual politician who gets into trouble ("Throw the book at them—feed them crusty bread and water," as my friend and talk show host Howard Monroe always joked), but they should understand that if the system is allowed to get out of bounds with the politicos, it will eventually do the same with the citizens.

We decided to tell the Bush Justice Department, Alberto Gonzales and Alice Fisher to kiss my ass—in legal terms, of course. We did not sign an extension and they did nothing. The simple matter is that they had nothing and wanted more time—to find nothing! It was a threat, a scare tactic, to interfere with my election. We called their bluff.

Having jumped that hurdle, it was only a week before the primary and we had to defeat Harris. In political financial terms, we had not a dime left to run TV or any media. Left over yard signs from previous elections and shoe leather sufficed—I was out, active, and alive. In my first parade in New Philadelphia, Ohio, I heard some people yelling in my direction as I was walking near them. Unfortunately, that day there had been a terrible headline above the front-page masthead of the New Philadelphia newspaper, *The Times Reporter*, indicating that I had taken a bribe, or something of that nature. The newspaper truck was ahead of us in the parade and, yes, they were giving out free papers so the people received the newspaper in enough time to look up and see me— another unplanned disaster. As I got closer, I realized the people were not yelling about Abramoff, but yelling about illegals saying, "Throw the bastards out of the country, Bob!" I was amazed. Frankly, very few people said anything about Jack. I think it also helped that I didn't isolate myself and was out among the great people who for two and a half decades had returned me to political office.

I needed to really blow the primary out and did through the good old-fashioned shoe leather of the great team of my Campaign Manager, Matt Parker; Katie Harbath, my Press Secretary after Brian Walsh resigned; and Ben Yoho. I could not have asked for more dedication or political intelligence.

Katie had served us well at one point by running our social networking for the House Administration Committee. She was a hard-pressing, fearless, energetic staffer. In time, we needed her in the District. She went on the ground to help with my embattled primary. *(At this writing, she works for the government division of Facebook and liaisons with the Members of Congress for Facebook.)*

Ben Yoho is a longtime friend of my son Bobby. He grew up in St. Clairsville and started as a volunteer when he was still a kid, and then later became a field representative for our campaign. He was with us to the very last day. *(Ben went on to work for Speaker Batchelder of the Ohio House of Representatives.)*

We took an impressive 69 percent of the vote in the primary. Aiming for the general election in November, Katie spun the issue correctly by capitalizing on DeLay's win. He was not in the trouble I was, as the Bush Justice Department did not seem to be pursuing him as doggedly as they were pursuing me. However, he was in trouble in a Texas court. Tom DeLay (of *Dancing with the Stars* fame later on) spent about three million dollars to take about 53 percent of the vote. Our win, even though against an unknown, was impressive because our campaign account was bled to the bone with legal fees created by the relentless Justice Department's Alberto Gonzales / Alice S. Fisher team.

After the Primary win, we were featured prominently in the media. My supporters and all of the county chairmen in the district held firm. We had a campaign blowout with my family and supporters in New Philadelphia, Ohio. We did an "in your face" event in Democrat Zach

Space's backyard and the national coverage, which abounded and included C-SPAN, was better than I could have hoped for. *(Zach Space later won the election for my former seat in the U.S. Congress.)*

We went back to D.C. in June refreshed, glad-handed by friends, and complimented by most Members of the Republican side. Even some friendly Democrats gave us private well wishes.

The Justice Department, in a way, went a bit dormant for a week or so. Matt Parker, my Campaign Manager, said I needed to have a meeting with Tom Reynolds, the head of the National Republican Congressional Committee (NRCC). Tom was one of the brightest and most aggressive politicians I had met. Matt and I had a cordial late afternoon meeting with him, and Matt watched as Tom and I polished off a bottle of red wine. Matt believed in something called Voter I.D., an effective process of finding exactly where voters were on issues such as energy or gun control. A company would make thousands of calls and narrow down what the voter thought about issues, then a follow up letter or pamphlet was sent, homing in on what the person had commented about and explaining where I stood on those issues. Matt was seeking money so we could do this. *(Matt later opened his own nationally successful consulting firm called Front Porch Strategies, and P.J. Wenzel joined him in the business. Matt is bright, and instead of running from working with me after my demise, he told potential clients, "If I could get Bob Ney elected that year in a primary, I can be successful for you." Matt is doing well today.)*

After striking out with Tom Reynolds (we were not able to get the money, but he was truly a friend and we had a great bottle of wine), at Matt's request I scheduled a meeting with my Chief of Staff, Will Heaton, John Boehner and me. Matt couldn't get to D.C. at the time. Before the meeting, Will received a phone call from Boehner's office asking if I would object to Dave Distefano's being there. I was shocked. What did Distefano have to do with this? At this time he was a lobbyist, and I was in trouble over lobbyists, so what would he do for me? Also, anyone who knows anything about Distefano knows that his gods are money and himself. He only does what is good for Dave Distefano. I responded to Will with, "Hell no—that's all I need!"

When we arrived at Boehner's office (the old DeLay office), surprise number two was there—Barry Jackson. Barry was no longer working for Boehner; he was working for Karl Rove. Boehner did not ask if it was okay, he just said, "Barry is family. He will be in the meeting."

We began talking and I told John that I simply needed to raise 150,000 dollars to win the general election in November—chicken feed in Congressional terms. Boehner said nothing. He just smoked and sipped his wine. Barry started with, "Karl [Rove] thinks you need to get this all behind you and the President [Bush] cannot support you unless you do." Karl Rove was the "architect" of the Bush presidency—a title that President Bush himself gave Karl when he won his first election. (Karl Rove ran the White House for all eight years of Bush's Presidency.) Now, Barry throws the "Rove" name at me. *Barry is bringing out the big guns,* I thought.

I said, "Well, Barry, you talk to Justice and I know that Karl does, so what do you know?"

Barry responded, "We may not know as much as you think."

He didn't deny talking to Justice, and he didn't deny that they had talked about my case. The hair on the back of my neck stood up. I said, "Barry, all due respect, but why are you here on a money matter that involves the House? What makes this an occasion for Karl Rove's number two guy to be here? I'm puzzled."

Barry said, "We're family. We're here to help, and you might think about ending all this and stepping aside."

I said, "Absolutely not—I am in this no matter what to the end, and no one is budging me." I turned to John and said, "What about the campaign money?"

He took a deep drag on his cigarette, looked at Barry, exhaled smoke, continued sipping his wine and said nothing as Barry piped up and said, "Don't think we can help." I left the meeting, not as much disappointed as baffled. Something was up. My radar did not figure it all out at the moment, but something was up and it was bigger than just me and my reelection.

Without warning, I received a phone call from Minority Leader John Boehner himself—who had apparently rediscovered his voice. John started cordially. "Bob, how are you and how is your family doing?" I explained that it had been, of course, horrifically difficult for my children.

Bobby had been working at a pizza place in Columbus, Ohio, and his bosses were becoming irritated with how many times TV cameras came in there. Kayla, a junior at Newark High School was followed to school in a car by the media. My second wife was scared by a news reporter who was a real freaky looking guy—the type that you would hang his picture up on the fridge and tell your kids, "this is your new babysitter if you don't behave."

After Boehner said a few polite words he got to the point. "Bob, we [he and Barry Jackson] realize what you have been going through and have been talking about your race. We know you are not a man of money and I am told one of your children has some medical issues." (I'm still not sure where that one came from.) "So I would like to make you a deal."

I didn't know where this was going or if I could trust Boehner. We were still holding our own, but we were out of money, so I listened clearly and attentively to Boehner.

"If you resign in the next day, I will personally guarantee you a job comparable to what you are making, and raise legal defense money for you that should bury all this Justice Department problem for you."

I could not believe my ears. Should I trust him? Why was he doing this? Was it real? I responded, "Let me get this right. If I resign, you will get me a job comparable to the Congressional salary and raise legal defense money for me? Not 'try,' but you *will* do it?" I wanted to be clear on this, as it could be one of the biggest decisions I would ever have to make. I was still winning; I just needed a relatively small amount of money. As a sitting Congressman and the Justice Department faced with a controversial but questionable case, it might just go away—it did with DeLay and other Members who were up to their eyeteeth with Jack.

John responded clearly, "Absolutely. That is the deal; you have my personal assurance and you can take it to the bank." He then repeated the "iron clad" offer. However, he stressed one caveat. "Let me make it crystal clear; if you do not take it in twenty-four hours, I will withdraw the offer and not make it again no matter what." He ended with, "Take care and buzz me."

There were Members who were aware of the deal and talked to me about it, so Boehner had confided in a small circle. After talking to my family, Matt, and doing some soul searching, I gave in and took the deal. When I called John back the next day, I confirmed that I would take it. I again stated the deal as he had told me it would be. I had to be sure. This was, at that time, a type of political and personal life or death situation.

John said, "Good." Then he said, "We want Joy Padgett" a sitting State Senator. He asked what I thought. I got along with Joy and we were close friends, but I felt compelled to be honest with him and tell him that another excellent choice was Jim Carnes, a popular State Senator from the Democrat portion of Belmont County who had a blemish-free career. Not wanting to be a hypocrite (I wasn't just blemished, I had full-blown acne), I still pointed out that Joy had a potential legal problem with a bankruptcy. My thinking was that one legal woe was enough, although I had nothing against Joy, as she was capable and seasoned. John dismissed Senator Carnes despite my statement and said, "No, absolutely not. It has to be Padgett."

I announced my decision not to run, as it was best for my family and all others. In my mind, this was true. I would have income and I could pay my legal fees, which were mounting to an amazing level—not due to my lawyers, but due to Justice's constant pressures and maneuverings. Later I found out from a friend that he had been asked by Justice, "How long do you think the Congressman can hold out until he is bankrupt?" I did what I thought I would never do. Because of Boehner's promise, I stepped aside.

The "hint" of a deal and my discussion with Boehner was a read-between-the-lines newspaper story. The scenario to follow turned into a rapid, unstoppable freight train that came down the tracks, driven by Justice. Because I bent to Boehner to resign, they would break me to plea.

I talked with Joy Padgett on the phone; she said that she had received the call to run and was thinking about it, and then quickly decided to do it as time was of the essence. I eventually sat with her and went over our campaign staff, how they functioned, all that they did, how everything worked. I offered my advice, service, whatever I could do behind the scenes, as I was toxic. Joy met with the campaign staff and then decided that none of them would be kept. I know the reasoning; it could be difficult to work with a staff that had been loyal to someone else, but I also know that she was influenced by some people higher up in the party—especially by Bob Bennett, Chairman of the Ohio Republican party at that time.

My staff was in shock over losing their jobs. They had done nothing wrong, nor was there a hint of their doing anything that could have been used by the media. They were absolutely clean, but tainted because they had worked for me—sort of a "guilty by association" thing. Matt Parker had moved on by this point, but the rest of them were vulnerable. Senator Padgett was not to blame for their being fired; she was pressured by the party to get rid of the "Ney people."

My drinking had escalated intensely. My anger, resentment, uncertainty, depression, and control issues were all intensified through the help of alcohol. I started a series of calls, mostly insulting, to Padgett and people around her. I should have let it all go. Those on my D.C. staff who were still there were paid out of government money because I was still a sitting Member and had not resigned—and due to no indictment or plea, I was not really being asked to step aside. I then made the official announcement that I would not run.

Padgett's campaign took a nosedive. Joy was attacked by Space for everything from knowing me to a bankruptcy, and she lost the election by 62 percent. She was a good State Senator and she and Don, her husband, are good people. I hated to see her lose, but she went on to do other good things.

(I have seen Zach Space once since I've been out of prison, when I was giving a talk in D.C. on the floor of the House to a group of reporters. Because I resigned, I am a former Member for life with floor privileges, which, I understand, some people don't like. Former Governor Arch Moore and the late former Member Dan Rostenkowski also returned to the floor at some time after being in prison.

Zach came back to the floor after finding out I was there, graciously said hello and offered his office if I needed anything. I was touched by his sincerity and genuine, nice-guy demeanor. Space served two terms, seemed to adapt well to the job, but was driven out by State Senator Gibbs in 2010 during the Republican tsunami. Zach Space is at this writing in a Columbus law firm, along with former Member Dave Hobson of Ohio.)

After stepping out of the election, I drank, waited for the Boehner job offer, and for the most part stayed in my house in Heath, Ohio, with my second wife and my daughter, Kayla, who was in high school. Bobby was in Columbus, and my family in the Valley; Mom, Dad, my sister, brother-in-law and their family, had to continue to endure press coverage. Television ads featuring the infamous Governor Taft, Noe, and Ney *(Noe was a coin dealer close to Taft who got in deep trouble for selling rare coins purchased by the State of Ohio)* abounded and were used not only in the Padgett race, but in many races in Ohio.

The phone silence from Boehner was deafening. I needed to have a job, as promised. I had always paid my bills, but I didn't save any money. All of my money was tied up in a thrift savings plan, which I could and eventually did liquidate with a huge penalty, and a U.S. Congressional pension that I couldn't take, even partially, for four years. My State of Ohio pension was cashed in long ago. After about six days, I picked up the phone and made a call to John Boehner's office. I never received a call back from him; I did not get a job, or the hint of one; I did not receive any support for money to be raised to pay my legal bills. The calls I made after that first one were not even returned by an intern. I had been lied to and ditched. I was the poster child, not only for corruption, but for naïveté. Nothing came except a call from my attorneys. I was to go to D.C. and talk with them.

I silently and stealthily went into Washington. I met with all four of my attorneys, William Lawler, Mark Touhey, David Hawkins and Craig Margolis. This was the bottom line: Justice had immediately turned the heat up. They were going to indict if I did not plea. It was as though they knew I was done; as though they knew that I did not have a job; as though they knew that I could not pay any more legal fees; as though they knew I was headed for bankruptcy. The John Boehner/Barry Jackson/Karl Rove-sanctioned strategy to deliver me had worked.

I made a plea deal in D.C. Federal Court, Friday, October 13, 2006. The date was so appropriate, not a good luck day when one wants to remember their plea date—of course no day you go to court is your lucky day; this one just had a bit more irony to it.

Chapter 29

☆ ☆ ☆

THE PERFECT STORM

"Sometimes God Calms the Storm.
Sometimes he lets the storm rage and calms his child."

—AUTHOR UNKNOWN

After reading the book *The Perfect Storm* and viewing the movie, I realized how factors come together to create a situation where multiple situations and phases of life all interact around some common entity to create the perfect storm. That storm can be good, bad, or sometimes in between. Some factors are in the realm of our control, some are not, and some are a combination of both.

I am not so naïve (or bold) that I would attempt to come off as the pure white knight who was taken captive and sucker-punched by the evil emperor and his forces. That version would make me seem more dense than I was throughout my political career—and that was certainly dense enough.

I received my teaching degree with a major in history, but have referred to myself as a "history teacher by degree"—not having had the opportunity, unfortunately, to be one. When I was in the Ohio State Senate and team-taught "Citizen's Lobbying" with Michael McTeague at Ohio University, I analyzed lobbying and elections for the students. Through the years since then I have been amused to hear the various ways that even the brightest of the bright politicos simplify elections: "Reagan won because of Carter and Iran," "The Republicans won in 1994 because of Clinton," "In 2006 the Republicans lost the House due to Ney," ". . . due to Abramoff," ". . . due to Foley," and so forth.

Neil Clark, the former Senate budget staffer, guru, and political strategist who took over the Ohio Senate for the Republicans in 1984, was one of the few people in politics, even beyond Karl Rove, who really understood the reasons for wins and losses. I adopted Neil's approach and analysis of elections and the multiple reasons behind victories and defeats. I also applied this to my everyday life, as well as to my downfall and eventual imprisonment.

While teaching those classes with Michael McTeague, I would ask students the question, "What started World War One?" The usual answer was, "The assassination of Archduke Franz Ferdinand of Austria." That was the *match*, but there were other causes, other factors that all came together and provided the *fuel*. The assassination ignited that fuel and began the Perfect Storm we now know as World War I.

I was the *match* for my downfall; I provided the spark that led to my imprisonment. However, other factors—controllable and uncontrollable —provided the *fuel:* persons, groups, fate, karma, or accidents, all swirled into the vortex that sucked me in. Granted, I jumped into that vortex with both feet—so we not only have a roaring blaze, but a "perfect storm" as well.

• The whistleblower, Tom Rodgers, a Native American of the Blackfeet tribe in Montana and an activist and advocate for Native Americans and tribal issues, was the catalyst that set this storm in motion. Tom is a good man and did what he should have done to expose what was going on with abuse of the tribes in the form of greed by Jack Abramoff, Mike Scanlon, and Ralph Reed. Mike Scanlon's former fiancée, Emily Miller, has been blamed by many for this and was portrayed unfairly in the late George Hickenlooper's movie, *Casino Jack*, as the scorned lover that took Scanlon down. That is far from the truth—the catalyst was Tom Rodgers, and rightfully so on Tom's part.

However, long before Tom Rodgers ethically did what was right, the storm was swirling around me. As DeLay got in trouble over the growing Texas controversy of campaign contributions illegally moved into other accounts, he also became a growing Abramoff protégé in the media. His trips to Marianas, receipt of contributions, and his staff being showered with "gifts" were beginning to get media attention. With my conviction, the heat was off DeLay. In a Texas Court, Tom was eventually found guilty of shady campaign money movements. It is now under appeal.

• Forces from the Left, specifically billionaire business magnate, investor, and philanthropist George Soros, saw the opportunity to spend some of his money to weaken me, and thus achieve what the Left wanted—and that was to bring Tom DeLay down. Soros spent, in an off-year election in 2005, tens of thousands of dollars in disparaging billboard ads, full-page newspaper ads in Ohio, television ads in D.C. and Robocalls to my district constituents. The billboards displayed a picture of me and some of the captions were, "Bob Ney took a bribe?"

Full-page advertisements in the Columbus Dispatch newspaper and Robocalls hit the same theme. The barrage was designed to get me to 'fess up about DeLay. (Soros and the Left assumed that I knew damaging information about DeLay that would put him behind bars. They also wrongfully assumed that Alice Fisher and Alberto Gonzales actually wanted information on DeLay, which they did not. If that was their goal, they could have gotten plenty of information from Jack Abramoff.) Even though the Soros attack was in an off-year election cycle, it caused me untold negative publicity, further weakened me in the district, caused additional public heat to "get" someone for the Abramoff affair and forced me to choose between hiring lawyers or fighting back with money and resources. It unknowingly assisted the Justice Department in getting a plea from me and letting DeLay and staff walk.

• John McCain started hearings in 2004 on something that was being looked at by the Justice Department. McCain, due to his past problems over the Keating scandal and because he was planning his run for president, seized an opportunity to look like the guy who cleaned up D.C. *(during his campaign he said he "got" Abramoff and me)*. When I got out of prison before the election, McCain stopped using my name because I was then free to attack him. *(I believe that there was an attempt to keep me in prison until after the election, and I believe that this is what the White House and McCain wanted.)* The hearings were a sham. He only called Abramoff —no Ralph Reed, who was also involved. *(In George W. Bush's Primary, Jack Abramoff went full force to support Bush against McCain. The support and help that Jack gave was, of course, in raising money—especially from the Conservatives and the Jewish community. Jack was so close to Bush that he was appointed to his presidential transition team. Jack was up front with his campaigning against McCain. The "Good Senator" McCain certainly reminded Jack of this in his own "payback" way during the Senate Abramoff Hearings.)*

And why was only my name mentioned? Why not all the other Members, including some of McCain's Committee Members who were involved with Jack? Their range of involvement included receiving contributions to their campaigns, letters signed for the issues Jack lobbied for, skybox tickets (Jack owned a skybox at the sports arena and would give out free tickets to his lounge and hold fundraisers there), former staffers who then went to work for Jack, and requests going both directions—from Jack to them, and from them to Jack. The list of members is impressive.

• When the first sign of trouble came as a result of the sham McCain hearings, I approached the House Ethics Committee under Chairman Doc Hastings and ranking member Alan Mollohan in a proper political move to have them look at my case. Yes, as Chairman of the House administration Committee I did fund the Ethics Committee budget, and yes, I did give them the largest increase they had had in decades, but that's Congressional life. I am not saying it smells good or is on the up and up, but that is how the system usually worked for all. If a Member gets into trouble, the Ethics Committee usually gets the first bite. I had private but appropriate conversations with both Chairman Hastings and Alan Mollohan. I could present my case and they would come to a conclusion.

The day I was to meet with them, Alan Mollohan called and said that he was tied up with Appropriations and we would meet later that week. The two leaders of the Ethics Committee got into further arguments and the Committee was hopelessly deadlocked, could not constitute, and I dangled in the wind.

The Department of Justice seized the opportunity to proceed because "nothing was being done" with me. The Ethics Committee's inability to address my issues at the time benefitted the Justice Department. They knew that if the Committee constituted and then made a decision in my case, it would force the Justice Department to await Congressional action on me. There have been plenty of past and recent cases where the Department of Justice does nothing while the Ethics Committee does its work.

In nearly all cases, then and now, when a Member goes through the Ethics Committee process he or she is referred to the Justice Department only if further action is needed. I would have certainly won with the House Ethics committee on the travel voucher issue, as it was in Heaton's handwriting and the committee understood how vouchers work; the figures are usually brought to the Members, and then the members sign the documents. The Justice Department did not understand the process nor, frankly, did they care.

• The August 31, 2005 recess appointment (an appointment by the President of a senior federal official while the U.S. Senate is in recess) of Alice S. Fisher and her trouble in getting the Senate confirmation as Assistant Attorney General created a crushing wave. She was nominated March 29, 2005, but due to much controversy, was not confirmed by the Senate until September 19, 2006. An online article by Firedoglake had this to say about President Bush's controversial recess appointment:

"Bush did give a recess appointment to Alice Fisher as Chief of the Criminal Division. On Wednesday, right smack in the middle of the Hurricane Katrina disaster when the country wasn't looking . . . Bush must've really wanted Alice Fisher in there."

President Bush's recess appointment allowed her to serve as Assistant Attorney General, Criminal Division, until the Senate confirmation. Someone had to go away for the Abramoff caper. In addition, Alice was attacked for being close to DeLay's defense team, and the controversy over her, Chertoff and the Guantanamo Bay torture was not helping her. My lack of following the rules provided a *scapegoat* and protected her ties to Tom DeLay.

• Alberto Gonzales was in trouble. When attacked in Senate hearings over the U.S. Attorney firings and his being political, the only name and defense he could invoke was mine. "This department, six weeks before the election, put Congressman Bob Ney . . ." Straight from his mouth, the portion of his quote, "before the election," says it all.

• I believe that the MEK and Iran issue added to the fray. There are some fascinating theories in a December 17, 2005 report by Wayne Madsen (a D.C.-based investigative journalist who specializes in *intelligence* and international affairs):

In Iran, the neocons got what they hoped for. Iran's President Mahmoud Ahmedinejad and his rhetoric about Israel being moved to Europe and the Holo-

caust never occurring is made to order for the neocons who want the United States and Israel to attack Iran's nuclear sites . . .

The neocons wasted no time in attacking Ahmedinejad. They falsely said that he was one of the U.S. Embassy hostage takers and that he was an international assassin who traveled to Austria to murder a dissident. Ahmedinejad, whose Muslim conservative base is similar to George W. Bush's base of a conservative group of fanatic fundamentalist Christians and some Jews who favor an expansionist Israel, ratcheted things up by playing the Israel and Holocaust denial cards.

I tend to believe that the Cheney neocon forces, the fact that Cheney's daughter Liz ran the Iran desk (in February 2005 she was appointed as the U.S. State Department's Principal Deputy Assistant Secretary of State for Near Eastern Affairs), and the fact that I was so outspoken about the need for communication between our country and Iran led to a covert exchange of information from Cheney's people to the Gonzales/Fisher Regime.

Liz Cheney had enormous influence while in the State Department concerning Iran issues. I was warned by "friends" within the intelligence community that all attempts to promote conversation and dialogue with Iran, some of which I have detailed throughout this book, was not setting well with the "Cheneys." With Liz Cheney's power inside the State Department, millions of dollars was secured to support opposition elements in Iran and Syria. She also met with discredited Syrian businessman Farid al-Ghadri, a Syrian dissident-cum-U.S. businessman from Virginia.

• Neil Volz and Will Heaton provided backup information and the ability for the Justice Department to indicate that they had people who would testify if we went to trial. Although they would be portrayed as people who got out of prison in order to fulfill the Gonzales/Fisher agenda, they were still a significant factor. The fear instilled in them by the Department, the pressure, and the additional personal pressure placed on Will by his mother, wife and father-in-law, an ex FBI agent (the "brotherhood" speaks strongly), all led to tsunamis of their own, and added to mine.

• Speaker Boehner, when he was just Congressman Boehner, knew that at one point people were saying that if we both ran for Speaker, it would be a tough battle. I know that Boehner seized the opportunity to get me to resign from running by promising to help fund my legal fees, therefore opening the path for the Justice Department to take advantage of a soon-to-be-unemployed Member of Congress—who was foolish enough to believe that Boehner was sincere about the promise to help.

• Barry Jackson, who at that time was Karl Rove's Number One man, saw the opportunity to discredit me. He had become alarmed at my strained relationship with Dave Distefano, and as Dave's mentor and "guardian," Barry could conveniently use my situation to put his and Distefano's questionable activities on the back burner. I was headed to prison and unable to be a credible whistleblower. Because of my long-standing relationship with Distefano, Barry had "motive and opportunity" to help me go down—and he did.

• The right saw the opportunity to clear DeLay if I went away. Advocacy groups who were close to DeLay and received support from him were able to make sure that the word of mouth initiatives weakened my fundraising ability, and thus my ability to raise money for my legal fund—and I had no personal wealth.

• The left saw me as a key to DeLay, so other advocacy groups moved on me. Melanie Sloan, Executive Director of Citizens for Responsibility and Ethics (CREW) will not reveal her funding sources. My troubles gave her an opportunity to raise money for her group—they were fighting the "king of corruption." Ironically, Melanie's focus on me allowed DeLay to skate. Unlike Alice Fisher, however, Melanie didn't do it on purpose—she was just inept and uninformed.

• The other crushing wave to help complete the storm was as potent as the sea. It took the form of a demonic presence. Oh yes, there was a demon involved. This demon doesn't care if someone is black or white, rich or poor, straight or gay, Republican or Democrat. It is a powerful force, tough to beat and ruthless in its approach and style. John Barleycorn was the old name, and alcohol/substance abuse is the modern name of this demon. I was drowning in my obsession with alcohol; I needed it as a crutch, a help, a guide. I worked to drink and drank to work. I am not saying that "alcohol made me do it" but I cannot deny the fact that my judgment would have been much clearer and focused had alcohol not been a part of my life. I simply did not care about rules, I didn't pay attention to my changes in behavior—they all became secondary. The effect of alcohol became my first priority.

In the end, I was and am responsible. I took free meals, as did my staff with my knowledge and permission, so I am responsible for them as well; I went the extra mile to make sure that former staff looked good, and in doing so, I violated the lobby ban.

What I did *not* do was tit-for-tat—contributions for actions. If I had, I assure you that bribery charges would have been piled on me by the Justice Department. I did not accept cash, gifts, cars, furniture, or trips in exchange for anything. It was, however, illegal, unethical, and immoral.

As far as others' actions go, I can only relate that to something I told the other inmates when I was in prison when they said that their neighbors sold drugs to the right and left of them, but only they were caught and prosecuted. "That may be true, but if you hadn't sold drugs, you wouldn't have been prosecuted." The same holds for me; some Members did things, but *I* shouldn't have. I stand in apology and sadness for what I did. I now know myself and I know what atonement is. Grace is in the heart of each individual in a different manner.

As far as my comparing myself with others involved with Team Abramoff and corruption in Congress—were we the rotten apples or is the barrel corrupt? And does it really matter? Jack Abramoff, who bragged on *60 Minutes*, "I spent a million dollars and had over 100 members in my pocket" does not expound on that and says, "I do not want to put other Members in jail." Is that due to Jack's grace, or the fact that he cannot put others in jail? The Gonzales department already decided who they needed in order to put this to bed. You decide.

Chapter 30

☆ ☆ ☆

ALTAR BOY WILL

*"Sometimes being a friend means mastering the art of timing.
There is a time for silence. A time to let go and allow people
to hurl themselves into their own destiny. And a time to
prepare to pick up the pieces when it's all over."*

—GLORIA NAYLOR

Writing about Will Heaton was one of the more difficult chapters in this book for me to write. I have so many mixed feelings and opinions about the person I thought he was when he confided in me, yet things were so distorted at the end. Did he act to save himself? Was it a staged event? Was it pressure from his family? Did he really believe it was entirely my fault, or was it a combination of all these things? I'm sure that he also looks back with mixed feelings about me.

I am told by people who are in contact with him that his wife makes it crystal clear that he did absolutely nothing wrong and everyone involved should not take any responsibility for it; it was my fault, period. I take responsibility, but I wish Katie's conclusion were that clear-cut and easy. Of course, I understand her defending her husband, and I do not believe that it should be any other way. However, Will was there and has his own beliefs—and they may possibly be the same as hers. To look back on one's personal history and try to assess it all is sometimes an unending, evolving process. Because Will and I have not had (and most probably will not have) conversations to clear the air, it brings different, separate conclusions. I'm not saying that I am totally correct in my assessment—only that this is my perspective, not having the benefit of knowing after the summer of 2006, what was and is going on in Will Heaton's mind.

The statement Will made to me countless times and that I believed was, "We have really done nothing wrong Bob—we will not go to jail." My Uncle Louis Radcliffe always said, "Bobby, justice and the law are a million miles apart." At the end of the day, we were a million miles from our goals. At one point, I agreed with Will's statement; but then, in the summer of 2006, I knew that for me at least, that statement would not ring true. I believed then, as now, that Will should not have done jail time, which he did not.

When I became Chairman of the House Administration Committee in January of 2001, I fully expected that the Committee's diverse oversight would be an interesting challenge and that the Members would be rather easy to satisfy, as it is also a Members' Committee. It proved to be a daunting task to keep Members happy and I saw that as a challenge needing a solution. In addition, what seemed to be routine in the past totally changed on 9/11 (as did so many things in America) and the workload was doubled.

Soon after we moved into what we deemed to be the spacious offices of House Administration on the third floor of the Longworth building, we started about the task of dividing duties. Neil Volz was my House Administration Staff Director as well as Chief of Staff for my personal office. I was aware that Committee Chairmen (nineteen at that time in the House of Representatives) had to deal with power struggles between the staff of the Representative's personal office and their committee staff. In the U.S. House there is a peacock hierarchy when it comes to the Committees. Everyone knows about it and it is openly discussed. Being on the staff of a Committee is a desired plum, just as being chief of staff to a member is. Neil Volz became one of the few who was in a dual capacity position: Chief of Staff for my personal office and a House Administration Committee Staff Director at the same time. It was a powerful combination and soon put him into the prestigious top fifty movers and shakers on the Hill. Every year *The Hill* newspaper in D.C. prints the "Top 50" movers and shakers list, and people salivated to be named on it.

(Speaking personally of desiring honors, eventually, through a poll of Members and staff of both parties, I was ranked the eleventh most powerful Member of the U.S. House of Representatives. Considering that the Republicans and the Democrats each have the "big four" in leadership, that makes eight mem-

bers on the list right there in the pecking order of power. Only two other members, one of whom was Chair of the Ways and Means Committee, stood in the
way of my number eleven ranking being elevated to number nine—just below
the leaders' positions.) My Chairmanship position helped propel me—and
Neil—to become Capitol Hill power players.

I quickly discovered by the first half of February 2001 that I was in
an unwinnable situation every time we cast a vote. In the U.S. House,
three bells ring to alert the entire House side of the Capitol that a vote
(or series of votes) is to be taken on the floor of the House. These bells
are built into most of the clocks in the Capitol and all Members' offices
contain clocks with a lighting system—red light if the floor is in official
session, and white light to indicate that the vote is on. Most of the 435
Members scurry like ants, walking across the street, underground, or on
the house "tram" (mini subway) to gather on the floor. During the voting sessions, Members usually find each other to discuss legislation, cut
deals, or just stand around having casual conversations. At times, the
Member's staff may have a specific agenda they want the Member to
accomplish. A staffer might say, "Congressman Smith has not signed
onto your bill yet. Why don't you go over and ask him?" Yes, staff are
the movers, shakers, or even puppet masters on some occasions.

My session time became a nightmare of endless requests from Members wanting items from furniture, to carpets, to refreshing of painted
walls, to technical questions on travel, to franking requests (Member
newsletters sent to constituents—I called them "happy day bullshit"
newsletters), to questions on travel, rental cars, carrying guns, and a
wide variety of other topics that could take up pages and pages of a
notepad. I would meticulously write these down, head back to the office
and then continue a grueling schedule of meeting after meeting with
constituents, staff, lobbyists, phone calls to the district, Transportation
Committee meetings, Banking Committee meetings, House Administration duties and meetings, personal office obligations, subcommittee
meetings and of course, more trips to the floor to vote and more Mem-
ber-requests—approximately six or more per vote. The previous amount
of requests backed up until I had a list of almost 150 unanswered
Member requests. I was becoming physically and (especially) mentally
exhausted; I seemed to be spinning my wheels and sometimes felt as if
I were standing in a room looking at all these things I had to do, but
unable to move and accomplish anything.

My drinking had escalated by this time. There were more events to

attend, more meetings scheduled, more dinners, more work. I was working to drink and drinking to work. Although I hate the term "functional
alcoholic," I understand it. I somehow kept up with all the work and
then rewarded myself by "unwinding" with drinks late into the night.
Then it was up early the next morning to do the same thing over again.
I served the Congress and my constituents, but I was spiraling down a
slide of increased alcohol, stress, weight gain, and irritability.

A quick way to end your political career (besides being voted out or
having the Justice Department down your throat) is to piss off fellow
Members of Congress. That was exactly what I was doing. I took the
dilemma to Neil and we decided to hire, out of the larger House Administration budget, a "body man." This was a concept popularized by Congressman Billy Tauzin. Billy was an entertaining Cajun Democrat from
Louisiana who turned Republican during the 104th Congress. He had a
body man. Technically, this body man was an Executive Assistant who
drove him around, waited on him at meetings, followed him to the floor
when he had official business, and acted as liaison between the personal
office and the Chairman's office (which, as I said, is often a hotbed of
jealousy). Basically, while Billy was awake and doing business, so was
the body man. This concept of finding a man or woman to be an Executive Assistant grew in popularity.

Neil and another staffer looked for a person to do the job. It should
be someone who was hungry to learn, saw this as an opportunity, was
not annoying, could keep the conversations they heard a secret, and
would be on the younger side because the hours were grueling and long
and most people with a family simply could not do it. The first person
that my upper management picked for me was a young man who was
more interested in himself than the job and was just not a match. We
kept him, but kept looking for someone else. Although irritating, at least
the guy was better than nothing—somewhat.

As we searched for a new person, someone in House Administration
said that a young man named Will who worked in Speaker Hastert's
parliamentary office was a hard worker, had been a page, was a quick
start, and even though he appeared to be young, he had been around
and was pretty seasoned. I checked out Will's work reputation with a
few people. *(A joke I made at that time to a woman who worked for the Speaker
came back to haunt me when Will's lawyers maliciously twisted the scenario to
make it look like I picked Will from day one so I could do illegal activities in
front of him and he would be too dull to realize it. The woman staffer eventu-*

ally wrote a letter to that fact. After she had given Will a good review, I jok-ingly said, "And another benefit would be that he would not understand when we would be having paid dinners with lobbyists." She laughed and said, "Yes, that is an added benefit." That later became another layer of Will's "Bob made me do it" defense.)

Will was sitting in Speaker Hastert's parliamentary office. This is not the personal office of the Speaker, but an office down the hall that houses and handles all the parliamentarians of the house and their research components. This is where Will worked. It is the technical part of the Speaker's office that oversees the legal side of the floor proceedings.

I had already spoken about Will, per protocol, to Ted Van Der Meid, Speaker Hastert's right-hand man. Ted was not at all pleased that I was going to offer Will the job, but he first wanted to see what Will thought about it.

I approached Will and said hello to him. He responded, "Hello, Congressman Ney."

I asked, "Would you have time today to come over to the House Administration Committee office? My Staff Director, Neil Volz, and I would like to ask you about a position we have."

Will responded, "I will be glad to come over and talk to you and be of assistance." I thought the "be of assistance" was a bit different, but maybe a fresh approach to saying that he was interested in the job.

When Will came to the office, Neil and I took turns bombarding him with the duties of the Executive Assistant, what it entailed, the salary, the hours, the responsibility. We then began to ask him about his goals and his thoughts about his future. Will suddenly, with a look of shock on his face, said, "Are you guys considering me for this job?"

We said almost simultaneously, "Yes, who else?" Neil looked at me, I looked at Neil, and then both of us looked at Will. I said, "Did you not know it was you we wanted?"

He said, "No, I thought you wanted to brief me on the job so that I could give you suggestions of people to hire!" With that, because Will was so stunned, we told him to take a few days to think about it.

Over the next few days, Will asked a few friends and colleagues about it. I believe that most of the answers he received indicated that it would be good for his future. He surely received some negative opinions as well, but our office in those days had a great reputation for fairness, working hard, playing hard, and getting things done.

However, I know for a fact that Ted Van Der Meid did not like the idea. For one thing, Ted wanted Will, who was a great worker, to stay in the Speaker's Office. For another, Ted felt that he and Will were close friends. Nevertheless, Ted, seriously beyond Machiavellian in my thinking, thought that through Will he could have his own *eyes and ears* in our office. Ted trusted no one, just as no one should have trusted him, but he felt that he had made a bond with Will that would give him, for a while anyway, the ability to have special access to our House Administration Office. Although the Chair of House Administration is personally appointed by the Speaker and can be removed by the Speaker, conflicts traditionally arose between the Speaker's office and the House Administration Staff or the Chairman. Ted was the ultimate pain in the backside for anyone who had to deal with what I perceived as his paranoia.

Will and I sparred occasionally over Ted Van Der Meid. I would question Will's loyalty: Was it to Ted or to me—to the Speaker's office or to House Administration?

Ted consistently tried to acquire information on what House Administration was doing. I believe that Will tried to keep a balance between Ted Van Der Meid and House Administration for the benefit of both, so it wouldn't culminate in a dogfight. I imagine there were times when Will was tired of both Ted and me.

One time Will said something when he was drinking about Ted that I didn't pay much attention to, as I thought he was joking. He said, "I have some things on Ted" and "Ted liked to invite me and other pages over to see his garden at his house, so don't worry if we ever have to take him on."

However, later in a report on the Congressman Mark Foley scandal concerning male Congressional pages, it was revealed that the Clerk of the House, Jeff Trandahl, had warned Ted Van Der Meid about his overinvolvement with pages in the Speaker's office.

Will Heaton served the office well. He was young but dedicated—aggressive but balanced. When Neil was moving on to be a lobbyist and I needed to find a replacement for Neil's position, I considered Will as my Chief of Staff. After talking to a number of people, including Neil and some "outside" former staffers and friends, it was decided that because of the abovementioned qualities that Will Heaton possessed, it would be a good move to give Will a chance at it. Will seemed to be, and I believe that he was, beyond his years in his maturity and his ability to learn and develop. (The times that were ahead and how they ended would try anyone; especially someone as young as Will.)

We did well as a team. He was liked by most of the staff, but resented by some in both the personal office and the House Administration office as being too young, and that he acted like a "stuck up punk." That statement, I believe, was initiated by jealousy. Dave Distefano had become Chief of Staff at the age of twenty-four, and Will was more mature, so I didn't feel that he was too young. *(At the end, disregarding his age was used against me. Supposedly, according to Will's defense attorneys, I chose him because of his young age so I could go behind his back to commit crimes or carry out other nefarious deeds. I cannot imagine Will believing that today any more than he would have at that time. There were too many important duties, plans, and responsibilities for someone in his position to have been selected for that reason. It may make a great case to dodge jail time, but it is not reality.)*

Will became a fixture with my children, a part of the family. As for his professional life, Will and I worked well together to accomplish some very good things for the people of the district. He kept a great hand on what I considered to be, next to voting, the most important duty of our office—constituent cases. I was taught at a young age that no one, but no one, took care of constituents like the late Congressman Wayne L. Hays *(whom I ran against and defeated in 1980 for the Ohio House of Representatives)*. His treatment of constituents served as an invaluable model to me.

A week before my high school graduation, I received a certificate from Congressman Hays. As everyone came in the door to our house in West Bellaire, my parents and I showed them the "personal" certificate from him, congratulating me.

I called his office one time about my grandparents who were on a waiting list to get into a senior housing accommodation in Bellaire. His office said that he would call around one to two in the afternoon. Sure enough, I received a call. I was not a big deal, no one politically, just a guy from Bellaire, but the Congressman responded to me.

This was a lesson I never forgot and one that I instilled like a magnet to steel in Will Heaton's mind and those who ran our office before him: "We work for the people of the Eighteenth District."

Eventually though, I noticed that Will became overtaken by the "control factor," as I called it—where chiefs of staff want to rule with a hard hand. I realize I totally fed that, as I had the same behavior problem. Will led in the demand to replace our District Director. I believe it was a move to consolidate his power and not have to be questioned by an experienced, older person. (Dave Distefano had done the same thing years before this in pushing my longtime secretary, Charlene Molli, out the door. Charlene was not fired—never—but was driven out by Diste-fano because she had my ear. Dave argued with Charlene constantly and told her she was not keeping up. It got so bad that she came to me and said she had to quit. She was dedicated, but just could not put up with his insolence.) It was the same scenario, but this time it was Will in the main role and it led to the departure of my District Director, John Poe.

I remember when the line was crossed by Will with my nod and con-sent. I recall ever so vividly how I brushed it off when I could have so easily said, "No!" Instead, I said, "Be cautious with it." Will told me that Team Abramoff, specifically Neil, told Will to his face that anything we wanted at Signatures (Abramoff's restaurant)—food, booze, people to be hosted—was ours. It was ours, not for the asking, but for the taking was exactly the way Will and I understood it; nothing to be deciphered or misunderstood—this was a clear crossing of the line for me, for Will, and for Team Abramoff. This was my time to lead, my time to say no, my time to do the right thing. I take the blame for giving Will the "green light" with Signatures.

As it all came tumbling down, unnerving roadblocks surfaced. Will and I started to mistrust each other. I had confided personal thoughts, ideas, and feelings to Will as he had to me. Everything was unsure. Will was scared. I waited late in the process to get an attorney and Will waited even later.

There were two times when I saw Will cry uncontrollably. Once was due to the fact that my Scotland trip WAS NOT FILED. The Govern-ment's case was based on a "false" filing by me. In eleven years I only missed having one trip filed—the Scotland trip. The Clerk of the U.S. House of Representatives, Jeff Trandahl, knew the system was anti-quated. He told me it could have been filed but the system was hay-wire—Will's was filed, Paul Voinovich's was filed, but not mine. After the Scotland trip, Will had brought the travel slip to me to sign. It was in his handwriting. I signed it, just as I had signed others for over eight years, all prepared by staff. This is the way it's done on the Hill.

We had a copy on hand and when the shit hit the fan, Will re-filed it (or filed it for the first time, depending on how you view it) without consulting me. I confronted him and went "off" on him. I said, "What the hell are you trying to do? Now we are going to look like liars. It will look like I never filed it instead of a clerk's error. You have indirectly fucked me!"

We were in my office and Will cried so hard that I felt bad and told him, "It's okay, you thought you were doing the right thing."

Will was then extensively debriefed by the Government and had a Justice Department "colonoscopy." I assume that he told the Government what he had done in filing my trip, but the Justice Department went full steam ahead for a plea from me for something that was technically, legally, not even filed by me. *(I knew, though, that the cost of the trip really did not pass the "smell test" so technically or not, in Will's handwriting or not, the buck stopped with me. Of course, when it stopped with me it came at me full steam—sort of like my sitting in a car on a railroad track and a high-speed train plowing through it.)*

As you read this you will think, *well, not filing is a felony.* Au contraire—it was revealed that Speaker of the House Dennis Hastert and Minority Leader of the House Nancy Pelosi missed trip filings; and Congressman Luis Gutierrez, in over a decade, NEVER filed any trips. Those filings, by the way, are House jurisdiction—except for mine. When Attorney General Alberto Gonzales wanted you, he disregarded the House jurisdiction, just as he disregarded anything else that didn't fit his agenda. It didn't matter that Will filed one a year later, it didn't matter that many Members of Congress didn't file reports, it only mattered that *I* was in trouble and *I* had a "bad" filing.

I felt that Will was heading toward a meltdown. His wedding was approaching, he had lost his grandmother, Mimi, and some of his family members were not happy about his marrying Katie. His father-in-law-to-be, a stern, controlling, retired FBI agent, came to D.C. sniffing out Government work for the new company he was working for. He, Will, another staffer and I met somewhat by accident at the Old Ebbit Grill in D.C. Katie's dad talked to Will as if he were ten years old, saying that Will would have to earn his way into the family and so on. It was degrading. The staffer and I left and were shocked about the incident.

Will was adamant that neither of us had done anything wrong—minor things, but nothing worth jail time. I made inappropriate jokes to Will about his going to jail and Katie visiting him. This was uncalled for and this type of humor certainly didn't give Will a feeling of security. It's just that I never seriously thought that he would go to prison—but I thought that I would.

We were both extremely upset with what was happening and tried to console and reassure each other that all would be okay—that what we had done was not that bad; that what we did was done by many on the Hill. But it came down to this: not only was Will innocent-looking and it would be hard to get a jury to convict him, but the Department of Justice needed a Member to go to prison—to be the one led away, not an *innocent staffer* who was "led astray" by an evil Congressman. I resigned myself to the fact that it was my fault, not Will's. I could have and should have run things differently—in the office and in the way we conducted ourselves. Despite Will's optimism, I resigned myself that I was doomed.

Will's attorney was right. Not only was Will the devout Catholic son of a fanatical Catholic (former nun), but he had the look and demeanor of an "altar boy." No surprise—this is the way the system works. To Will's benefit, a jury would have been hard to convince. I am pleased it was turning out for him this way. One more person doing jail time benefits no one.

Will received a couch as a gift from a former Member of Congress, now a lobbyist. I discovered that this lobbyist had received a five million-dollar appropriation for a client of his, submitted by Will under my name. It did benefit the 18th District, but because we were in trouble, I thought the couch being given to Will by a former Member/now lobbyist was a chance we did not need to take. Although admittedly late in the game, I was finally watching everything so as not to give the Justice Department new "fuel for the fire."

Will said, "Don't worry, the former Congressman has some 'sensitive' personal issues he confided in me, and he would never want them revealed." Will's tone shocked me. This thing was undoing us all. This just was not Will's usual style or the way he operated or reacted to situations. The entire mess was taking a toll on everyone involved.

Chris Otillio, who was my Legislative Assistant and had been on the London trips with us, was subpoenaed by the Justice Department. They could have simply called people in, but instead they issued subpoenas—those then had to be read on the floor of the House on C-SPAN, to the entire nation. Might makes right—break the person down piece by piece—all is fair in the world of Alberto Gonzales. Intimidation is the key, and this was just another tactic.

Otillio got his turn at the barrel end of the shotgun. I don't know if Chris Otillio is practicing law today, but I hope he's more convincing in a courtroom than with what he attempted to pull on me. He told us that the Justice Department called him and he was taking the day off to talk to them. He simply did not show up to work again—ever. Will and I texted him or e-mailed him to see if he was coming back, as he had pending work for our office and we needed to have that work, even if he was quitting.

Chris was now a captive of the Justice Department, and of course, we knew it. He finally called me after almost five days. He said, "What should I do? What should I say?"

I asked, "About what?"

He answered, "About what happened in London—about reimbursement for the chips; what I did at the casino; what you did."

I responded, "I'm okay with what happened with me and what I did."

Trying again, he said, "Boss, I wonder if there was video there?"

I was growing tired of this lame attempt at entrapment and said, "So what if there was?"

He repeated his plea, "Please, boss, tell me what to do—tell me what to say."

Chris was obviously wired. He was trying to get me to tell him on tape what to do and what to say, which would be an additional felony charge of tampering—of my trying to obstruct justice by manipulating him to say what I wanted him to say to the authorities. This would have given me five more years at least. The Justice Department was having trouble nailing me down, so they did whatever they could to add additional charges. It was clearly an amateurish attempt to *sting* me. I said to Otillio, "Chris, tell the truth and get an attorney."

Will came into the office within ten minutes and I told him that Otillio was not coming back. We got into a crowded elevator and rode to the downstairs parking area of the Rayburn House Office Building. We were alone in the garage when Will said, "What did Chris say?" He also added, "God, I hope we are not being taped."

I said, "Will, they aren't the NSA. We are in an underground parking garage. But Chris was wired."

Will said in a surprised tone, "Are you sure?"

I said, "Oh yes. He was definitely on tape trying to get me to obstruct justice. He will not be returning to work."

Will then said, "Damn, their case must be light to try and do this to you. I wonder if he will call me?"

"I don't know, but if he does, he will most likely be wired."

Will said, "This is getting bizarre. What bullshit! If he calls, I know what to say."

(During Will's plea/sentencing, while I was in prison, it came out that Will

told Otillio on tape "to do the right thing." Even though Will knew from our conversation that Otillio was probably wired, his attorneys used this to make it seem that Will was just being honest in telling Otillio to do the right thing.)

In June of 2006, Will invited me to his wedding, called me, even offered to pay for my plane tickets. I knew that his mother disliked me intensely, and Will had related to me that Katie didn't like me, so I told him that I appreciated it, but it was best for all if my wife and I did not come.

Will invited me to what turned out to be the fateful "wired" dinner. (See Resources for the link to the Washington Post article.) We talked at length that night. It was a consoling, low-key, quiet time of surrendering to the inevitable. It felt like two friends trying to figure out what would happen next. Bit by bit we went over the reasons why we wouldn't go to prison. I told him that I had accumulated some receipts in a half-hearted attempt to show that I had paid for some drinks at Jack's restaurant and other restaurants in town. Most of the conversation was not significant, but toward the end Will brought up some issues about the Casino and Otillio. I felt uncomfortable, and in the back of my mind I thought, *my God, he may be wired.* I dismissed the thought and we left.

I didn't know for sure that Will was wired that night until after I was in prison and read the press report, so it was not in my mind to make a deal. By the Justice Department's own admission, it was circumstantial at best. *(Will's lawyers built the tape into his defense—he had been so "honest" with Otillio when Chris was wired, and now he was cooperating by providing evidence against me with this tape, which they claimed helped in my decision to do a plea.)*

Neither was true, but I do understand why they took the "Altar Boy Will," "The devil (Ney) made me do it" defense. Will was being forced by family pressures.

Will came to my office in July of 2006 to resign. For the second time, I witnessed his crying uncontrollably. He told me that neither of us had done anything wrong, but his lawyers told him he needed to resign immediately.

I understand his lawyers' making him out to be the White Knight. But I have to believe that Will knows his original belief and statement to me that our deeds were not at the levels purported was an honest assessment.

I understand pressure and fear. The letters of support from Will's relatives were understandable, but some of them, in my opinion, crossed the lines of decency and truth. I have copies of these letters, and some of them say a lot more about the nature of the ones who wrote them than they do about me.

Will is a good person, has good motives, and although he overplayed "The devil made me do it" card, he is someone who has a bright future ahead of him as he searches for his independence and achieves his goals. He has a decent, good, inner soul, and I am sure he has learned from this and moved on, not to repeat the mistakes we made.

Chapter 31

☆ ☆ ☆

ONE DAY AT A TIME

"God grant me the serenity to accept the things
I cannot change; courage to change the things I can;
and wisdom to know the difference."

—REINHOLD NIEBUHR (SERENITY PRAYER)

My friend Ellen Ratner had not only been worried for me, but also about my drinking. Ellen's background is interesting. Those who only know her from Fox News Channel, or as the Talk Radio News Service White House Bureau Chief, do not realize that she was formerly a substance abuse and rehabilitation counselor.

Ellen attempted an intervention in 2005. She planned to have two or more Members of Congress, at least one Democrat and one Republican, ready for me when I arrived in Georgetown to "meet" with her. I sensed that something was up and that it could be an intervention. Despite Ellen's insistence (and believe me when I say that Ellen can be more insistent than any other human being you or I would ever encounter), I refused to go and had a solid excuse for not being able to. She became so alarmed and suspicious that she made a trip to Ohio (soon after she had just had eye surgery for a detached retina!) and said she would like to stay at my house for a weekend. I made certain that whatever I did when she visited, I did not drink. I also made sure that, with the exception of a token amount of alcohol in the house, most had been hidden in the storage room.

The weekend was a blur. Although I always enjoy time with Ellen, fighting the desire/need to have a drink was mind-boggling. She confronted me during her stay and didn't mince words. "I think you are drinking tons of booze and you have a big-time alcohol issue."

I assured her, apparently not so convincingly, that "All is good. Everybody drinks in D.C. and it just got out of control for a bit."

Her comeback was, "Yes, but at my birthday party you were loaded, and I have heard from the Hill that you have a drinking problem."

I told her that I had a problem and I was getting a hold of it. I could tell that she was suspicious, but I believe that the willpower I had summoned to keep from drinking that weekend threw her off track. She left. I drank.

My problem with alcohol became an alcohol problem on steroids from 2005 to 2006, escalating into blackouts, anger, depression, extreme sadness—you name it, I experienced it. I had been a drinker through the years, but I had been drinking more and more during the seven years prior to this time. Like any addiction, the worse it gets, the more one denies it.

I had to make a decision about the plea, and I had a limited time to do it. (*I didn't know at this time that the pressure for my pleading guilty stemmed from Alice Fisher's need to get the confirmation for the Assistant Attorney General. This explained why the Justice Department insisted on a plea deal and the ability to announce it. As I explained before, my plea took care of many "troublesome little details" for Alice Fisher and Alberto Gonzales.*) However, the plea date was delayed by alcohol—or more specifically, my addiction to it.

Ellen had stirred things up, was not taking no for an answer and demanded I seek help. I then took a long, hard look at my life. I had no income, thanks to Boehner's empty promise, and I was with certainty headed to prison. After a night of drinking when no one was around, I concluded that it was better for my children financially if I were to die before going broke. If I ended my life before leaving Congress, my remaining salary would kick in and my insurance policies would pay out large benefits, even with suicide as a cause of death. I had never before planned to kill myself.

In my mind, the plan was unique, perfect and damning—the ultimate payback to Bush and Gonzales. First, I would deny Alberto Gonzalez the benefit of a *prize* to please his right-hand maiden, Alice Fisher. Second, I would lay out all I knew about Bush and his dealings via his surrogates like Barry Jackson and the crew that drank and ate off of Jack

Abramoff. I planned to do it right in front of the Department of Justice building with a letter in my pocket and one in the mail to the media, just in case someone from Justice found it on me and disposed of it. I planned to do it the next day. My twisted mind was in full throttle.

My plan got sidetracked that day when Matt Parker knocked on my door to invite me to coffee at his house. His wife, Marina, was there. I broke down when Matt and I talked about the plea. I didn't mention what I had planned, and after talking to Matt and hearing what he had to say about life, living, and God, I put the plan away. With Ellen's pushing, Matt's coffee talk, and a call from Bill Lawler, my attorney, I made a decision that was the best thing I have done to this day and throughout the entire bloody mess.

Bill said, "How are you?"

"Not so good. My kids would be better off if I wasn't here."

He said, "Wait on the line a second."

With what seemed an eternity, Mark Touhey, Bill's law partner, came on the line with Bill. We talked about the plea, then Mark said, "Bob, I think you are a fine person who is getting screwed in all of this, and I think you will get past it. I have dealt with alcoholism issues that friends and clients have had. I am not judgmental, but we need to get you help. As your lawyer and friend I cannot in good faith let you formally go to court with this plea until your mind is clear to focus on what we are doing."

With that, I was on my way to D.C. the next day to be evaluated. From there, it all went like lightning. Without telling anyone specifically where I was going, just that I was going, I was on my way to rehab. There was no more going down with the ship. I had raised the white flag. My attorneys suggested Virginia, and Ellen knew of a slew of good places. I preferred Shepherd Hill in Newark, Ohio, not because it was ten minutes from my house, but due to its wonderful reputation. I knew of it from my college days when I went to school with Kathy Kennedy, whose father, Dr. Kennedy, was a founder. But one fear overtook me— that the press would sniff out Shepherd Hill and camp out there. I opted for the Cleveland Clinic.

David Popp, my current and final Chief of Staff, drove in to stay with my family in Heath, Ohio. The Campaign Staff came to my home and we had an emotional good bye. I drove myself to Cleveland, was checked in, taken to my room, handed the 12 Step recovery "big book," and there it began. As a sitting Member of Congress, I was allowed to keep my cell phone in the event of some crisis occurring in D.C. How ironic was that? I was a crisis. I thought, *What the hell could I do about anything at this stage in my life?*

After only two days, I found that I could not stay there anymore because my insurance company wouldn't pay for it. My lawyers begged me to stay and I should have, but I just could not come to terms with owing money to stay there. (Many people going through rehab justify not sticking with it due to financial issues—not thinking that in the long run, the cost of using is more than the cost of rehab, and it can also cost a life, which is priceless.)

I showed up at my house and I believe that I surprised David Popp, Matt, and my wife more than anyone. There was one thing on my mind—not the plea, but having a drink. Before I could go down that path from hell again, my sister called and said that my mom had a perforated colon, was going to undergo emergency surgery and I needed to come to the hospital in Wheeling, West Virginia, as soon as I could. I headed to the hospital, Mom survived the surgery, and at 10:30 p.m. I headed west from Wheeling toward Heath, Ohio, which is thirty miles east of Columbus. After driving for about forty-five minutes, I saw the Route 209 exit. Without hesitation, I got off at the exit, turned right, drove to the Guernsey County Courthouse, made another right and headed straight to the Point Bar.

The city of Cambridge in Guernsey County is a wonderful place. It was solid for me in election after election. It is the home of a tremendous State Senator, the late Bob Secrest (an amazing, unflinching supporter of veterans) and his nephew Joe Secrest, my friend who served as an Ohio State Representative with me. It was a quiet, eastern Ohio town that had a homespun environment, and I had friends there. But this night there was only one *friend* calling my name, and that was a drink. I pulled into the parking lot of the Point Bar, turned off the engine and I knew what was going to happen next. My mom had lived, so I was going to have a drink to celebrate. It had been a tense evening. *(Of course, later in rehab and the 12 Step Program, I learned that had she passed away, I would have gone into the bar to drown my sorrows.)* Either way, I was heading in there. I remember thinking, *Okay, I am in trouble already; what if I drink too much? I am an hour and a half from home and it would not be good to get a DUI right now.* Then the perfect plan popped into my head. My friend John Bennett and his wife, Janice, lived within five minutes of the bar. I could call John and stay at his place.

As I was about to get out of the car, something occurred that I now know as my "Higher Power moment." I said to myself, *"What the hell is wrong with me? Why am I doing this? God, I can't stop drinking—this is insane."* If insanity truly is doing the same thing over and over and expecting different results, then I was insane. I was frightened. What was I doing? Where would I end up? I started my car and headed home.

Everyone was in bed. I went to my computer, got on the Internet, typed in "rehab" and started calling. I pushed Shepherd Hill out of my mind. I still wanted to go there for many reasons: it would be close to my home, it would be quick, it would be safe. Nevertheless, foolishly, I let the media factor keep me from calling. I called around to the places my insurance company covered, and on the third call I got a "live" voice at nearly midnight. I heard, "Woods at Parkside." It is a rehab facility in Gahanna, Ohio, about 40 minutes from my home. After telling that person my situation, I was connected to someone on duty.

The woman was pleasant and after answering a series of questions, including "Do you currently want to kill yourself?" and my answering, "No, but there are a few people I would like to take out."

She said, "Are you serious?"

I said, "No, just trying to keep my sense of humor, twisted as it may be."

I went up to Woods at Parkside and made another decision that Ellen, my lawyers and some friends disagreed with, which was to go as an outpatient. The Justice Department was told that I would not be formally finalizing an "appearance" for Alberto Gonzales in court until at least October. We thought the Justice Department most likely would come back at us for my being an outpatient versus an inpatient and might demand quicker action.

The press, some friends, and general citizens considered this all a ruse, and I am sure that Justice did as well. It seems that when politicians and celebrities get in trouble, they always blame it on alcohol and go to rehab. My fate was sealed, the deal was done, I was doing a plea and going to prison, but what was becoming important to me was that I stay sober. I told my lawyers to convey to Alberto and Alice that they could kiss my ass—indict if they want, arrest me in cuffs if they want, but I needed to clear my mind and focus to be sure that I was of sound mind to go through with this plea.

Alberto and Alice yielded and got the press attention they needed; evidence that they were doing their job. Don't you know that the master manipulators running Congress were not the oil companies or pharmaceutical companies or Wall Street? Jack Abramoff and Bob Ney were the perps, and now all corruption was ended. Hallelujah!

When a politician goes to rehab, most people believe that he or she has but one interest in mind, which is to get a better deal in court. That is not always the case, and it was not our goal—not for one second. Even Neil Volz, who himself drank heavily at that time and knew what stress and drinking to alleviate it did to him and to all of us, doubted my motives. He states in his book, *Into the Sun:*

> Matt Parker was the former staffer I had been told remained closest with Bob. In a letter to Judge Huvelle, Parker wrote about the Congressman's appetite for alcohol. Since it was a key part of the Ney defense, and written by the guy most under the Congressman's influence, I was skeptical that the letter really represented Parker's own words. I figured a more likely scenario was that Bob told him exactly what to write. Whatever the case, I overanalyzed every aspect of his letter.
>
> *Unless someone partied with Bob, I never spoke about his drinking when I was in Parker's position,* I thought, before waiting a second. *What am I talking about? Bob is going to jail,* I continued. *I've never been in a position like Parker's.* Such a realization made me even more intrigued by what he was really trying to say with his letter.
>
> *"When the scandal first broke in 2004, the Chairman began to drink more heavily,"* Parker wrote to the judge. *"Bob was a functioning alcoholic who could rarely make it through the day without drinking and would often begin drinking beers as early as 7:30 a.m.,"* he continued. I could feel the anguish of the scandal in his words, the words of yet another young Ney staffer. The image of Bob and Parker drinking brought back memories of my time with Ney, both good and bad. *We did like to party,* I thought, and smiled at the memory. That was unusual. A frown or sarcastic comment was now a more likely response to any thought of Ney World. The question at hand, though, was whether Bob's drinking was an acceptable reason for Judge Huvelle to give him leniency.

Woods at Parkside had a good outpatient treatment program. I made the forty-minute drive from my home in Heath to attend my first day. The lecture portion was interesting, as it went into all the scientific, chemical reactions, consequences, and causes of addiction. It was followed by group sessions. I went upstairs to be assigned my counselor and my Higher Power kicked in and gave me John E. He was a stocky-built, African American, about 38 years old, who wore *dreads* and had an overpowering presence. He and I talked privately for a bit so he could get an assessment.

John's group sessions were truly fascinating and his story was amazing. A recovering addict himself, he went through several arrests and on about his fourth stint he was looking at a lot of years in the pen. Through a new program in the prison system, he got a chance to exchange a decade of incarceration for freedom. In prison he had gotten into 12 Step, a well-known recovery program, and had demanded he be allowed to set up meetings when they had none available. At Woods at Parkside, John promoted and pushed 12 Step recovery meetings. He required that we go to three of them a week, get signatures from those conducting the meetings and return the slips to him.

Years before, in 1985, we had hearings in the Ohio Senate on substance abuse and money available for the State of Ohio Drug and Alcohol Department. The Chairman of the Finance Committee is a guy I respect tremendously, Senator Ted Gray of Columbus, Ohio. He was humorous, fiscally a conservative, and an "outside the box" thinker even before it was popular. He was fair if you could adequately explain your issues, but dismissive if you were just fudging it and after the money. When the hearings were finished, Ted and I grabbed some lunch and discussed the issue of substance abuse. As a State Senator, I would get visits and calls from constituents seeking guidance about their loved ones and asking what the State could do to help with their substance abuse problems.

Ted said, "I am not saying these programs with the government don't have some value, but Bobby, in all reality the only thing that has a chance to work is AA [Alcoholics Anonymous]."

For years after that, when constituents came into my office and asked a question about substance abuse, I would talk about the State program and give them information on rehab. Then, I would with certainty repeat Ted's words verbatim about AA.

In 2006 as I sat listening to my counselor, I wished I had followed Ted's advice myself.

I religiously attended the outpatient sessions, took deliberate and precise notes, attended group sessions, and embarked on my first 12 Step meeting. With paper in hand, I went to a meeting near DCSC, a federal defense supply command post near Gahanna, Ohio, where Woods at

Parkside was located. It was a noon meeting complete with lunch, all for a voluntary dollar in a basket. I thought that was a deal. All I knew about 12 Step recovery meetings was what I saw in a movie. They drink coffee, smoke and listen as a man or a woman stands up, goes to the podium and says, "Hello, I'm Jane [or Bill], and I am an alcoholic." They then tell terribly personal things and cry, and then all applaud.

The speaker for this noon meeting told her story about her life, none of which I really related to. It was just like my two days in the Cleveland Clinic when I thought, *What am I doing here with these losers? They are unemployed, unloved, and they are "real" addicts.*

But maybe I was worse off than I thought, because I had zero recollection of a phone call during that time with Matt Parker, my District Director for the Congressional Office. I was shocked when I heard Matt in 2010 tell the story with deep emotion of when I was at the Cleveland Clinic: "Bob called me from re-hab. I was at a football game with my wife, Marina. I stepped out, took the call and Bob said, 'Matt I do not belong here, come pick me up now and get me out of here, I do not belong with these people, please.' I said, 'Bob, it's best for you to be there.' Bob then launched into a rant, yelling, threatening to fire me, reminding me that he was the boss."

Matt finished by saying, "I had to do one of the hardest things there was to do and tell him no. I ended the call and went back to my seat. I was emotional and Marina asked me what was wrong. I told her that I would tell her later."

Matt, of course, did the best thing for me at that time and I will always be grateful for that tough love.

I left the noon meeting thinking, *Okay, this did not relate to me, but I did like the meeting, the feeling of community, the atmosphere, and the fact that I was in a place where people didn't seem to judge others.* I was paranoid that someone would recognize me, although anonymity was stressed at the beginning of the meeting. I still was not getting it.

As usual, the next day was outpatient and group with John E. He had fascinating stories, phrases and sayings, and he could relate his life to each of ours in many ways, even though we were raised differently, were of different ethnic and racial backgrounds, and had different types of home and neighborhood situations. John would say, "If you are new into sobriety, don't hook up with someone with less time sober than you—two dead batteries don't start a car." He related horrific stories in his life of denial. One such revelation was after he was shot during a drug deal gone bad. He was sitting with his leg in a cast a week later, doing drugs with a friend and saying, "This wasn't that bad." He stressed that denial is huge with addiction. This was starting to sink in.

Years before, I could not get enough of hearing Newt Gingrich speak. I listened to Newt constantly by attending every meeting I could to learn as much as I could. Twelve years later I was listening to a former prisoner, now drug counselor, with the same passion and intensity that I had while listening to Newt, except the words had a much different theme. John had become my new "Speaker."

I was not returning to D.C. for business, but I was working on constituent cases. I felt deeply about taking care of their needs to the end, although it was impossible to vote in the House, I could and did work on their cases and call them to see what they needed when they contacted us for help. All other free time was spent at rehab, with my family and going to 12 Step meetings.

Yet the compulsion, the obsession to drink was constantly with me. I was white-knuckling it. "One day at a time," the 12 Step slogan for hope and how to find it, became one *hour* at a time to keep from drinking. I intensified the number of 12 Step meetings I attended to the point that by the following Monday, John looked at my signature slips from the 12 Step meetings and saw that I had gone to twelve in one weekend. He said, "No need to sign slips anymore, just keep doing what you are doing."

I said, "John, I am getting addicted to 12 Step meetings!"

He said, "No, you are getting addicted to the results of 12 Step meetings." He was right. After a week of driving forty minutes to Columbus, going to five or six meetings, then driving back late at night to Heath, Ohio, I decided to do what I had refused to do before—attend a meeting in Newark, Ohio, the adjacent community to Heath where I was living at the time. (*After prison, I moved to Newark where I reside today.*) I had been opposed to attending meetings in Newark because when I was new to recovery, I didn't understand that I would not be put on trial, judged, or harassed by other "recovering drunks and addicts."

When I finally got the nerve to go to a 9 a.m. meeting in downtown Newark (locally referred to as "the pit," based on its location in the basement of a Church), I went in as if I were an F.B.I. informant scoping the place out and not wanting to be discovered.

I saw that it was to be an open topic meeting. I was nervous; I expected to be the center of attention; everyone knew who I was; I had done terrible things; they didn't like me; and on and on my mind rolled.

There were to be three topics:

1. Step One—realizing that we are powerless over alcohol

2. Higher Power

3. Gratitude

The first topic made me think. I had managed to always overcome all odds, be focused, achieved what I wanted, and be able to fight the good fight. I was not a powerless person whatsoever, or so I thought.

Higher Power, I was not sure about that one. I had not found one yet. I believed in God, but needed to study more about this "Higher Power" stuff.

The third one, I really struggled with. I was going to do a plea, I was quickly going down the tubes financially, my family was being put through the wringer, jokes abounded about my alcoholism and situation, I was surely going to lose the house we had bought a year before, and I would soon be in prison. Gratitude was out of my realm of comprehension.

An older man, with a heavy Boston accent and robust voice was sitting next to a very graceful looking woman that I later discovered was his wife. Bill and Judy reflected on the topics and between the two of them, I could see a bit more clearly how these topics did affect me. I had raised my hand when we were asked if this was anyone's first time at this meeting. "Old Bill" as he was called, gave me a very important *coin*, and I have carried it in my wallet since that day. It is aluminum, and about the size of the old half dollar. On the front are the words, "Never Alone Again," and on the back is the Serenity Prayer.

In answer to the first topic, I heard about not fighting this, about not being a warrior against this disease, but about surrendering to the unmanageability of it all.

The second, Higher Power, was my definition of God or spirituality.

Gratitude, the third topic, was being grateful that I was alive, and that the "sweet messenger of hope" would be around the corner if we are grateful and not absorbed in self-pity.

As I was leaving the meeting, a guy named *Wes* walked up to me and said privately, "I know who you are. I have been in your office for veteran's meetings in the past. You are a good man. Welcome."

I felt relieved and started the long, embryonic process of experiencing the 12 Step program at work. There were behavioral changes, and I knew that something, I wasn't sure what, could be around the corner. All of the sudden, Washington and the Justice Department seemed as if they did not exist. I was in the first stages of realizing that what really counted was to be able to live on.

I went to meetings daily at a madman's pace, from Newark to Columbus and back. They tell you to do ninety meetings in the first ninety days of your sobriety; at least one a day. I was averaging six to seven a day. I still struggled daily to stay sober. Cravings were routine and *triggers* like the beer aisles at grocery stores, advertisements, T.V. shows, all added to the desire to use again. I fought the cravings and soon learned that it strengthened them, so I let them come, played the *tape* (in 12 Step recovery, whenever one thinks of "using"—drinking or drugs—we play a mental *tape* backward: *What happened before when I was drinking?* and then forward: *Where will I end up if I use again?*). The cravings would subside after about fifteen minutes—until the next round came. I prayed, meditated, went to meetings, cleaned the house, talked to friends, avoided restaurants, beer aisles, and anywhere else there was alcohol.

My counselor demanded that I get a "sponsor," someone who was in recovery and could guide me out of hell. I found Russ P. in Newark, Ohio, who is still my sponsor, and has helped me beyond words.

My lawyers called. It was nearing mid-October and time to get the "show" in D.C. moving; time for me to "do the time for the crime"; and time for Alberto Gonzales and Alice Fisher to be able to put me away and surreptitiously close the book on those Members that they dared not touch.

I went to D.C. on Thursday, October 12. I spent the day with my attorneys, who briefed me as to what I could expect, and what I wanted to say to the judge about my plea.

But on Friday the 13th of October, 2006, nothing could have prepared me for the press *feeding frenzy*.

★ ★ ★

I met with my attorneys Mark Touhey, Bill Lawler, Craig Margolis and David Hawkins at Vinson and Elkins's law office. I had a bagel and a cup of coffee. We would be heading out in a Lincoln Continental, the same kind I had been used to riding in for a few years on Capitol Hill. That was about the extent of anything I could relate to that day. I have had two speeding tickets in my life, and with the exception of one brief court appearance as a witness in one case, I had never stood before a judge.

We arrived at 333 Constitution Avenue to media madness. The area in front of the courthouse was jammed with reporters. This courthouse entrance had been newly redone, and there were no roped off areas separating us from the "press" of the press. There was no security outside to clear a path for us. I could have been taken through a different entrance, so regardless of whether Justice planned it this way, the chaos certainly provided a dramatic visual for the day's events. Later, one of the security guys said he had not seen such chaos and crowd pushing, even with the D.C. serial killers.

I got out of the car and the media swarmed around—actually pressing against me. Some cameras crashed together, pieces of plastic lay on the ground, my lawyer David Hawkins received a cut on his hand, I was almost hit in the face, and we could barely move. Reporters were shouting out questions, but I was oblivious to them; I just kept moving with a strange look on my face as I saw it later on YouTube. It was a combination of nervousness and numbness. My frame had bloated to 234 pounds, I was on high blood pressure medication and Lipitor for high cholesterol, but I entered Judge Ellen Huvelle's courtroom thirty days sober.

As we went through the motions, I was calm and my voice was strong. I entered into these proceedings without feeling guilty of taking someone else down—of roping someone else into this. It was all about me and what *I* did. I spoke when quizzed about the entire affair, but I refused to cooperate in dragging Members and staff down for no reason. (*When negotiating my plea in mid-September, the names that the Justice Department wanted information on were absurd and included three Members— one Democrat and two Republicans—who had nothing to do with Jack Abramoff. The Members who were joined at the hip with Jack were not mentioned. I suspected a witch-hunt to put more trophies in Alberto's corner and to help his "friend" Alice get her appointment, then a successful pay raise at some firm when she left the Justice Department. Both speculations proved correct.*)

When the Justice Department has you by the balls, they do not let go. However, once I went to the plea, I was done—I would not be summoned back endlessly. Not knowing when it would be over had to be difficult for others involved in the Abramoff case, which led me to sympathize with them. When one turns on others to help his or her own plight, it can be called "coming clean," but sometimes it is not. It can also be a matter of enabling the prosecutors to name the people they want, and then they try to build their case.

Just to be clear, the temptation to give bits of information on Members and others so Justice could spin them and manipulate them was there, but I opted for my comeuppance without dragging someone else down with me. Justice didn't want to hear anything anyway—not about Tom DeLay, Barry Jackson, or Dave Distefano.

U.S. District Court Judge Ellen Huvelle, a Clinton appointee to the bench, had a friendly, but no-nonsense style and a dry sense of humor. One of my former employees actually did an internship for her, so I had heard some good things. The charges were read and I was systematically asked if I agreed. I agreed by answering, "Yes, your Honor," repeatedly. I was worn down in every way. I wanted to get this over with—they had won and I was going to prison, so what difference did it make? When you plea, you plea to the government's case. This is where one has to be careful. If you plea and accept each charge and later dispute it all, you technically perjure yourself. Therefore, despite Alberto Gonzales's techniques, tactics and motives, I was accepting my guilt and starting the process of change.

My attorney had made it clear to the media that we were not blaming all of this on alcohol, but it didn't matter, as the press and others still said that we were blaming it on alcohol. Here are my attorney's words:

Statement of Mark H. Touhey III and William E. Lawler III, Counsel for Congressman Robert W. Ney

The Plea Agreement Congressman Ney has reached with the government reflects his decision to deal with the effects of his past conduct and to start preparing for the next stages of his life.

Bob Ney is a decent, hardworking, lifelong public servant who has made serious mistakes and he wants to take responsibility for those mistakes.

For over two years, the government has exhaustively investigated every aspect of Congressman Ney's life and work. While the plea agreement is very serious, some of the very worst impressions and rumors about Congressman Ney that have been thrown around simply are not true. The actual facts will show that Bob Ney made serious mistakes in judgment and action, but the facts will also show that Bob Ney worked hard for the people of his District. His work has ranged from helping military widows seeking fair benefits to ensuring that children get access to decent housing and education.

Congressman Ney has come to realize that alcohol dependency has affected his judgment, but he is not running away from his conduct or offering excuses. Congressman Ney accepts responsibility for his actions, and we hope that the treatment he has begun will enable him and his family to face the future in a healthy and productive way.

It was done, we went upstairs, and I surrendered my blue American citizen's passport. I then said, "Do you want my other one?" I saw this look of surprise and I thought, *a bit naïve*. Members can have three passports if they choose: a blue one that most citizens get; a brown one that says "Official" on the cover and has a statement in the back about being a Member, which allows diplomatic immunity overseas; and a black diplomatic passport that allows diplomatic immunity, but restricts travel to some areas, like Cuba. You can get into the country with a brown one, but not a black one. I carried two. I then surrendered the brown one. I could have kept it and flown the coop, which of course would have been absurd. I was released on my own recognizance and headed back to Ohio.

Some of my friends, and even the press, said I seemed calm, cool, and almost serene. The entire time I had my hand on Old Bill's coin, imprinted with the words, "God grant me the serenity to accept the things I cannot change, the courage to change the things I can, and the wisdom to know the difference." I did have some serenity; my mind was on a different plane. I respected Judge Huvelle and her position, but I was thinking of a higher authority, a Higher Power than an earthly judge.

The trip back to Ohio gave me peace and the knowledge that even though I would have to go through Members calling for my immediate resignation from the House, I had no intention of doing so. Technically, because I had entered a plea, I didn't have to resign until sentencing. I could rescind my plea at any time and go to trial.

★ ★ ★

November and December were quiet months for me media-wise. There were larger fish to fry—namely the election. A new, Democratic majority was ushered into Washington in 2006. The *talking heads* speculated about how this happened. My name came up as well as Duke Cunningham's and Mark Foley's (other Members in hot water, although over different matters), but the focus was mainly on the war and Bush. The Democrats were, under Speaker-to-be Nancy Pelosi, putting out the mantra about "draining the swamp" of corruption. It was a theme to be carried out for two years—until they filled the swamp back up themselves with many of their own Members. From income tax issues, improper financial filings, sexual advances, taking pictures of their *wieners*, "tickling" staff contests, you name it, the scandals continued. Most were from their side, but one *shirtless* Republican who was unable to stay off Craigslist joined the melee.

My daughter was a senior in high school and I secured a small apartment in Newark, Ohio, for her and moved some furniture into it from our house. It was tiny and easy to equip. My wife moved to her sister's place. I had our large home up for sale and while hoping and praying someone would come along, I began the slow, deliberate, process of packing up decades of our belongings one by one, item by item. I would like to say that it was therapeutic, but it ranged from hell to bliss—looking at our entire life, piece-by-piece, box by box.

My days were spent at 12 Step meetings and packing. I usually started my day with a morning meeting in Granville, Ohio, at a Church near Lake Hudson. Then I followed up with additional meetings at "the pit," the place in downtown Newark that I referred to previously. It is the central office for a recovery group. I found these meetings to be particularly spiritual as it allowed me to reflect on the day ahead, and focus on the little time I had left until my January 19, 2007 sentencing date. Time was to be valued—day-by-day, one day at a time.

David Popp, my last Chief of Staff; Jennie Vollor, our wonderful "southern belle" office manager; and some remaining staff were carrying out the monumental task of boxing and shipping hundreds of boxes and items from D.C. via House Administration (as they do for all exiting members), to storage bins in Heath, Ohio, near my house. The District Office under the direction of our District Director, Bob Wallace, with the assistance of Nancy Fry, Jody Bobek, Joy Dillon, Dennis Watson, Lesley Applegarth, John Bennett, and J.P. Dutton were clearing out four District Offices and sending the material to Heath.

I had a near-relapse in December, not due to the Christmas season but due to a letter from the IRS saying that I owed 297,000 dollars to them over the Scotland trip. I had no idea who paid for that trip and despite what the Justice Department was trying to pull, they knew that was true.

I was in such despair at the incredibly huge amount that would surely follow me to my grave. That very morning I had attended a 12 Step meeting at "the pit" in Newark, Ohio. Shawn C., a young man who chaired the meeting, spoke about his working around and with alcohol while in recovery, and told how he handled it. I was impressed. I spoke to him and told him that I was new into recovery. *(He and I still play racquetball occasionally and see each other at meetings.)*

Later that evening, after receiving the letter, I drove to Heath on Route 79, planning to go to the Kroger store. I saw the restaurant Ruby Tuesdays, pulled into the parking lot, got out and walked toward the door. I didn't do what I should have, which was to call my sponsor. Instead, I decided that a drink was needed; that I deserved it for what had happened that day. I had been sober all of three months or so and *white-knuckling* it, so Ruby's was as good as anywhere else. I entered the door not caring, not thinking, not hoping, not calling my sponsor, not playing the [mental] *tape,* just bee lining it for the bar. My Higher Power had other plans. As I got near, who was bartending but Shawn from that morning's meeting. He had his head turned toward a waitress, talking to her. I spun around, not wanting him to see me, headed out and went where I belonged—home.

The next day I headed to D.C. to do my PSI (Presentence Investigation Report). Anyone who is sentenced goes through this procedure. I had no idea what it was; I just wanted to get it over with.

I met my attorney Bill Lawler for coffee in the federal courthouse cafeteria just before going upstairs to meet with the probation officer who would be writing my report. Bill is a good-natured, religious, all around wonderful human being. I have often jokingly said, "How he can be an attorney is beyond me." The same can be said, of course, for good-natured politicians.

He was very, very focused that morning and said, "This is beyond important to you. We need to go over this and I need you to carefully listen to me."

I said, "Fine, but I need you to see this." I pulled the IRS letter out of my briefcase and handed it to him.

Bill said, "Fine, I will look at this later."

In a panic, I interrupted him. "This ruins me forever. Justice said this would not happen, they lied, they lied!"

In a stern voice that I had never heard him use before, he said, "Don't you get it? They lie! They lie a lot—now focus. Now!" I broke down in tears for the first time, right there in the cafeteria of the U.S. Federal Government Courthouse.

We went upstairs, a nice young lady asked me tons of extremely personal questions, I answered honestly and we left. *(I later realized that Bill was correct; the PSI was critical, as it went to Judge Huvelle and my economic status was taken into consideration for setting a fine. I had committed a victimless crime, no government money taken, so there would be no restitution, just a potential fine. But more important, the PSI would weigh heavily on whether the Judge would utter the necessary words during the process, enabling me to get help through prison rehabilitation. Judges cannot mandate that a person receive treatment; they can only suggest. Judge Huvelle's recordation was critical, though. Without it, I might never get the help I needed.)*

After my incarceration, the whole IRS thing went away. The Justice Department had signed an agreement stating that I had no knowledge of who paid for the Scotland trip. Now it was the Justice Department that had a problem: If the IRS pursued me and asserted that I knew the trip was for personal gain and was paid for by someone privately, which of course was not the case, the IRS would be contradicting the Justice Department. At the very least, it would look like different parts of the government didn't know what was going on. Or, even worse for the government, it would look like the Justice Department submitted an inaccurate Agreement to Judge Huvelle. So, the government could look either incompetent or deceitful—not a great choice, which probably led to the IRS's dropping it.

January 19, 2007, I appeared at court and once again traversed the press line, which was much more controlled this time. Scooter Libby (indicted former Chief of Staff to then Vice President Dick Cheney) was soon to be at the courthouse also, so, they had it a bit more under control with the press semi-roped off. We entered the Courthouse. I was still a former Member and I was wearing my Congressional Pin—the pin that Members wear on their lapel—of a design that I approved or disapproved every two years while I was Chair of House Administration. I had the words my lawyers and I prepared for my time before Judge Huvelle. And in my pocket was Old Bill's Serenity Coin.

We went into the courtroom. Matt Parker, David Popp and Ellen Ratner were there. I told my kids they could come if they wanted to and they said it was up to me. I opted for them not to. If they came, my mom and dad would want to come, then my sister, my wife, cousins, nephews, nieces . . . you get the picture. It's not that I didn't want them, but the emotion would have been too much for everyone.

Webb Hubble, former Assistant Attorney General under Clinton, told me that his daughter had insisted on coming to his sentencing, but began to pass out as the sentence came and they had to stop the proceedings. I opted for something I thought worked best for our family.

Prior to the Judge's appearing, I was sitting up front and the court sketch artist was working his trade (*I later attended his book signing in D.C. when I got out of prison*). I received a message that I needed to tell Ellen to "settle down." Matt Parker told me that Ellen sat next to a woman, two grade school kids, and an older lady. I saw them; they sort of stood out, and I wondered who they were. Ellen introduced herself to them, and the younger woman of the two said, "I am Mary Butler's sister, and these are her nieces and her mother." (Mary Butler was prosecuting my case for the Justice Department.)

Ellen said, "Does your sister get sick in the morning?"

The woman said, "What?" Ellen repeated the question and the woman said, "Excuse me?"

Ellen then said, "When she looks in the mirror and sees what she has done to this man." Ellen continued, "So you took the kids out of school for Mary's big case, huh? A big deal for her huh?" She then ended with, "I hope your sister rots in hell!"

The sister was speechless. I told Matt, "It's okay if Mary wants her sister here. Mine has been through hell, so hers can get some verbiage too."

Ellen is unfiltered and you just have to love it—although I have sometimes been on the receiving end!

I stood before the Judge, and the charges against me were read. I said, "I accept responsibility for my actions and I am prepared to face the consequences of what I have done . . . I have made mistakes of judgment and acted in ways that I am not proud of. I never intended my career in public service to end this way, and I am ashamed that it has. I never acted to enrich myself or get things I shouldn't, but over time, I allowed myself to get too comfortable with the way things have been done in Washington, D.C., for too long."

Then Judge Huvelle said, "Whether or not you've served your constituents well, on some level you have seriously betrayed the public's trust and abused your power as a Congressman. You have a long way to go to make amends for what's happened." I knew the sentence was going to be on the high end of the scale in the grand scheme of the plea.

The Judge then noted from the PSI by her own employee that I was "financially insolvent" and no fine was recommended. I got a 6,000-dollar fine payable in two years.

I thought, *Wow, how can I ever pay that?* To make it worse, I realized that a year before this I made that amount in fifteen days of one month. Now it seemed unattainable. I couldn't buy a cup of coffee; I was totally dependent on family and friends for food. I had drained my thrift savings to pay large, overdue bills; to pre-pay Kayla's apartment, utilities, and whatever she needed; and I had given my last thousand dollars to the kids—500 to Kayla, and 500 to Bobby. But as I watched my very capable attorney, Mark Touhey, politely argue with the judge for no fine, or at least more time in which to pay it, although I appreciated it, I said quietly to Bill Lawler, "It's okay. It's okay, I just want to go."

It *was* okay. It did not matter in the big picture. I needed to focus on more than money, more than a prison sentence, more than an earthly, judicial figure of authority—I needed to accept responsibility, realize that I put myself here by making the bullets that were fired at me, and most of all I needed in a very large, important way, to stay sober.

I have a favorite expression that I alter slightly, but it is so true: "Throughout our lives we have good and bad moments, but at the end of the day, it is the moments that take your breath away that count. May you have many." I later heard this repeated in prison by Sheila Land, a rehab counselor. It sounded wonderful then as it does now. It rings of the spirituality of truth and sends along the "sweet messenger of hope," no matter what is occurring in our short time on this earth that we deem to be "life."

As I walked out of the courtroom, amid the court reporters, the press, the gallery, Mary Butler's sister and mother, I had one of those moments that took my breath away. There in the last row to my left, was a refugee who had escaped from a repressive country where he was jailed for daring to become a Christian. He arrived in America without knowing a word of English. Through God, karma, fate, whatever you want to call it, an American brought him to my Congressional office when he was down to his last week of money. I got him a job. He always called me "Boss" and said he owed me his life for what I did. I was happy to help him and expected nothing from him. But, there he sat, looking at me, wearing a slight smile. It took my breath away; it summed up what I knew of the human spirit amid despair and tribulation. It spoke to me; to my inner peace, of what I really knew—that deep down, many people have an angel in their heart—and that I know what is so amazing about grace. I glanced away because I didn't want the press to pick up on my looking at him and try to figure out who he was. I called him later and thanked him. He said, "No problem, Boss, I owe you my life." Payam Zakipour is now an American citizen, married, and goes by his new American name, Kyle Washington.

I was officially booked and given the date of March 1, 2007, to report. I would transition from being an 18th District of Ohio Congressman to becoming a federal number. After leaving the courthouse, I headed back to Ohio. I really wanted to be taken straight from the courtroom to start my sentence, but I had to wait and self-report. It is comparable to walking up to the noose, putting it around my neck and jumping off the platform versus the lever being pulled.

My house had a buyer, but Countrywide Mortgage Company was not in a short sale mood. I was short $25,000 to be able to walk out of the house, mortgage paid, not making a cent. Finally I said to the man at Countrywide (ironically, Mr. Bush), "Okay, I owe you $303,000. You can eat $303,000 or $25,000, it's up to you. And by the way, March first I can't call you and you can't call me." No deal. (*I gave power of attorney to Matt Parker, went to prison, and several weeks later they yielded.*) When you are flat broke and not filing bankruptcy, but still unable to pay, you get calm, you surrender and you do what you can. That is what I did with all the bills.

(*I had some very uplifting moments during this time of transition and loss—moments of outpouring from many people; some whom I had known and some I had not. I recall memorable expressions from that time. One came from a long-time friend, Scott Krupinski. Scott contacted me and said, "Anytime you want to talk, have coffee, I have an ear for you—in fact, two of them."*

Former Congressman Charlie Wilson from my home area of St. Clairsville was extremely kind in making phone calls to my parents. He also sent me an inspirational story that concerns a mayonnaise jar, golf balls, pebbles, and sand, illustrating what is important in life. You will find the link in Resources. It will be worth your time to read it.

My friend Doctor Terry Wallace reminded me of what is written on his business card: "Carpe Diem"—seize the day [or even the moment, as it may be]. And so I did seize the moment . . . be it a good one or not.)

Before my sentencing, I had negotiated with a moving and storage company for everything we owned. The owner of the company came to my house, assessed everything, and then said, "Where are you moving to?"

I said, "Prison."

He looked shocked and said, "Sorry."

I retorted, "It's okay. I got sentenced to three years for beating the hell out of a guy over a quote I didn't like for moving these items." He stared at me, I smiled, and then he laughed. I did keep my sense of humor, although dark at times, throughout the entire ordeal.

The moving van arrived the week before Christmas. Freezers, four bedrooms of furniture, two rec rooms of items, pool table, foosball, dining room set, tables, great room, Italian design furniture, lawn equipment, curio's, antiques, and on and on. Oh yeah, and 495 boxes that I personally packed.

Looking on the bright side of things, the kids and I agreed that it would have been far worse to have lost our house in St. Clairsville, Ohio, where the kids were raised—many great memories still lived on between there and the recesses of our minds.

The vans arrived, the stuff went out, I systematically and meticulously cleaned 5,000 square feet, went to the door, took off my Ohio state ball cap, waved it into the air with my left hand, blew a kiss to the house with my right hand, and yelled out to an echoing, empty, sans human-being interior, "It's been great. Thanks for the memories." As the evening drew near, I shut the door, locked it and dropped the keys off at Matt and Marina Parker's house. I headed to my daughter's place to prepare for Christmas week and do some more 12 Step meetings—about five a day. It was the holidays—a great time to relapse for one who is a member of, not Congress, but my new associates' group, the "one day at a time club."

My days were spent with the kids, my family, and visiting some friends, plus my usual 12 Step meetings. I was in the "Valley" (Belmont County, Ohio) for the rest of the holidays. We exchanged gifts. My daughter bought me something that could be used later when I got out of prison, as did my son. But Bobby also gave me a lottery ticket. I scratched it off and about hyperventilated when I saw that I had won 10,000 dollars. I was so excited about not being broke anymore, and then realized it was fake. I didn't get angry. You really have to know Bobby to appreciate his sense of humor!

The New Year came, and according to a family tradition, a belief started by my mom and dad, whomever you spend New Year's with, you will be with the rest of the year. I saw all of my family that next year while I was in prison, so the traditional belief panned out.

January and February were consumed with checking last minute items, preparing to leave, thinking over every detail because once you are "locked away," taking care of things is not like picking up the phone.

I visited a lot with Tim Ritter, my good friend and college roommate. I took comfort in spending time at his house and enjoying his wonderful friendship and hospitality—dinners, movies, and partaking of my second addiction, gelato from DaVinci's in Upper Arlington, Ohio.

Having had experience with campaign events and planning, I made a huge "to do" checklist and followed it thoroughly. I only forgot one thing, and it was major—get dental checkup prior to entering. That little slip cost me a tooth in prison as a result of no access to treatment. I know, I know—as I told you before, my friend Howard Monroe says ". . . feed them crusty bread and water." Howard was not far off. I swear he must have seen the prison cafeteria.

One of my all-time favorite books, *The Winter of My Discontent*, was assigned reading when Tim and I were in Liberty Antalis's English class at Ohio University Eastern. I thought about this the last week of February of 2007. I had thought of March 1 as the day I would be entering prison. Then I realized that I was escaping *from* prison—the prison of my addiction and all that was wrong in my life. As painful as the process had been, somehow I knew that I would not look back on it as the winter of my discontent, but rather as the winter of my evolving intent.

PART IV

☆ ☆ ☆

POST-CONGRESS

*"Don't cry because it's over,
smile because it happened."*
—Dr. Seuss

Chapter 32

☆ ☆ ☆

MORGANTOWN FEDERAL CORRECTIONAL INSTITUTION
MORGANTOWN, WEST VIRGINIA

*"In my country we go to prison first
and then become President."*

—NELSON MANDELA

THE TRANSITION

Leaving one's family for any reason is difficult and emotion-laden for everyone. I said my goodbyes to my son, Bobby, at his apartment up in Columbus where he was residing. We went to get a bite to eat and my cell phone rang; it was Steny Hoyer (D-Maryland) calling to see how my family and I were doing. I told him I was with Bobby, and he wished Bobby, Kayla, and the entire family the best.

I left Bobby, which was difficult. Although his girlfriend, Julie (now his wife), was in Columbus, it was still hard to leave him. I felt a tremendous surge of guilt. Not that Bobby wasn't capable—he had always been a hard worker, but I had been giving him financial support for school and his apartment, as was his mother. My share of the money was gone and I felt very bad about that.

I then drove a half hour down to Newark to see Kayla. It was during a break between classes and I was able to catch her and her boyfriend, Adam (now her husband), crossing the green on the high school campus. I hugged her. It was especially hard to see Kayla, only a senior in high school, stay by herself in Newark. I had hoped she would return to Belmont County to be with her mother, Candy, who lived an hour and a half from Newark—but she didn't want to miss her last year at Newark High School. Thoughts of my not seeing her receive her diploma surged through my mind.

I told both Bobby and Kayla that I loved them, that I was proud of them, and sorry for what happened. They were both very understanding and brave about the entire mess. Not having to worry about money as they were growing up, they certainly adapted well to not having a lot of money at their disposal, but they had plenty of emotional support from both sides of their family as well as from their mother, Candy, and that was a great comfort to me.

(I had received a "gift" from Candy about two weeks before this. I was headed to a 12 Step recovery meeting, hanging on one day at a time and determined to enter prison sober, when my cell phone rang. It was Candy. We had a wonderful conversation; talked about the kids and politics. She told me to remember that I was the best at politics the State of Ohio had seen in ages. Her words were chicken soup for my tortured soul—more than she knew. I wished her and her husband, Matt, the best.)

I headed to Bellaire, Ohio, where I was born and raised. I knew my family supported me and would all want to be with me when I was dropped off at prison, but there was no way that I wanted that to happen. To have them all go up there would have been an emotional upheaval I didn't want any of us to experience—so I went to Bellaire with Matt Parker and David Popp, two friends and former staffers.

I walked into the house I was raised in, and a flood of memories came back from the third grade, the year we had moved there. I imagined that my dog Shep would burst into the room at any moment. I would turn around and see my boyhood friends Bruce Velt and Mark Giannangeli in the yard waiting to ride bikes—and this mess I was in would have just been a terrible dream.

My mother and sister had already been crying. Everyone was in the front room, and we had an emotional good-bye. I was so lucky to have the unconditional support of Mom and Dad, my sister Emmy Lou, her husband, Rick, and my second wife. I headed out the door with Matt and Dave.

The three of us designed an elaborate plot to thwart any plans the media might have of swarming the prison area outside Morgantown. It involved a sincere e-mail of regret and thanks I sent out to about forty friends. However, in that e-mail I planted some erroneous information that would be beneficial to a couple of the recipients. These two people would (and did) absolutely leak anything to the press that I sent to them *in confidence*. (As it is said about some people in D.C., "If you want a friend, buy a dog.") The following is an article that appeared in *The Hill* by Jackie Kucinich about that e-mail, including my original e-mail— without the *extra* information:

CHANNELING GARTH BROOKS, NEY SENDS FAREWELL E-MAIL

By Jackie Kucinich – 02/28/07 08:49 AM ET

Former Rep. Bob Ney (R-Ohio), who will report today to federal prison in West Virginia, issued an emotional goodbye e-mail (see below) yesterday to friends and colleagues. He thanked them for their support over the past six months and told them he had "gained a higher power" to help him through his incarceration.

The e-mail closed with a quote from the Garth Brooks song, "The Dance" . . . Ney will serve a sentence of 30 months on federal bribery charges. He resigned from Congress in November after pleading guilty to one count of conspiracy and making false statements.

In his letter, Ney expressed a mixture of hope and regret.

"Someone asked me the other day, if I wish I had never run for office," he wrote. "I answered that I am glad that I did. . . . Nothing can erase the wonderful memories, thoughts, constituents, and changes that we, working together with the Republicans and Democrats, have been able to do."

He expressed sorrow for the crimes he had committed and said he was willing to accept the consequences of his actions.

"My family and I have lost everything on an economical basis, house, health care, possessions, but so have other people, people in the district, many, have lost all," he wrote. "And yes, that is painful for anyone that has gone through it, but, I am so fortunate to have my wife and children, we are so rich with family, friends like you, loved ones that are there for us, and full of hope for a good future.

"The darkest days are not ahead, I have gained a higher power, the god of my understanding, is with all of us and that allows me to view tomorrow, although as a day of loss of freedom, as a day of enlightenment and of life to come," concluded Ney.

Ellen Ratner, a close friend of Ney's, said the former congressman is particularly grateful that he is sober. Before his sentencing, Ney completed a month in an alcohol treatment facility.

"He has thanked me numerous times for helping him achieve his sobriety," Ratner said. "I'm just mad at myself for not doing it earlier."

Ratner said she dined last week with Ney and that she comforted the lawmaker and told him that his incarceration could be a positive experience.

"Obviously he is scared, but he believes he is going to get through this," she said. "I think he has learned and knows that it can be an extremely positive experience, by using it as a time to reflect."

"Bob made some serious mistakes, and he and his family are paying a steep price for them," said another Ney associate, who did not want to be named. "But he's taken responsibility for his actions and he still has many people who care deeply for him. Over the course of his long career, Bob helped countless people and thousands of lives were improved because of his hard work and compassionate spirit."

The associate added, "It's very sad that all of that will be overshadowed for the foreseeable future, but hopefully one day more people will look back and recognize that this is a decent man who did a lot of good and who is determined to make amends for his terrible mistakes in judgment."

Ratner agreed. "I don't think we have seen the last of Bob Ney," she said. "I think people are going to see that he is a very good person. It may take some time, but they will."

Ney first signaled the problems that lay ahead when he resigned from his chairmanship on the powerful House Administration Committee last August and announced he would not run for reelection. Ney later admitted he accepted thousands of dollars of gifts from lobbyists in exchange for legislative favors, and he formally confessed his wrongdoings in November. On Jan. 19, he became the first lawmaker sentenced for involvement in the scandal surrounding former lobbyist Jack Abramoff.

His ex-chief of staff, Will Heaton, was sentenced on Monday for his role in the scandal, which included concealing thousands of dollars in gifts from lobbyists for himself and Ney.

Here is the e-mail:

hello,
i will not have access to e mail so this will be my last for a while. i wanted to drop you a short e mail to give you my address:
    i also wanted to thank you for all you have done for me and my family. your kind words, thoughts, and prayers throughout the last six months have helped all of us quite a lot.
    someone asked me the other day, if i wish i had never run for office. i answered that i am glad that i did. nothing can erase the wonderful memo?

ries, thoughts, constituents, and changes that we, working together with the republicans and democrats, have been able to do. working to bring jobs to the district, helping constituents with issues, and trying to change law to help people has been the greatest memory ever.

would i change things if i could, sure. am i sorry for things that happened, absolutely, and i will pay the price. but, i am grateful for many good people in our office that helped the district and grateful for a free nation, the men and women that protect it, and a wonderful constituency in the district that i used to serve.

my family and i have lost everything on an economical basis, house, health care, possessions, but so have other people, people in the district, many, have lost all. and yes, that is painful for anyone that has gone through it, but, i am so fortunate to have my wife and children, we are so rich with family, friends like you, loved ones that are there for us, and full of hope for a good future.

the darkest days are not ahead, i have gained a higher power, the god of my understanding, is with all of us and that allows me to view tomorrow, although as a day of loss of freedom, as a day of enlightenment and of life to come.

as garth brooks said in his song the dance, *[The refrain from the song was included here—it illustrated my feelings better than I could—that had I known how everything would end for me, I might have never gone into politics, and I would have missed so much that was good in my life.]*

my family and my life is starting new, thanks for being part of it.

god bless,

bob ney

The false information said: "If you want to contact me by e-mail, I will be arriving on a US Airways flight from D.C. to Pittsburgh and will arrive at Morgantown on March the 1st at 1:30, so send me e-mail prior to 1:30."

In actuality, when Matt, Dave, and I left my parents' house on February 28, the night before I was to report to prison, we were less than two hours away from Morgantown. We stayed at a motel ten miles from the prison; I would enter Morgantown on March 1 at about 10 a.m., not 1:30 p.m., as I had stated in my e-mail.

We checked into our motel, ate, and then went to a bowling alley where we bowled and played some pool. I suppose I was as relaxed as someone can be on his last night of freedom.

The next morning, being the breakfast lover that I am, we went to the Bob Evans Restaurant near the prison for my final "good, authentic" breakfast. As we sat in the booth, Matt and Dave were talking and I was reading the Morgantown paper. My picture was at the top of the mast and an article about my heading to Morgantown. By this time I had stopped reading articles, but for some reason I started through this one.

It was all about my going to the same prison where Richard Hatch (former *Survivor* champion) was incarcerated (the newshounds were obsessed with mentioning this), and how my life would be so different from Congress. I thought, *No shit!*

Then, as I read further, the next paragraph surprised the hell out of me. It said, "Ney will be in one of four prisons in the country that has a pilot program for e-mail." I let out a yelp. "I am on vacation!" I had joked that after years of a grueling schedule, plus constant work and stress, if prison had e-mail, I would consider it a vacation. I could maintain contact with the outside world. *(Although there was no Internet in prison, we were able to write to a limited amount of people. It was read by someone in authority, and then sent on for us. Whenever there was a response to our e-mail, it also was read and then sent to us. Prison is the ultimate boredom—Groundhog Day again and again—so e-mail was exciting!)*

We left the restaurant, and were about to get into the car in the Bob Evans parking lot and head to the prison. I told Matt and Dave that I wanted to make my goodbyes right then, because once the car stopped I had to get out of it quickly and they had to leave immediately—prison rules.

I said, "I know this didn't turn out the way we all wanted, but you guys did the greatest job ever possible and I thank you for it and your friendship." With that, we all three did what I did not want to happen— we hugged and we cried. Down the road we traveled; my last car trip for a while. The car stopped at the entrance, I waved goodbye to Matt Parker, my former District Director (by that time Matt had moved on to a great public relations firm), and to David Popp, my last Chief of Staff (of about 90 days) who, like Matt, stayed to the end to close things out.

I had no idea what to expect next, but the ruse had worked—there was not one single member of the "pesky" media at the prison gate. I walked up to the window and said, "Bob Ney, self-reporting," as if it were some type of basketball camp and I was there for the first day.

The guard replied, "Yes, I knew you were coming." He told me to sit inside and wait. I sat on a stool as he continued his work, and after about ten minutes another corrections officer came through the door. He said to follow him and I did. We walked down a small, asphalted road as thousands of things started going through my mind. I knew not to engage him in chit-chat, and also knew to address him as "CO" or "Corrections Officer." *(Prior to going into prison, Mark Hrutkey, an attorney from West Virginia who had been an inmate at Morgantown at one time, sent me his personally written book that told me in precise detail how Morgantown worked and how I could best survive. I also had the benefit of advice I received from Webb Hubbell, a friend of Ellen Ratner's.)*

The silence didn't last long before the CO said, "I knew Joel Potts, your first Campaign Manager. I'm from the Valley." Joel is from Shadyside, Ohio, near Bellaire where I grew up. Joel did an excellent job as my first Campaign Manager in the 1984 Ohio Senate race against Bob Olexo. Hearing the name brought back a ton of "Potts family memories" and provided some type of link between my old world and this new one.

I said, "Yes, Joel is a great guy," and that ended our brief discourse. I thought to myself what a small world it is, and that politics is everywhere.

The next few days could have gone worse, but I had been well prepared, even though I almost didn't receive this invaluable preparation via a personal visit with Webb Hubbell in D.C.

A few weeks before I was to leave for prison, Ellen Ratner called me and insisted—and I mean insisted—that I meet with Webb Hubbell, the famous fall guy for the Clinton Administration. *(I truly believe that the Hubbell case was a travesty and Clinton should have pardoned him. Hell, Clinton pardoned the two ladies that bombed the Senate in 1982!)* But by this time I just wanted to go to prison. I didn't want to talk to anyone. I didn't want to discuss any part of prison life. I didn't want to hear what was ahead. I just wanted to do my time and get it over with. Ellen won, of course, and off to D.C. I went.

(This was not the first time I met Webb. I was on the Whitewater Investigation Committee and Webb was being held in the anteroom of the House Financial Services Committee. That day Mike Oxley, Republican Congressman from Ohio, and I went back to the anteroom and saw Webb sitting there in his suit, handcuffed. He is in the Capitol with security out the ying yang and they had him handcuffed prior to his testimony that would take place in about 15 minutes! Oxley [Ox, as we called him] had been an FBI agent and is a great guy and just a real good Joe by nature. He asked them to uncuff Webb. The U.S. Marshalls started in about protocol, blah, blah, blah, but as a Congressman,

Oxley trumped the Marshalls and Webb was uncuffed. As Ox and I headed into the Committee to take our chairs, Oxley said, "This guy really got hosed." Webb testified and by the time he was done, I felt the same.)

So there I sat, about-to-go-to-prison Bob Ney, with Ellen Ratner and a free Webb Hubbell in a complete role-reversal. Webb started by saying, "Let me assure you of something off the bat. You are relatively safe and no one is going to drag you into the shower rooms. The worst part is the first three days. You will be taunted and they will test your patience—both the inmates and the guards. The guards will let you know, like they did me, who the boss is now. Just keep your wits, follow your instincts, and fight boredom."

For over three hours, Webb filled me in on every detail and aspect of prison life—from the commissary accounts, to phone lists and visitors lists, to handling tough situations with humor, and on and on. Every single detail that Webb told me was true. His advice and Mark Hrutkey's book were invaluable to me. (Hrutkey's book is now available to others as well. See the link in Resources for this chapter.)

As I entered the waiting area, I knew that the most degrading part was coming up very soon. The guard inside turned to me and said, "Where's the media?"

I said, "They will be here around one o'clock," and then explained to him the ruse in the e-mail I had sent.

He smiled a bit, then handed me a small box and said, "Here is some hate mail." (I read it later. It was from some people in California and Massachusetts hoping that Jack and I were going to be gang-raped, beaten, put in for thirty more years . . . just the usual enlightening hate mail, which I assumed came from the more liberal side of the spectrum, although I'm sure that some conservatives felt the same way.)

Then came the *inspection:* I was totally stripped down, standing there in my birthday suit, all possessions gone except for eyeglasses. Had I worn my wedding ring, I would have been able to keep that, but I had been told that they usually get stolen. Then the guard said, "Raise your nut sack and then bend over."

When the once-over was finished, I was given newbie clothes. They are a cross between balloon-looking Afghanistan pants and a top that looked like a hospital gown. The shoes were cheap slippers. All newbies make an easy target in these clothes and, as Webb had said, are taunted. I obviously wanted to get out of these and into regular prison clothes as quickly as possible, and especially before the weekend, because the prisoners that dole out the clothes don't work on Saturday or Sunday.

The guard from the compound below came up, checked me in, and asked me a series of questions. Some were health related, and some were about my knowing any prisoners at Morgantown. I knew of none personally. As soon as the paperwork was done, I was no longer the Honorable Robert Ney M.C., but inmate number 688288-061. (*My new ID was more valuable for the next seventeen months than my social security card.*)

A lady came down the hallway and took the guard aside. She asked him something and I could hear him in a stern voice say, "I am treating this man no different than anyone else that's here. I am not doing that."

She responded, but it was in a lower tone of voice and I couldn't hear what she was saying. He answered loudly, "No way!"

The guard came back to me, asked me some more questions, had me fill out some paperwork, and then said that the prison provides another prisoner who would escort me to my next step. As I waited, another guard of a higher rank—sergeant, I believe, walked by in the outer hallway. The guard who had interviewed me stopped him and they spoke. The sergeant must have already heard about the argument between the guard and the lady because the guard said, "I hope you got my back. I am just not treating him any different and will not agree with humiliating him needlessly."

The sergeant responded, "Got ya."

I then met my first fellow prisoner, who was to be my escort, and he said, "Follow me." As we walked, he said he was "close to the door," which meant he was soon to leave. He also said that there was a lot of hype in the prison compound about my coming there. He gave me some advice on not trusting people and not pissing the guards off. We entered the "Mainline," which is the eating area—he in his mandatory 8 a.m. to 5 p.m. khakis and brown shirt and I in my newbie clothes. It was about to close, which meant that if I didn't eat right away, I would not eat until 6:30 or so that evening. There were very few prisoners in there. We hurried to get trays, and I sat with my back to the few prisoners in the serving line. As we talked, my escort glanced up and got a look of shock, then fear on his face.

From behind me I heard, "Get the fuck away from him."

In a much quieter tone, my escort replied, "Sir, I am the escort."

Shooting back, the voice behind me repeated, "I said get the fuck away from him. Fuck him—let him find his own way."

My escort said, "Yes, sir," got up, never said a word to me and left.

I wasn't addressed by the harsh voice behind me. I got up, saw where to dump my tray, and proceeded to walk out the first door to my left, which was locked. As I turned to my right to go toward another door I glanced over and saw the back of a very short man, the owner of the mysterious voice, who was in a suit, walking to the back area that led to the kitchen. *(The next day I saw that same guy walking around, and I asked someone who he was.*

"Oh, that's the warden." The owner of the mysterious voice, Warden Dominic Gutierrez, was abruptly dismissed about two months later. Rumor had it that I had him removed. Wow—I was all-powerful even in prison!)

I found an open door, walked outside, and stopped the first guy I saw that was in prisoner's clothing. I asked, "Where do I go now? How do I get clothes?"

He asked me where my escort was and I said, "I have no idea. Some guy yelled at him in Mainline and he left."

He then asked me what unit I lived in and I said, "I have no idea— they didn't tell me that either."

The prisoner looked baffled and indicated that everyone, when they first arrive, has an escort who gets them settled. He said, "We have to hurry because the laundry has closed." (The clothes the prisoners wear are distributed from the laundry.)

I followed him—at this point I would have followed him into the little creek that ran through the compound! As I walked behind this inmate, who was helpful, but a total stranger to me, I became painfully aware of my helplessness. I had always been a confident person who led the way; someone who came up with the plan, spearheaded ideas, was part of an important Congressional process. I was now totally out of my element—lost, afraid, unsure, and following a stranger hoping to get some different clothes. I felt as though I had been beamed to another planet. We headed to the back door of what turned out to be the laundry. When we knocked and went in, there was a flurry of prisoners doing different tasks. I later learned that not only do prisoners work different prison jobs, but the prison system has other jobs for them—data entry work on word processors, call centers, and so forth. "Prison Industries" seems to be a modern-day form of slave labor that makes somebody some money, somewhere up the food chain.

I saw a gentleman who looked like he was in charge, sitting in a chair behind the workers. He seemed to be in his early 60s, a distinguished-looking African American. He looked at me and asked the same question they all asked, "Where is your escort?" I went through what was now becoming my standard line. He spoke eloquently and dramatically and asked, "Are you a Republican?"

I quickly answered yes. He said, "I thought so. Congressman Ney, we have been waiting for you."

I replied as fast as I could, "But remember it was the Bush Administration and Alberto Gonzales—the Republicans—that put me in here."

He smiled a large smile, indicated that he knew that, shook my hand and said, "I'm a Buckeye. I am the former Mayor of East Cleveland," [Emmanuel Onunwor] and he was. (Having been convicted in 2005 for public corruption and tax evasion, he was sentenced to nine years in prison.)

I was measured, suited up with khakis, and given shoes by a polite young man who seemed to be extremely curious, as he had heard about me. He asked what it was like to be a Congressman. I said that it is an interesting job, but the people are the ones who are important.

Once I was outfitted, the "Mayor" made a call on an internal phone and then said to me, "You are in Gerard unit."

Another man gave me a *bedroll* of sheets, pillow, and a blanket and said, "Come with me."

MY NEW HOME

I arrived at my new home at 5'8" weighing 234 pounds, with skyrocketing cholesterol, on medication for high blood pressure, broke, battered, weary, depressed, apprehensive, angry, resentful, and sober 12 days shy of six months. Yet somehow I felt that the worst was behind me.

I went up to my unit, got some stares and a few cackles, walked to the end of the hallway, and then turned the corner. I faced a room with a door—not cell bars. The door had a window in it, and looked identical to an average schoolroom door. I walked into the room that was barely large enough for two people, but it contained two bunk beds, four lockers, and a desk that looked like a small school desk. Into the room bounced an inmate. He was about 27, thin, tattoos galore and wearing a big smile on his face. In his hand was a lock.

He said, "Welcome to Gerard unit. We've been expecting you. The entire prison here at Morgantown saw you on TV. You have three roommates. They are at work." He handed me the lock he was holding and said, "Here is a lock for your locker. And, oh yeah, don't trust anyone!"

He left and immediately another guy came into the room. He was about 30, African American, looked at me as if he had seen a ghost and said, "Are you a Congressman?"

I said, "Was."

He then handed me a clipboard, said, "Welcome" and left.

I, being a new inmate with just a bedroll and no other clothes except the ones on my back, thought, *Okay, be enterprising—you never know what you might be able to scrounge around here that can be useful.* I walked down to the bathroom. As I looked around at the totally unfamiliar setting with the other inmates moving about, somehow I felt like MacGyver (from the TV series). I had a clipboard and fantasized that it could be turned into something useful or made into a weapon to save my life. I also thought that not very long ago if I needed supplies, phones, materials or goods of any kind I just called Charlene Molli, Maggie Riith, Paula Sievertson, or Jennie Vollor, all of them Office Managers of mine through the years, and my every need would be taken care of. Now I would need to scrounge the occasional, lucky paper clip found on the ground. Although, I was quite proud that in only fifteen minutes from entering the unit, I had grasped what it was all about. What a chameleon I was! My political days and all that I had learned in Congress were paying off to allow me to have "street skills" in prison.

When I returned to my room, the lock on my locker that I had been given was gone, and my bedroll, pillow, sheets, and so forth that were in the locker were gone as well. Bounding into the room came the inmate who had given me the lock. He was holding the lock and my bedroll and he said, "I told you not to trust anyone." He handed my things to me, smiled, and left.

My roommates (cellies, as we called them) came one by one. Hank was a guitar- strumming Valley boy from Follansbee, West Virginia, and a likable, helpful guy. He had been a deliveryman who made the rounds carrying food products for vending machines. (*He is out now and has a productive life in the Valley. He took me to my first 12 Step meeting in prison and knew the program well.*)

All were great to me, and patient with my city, non-street ways. I think they were amused at the way I looked at prison.

I remember my first morning in the unit. I fixed some instant coffee, stepped out onto the cement area outside the door of the unit to smell the air and try to get into the mood of appreciating being alive and making the best of things. One of the inmates yelled, "What the fuck you doing, dumbass?"

I thought, *Here we go,* and replied, "Hello, having some coffee."

He said, "That's fine, but until they call breakfast you are not allowed one foot outside the door and if they catch you, you go into solitary for thirty days and this unit gets penalized and when you get out you will wish they kept you there for another thirty for all the shit you will get from the guys." Then he barked, "Get in here!"

I was in shock. I was looking at this place through glasses that said, "Life is normal; this is just a different version of what I am used to." I realized at that moment that life in prison was going to be one hell of a roller-coaster ride.

The next three days were filled with listening to a few people, especially my cellies, tell me what I needed to do to make it. Priority number one was to get a job. You basically have one week to find a job opening or they are going to stick you in the kitchen. If you go into the kitchen, there are a lot of fights and arguments there, crowded spaces, and a lot of food theft. This can lead to many strip searches, pressure to steal for other inmates, or be a "pussy snitch" when you are lumped into *group* problems:

(In prison, if you are even near a theft situation, it is as if you stole also; if you are near a fight, you are part of it too. If you are playing Ping-Pong and accidentally hit someone with a paddle; if you get a cut, a mark, or something of that nature and do not report it and later a fight ensues; when you are stripped down and an "unreported" mark on your body is found; if a guy passes out, falls to the ground, and you touch him—all these things can result in all involved being dragged off to solitary in the SHU [Security Housing Unit]. The length of time in the SHU can depend on how long it takes to determine whether you had something to do with the offence or until you "get it.")

The SHU is a freestanding, blond brick building with a red metal roof. You are placed in a cell that is barely big enough for one person, but you may be in there with another guy. A toilet is beside the bed, so privacy and the odor control factor are non-existent for you and your cellmate. The SHU is isolation and includes limited privileges. The only time you get out of the cell is for a one-hour per day "dog walk" for exercise. Even the toughest of the tough don't like the SHU.

The problem is that if a CO (corrections officer) doesn't like you for any reason, including an "eye assault" (looked at him in a perceived "threatening" manner), you go to the SHU. You could be put in there for any reason and without anyone questioning why. It scared the shit out of me. From that day forward, I made sure I had my coffee inside, not standing outside, which could get me into the "red roof inn" as the inmates called it. (For an in-depth description of SHU, see the Bad Lawyer NYC Blogspot link in Resources under the Morgantown chapter title.)

The next morning the call to "Mainline," the prison cafeteria, was made. Running was against the rules, but guys tried to "fast walk" to get to Mainline. After eating there for a week, why anyone would be in a hurry to get there was beyond me. As I once joked after being there for a while, the only reason to run to Mainline is if they announced, "Women or pardons are available at Mainline today."

As I entered Mainline, I saw to my left that there were predominantly African American and Hispanic inmates. Specifically, African Americans were in the left front; Black Muslims were in the left middle; and the Latino community was behind them. On the right side, were the white inmates; up front were the white-collar crime guys—stockbrokers, lawyers, professors, accountants . . . politicians.

In the middle of Mainline was a common milk area with a salad "buffet" in the afternoon and evening. There was a line for the left side of the room, and a line for the right side. Inmates dished out the food portions so everyone got the same amount—unless you were lucky enough to know someone and got a bit more.

I remember one day a male prostitute, an African American from D.C. who was sentenced for drugs, was in line. His nickname was "puffy cheeks" due to the fact that he had cheek and buttocks implants. He was halfway through the process of a sex change, and had what looked like breasts. This guy had a tough time in prison, but seemed to have an "I don't care" attitude—which was an attitude one would need to be him. He wanted some more cereal so he stood there, looking at the guy serving the food. He was not moving until he got some more. He glanced at the guy, motioned downward toward his plate, nodding for more. The white corrections officer who liked to deem himself a cook of sorts, looked at him and said, "Move on monkey fag." The inmate just looked at him, angry of course. The white CO looked at him and said, "Don't look at me, monkey. Move on before I throw that faggot ass into the SHU." I thought, *Okay—corrections officer, Bush Administration—I guess the diversity, race, and compassion factors don't count here.)*

My first instinct was to say something to the corrections officer. Pre-prison I would open my mouth, bark out my opinion, and debate people. That was my job, my natural instinct as a Congressman and a politician. But common sense, an awareness of my surroundings, my lack of power, and my loss of rights (including the right to express my opinion), reduced me to merely hold out my bowl for a helping of oatmeal. I walked away appalled at the out-front, in-your-face racism and cruelty of the guards. I assumed that the "Bushies" in Washington, in the White House and in the Justice Department would not be concerned about the behavior in Morgantown, even if told of it. They especially would not care if it came from my "criminal mouth" through the form of a complaint letter. Reality told me that it would get me the next open spot at the "red roof" inn.

After getting my breakfast the first morning, an inmate approached me and said, "Mr. Blackwell would like to see you." I felt like this guy was the maître d' or was a Congressional scheduler trying to arrange a meeting between "Mr. Blackwell" and me. It turned out that the Mr. Blackwell he was talking about was Roger Blackwell, Ph.D., and I knew who he was—a respected professor of economics from my alma mater, Ohio State University. He was an accomplished author, health care expert, business owner, entrepreneur and inmate. He had a stock issue with Max & Erma's (a casual dining restaurant chain) and some small inside trading deal that turned into some large mountain from a molehill. An inside source had told me, and this was a credible one, that Roger had pissed off the feds and a few high-placed people and got the kitchen sink thrown at him. He is a smart, likeable man who gave back tremendously to others in prison.

At his table was Reuben, a former successful "boy wonder" stockbroker. Reuben and I became friends. He is a brilliant man with a good family and a wonderful wife. He is a solid Christian and he gave me priceless advice, great spiritual words, and strength to make it through Morgantown Federal Correctional Institution. Reuben spent his time reading, working around the books, and framing his personal activities in a remarkable way to mimic life outside of prison. He scheduled weekends off from daily chores, met with people to give advice after they scheduled time with him, and translated works in various languages.

Dr. Blackwell gave back to many inmates by providing classes for their GED tests in order for them to achieve a high school diploma. *(Today, both he and Ruben are successful men on the outside.)*

Richard Hatch, the first *Survivor* winner (television series), was also at the table. He had won one million dollars, but refused to pay the taxes on it based on his allegations that CBS was supposed to pay them. He was convicted in a federal court in Maine and sentenced to Morgantown. He had "celebrity" status of a sort at Morgantown and was endlessly talking about his appeals and how he was "about to leave at any time." I think it was a "shtick" he did to keep his sanity. Another man at the table was a lawyer from New York.

Sitting down at that table turned out to be so much more than breakfast—it was an epiphany for me. I walked into the Mainline that morning thinking, *How do I get a career when I get out? How do I get money back? How will I ever again earn what I did? How will I pay bills? How will I buy another house? How can I take care of my family?* I then thought, *I have to find the solution; I need to rack my brain, get it done, solve it now. I cannot live in poverty with no purpose, no ability to pick up the pieces.* I told myself, *Think, plan, project, solve—come on Bob, get the solution now!*

I sat at that table bewildered and hungry—not only for food, but also for some brainpower that deep within the recesses of my twisted, tormented mind hungered for the light of day—for the answer.

After we began to talk, Roger told me that maybe there was room at the Education section in the prison where he was working. (It didn't pan out because the corrections officer he had to work for just did not seem interested. She was, and I'm being generous here, a complete asshole flake. When I approached her via Roger Blackwell, she acted as if I were going to have to pass the law bar to work for her. She was very unprofessional about what the program involved, almost making light of it. She left it "up in the air" about my being able to help there.)

I asked Roger about it later and he said, "That's the way the corrections officers are, they really do not care a lot." He indicated that she was actually one of the better ones. He left to start his day and I decided I wanted nothing to do with her, so I began the approach toward another job. However, I appreciated Roger's offer to help.

As the conversation continued at the Mainline table, the lawyer from New York who was at Roger's table started talking about the home that he had lost, the Vail vacation home that was history, the loss of his attorney's license, the mounting bills. He just went on in a blistering, painful, hopeless, series of statements that really were intended to beg the answer from someone as to how he was going to re-create what was.

Someone at the table said, "You start again."

The lawyer, in a frustrated, high-pitched tone said, "Please. I am forty-nine years old. How do I start again? Where in the hell am I even going to live after I get out? I don't have a house."

Without analyzing, thinking, pondering, or considering that those had been my identical thoughts that very morning, I said, "Hell, you start again. You're forty-nine; I'm fifty-three. When we get out, we get an apartment. What we really need to do is open up our eyes and realize that this is about today, one day at a time, staying in the moment, making the best of today."

My mouth seemed to belong to another body; it must not have come from me. Someone else planted that thought in me and just used me as a *wisdom host*. I answered my own perplexing situation by hearing someone else say what I was thinking. I was able to give him an answer that I could not give myself.

That was a major turning point for me. Naturally, I thought daily of my family, my friends, the outside world, but from that breakfast on that first day I did not remain on a path of bemoaning my problems; I did not whine endlessly about where I was. Wasting brain cells by lamenting the internal conditions there in Morgantown did not become my routine. That morning I freed myself to be all I could be in prison, taking opportunity from despair.

I tweaked the lesson I had just earned somewhat when I walked outside after breakfast and a prisoner pointed at me and said, "You bastard, you supported the Meth Bill about stealing Sudafed—you put me in here!" My thought was, *To hell with next year . . . I need to survive today!*

I was assigned a top bunk, although when you are over fifty you are supposed to have a bottom bunk. The bunks did not have a ladder to get up to the top bunk, so one had to do some minor acrobatic maneuvers to get there. My first and second nights were rough. Due to my weight gain, I was not in the best condition to get up to the top. A cellie had to help me. Not only was it embarrassing and degrading, I just could not expect someone to have to do that for me.

The next morning I went to the recreation center to see if I could talk to Mr. Larry Workman, a corrections officer, about securing a job there per my cellie Hank's advice. There was a clerk in the office area of this section. (The clerk is an inmate who maintains records of those working, and all of the technical details to run that area.) I sought the clerk's advice on how to approach this. He seemed well educated, and was articulate and knowledgeable about the workings of the prison system. He told me that he had been a judge in Fairfield and Licking counties,

Ohio. Licking was the county I last lived in. I then remembered his case; at least what I had read about it.

The Recreation Department appealed to me because it housed the computers that controlled the e-mail system. If I worked in recreation, even though they weren't hooked up to the Internet, I could use them for e-mailing. (If you worked outside of recreation, you could only use the computers after lunch and in the evening.)

I got called to fill out my paperwork, which I did. I submitted it, hoping to be selected. I had not had to apply for a job for years. I just used to *run* for mine. When I say, "apply," it isn't the same as in the outside world. I wrote my name, prisoner number, and the name of the unit I lived in. I then talked to the boss of the section, Larry Workman. He asked me where I was from and then said, "Okay, you're hired."

Amazingly, my quick interview was over, and my new career in recreation was full steam ahead. That evening I started to walk around the main yard, which I called "Times Square." It turned into a nightly, mandatory, hour and a half walk for me. Many nights I walked and contemplated life with my friend Todd Kline, who was also from Ohio.

Eventually, a lot of my fellow inmates asked me questions about jobs, the outside world, politics, and how things worked in general. I used to have them walk with me as we talked so my exercise would not be put aside, and their questions would be answered. I had to do something about my physical health—not just my mental health. Answering my peers' questions helped make me seem not so unique; not so much of a curiosity, and it was a good thing to do. My sharing the experiences and knowledge that was foreign to their world was a way for me to give back. It was, in my mind, a way of atoning for what I had done to my constituency by my actions. I could not help or give back to them anymore, but I could give to another group.

I was asked a wide variety of questions about politics: Who would win the primary, Obama or Hillary Clinton? What was Bush like? Was Alberto Gonzales as big a jerk as he looks on television? Who was the greatest person I met?

Another timely issue was percolating, and eventually the law was changed, on guidelines for *crack* sentencing. The sentences were harsher for crack than for powder cocaine due to the high-profile death of Len Bias years ago. He was a famous, upcoming basketball player who had done cocaine and died. The aftermath was to blame crack and make far stricter sentencing guidelines than for cocaine powder. This law did not make sense and I spent a lot of hours talking about the ramifications of the law, what I heard when I was in Congress, and so forth.

I was also asked about how to start a business, how to get Pell grants, what would be the best healthcare job to pursue, what I thought about the economy, and how could one buy a house? I enjoyed answering the questions and interacting with my fellow inmates. I answered constituent inquiries for over two decades, so I was used to it. I also felt that by sharing my experiences, hopefully if would give my new friends some guidance as they reentered the real world.

I spent weekends, which were horrifically boring, walking for three to five hours around and around the baseball field track. Up there we could walk as fast as we wanted, or even run. We couldn't do that down on "Times Square."

During the first week, when I was applying for a job with recreation, I walked past the gym area and saw about twenty-five guys in the class doing aerobics. The other inmates were making fun of them, calling them "sissies." Later I joined the "sissy" aerobics class. The inmates who were knowledgeable about personal training and exercise (and a lot were, due to prison boredom) provided ample instruction to me on yoga and aerobic workouts. The meditation books in the library and conversations with a couple of spiritual inmates taught me how to meditate. I attended organized yoga and aerobic classes in the gym five days a week. The meditation was easy to do in my bunk when I awoke early and had time before we were allowed to start moving around to get ready. The morning time was the only quiet time of the day. If I woke early enough, it was an extremely peaceful, quiet setting.

I was settling in, and I realized that a lot of the "blue collar" inmates (drug offenders) were better adjusted to prison and psychologically healthier to be around than some of the "white collar" criminals—some of whom, not all, whined a lot about their present situation.

As time went on, prisoners left and prisoners came, like a steady routine. When I got to know a lot of people on the prison compound, and they then left, I called it "leaving the matrix," after the Keanu Reeves movie. One day they are there, the next day their name is called, you look at their bunk area and not one trace of them is left—they left the matrix.

I established regular friends: Reuben; Harry; Mike; Jamie; Jeff and Greg, whom I worked with in the Recreation Department; Charles at the library, and many other inmates.

Then, when a new group came in, I became very good friends with Zamil, a former Afghanistan freedom fighter who lived in the D.C. area, and Kevin Haas, a bright, delightful, humorous guy from Chicago who made prison life bearable, especially on the weekend mornings. Kevin and I would meet every Saturday morning outside our living quarters and have coffee at the bench area in the grass. It was our "country club" morning. In memory of my mess of a Scotland trip, I called it our "tee time." We met weekly, almost without fail. It was a relaxing time when we could be lifted away from Morgantown, talk about the future, our families, thoughts, plans, dreams, what got us there, and what would take us out of there.

I had applied for RDAP (Residential Drug Abuse Program), which was prison rehab. There are only so many slots and it is horrifically competitive. As high profile as I was, I had to be careful due to the prison rumors that I was getting into RDAP because I was a former Congressman.

It's interesting what happens to a person when they adapt to the world they are in. Some may say, "Who cares what other inmates think?" But we live in the *world* where we are currently taking up space. Prison is a world unlike the one on the *outside*; if you don't like your neighbor in that world, you simply don't talk to them. In prison—on the *inside*, the neighbor you don't like may be your cellmate.

It came time for me to interview for RDAP. I was like all others in thinking that if I got into RDAP I could possibly get out of prison nine months early. If approved, I would be released around February of 2008. The catch was, you would serve six more months on the outside in a halfway house, but you could eventually get home confinement in that setting. The important thing is that you are on the outside versus the inside, which is the best way to complete your sentence. (*Although in my case, the halfway house became worse than prison in many ways. More about this in the Halfway House—Halfway Home chapter.*)

However, there was another reason I wanted RDAP, but I shared this with no one, as they would not have believed me. I wanted it as a way to change my behavior, to start new; to get control of my alcoholism, to utilize my mind to see what was wrong—what was making me tick. I saw the program as an intensive way to find my bearings, to remember where I came from, who I could be, and how to change my life pattern. This was a temporary opportunity to receive the tools I would use to make a permanent change. My attorneys, Mark Touhey and Bill Lawler, encouraged me to do it. Mark stressed that this was a great program, and that normally, on the outside, it would cost a fortune.

It was my day for the interview to see if I would qualify for RDAP. Judge Huvelle had recommended it and that was a step, but now I had to get qualified by meeting with Dr. Baker, the head of RDAP. He was different, almost an über-introverted man who at times seemed aloof and distant, but he was very brilliant and ran a good program. I believe that he was interested in the development and change of the individuals that he had in the program. He was head of the internal board that made decisions once you were in the program as to whether you were kicked out if you got into trouble or were not performing well. He had to contend with budget limits and internal crap, just as anyone else in the government does, but he was trained in human behavior and he was effective. I assume that his doctorate was in psychology. Although he was hard to read, he was an interesting person, extremely quiet, and had a very, very dry sense of humor. One day in class, an inmate talked about meth (methamphetamine) and how he had sold it. Dr. Baker smiled a bit and said, "You are the reason I can only buy so much Sudafed at the store."

The inmate laughed, pointed at me, and said, "The Congressman is the reason—he voted for that law." Everyone cracked up, laughing.

My interview, of course, did not go as per usual. My friends thought it was due to the "system" trying to screw me; I think it was more a matter of Dr. Baker's protecting himself from criticism if I got in—or if I did not. There were times when the "system" (the long arm of Gonzales/Fisher) was reaching out to me from D.C., and this was one of those times. No matter how I adapted, no matter how I blended in, no matter how I remained low key and humble, I simply could not escape politics or who I was when it came to the prison management.

I was approached on many occasions by inmates who bitched about Bush or asked political questions about the elections, or corruption. There were also disputes with corrections officers or issues with the food, the Visitors Room etc. when inmates said to me, "You have connections, do something about this."

I responded, "Hey, my connections are shot. I am just like you in here, doing my time." A couple of times when I was berated by some inmates when something bad happened, like a man dropping dead and not being treated fast enough, or an older prisoner not having adequate treatment, some, not many, became verbally abusive. In those cases I had to respond, "You do you, I will do me," which is prison talk for mind your own business, take care of yourself, leave me alone. Sometimes other inmates would step in to defend me.

Nevertheless, they had a point; I had been a lawmaker and was a part of not looking into this system as it existed. I still think the prisons are not properly monitored. It is a matter of the unions getting more staff versus the needs of the inmates. Therefore, the political system is more responsive to the guards. Be it right or wrong, standing up for prisoners does not get them much in the way of public kudos (or votes).

The RDAP interviews are standard. They take about ten minutes, max. The drug and/or alcohol history is sitting in front of the board from the PSI (Presentence Investigation Report), which is what my lawyer Bill Lawler had begged me to focus on, and now I knew why—the inmate's story has to match the information given on the PSI.

A prisoner is not allowed to have his PSI with him for security reasons, as it contains his personal history. If, for example, he were a pedophile or a "snitch" for the government and that information leaked out, it could cause him serious harm.

I had forgotten exactly what I had said in my PSI about alcohol abuse. What else did I forget?

I was so nervous about this that I devised an elaborate plan with one of my visitors to read my PSI and then write me a letter about "a friend" of mine who had gotten into trouble with alcohol and a bit of drugs. Of course, these were the details from my own PSI. I was paranoid about the RDAP interview; make no bones about that. *(I discovered later that I was right to be paranoid about the possibility of Gonzales/Fisher interference. More on this further along in this chapter.)*

I sat outside Dr. Baker's office and watched through the glass window at the six or so inmates before me as they went in to pitch their cause. I wore a watch in prison— something I never did before on the outside. *(When I saw Matt Parker after I was released, the first thing he said was, "You have a watch!")* I used the watch to time the prisoner's average length of an interview. It was about thirteen minutes.

My turn came but before I went in, a man I had never before seen on the compound went into Baker's office. They chatted for what seemed like a lifetime, and then I was called in. The man was introduced as the head of RDAP for the regional prison system. He just "happened" to be in the area during the interview and wanted to sit in. Strange, he did not want to "sit in" with the rest of the inmates. I had an excruciating, one-hour interview. Questions were asked by both men about anything and everything—alcohol, life, family, growing up—except what I thought about Alberto Gonzales and Alice Fisher's waterboarding people. Thank the Lord, I was not asked about that one.

At the end, Dr. Baker asked a question that, as we say in prison, got me off "square" (balance). He said, "Why have you never had a DUI?"

I tapped into my humor reserve, as I had many times before and since, and replied, "I had a driver most times, partially paid by you as a taxpayer. Thanks."

He smiled ever so slightly and said, "Anything else that you can provide to document your addiction?"

Anything else? Anything else? What the hell did he want—for me to pull out a joint and a bottle of booze, which, by the way, were available in prison for the right price? The underground cigarette market was one tuna packet per cigarette (tuna was about a dollar a packet). The weightlifters wanted tuna for the protein, so tuna became money and people traded tuna for other items they wanted. It was one big barter system. I was told that alcohol was about 200 dollars a bottle. A bag of "goodies" (cell phone, mp3 player, weightlifting powder), could run up to 5,000 dollars. At that level, it went beyond tuna packets. Money had to be exchanged on the outside from an inmate's family. Cigarettes were routine; the big goody bags were not. I would estimate that about 20 percent of the inmate population smoked.

However, I kept my composure and said, "Sure I can provide more—just Google my name." The interview ended and I left feeling very unsure whether I was going to make it into RDAP.

I got the notice in about a month that I was in! Kevin Haas, Zamil, and I moved into the RDAP unit that same day. Everyone in RDAP lives in the same unit so that all who are in the alcohol/drug program, about 280 people, are under one roof.

There are three classes; phases 1, 2, and 3. Complete phase three, you graduate and are out the door for a six-month stay in a halfway house. It is an extremely aggressive program (inmates in the program were encouraged to be verbally combative with one another) that goes daily for three hours, but we lived it 24/7, under a strict set of rules and zero tolerance. Other inmates cut through the rec center to go to Mainline to eat, but we could not. If someone did, he had to *bring himself up* (admit he had done this) to the "group," which is his class of thirty guys on one side of the room—a foot in between—and thirty more on the other side of the room. All are packed into one room, sardine-style, for three hours daily. If an RDAP inmate breaks some rule but doesn't bring himself up to the group and another RDAP inmate has seen him do it, he has to bring the offender up to the group. If he doesn't and both are caught for not reporting, they are both in trouble and can be thrown out of the program, sent back to their old rooms, and must serve all their time.

We had books, journals of sorts, that were filled with questions about what substances did to families—the dangers, the impact on society; questions about behaviors and improper attitudes. The series of six or more books were good self-help and 12 Step Program–type materials. I was brought up once for not reporting on myself by another inmate who was heard to say, "I'll get the Congressman." I had left my cup of coffee in the microwave when we were all called back over the P.A. system to our sleeping areas due to a "bed check" for some unknown reason. Whenever we were "called back," we had to drop whatever we were doing and head back to our area immediately. The accusing inmate argued that I thought I was "privileged" and "entitled" to leave my cup there to hold my place in the long microwave lines. The other inmates defended me, and Ms. Sheila Land, the counselor/corrections officer who ran my group, thought I had just made a mistake. As a punishment, I got "learning experiences," which amounts to writing a paper or doing a task to teach me the harm of my ways and to make up for my wrong.

The paper had to focus on what I did wrong and what I should have done in the situation. I also had to point out what character flaw I exhibited. In this case, I was feeling entitled to leave my cup there and was exerting control. As I wrote, I at first thought it was bullshit and making a big deal out of nothing. However, it began to sink in that little things lead to big things. Entitlement over a cup of coffee could lead to thinking I was entitled to do as I pleased in other situations. I thought back to Jack Abramoff and his restaurant. *Wasn't I entitled to a drink? It wasn't a big deal, just a little infraction.* I then realized that this was not bullshit; it is what led me to problems years ago. Little things became big things: I felt I was entitled, that I was in control—which led to behavior problems that crashed my career. The lesson was this: Do the right thing when no one is looking. (*It applied to my life in prison, it applied to my past, and it applies now.*)

The way the program was set up and administered was fairly good and sound. Unfortunately, not all counselors were good ones like Mr. Sowden. There was also Sheila Land (the "beauty queen," as we called

her), and if you were really unlucky, the totally—and I mean totally—
volatile Mr. Livengood.

As I said, Sheila Land was also a corrections officer and a "towny,"
as they called those who were from Morgantown. She wore *painted on*
tight jeans and tops. Frankly, she was easy on the eyes and she knew it.
The prisoners knew that she knew it, and appreciated the daily show.

She was a half-hearted counselor who really enjoyed having control.
That was evident. She and I sparred. One part of the RDAP program
involved the honesty of the participants in bringing up matters that had
upset us. If the CO/counselor (in this case, Sheila Land) knew of an incident that had surely bothered me but I didn't bring it up, she could say
that I was not following the program and therefore I could not be released
early. (For a graphic portrayal of the RDAP program, James Laski's book,
My Fall from Grace: City Hall to Prison Walls is a good source.)

On one particular morning when I had seen Will Heaton's face in the
newspaper, smiling from a car window as he left court, yeah—it bothered me! The media played up his defense as the *honest* guy who wore
a wire. Since the newspapers went all over the prison, I knew Sheila
would have seen it, and I knew that I had to bring it up. Her response
when I did was, "Poor, poor, pity Bob." That became her mantra. When
the inmates wanted to tease me they would say, "Poor, poor, pity Bob."
I especially got a kick out of it when my friend Todd Kline would say it
with a robust smile.

Sheila often said to me in front of the group, "You ran the House but
you could not run your own house." She said it again the day we
received our certificates (we called it a diploma) guaranteeing that we
are leaving. An inmate can say anything he wants that day and it's safe.
I was speaking to the group, telling them how much I appreciated them
and the program and how I would not miss the prison but would miss
them, when Sheila began to interrupt. I looked at her and said, "Will the
gentle lady from Morgantown yield?" (This was a play on how one
Member addresses another Member on the floor to interrupt and ask a
question.) She looked at me, and I said, "This is my time. Please be
quiet." The class erupted in laughter, and even she got a kick out of it.

Even with Sheila's games and power trip, she did do some good
things for me and for some of the men in the program. If I had one criticism, it would be the need for closer supervision over the supervisors
for the benefit of all. There can be (and were) some abusive situations
when corrections officers are in control of a person's life.

You are at their mercy. If you contact a Congressman, your life becomes hell. They can change your job or put you on the worst clean-up crews. If you make a tiny mistake, you could end up in the SHU. If they wanted to, you could be determined as aggressive or a behavior problem and could be shipped out of state to a worse facility. They had many options to make life miserable. We all knew this is how it had to be. They had total control over every aspect of our lives, including making us strip as many times as *deemed necessary* to see if we were hiding contraband. It was irrelevant if we were right or wrong; we were inmates and that was the reality.

An interesting incident took place one day that involved a corrections officer, me, and a definite change in protocol—at least temporarily. On Fridays, Saturdays, and Sundays, families could make visits. Each prisoner is limited to six visits a month, so our visitors' list could not be long. This isn't like what you see on TV and in the movies where the prisoner is behind a screen. It is a huge room with plastic chairs in it, and nothing else. We could sit and talk with our visitor, hug, or appropriately kiss someone hello and goodbye, but that was the extent of it. The first time my mother and dad came, we were all sitting together when suddenly "Red Face," as we called Officer Hopkins, was standing just to my right and to Mom and Dad's left, looking straight ahead. He looked like a scene out of the movie *Full Metal Jacket* where the drill instructor reads the recruits the riot act. Red Face then yelled, "Ney, come with me." My mother and father were startled. I stood up and followed him. As I got to the door, I saw a former Member of Congress smiling at me. Red Face stood between us as if he were the bouncer for a bar.

The former Member was oblivious to what the procedure was and said, "I was just driving through and wanted to say hello."

I said, "Sorry, I didn't know you were coming. I have to put you on a visitors' list or you can't get in."

He said, "Okay, do that. I would love to come see you." He then shook my hand and left.

Red Face then looked straight ahead, and in front of another CO (corrections officer) he said, "Next time, put him on your visitors' list."

I replied, "Yes, I didn't know he was coming."

I don't know if he believed me or not, but I had to chuckle later because no one—and I mean no one—gets through the first door, let alone inside the second one to say hello to an inmate who doesn't have them on a visitors' list. The former Member had to have played the "former Member ID" game and the guard didn't know what to do, except get angrier and more red-faced.

Later, a young inmate tearfully confided in me that this same CO (Hopkins) had made him bend over completely naked for at least five minutes, looking at his rectum. He did this to several others, one man for over twelve minutes for no reason. My friend was helpless to report it or life would come down on him. Word finally got around about this incident and others. The guard was moved to another section, I believe out of fear of too many incidents.

The lieutenants supervise other corrections officers. One of them, Lt. Shaw, was exceptionally nasty. He tormented, chided, and demoralized prisoners with no one to temper his constant brutality. Shaw would come to the Visitors' Room and stare at the visitors, further enabling Hopkins in his intimidation campaign. Visiting with loved ones is extremely important in the process of rehabilitating a prisoner. The fact that families were allowed to be *tortured* and intimidated during this time was inexcusable.

Most of the guards could get away with intimidation. I completely understand that prisoners have committed crimes, but that is not a reason to treat people like cattle. Punishment is part of the system, but rehabilitation to prevent them from returning to be a taxpayer burden is also a goal. The greater part of the focus is on discipline. There were plenty of good corrections officers, but many others used intimidation at will for correction purposes because they were allowed to.

One morning I went to do my laundry, mistakenly thinking that we were allowed to walk around. (In the mornings when the televisions were turned on for the news, the prisoners were allowed to proceed to the showers, to the laundry room, or to warm up their coffee.) I saw that the televisions were on, but did not realize that the guards had forgotten to turn them off the night before. I went out the door that was right outside our area and over to the laundry room to get a head start on my laundry. Then to my horror and shock, I saw the two morning patrol officers who made the beat inside where we slept. The routine was for them to make their rounds, take a count of prisoners, and then turn the televisions on as a signal for us to be free to go about our business. As soon as I saw them I realized there was a mistake of some kind.

They said, "What are you doing?"

I answered, "I thought you had made your rounds and I could do my laundry. I am really sorry." One of the officers replied, "You sure fucking are. You are one sorry son of a bitch."

The other guard, the nicer one, asked, "What is your name and number?"

Before I could respond the first guard said, "I know who the mother fucking Congressman is. You sure are a big deal now . . . a sorry deal for sure." He then said, "You have a shot," and walked away.

A "shot" is an offense you are written up for, and it can put you in the SHU—in solitary confinement. For me, if I had to stay in solitary for over ten days, I would be knocked out of rehab and not receive credit for the program. I spoke with another officer about this and he went to bat for me.

This may seem trite, but when you are in there struggling to do the right thing and to change your life, this type of authority can cause a person to have mental issues. Far worse was done to others, as Ricky Campbell will describe later in this book.

Some inmates had to cut timber on federal land and then load it onto trucks that the corrections officers took, illegally, to their homes for their own use. One of my sponsors in the 12 Step Program, a prisoner from South Carolina, told me that an officer who had him and other prisoners cut wood all day informed him in no uncertain terms that if he bitched or told anyone about it, he would have him shipped out to a tougher facility.

There were also drugs and alcohol in the prison, and I believe that there had to be someone in authority on the inside who made bringing the contraband in possible.

The apple rots at the top, and the Bush White House didn't care about human rights—all they knew was that the prison system was under Alberto Gonzalez, who couldn't have cared less about prisoners. He manipulated and shredded the constitution when it came to torture, so why should he care about, as one guard called us, the "dirty asses" in prison.

★ ★ ★

The excitement in RDAP grew. There were concrete steps we took after six months in the program, and one of these was to list where we were going to work, if we knew, when we got to the outside. Ellen had visited me in prison. We talked about where I was going to work and what

I was going to do. She wanted me to work for her and with her at Talk Radio News Service; first out of Ohio and, as time progressed and the government allowed, travel occasionally to D.C. and New York to do some work there.

Before I went into prison, a representative of Allen Stanford's office called me. I had talked with Allen after I got into trouble. It wasn't like an Abramoff situation, with staff ties and requests made to each other for help. Allen was very much on the up and up with me. His staffer said, "Allen thinks this is all overblown. He knows you, knows you are a decent person, and when you get out you will have a job." These were reassuring words when I went in, but you never know how time will change things and how the offer will work out.

When Ellen offered me work, I declined and told her about Allen's offer. She said, "You don't want to work for the corporate world. Radio would be right up your alley. I can't pay you what he can, but radio is better for you. It will help get you back out there where you are not such a mystery. Come to Talk Radio News."

I thought to myself, *I am sitting here with an offer on the table for some decent money, tucked away out of sight in the business world versus the exposure I am so tired of if I take the Talk Radio job.*

Then I remembered something from September of 2001. I never liked to stay in D.C. on the weekends—I wanted to be at home in Ohio. Even if I could go home for one day, it was worth it—and I really didn't like having to be in D.C. for two or more weekends in a row, but sometimes it couldn't be helped. Ellen's 50th birthday was on August 28, 2001. She was to have a party in D.C., but postponed it to September 8. I had to be in D.C. the weekend of August 31 for a wedding. I had plans to be in New York on September 11, 2001 to open NASDAQ at 7:30 a.m., then go up to the restaurant at the top of the World Trade Center for a little reception, come down to do a noon fundraiser and then close the Stock Exchange. I wouldn't be able to go home between Ellen's party and the trip to New York. Because I was given two options for that trip, September 4 or September 11, and because I could go to Ellen's birthday party and still be home for one day, September 9, I changed my plans and went to New York on September 4 instead. I missed the horror of 9/11 because Ellen changed the date of her birthday party.

I thought about my longstanding, wonderful friendship with Ellen and her persuasive "will not take no for an answer" attitude. (*I met Ellen in 1995 through Howard Monroe's radio show, WVLY-Wheeling, West Vir-*

ginia. I was on his show and Ellen happened to call in. Howard put the two of us on the air together. She joked with me that she didn't like Republicans, but that I was cute. Howard said we should meet, Ellen came to my office, and that was the beginning of our friendship.) There was also the lure of being *quasi-back* publicly and the fact that had I listened to Ellen on several different issues both personally and professionally I would not be in such trouble. I accepted her gracious offer.

The next day I filed my job intent, as I had passed the six-month mark in RDAP. I received a loudspeaker page: "Ney to RDAP office." I was paged by the corrections officer who handles our halfway house placements. He had been there for years and was very no-nonsense, short-tempered and stern.

When I walked into his office he barked, "Who the fuck are you talking to and why the fuck is Charles Mosher putting his fucking nose in my fucking business? You think you can pull Congressional shit here? You think you have some power, that you are some big, swinging dick here?"

I was stunned. I had placed no calls to anyone. I had no knowledge of who Charles Mosher was, did not want to know who he was, nor did I care who he was—except this "Charles Mosher" was causing me to have a very unnerving day. Three months from my departure and this could get me written up in RDAP and who knew what else. I responded, "Sir, I assure you, I do not know him, I did not call him, I have nothing to do with this."

He asked, "Who is Ellen Ratner?"

I said, "My friend, and she runs Talk Radio News Service."

He said, "Does she know Charles Mosher?"

I answered, "I have no idea. Who is Charles Mosher?"

The corrections officer replied, "Some federal probation officer *cocksucker* from Columbus who is *not* telling me my fucking job! I have been here for years and I am not putting up with this shit. Do you understand?"

After hearing this I said, "Sir, I swear to God, Ellen has nothing to do with this. She would not know him; I don't know him. We had nothing to do with this."

He lightened up and said, "I will deal with this asshole once I call his boss." He stressed that he never receives calls from a federal parole officer wanting these details. The halfway house handles this information and the federal parole office takes over when someone leaves the halfway house. He then told me, "Right now, you just list a job. You don't have to do that to get out of here, but it's okay. Whatever is going down here with his calls to me and all these questions is unusual. Okay, you can leave. I'll take care of this."

Charles Mosher took unusual steps concerning my probation long before he should have. A federal probation officer is more directly under the attorney general than prison corrections officers are.

The job saga continued when I was summoned the next day to the office of the top dog over our unit and a "thorn in the side" of many of the other corrections officers who didn't like him. He was known as an African American who did not care for white prisoners at all, but he didn't like black prisoners either, so it was equal opportunity hatred. This wasn't along the lines of "Who is Charles Mosher" or "Why did you call him," but rather along the lines of "Someone from Justice called me."

When I walked into his office he said, "Who is Ellen Ratner, how do you know her, what are you going to do for Talk Radio, and how much is she paying you?"

I said, "Ellen is a friend of mine, I don't know my exact duties, and I didn't discuss pay at all."

He said, "Come now, Congressman, come now, $150,000 dollars I assume?"

I was flabbergasted and said, "I am broke, I had a long-term career that no longer exists, I just want to work—I don't care what she pays me." I then spoke politely and asked, "What is going on here?"

He said, "We here [at the prison], the feds in Columbus, and in partic-ular, the United States Attorney General's office, need to make sure that you are doing nothing to disgrace the Attorney General or his associate and that you are not being paid an unusual amount of money for your services." He concluded by saying, "Get me a description of your job and how much you will be paid. I assume D.C. will check out your employer."

I was so pissed off, but needed to control my temper since I was stand-ing in front of a guy with an ego so big that he probably looked in the mirror daily and said, "You are one hot stud." I felt like I was in the middle of an insane asylum and the inmates were not the crazy ones.

As I went back to my room, I carefully—very carefully—thought about his words while they were still fresh. They told me quite a lot, and maybe he did it intentionally to send me a message of "We are watch-ing you, your behavior, and your friend Ellen." The important word he used was "we." He had said, "*We here . . . and in particular the United States Attorney General's office . . . need to make sure that you are doing noth-ing to disgrace the Attorney General or his associate [Alice Fisher] and that you are not being paid an unusual amount of money for your services."* He had concluded with, *"I assume D.C. will check out your employer."* Clearly, Alberto and Alice did not like the new involvement of Ellen Ratner— her media prominence, her Congressional connections, her philosophical bent. They were shooting a message across the bow.

(*I have since spoken with a reliable, friendly, former federal employee who worked for the Justice Department during the Bush Administration and he told me that all of this back and forth business among Charles Mosher, the Justice Department, and the prison system was unusual at that stage of the game.*)

The entire issue dropped when I called Ellen on the phone from prison. She indicated a salary, modest, but more than I expected, and duties of simply being an analyst for her. Ellen's voice on the phone had a sound of questioning in it like "What is this all about?" But we were being taped, so caution was imperative. Ellen is extremely perceptive, almost a sixth sense, so I knew without telling her that she would pick up that some monkey business was underway.

The last three weeks of my incarceration, things started to unravel. One night as I was walking with my friend Todd Kline around "Times Square," one of the top guys at the prison, (I will refer to him as "my Management friend"), motioned for Todd and me to come toward him. As we walked closer, he said abruptly to Todd, "Not you, just Mr. Ney." Todd left and I followed him into the J building, as it is called, which houses meeting areas and corrections offices.

(*I had met my Management friend on my fourth day at the prison when he stopped me one day and said, "Hello. You are Congressman Ney. I remember you from Congressional days when I was with the corrections officer union. I was from Texas. You got screwed. You took the fall for DeLay and the Bush Administration. Please, if you have any problems, let me know." That did brighten my first week there, I must say.*)

When I went into his office, I felt relaxed. Sometimes he would stop me to ask my opinion on the Democrat primary, who would win the election, politics in general. This time he had a serious look on his face, not angry, just serious.

He said, "Congressman, this could cost me my career, my job, but I have to be honest with you. I overheard a conversation with D.C. in the warden's office. I don't know what all is going on, but D.C. is trying to keep you in here until after the elections. They are going to try and stop you from leaving. You must get an unrecorded call to your attorneys soon or they are going to hold you in here."

He said he wished he could help further, but that was the best he could do; he wanted to warn me.

I said, "Thank you, and God bless you."

I went back to my room in disbelief about what was coming down from Alberto Gonzales and Alice Fisher, and I assumed John McCain had to have his fingers in this somehow, or at least those of his campaign people. Maybe they were afraid that after all the McCain statements of "I put Jack Abramoff and Bob Ney away"; after all of John's attempts at projecting the image of *Clean John*—not the *Dirty John* that took all the Keating trips; not the *Lobby-Money-Sucking John*—I would be out of prison and free to share my theories and the stories that existed.

I was not sure what was happening. Was my Management friend wrong? Why would he lie? Was I going to be set up in here? Beaten? Framed? I went into a state of paranoia. I thought of things that could happen to me. I truly feared for my life—the orders were coming from D.C. to Morgantown.

Soon, my worst fears were confirmed.

THE MATRIX

I shared my fears with Todd Kline and my cellmate in the Rehab dorm, Will. Will was one level ahead of me in the program and helped me immensely. Both of them could keep a confidence, and that was unusual in prison. Todd was in the RDAP program with me and would be exiting with me. Will was from New York City. His background was Dominican and he was the best cellie an inmate could have. He was orderly, polite, clean, knew his way around, was street smart, had a beautiful son in New York, and had been "down" (what we called serving time for a pretty damn long sentence), at least in my thinking. Will watched after me, advised me, and helped me look at things in a logical way. *(Today he is back in New York City, doing well, and enjoying life.)*

I also spent a lot of time toward the end with Chuck, a man from Richmond, Virginia. Chuck had an extremely long sentence. Anyone else would have been mentally affected by the length of time he served. His child grew up in Virginia while Chuck was in prison. I was fortunate enough to meet his son and wife on visiting day. They had all adjusted so well—it was an amazing thing to witness. Chuck was, and remains to be, an inspiration to me of the spirit within to endure hardships. *(He is now reunited with his family in Richmond, Virginia, and is involved with his community.)*

With Todd, Will, and Chuck, I was able to vent my thoughts, hopes, and doubts. It made me feel that in my time left, I was taking my progress to one more level of fine-tuning my changes.

I was unsettled by all that I had heard, but decided that maybe it was all hype. It did sound unbelievable. Maybe the Charles Mosher call was a coincidence. Maybe the corrections officers were just putting me on. I wasn't sure, but I decided to chill and stay in the moment, day by day.

Next came the mandatory DNA tests and final preparations for those "close to the door." We were abuzz with anticipation.

Within a few days the halfway house approvals came for the sixty of us. One by one, they called the numbers to go over the details. Everyone had the same release date, February 1, 2008. The first ten or so of my group were called, then the following day, twenty or more. Everyone was showing their confirmations to one another and getting their bus tickets or other transportation arranged. A day or so passed and there were fifty-nine approvals. Only one person didn't get one—I was that person. There was no notification and no explanation was given. It simply did not happen. When I inquired, I was told that there was no room at the halfway house *and* some things were not yet approved. No other answer would be given, no other inquiry by me accepted. It was what it was. My Management friend's words to me weeks earlier came home to roost.

The following night, after I had calmed down about not being able to leave, I went to supper at the Mainline. By this time I was down about sixty-two pounds and having my clothes altered bi-weekly. One of the really nasty lieutenants looked at me and said, "Ney, is that you? Doesn't look like you. Is that you?"

I said, "Yes, lost some weight."

He said, "Good for you, but you aren't getting out of here on time." He laughed and moved on as he said, "I'm watching you."

I panicked and sank to a new low. I was hopelessly at a loss as to what to do. Then I summoned some strength. I prayed, thought, meditated, and decided that this was it. I was tired of Bush, Gonzales, Fisher, McCain, Abramoff, staffers, the press, and just about everyone and everything that was not right in my life. I needed to regain my composure, focus, and rely on the "sweet messenger of hope" to do something about this before it escalated to the point where it was too late.

I needed an unmonitored phone call and needed one now; and if I got it, I had a plan I needed to have carried out. I asked for a call to my lawyer. The CO who handled that was not in that day. I waited daily, doubting I would get it, but still trying. The CO finally got back to me after I put in an official request to see her. My time was to be at three o'clock in the afternoon.

I had already had a monitored call (one where the CO stayed in the room) during my final two months at Morgantown when Kendall Day, one of the Bush lawyers for the Justice Department that prosecuted me, got the bright idea to take me out of prison for the purpose of a deposition or grand jury for someone else's case. It would have been a convenient way to ruin my chances to leave prison early, and potentially get the shit kicked out of me when I returned. It would have been perceived by some that I left to "snitch," even though I would not have cooperated. My lawyers and some House threats of "Speech and Debate" stopped federal prosecutor Kendall Day's sabotage effort. The Speech and Debate clause is in the U.S. Constitution and states:

Members of both Houses of Congress . . . shall in all Cases, except treason, felony and breach of the peace, be privileged from arrest during their attendance at the Session of their Respective Houses, and in going to and from the same; and for any Speech or Debate in either House, they SHALL NOT BE QUESTIONED IN ANY OTHER PLACE [caps mine].

The intended purpose is to prevent a president or other officials of the executive branch from having members arrested on a pretext to prevent them from voting a certain way or otherwise taking actions with which the president might disagree.

I think that's when they went to Plan B—just say no—no halfway house, no bed space, and eventually a no-go from RDAP.

When I showed up for my three o'clock appointment, I got in a long line. It was a Friday and my sister, Emmy Lou, and my brother-in-law, Rick, were on their way to see me. Then the female CO came down the hallway in an obvious panic. Soon an inmate was brought in, the door closed and we could see her on the phone, then him on the phone, then her on the phone; it was like a tug of war. She then came out into the hallway and said, "I have an emergency. All of you [your appointments] are cancelled."

My spirits were low. I got dressed for my visit and went up to the

Visitors' Room. I had a nice visit with my sister and Rick. As I looked to my left, I saw the subject of the emergency—the inmate that had been in the CO's office earlier. He was in his prison sweat pants, which, as part of the dress code, are not allowed in the Visitors' Room. He had a green garbage bag full of something with him. After Emmy Lou and Rick left, I had an opportunity to speak to him.

I asked, "What's going on?"

He said, "Hell if I know. She called me in, Washington was demanding that they discharge me right now, and she was going crazy. A few more people called, some new people came on the line, and then she told me to call my family, gather up my stuff, and leave."

(I found out later that my friend Jim Owen [a respected attorney in Columbus, Ohio, who has orchestrated the release of many innocent people from prison] and others exposed Ohio federal agents who fraudulently arrested and placed people before grand juries to send them to prison. They photoshopped their faces into still photos, paid people to lie, and so forth. The hideous crime they committed against these people was not only an embarrassment to the Justice Department, but big trouble for the feds as well.

The prisoner I spoke with that night was one of those who had been set up— I believe he had done four years by that time.)

On the following Monday I started the process for the unmonitored call again. I could not get in to see the CO, as she kept cancelling. There was another CO who handled the calls, but he had been on sick leave for cancer treatment at the time I was trying to get in. Everyone said that he was one of the decent ones and a fair man.

On the day that this CO returned to work after his sick leave, I just happened to have volunteered to do a 12 Step meeting and needed to pick up some materials for it before the office closed. I was passing by this CO's door on my way, and decided that regardless of the punishment, I was going to go into his office and then figure out what I would say.

I knocked, and he said, "Yes?"

I then mustered up every political/mental/reasoning/communication skill I possessed, put on the *calm* look, and did what any good current or former politician would and could do—I flipped the half bullshit /half lie switch and said, "Hello, Mr. CO [Corrections Officer], welcome back. I was told by another CO that if I saw you I could get the unmonitored call that she was to make, but she was detained."

He looked at me and said, "Sit down. Now, what's the number?"

I felt that my heart had stopped beating! This was going to happen, and without dragging my lawyer to Morgantown, without passing along the *he said/she said* misconstrued messages to my lawyers through visitors—this was going to happen.

He dialed Bill Lawler's number, and Bill picked up. Then to make things even better, he walked out of the room. I explained to Bill what was happening. Bill said the halfway house had confirmed there was a bed open. The prison was clearly lying.

I asked Bill to relay all of this information to a very powerful, politically connected attorney in Columbus, Ohio, who had superb state and federal contacts at all levels and was the type of guy who would have no problem playing hardball.

★ ★ ★

Out the door, one by one, my entire class left without me. I was the only one not allowed to leave.

Then, out of nowhere, three days later I was on a one-day mad dash to do everything it normally takes two weeks to do. The process was moving at warp speed. Somebody got to somebody. I know one possible tactic was to call *The New York Times* and start questioning the local Morgantown prison authorities, hoping a leak of improper conduct would emerge.

I received my release date. I was mentally worn out. I just spent the four days reading, resting, walking, and watching television, which is something I rarely did. On the next to the last day, I was the only one in the TV room and I could see Dr. Baker (head of RDAP) just outside. He had been standing around for a few minutes, and I sensed that he wanted to talk.

I went outside and one of the few times since my initial interview, we had a conversation. He asked how I liked the program and I told him specifically what I thought was good about it. He asked if there were any criticisms I could offer to help the program. I said that I thought the counselors, some of them, could use some follow-up training because if you do anything for too long, you need to be refreshed. I also told him that I thought it was such a good program it should be mandatory for everyone, in order to change their behavior.

He then made a "cover your ass" statement, but I am still grateful to Dr. Baker, as I think he was my unknown ace in the hole, and had it not been for his integrity, my exit would not have happened. Dr. Baker said, "Mr. Ney, you did the work, you deserve to leave. You earned your exit. *They* do not agree, but as I told *them*, you need to be treated like all others, and I have crossed my t's and dotted my i's." He turned and left.

(I saw him one other time, when I was covering the CPAC (Conservative Political Action Conference) in D.C. for Talk Radio News and he was walking down the aisle. I was wearing a suit, far from the brown shirt and khakis he was accustomed to seeing me wear, and he looked far from Morgantown. He was there with his wife. I smiled. He smiled. I said, "Hello, Dr. Baker, surprised to see you here [at a conservative conference]."

He said, "Well, I have my views too," and he rounded the corner.)

★ ★ ★

Memories—Morgantown, Dr. Baker, the inmates, the good experiences and the bad—all faded when I heard over the PA system these glorious words: "Ney to the exit room." This was it. Two weeks after my Rehab class, I made the final walk through the compound, turning a page, leaving it all behind me. Now I understood how the other inmates felt as I watched for months when they headed to the exit room.

I walked into the previously forbidden, off-limits area of an administration room where people check in and out. This is an area a prisoner never gets near while serving their time in Morgantown. As I walked up to the window, one of the female corrections officers said with a smile, "I am a big bitch—make sure you put me in your book."

I then walked into another room, carrying a signed slip. In a very low-key, matter-of-fact way, an officer handed me a box. It was not low-key for me. I knew that contained in that box were all the earthly possessions I walked in with—before being stripped to my birthday suit and donning federal prison clothes. Now, my personal touch with the world I had left behind was in a small cardboard box.

I touched the top as though it were a treasure chest. Before opening it, I had a weird moment of hesitation. It wasn't as if it were a Christmas gift I was eager to receive, but rather an unknown, almost scary something that had the potential to make me feel happy or sad. It was nostalgic for me, as though a decade of my life had been lost and the key to finding it was in that box. I opened it and felt the *electricity* as I touched my clothes—one step closer to another world that awaited my return.

I changed into my *own* clothes—my now six-sizes-too-big jeans, my brown loafers, my hoodie—and "unplugged myself from the matrix."

Recollections of Friend and Former Prison Inmate, Ricky Campbell

I made some good friends while I was at Morgantown Federal Correctional Institution, and Ricky Campbell is one of them. I asked him to write down some things he remembered of prison life and send them to me. The following is what he wrote:

I had contracted Hepatitis C through a tattoo I received back in the late 70s before they had standards on how to sterilize the equipment. I had found out about it just before I got arrested and was set up to begin my treatment program in prison. Once I got to see someone, I was told that I had to wait until I had full-blown liver disease before I could receive the interferon treatments. I got the treatment, but my liver was shot because of the wait. My hair fell out by the handfuls and then started to turn white. I have never been that sick in my life.

One guy who was trying to get treatment had to wait so long that he was too sick to take the treatments. He died three months after he got out of the halfway house.

In Randolph unit, there was an older black gentleman from either Detroit or D.C. who had a year and a day left on his sentence. He died before he got out. He was a diabetic who had a staph infection that antibiotics would have healed. They kept taking pieces of his foot until he finally died.

A fellow had a heart attack and it took the staff 10 minutes to get to him. The inmates were trying to save him. Then, after the staff got to him, they didn't call for an ambulance for another 10 minutes, and the ambulance took 18 minutes to get there. They listed him as passing in the ambulance, but he was dead by the time the lieutenant called central to call for an ambulance. I watched this and timed it myself. The policy is that no inmates die on that compound—they all die on the way to the hospital.

I have lost three teeth because the policy is to pull them and not fill them. By the time I got out, the teeth had gotten so bad that I had no recourse but to pull them.

Then there is the issue of the food. All too often it was out of date. I had a friend who worked in the kitchen that brought me a corner of a bag that had had donated fish in it. It said that the expiration date had passed and it was to be used for BAIT ONLY.

The staff was supposed to eat the same food that we had to eat. When I worked on the alarm systems, I was in the Officer Dining Hall on several occasions and had even eaten some of the hamburgers in there. There was a major difference in what they ate and what we ate.

If you compared what the stores charged the prison with what we would pay on the outside, you would see that the prison paid almost double. I still have several of the stores' sheets that list the prices.

The ducks and geese [that were on the prison property] were to be protected and if the population became too large, they were to be captured and removed. The landscaping crew was supposed to go to the nests and crush the eggs. Some people called the Department of Wildlife and they came in and stopped that. But then that jerk CO [corrections officer] they called "Batman" had the landscaping crew going around spraying the eggs with some type of oil-based solution that killed the chicks in the eggs.

Someone should look into who owns UNICOR [Federal Prison Industries]. It was my understanding that UNICOR was a corporation that only federal district attorneys, judges and certain Congressmen could buy stock in. I do know that the wood shop was shut down because a Congressman in Michigan owned several factories that sold his product to the federal government, but when these UNICOR woodshops came on line they took over 3/4 of his business. He filed some type of action that forced them to take out the woodshops, which were teaching the uneducated prisoners a real workable trade, not something like how to make a t-shirt. This information came from the CO that ran the shop when it was shut down.

People would come from all over and not get to visit their family [prisoner] because the visiting room was too small and it wouldn't hold everyone, or they wore flip-flops, or they wore the wrong color of clothes. And I'm not talking about adults, I'm talking about children. Many of them had traveled for 6 or 8 hours to see their fathers and they were turned away.

Barbara Walters' exposé on "Club Fed" is what caused the prison to be turned into the hellhole it became. I had more than one CO tell me that. I have forgotten so much of the horror. A few of the men and women COs treated me like a man, but for the most part I was treated like an animal.

It is still a daily struggle even to come out of the house. I was shocked at how people treat you once they find out that you have been in a federal prison.

Chapter 33

☆ ☆ ☆

HALFWAY HOUSE— HALFWAY HOME

"Nobody can hurt me without my permission."

—MAHATMA GANDHI

Rather than have someone pick me up and undergo press scrutiny, I opted to take a bus from Morgantown Federal Correctional Institution to Columbus, Ohio, where I would reside in Alvis (Halfway) House—my new "home away from home." The stories abounded inside and outside the walls about limos picking me up, a press stampede, and so on. The reality was that only Mr. Robinson, who managed the public relations for the prison, was near the door. He said, "We have had a lot of calls about you leaving. Good luck and I don't want to see you back here, Mr. Ney."

I said with a smile, "Don't worry Mr. Robinson, you won't. If something else happens, I am fleeing to Mexico. Thanks."

He was an interesting man; educated, sharp, and enjoyed discussing some "off the record" facts about politics. The times I occasionally spent in his office were conversationally stimulating. We talked about the presidential campaign. He was African-American and conservative. I remember the time he let me know that Congressman Paul Gilmor had passed away. I had served with Paul in the Ohio Senate and in Congress. Paul and his wife, Karen, were longtime friends.

I saw my supervisor, Mr. Workman, on my way out and thanked him for being so fair. He just nodded and said, "Good luck."

I glanced back, waved, got into the prison car, and looked straight ahead. A trustee inmate drove me to the bus station. We didn't speak. When I was dropped off at the Morgantown bus station, there was no media. I had my ticket in hand and forty-five minutes to kill. I just stood there—waiting, I guess, for someone to say, "Go ahead, it's okay. You can walk around." I had twenty dollars with me that had been sent to my prison money account and was given to me when I left. I walked for about three minutes to a grocery store, bought some beef jerky and got on the payphone. These were my first calls outside the controlled, prison-system phone bank. I called Mom and Dad, Bobby, Kayla, Ellen Ratner, and Payam Zakipour (*American name, Kyle Washington*), my Iranian-American refugee friend who was at my sentencing. There were several more people that I wanted to call, but I was running out of time. I headed back to the bus station and boarded the bus. As it took off, it felt very weird—it was the first time in a year that I was on something that moved this fast. I wanted to say, "Slow down!"

We stopped in Wheeling, West Virginia, for a few minutes. We were at the Robert C. Byrd Intermodal Transportation Center (bus station). I was in "Byrdland" as my friend Dimitri Vassilaros used to say when he hosted his radio show in downtown Wheeling. I could see the Wheeling Intelligencer newspaper office and chuckled as I fantasized about walking over there and saying to Jocelyn King, the political reporter, "What's new?" I actually wouldn't have minded giving a story to the Sunday contributor, Al Molnar, or talking to Mike Myers or John McCabe. I would have told them all about prison, the people I met, the experiences I had, and after that they would have grilled me about Jack Abramoff. I would startle them by announcing my reelection bid!

Of course, this was a fantasy. Even if I had wanted to do it, it is illegal to talk to the press without permission while in the halfway house. In addition, there is a rule that gives the Department of Justice a broad brush with which to send felons back to prison—one can do nothing to disgrace or bring dishonor to the Attorney General while under their control, such as a halfway house or probation. In other words, I could have said nothing derogatory about prison. (Although, how could I, even as disgraced as I was, bring any more dishonor to Alberto Gonzales than he had brought upon himself?)

As I waited for the bus to begin its journey from Wheeling onward, I took a minute to stretch my legs. No one recognized me. I saw not one familiar face on the bus. What a change from a year before when I had "celebrity" status in the Ohio Valley, regardless of where I ventured.

Within ten minutes we were passing St. Clairsville, Ohio, where we raised our kids and had a great life for many years. As I gazed out of the reflecting bus window, my mind flashed back to growing up in Belmont County and the great family and extended family that helped build my future. I saw the familiar area that at one time hummed to the tunes of factories; the bustling little downtowns; glass houses; textile plants . . . all but shut down by now. My brain was filled with pleasant vibes— much different from the environment that was left behind a few hours away at the prison. I thought about how close family and friends were, practically within reach from my bus seat. And I thought about how I was free but not free. Freedom comes in stages, requiring patience for her full flavor. She, "freedom," is like a good wine; it had to age a bit more.

On to Cambridge, Ohio, my old stomping ground, where we stopped to pick up some more passengers, and then, finally, Franklin County. I could see the city of Columbus where I spent some great years at Ohio State University, the Ohio House of Representatives and the Senate. More sweet memories flooded my brain of people, places, events, buildings, landmarks, nights, days—and then the bus moved no more.

I waited until everyone got off the bus, preparing what I would say to the reporters because I knew they would be around somewhere. I mentally planned how I would answer their questions, and definitely planned to cite the "gag order" by the Justice Department. I decided, however that I would be upbeat and simply say, "Life is good." I cautiously peered around the door of the bus, moved out quickly and went behind the bus station. Maybe they were waiting out front. I would not go straight to High Street, but would go down a block then up toward the Hyatt on Capitol Square to get a cab. Unlike New York or D.C., I couldn't summon one on the street and I had no cell phone (not allowed), so I would have to go to the Hyatt where the cabs stood in line. *Dammit,* I thought, *the media knows this.*

I thought about the Hyatt and more sweet memories, but these would all end as soon as the media saw me coming. I walked swiftly to try to beat the yet unseen reporters to the Hyatt, hoping to hop in a taxi before being accosted. I spotted a cab and needed to hurry, as I had a deadline to get to the halfway house and report in. They only allowed a short amount of time over what it would take to get from the prison to Columbus; if I were late, it could mean being sent back to prison for a reporting violation. I jumped in the taxi. When we got to Alvis House, I made the taxi circle the block. No one—no media, no people—I looked around and said to myself, "I am a *nobody*."

It felt good, bad, and something in between. I didn't desire media attention, but after years of the public spotlight, it was in itself a weird, hollow sensation. I was a private citizen, not a public, sought-after figure. I was officially stripped of the Congressional spotlight. I mused that somehow society functioned and continued without me.

When I got to Alvis House, I checked in, was drug and alcohol tested, filled out forms, and got assigned to my room area. I shared a room with three other people. Like most of us, they were trying to do their halfway house time and find a new line of work.

The room was larger than the four-person prison room. It had two bunk beds, two dressers, a window that looked out to the road and, incredibly, a television in the room—not one to be shared by seventy people as was the case in Morgantown Federal Prison. The atmosphere was more relaxed in the halfway house. There were no prison guards, just staff. One difference, however, was that some hard-core individuals, some who had spent two decades in prison for murder, were now mixed into our population at Alvis House, so the dynamic was a bit tougher. I watched my step a lot closer as far as not pissing someone off. Yet most of the people were rather docile, trying to reconnect to life, and soon most would return home.

Alvis House was still confinement and rules, oversight and regulations, limits and boundaries—much like Morgantown, but the big difference was the ability to work; to be able to see society, restaurants, highways, grocery stores, people wearing something other than prison khakis and, of course, to see my family much more often.

One of my roommates, Jacob, was a great guy. We attended 12 Step meetings, watched movies and ordered pizza with the other "residents," as we were called. I had graduated from being an inmate to being a resident. Jacob and a few of the guys made the halfway house bearable, but that was about all that was positive, with the exception of my great, fair, caring counselor, Melanie Hartley. Either I lucked out or they assigned me to her on purpose. As the front desk lady told me when she walked into my room on my second day, "You don't seem that bad or such a problem."

I said, "What?"

"We were all called into a meeting to talk about how to handle you—

to see what you say, visitors, that type of thing. First time I have seen that here." Then she walked out of my room.

Melanie, my counselor, met with me the next day. Ellen Ratner flew in and had Meredith from Talk Radio News with her. Jay, also with Talk Radio News, came in the next day. It was great to see Ellen. She spoke with my counselor and told her how I had been screwed. Melanie politely nodded and the two seemed to hit it off. Melanie assured Ellen that my treatment would be fair.

I will say that Melanie was always fair, but unfortunately, the rest of the place was a psychotic exercise in pure, unadulterated madness. The management refused to let a man who had no teeth go to the dentist to get a set of dentures, but they expected him to go to job interviews; they then denied him bus tickets to do so.

One day I was scheduled to go for my weekend visit, but someone messed up my paperwork. Kayla had started a new job and was waiting on me to come home and babysit my granddaughter, Aaliyah. Although it was approved, they refused to let me leave due to an employee carelessly not signing off on it. They refused to call the supervisor at home by telling me that they did not have her number.

One of the front desk girls had her boyfriend come in at three a.m., and several of us saw them. Some of the staff routinely made fun of the residents and called them dirtbags. The cook came to work heavily intoxicated on several occasions. It was a nut house.

Within a day or so of my arrival, my federal probation officer (PO) showed up unannounced with his supervisor. I asked innocently if they were from Cincinnati. One of them said, "Why would you ask that?" I was simply making small talk.

I explained, "The press reports kept saying I was reporting to Cincinnati." He seemed extremely curious about this—and puzzled.

He continued to quiz me. I quickly learned to say nothing beyond answering questions, and not to elaborate on my answers.

The other *gentleman* was none other than Charles Mosher—the Charles Mosher who caused me heartburn, grief and sleepless nights when I was in Federal Prison, due to his calls to the facility. He looked to me like a *White Shirt Fed* (stiff-necked, perfectly starched shirt, a control freak who is not only "by the book," but nasty about it).

I looked at Mr. Mosher and his supervisor as "Bushies." In my thinking, they were not law enforcement; they were just part of the Gonzales/Fisher Nazi squad.

Mr. Mosher started in. He hammered me, grilled me, and told me that I had to go to AA meetings, which I told him I had scheduled. He asked where and said he may have to go see the meetings. He told me he had no idea how I was allowed to work for Talk Radio News and kept asking me ridiculous, mundane questions about my work. He used a high-pitched tone of voice that started loud and got louder and told me how I would not do this, I would not do that, I would not go on radio, I would not blog on the Internet, and told me what would happen to me if I did.

I was done. I was finally finished with all this shit. This was the lunatic who damn near got me thrown into the hole in prison. With absolutely no provocation, he was talking to me as though I were a serial killer. His tone was threatening, and his body language aggressive. I then looked at him and his supervisor and did what I was warned by other inmates that I should never do—I lashed back at him.

Over the course of my life, there is a word that I did not allow to be said in my home or in our offices, and that was the "N" word. I didn't ever say it myself, but I did that day. I looked them in the eye and said, "I know what you people are about: liberals are filth, gays are f_ _ _s, inmates are dogs, Alberto is God, Bush is the savior, and blacks are n_ _ _ _ _s."

They were stunned. The supervisor just looked at me, and Mr. Mosher was beginning to boil. I continued, "I am on to you 'Bushies.' You have respect for no one, so do what you want, and I will do what I do, and what's fair is fair." (*I didn't pull that line out of my ass. This was a famous line that the late, beloved Speaker Vern Riffe of Ohio, the most powerful Speaker of any Statehouse in America used to say when he wanted to make a point— that you can go ahead and do what you want, and I will decide what is the fair solution at the end.*) First, this did not make sense to them unless they had served with Vern, and second, I have no earthly idea why I said this except that I needed to say something.

Mosher blew his top. He started to yell something—I'm not sure what because I was about to tune him out when his supervisor put his hand out in front of him and said, "Mr. Ney, we just want this to go smoothly. We just want you to work, and you need to be patient and work with us." He was shockingly conciliatory.

I calmed down and said, "Listen, I know that if I worked at Waffle House this would be a lot simpler (I love Waffle House, by the way), but I do not. And yes, I too just want to work." Not another word was said and they got up and left. I went back to my room, shut the door, and thought, *Oh no, I am so screwed.*

My counselor told me later that it was unheard of for them to come in like this. She also said that I was "theirs" (the staff at Alvis House) until I left there, and the probation officers had very little to do with me until then, except for some coordination or visits to work sites and home sites. She said she was going to express to them that this did not seem the usual protocol to follow. That was reassuring to me.

The next day was a whirlwind of pressure and a personally imposed deadline. Mr. Mosher had said during his Alvis House visit, "And when you are off probation, we may need to request permission directly from the Attorney General to allow you on radio." I knew then that they simply did not want me talking, even when I was legally out from under them.

I was under the gun, time-wise, to get my job going. It would be do or die—the Justice Department would pull the plug. I only needed permission from Alvis House, and I knew that once that was obtained, there was very little that the federal probation officers could do except protest it. Ellen Ratner, I knew, would be ready to threaten a federal lawsuit. She doesn't scare easily.

I was given a window of about three hours in Newark to get a car and get an office. Not just any office, but one in which I could be supervised for the entire day. You have to understand the federal system. I have concluded that either they intentionally want you to fail so that you go back into prison and perpetuate all of their jobs, or they are just idiots about how a person can restart his or her life. I believe it's 50 percent idiocy and 50 percent job security.

Let's say that you were an experienced construction worker or a heating and air conditioning repairperson. You will not be able to work in that field. You must be supervised, which could easily be done at construction sites, except that there *has* to be a landline telephone—yes, landline, not a cell phone. Although the PO may know your supervisor, trust him or her, and everything has been approved, it is irrelevant if there is no landline telephone available. This tremendously limits your ability to work.

And here's the rub . . . if you don't get a job within two weeks, you may be sanctioned and not allowed out of the halfway house (which really helps one to find a job!), or sent back to prison.

Trying to find an office setting with supervision is also difficult, unless you know someone. The halfway house was forty-five minutes one-way from my daughter's apartment in Newark, Ohio. Finding a space in Newark was my goal as I could quickly satisfy all my requirements for the halfway house and be home in one month, versus six months. I would only have to drive the daily hour and a half roundtrip for about one month, then I would be in-home confinement in Newark, save all that gas money, which could be applied to my living expenses, and be at "home" with Kayla, Adam, and my granddaughter, Aaliyah. But *Alberto and Alice* had other plans for me.

Kayla picked me up at the halfway house and we started the thirty-minute drive to Newark. The trip there and back would eat up one hour of the three hours I was allotted to get this done. You cannot be one minute late returning to the halfway house.

I was to call when I arrived in Newark—from a landline. If I had to leave and go to another office, I had to call again on a . . . well, you get the picture. Have any of you tried to find a pay phone recently, especially in small towns?

I arrived in Newark and went straight to a realty company because I knew the owner. He said I could use his office as I pleased. I racked my brain on the way down about who to call. The first call I made was to the business office of a former State Senate colleague, former Senator Nancy Chiles Dix. Her secretary said she was out of town and unavailable. I asked the secretary if she could recommend someone for me to call, as I desperately needed to secure an office right away. She said she would call me back. The ten minutes it took for her callback was quick, but to me, under the gun as I was, it seemed like a month. I assumed she had called Nancy, but I wasn't sure. She gave me a number to call. His name was Jim Hoekstra and she said he handled a lot of property. I thanked her, picked up the phone and dialed the number.

Jim answered the phone and I just started talking without thinking to introduce myself formally. I said, "Hello, my name is Bob and I need as soon as possible to secure one office, can be small, just need one to work out of."

He said he knew of one that was open in an insurance business and a lady there had just told him she wanted to find a renter. I said, almost casually for some reason, "Oh yes, I also need supervised, so there has to be someone in that office area that can do that, as I am under federal probation." Great way to impress someone and get his help!

He said, "What is the nature of your crime?"

I said, "Falsification of a document and honest services fraud." (*This was a law against "fraudulent schemes to deprive another of honest services through bribes or kickbacks supplied by a third party." If the Justice Department could have charged me for bribery, they would have, but there was none. Therefore, they used the wide brush of honest services fraud, a law that on June 24, 2010, the Supreme Court unanimously ruled to be unconstitutional—the law was too vague to constitute a crime unless a bribe or kickback was involved.*)

Jim then said, "Who is this?"

With a slight hesitation I said, "Bob Ney."

He then said in an upbeat voice, "Okay, I think you were a scapegoat. Wishing you the best. I do know of that lady that has the office open, but I think she's a Democrat. She has a Hillary sign in the yard!"

At this point in time I didn't care if she had Hillary, Obama, or anyone else, as long as it wasn't a John McCain sign, but I didn't have the heart to tell him because he was so nice—a real gentleman. I got her number and name, Melody Ghiloni, and thanked Jim profusely. (*Jim is a compassionate, good, honest man and we remain friends.*)

I thought that lady luck was with me. Jim could have been head of the local Obama campaign. I dialed the number and heard this clear, confident, vivacious voice say, "Melody here!"

I said, "Hello, my name is Bob Ney. Jim Hoekstra recommended I call you. I am looking to rent an office space." I thought I would not push the "need a supervisor" part until I saw her face to face. She said that she had a small office space, and how did two days from now at noon work to come over. I said, "How about in five minutes?" I told her that I was in a real time bind. She said okay and told me to come on over.

I made my "I am leaving call," which was not simple because the lady at the front desk, "Resident-hater" we called her, put me on hold for five minutes—most likely on purpose—until she took my call. Five minutes to me at that point was five too many.

We arrived at Melody's place, which was a Farmers Insurance business. I walked in and there was Melody—tall, bright-eyed, upbeat, and friendly. She said, "I don't know who the hell you are, I am from New York originally, and have no idea who this Jack Amaroff, Abratoff, whatever the guy's name is, but my husband, Albert, when I called him said, 'Bob Ney? Good guy, help him out.'"

I smiled, silently thanked God, and looked at the small backroom office. I took it and then said, "Oh yeah, can you supervise me?"

Melody laughed and said, "Okay, let me know what I have to do." I left, and headed back to the halfway house with Kayla without getting a car, as I was out of time—but I returned feeling pretty well satisfied.

On another day out, I got my car from Coughlin Cars of Newark. The man there was helpful in getting me a used 2002 Chevy Impala with 75,000 miles on it. Far different from the decades of new cars that I had bought or leased, but it felt like a new Cadillac to me!

Things were looking up. I talked to Melanie, my counselor, and was following everything to the letter. The next day I started working on getting permission to go to the office.

The first day at my new "digs" I was to arrive at 8:25 a.m., which had to be written on the extensive halfway house paperwork schedule beforehand. Then, I would have to call the halfway house within five minutes of arrival. I would receive periodic calls throughout the day from the halfway house to be sure I was where I said I was (thus one purpose of the landline), and then I was to call the halfway house as I was leaving the office, giving me thirty minutes to get back to Alvis House. God help me if there was a traffic jam or a wreck. I would have had to get off the Interstate and find a landline. Everything in the system is geared to drug deals. They don't want you to have a phone—like you couldn't make deals from someone else's phone? But hey, it's the feds.

I had been part of this system that created useless and antiquated solutions that simply perpetuated spending billions of dollars hiring more people and creating more regulations that were one-size-fits-all.

When I arrived at the office that first morning, I nearly had heart failure. No one was there yet. No big deal to a private business owner, but I was in a panic. "Anal Man" was on the front desk. This guy at Alvis House was not only *by the book*, he was psychotically by the book. He was the type of guy that I would not have hired when I was in Congress to clean the toilets. He looked like a nervous breakdown waiting to happen. He was about thirty-two and got the nickname "Anal Man" because he was so uptight and spastic. I used to say that he was so anal you couldn't get a toothpick up his asshole with a jackhammer, which brought some comic relief to my fellow residents.

Melody's office manager got to the office at about 8:40, but now I was five minutes late to call in. I had thought about going up the street to call, but was worried that I would be accused of lying because the phone number would not show "Farmers Insurance."

I rushed into the office, called Anal Man and he said, "Why are you late?"

I said, "The owner's manager just got here." He then asked why.

I thought, *Why? Why? You asshole idiot, because she can!* But I responded, "I don't know, It's a private business, not Alvis House."

He said, "I just don't understand this, why would she be late?"

I fantasized about driving up there and screaming at him, then dunking his head in the toilet several times. There, I felt better and said, "Okay, got to go," and hung up the phone. I assume that Anal Man is still trying to figure out why the office manager was late.

The layout of the offices was good. There was a reception area and Melody's office to the left. To get to my office, one would walk through a conference room and a small kitchen. My office was small—really small—I think it may have been a pantry at one time; but I was thankful for Melody and happy to have it. Everything is a matter of perspective: When I was in Congress I had a House Administration office of my own, a hearing room and a conference room that sat twenty-five people; in the Rayburn building, I had my own personal office with a conference area; in the district in Ohio I had five offices. This was quite a contrast for me, but I loved it—and it was certainly better than the 5 by 9 living area I shared with another guy in prison.

There was no door on my office, which was fine, as it made it more convenient for me. I had a small, glass top desk and a landline telephone that was Melody's business number. I was having my own landline installed, which was Talk Radio News Service's phone, so we didn't have to bother the receptionist with my calls. I was strictly to do research. I set up a coffee machine and Kayla brought me food supplies, as I was not allowed to go from the office to the grocery store. I kept some soups, canned tuna and Cheerios in the kitchen. I was set and settled in.

As soon as my new phone number was activated, I gave it to Melanie, my counselor. It was secondary, as she had Melody's Farmers Insurance number. Since Melody was my supervisor, I really didn't even need to give the second number but I followed the rules explicitly. I knew that I was under scrutiny from afar—in Washington.

When I left work that evening, I followed all protocol. I called from the Farmers Insurance office and reported that I was leaving and I arrived at Alvis House within one-half hour. I was preparing for dinner when I heard my name called to come to the front desk. Resident-hater was smiling and said, "Mosher, on line two."

It was my probation officer, who was not supposed to be taking over until the day I left Avis House. I picked up the line and said hello.

The response on the other end of the line went like this: "I expect when I call your number I get a response!" His voice was manic, screaming, threatening.

I said, "Excuse me?"

He said, "I called the office you are in and got an answering machine!"

I said, "I know, they are gone for the day."

"No, I called before you left for the day. Where were you?"

Well obviously, they must have had some other calls and I assume the other line went into an answering machine. I never answered their office phones. Or maybe the office manager had to go to the restroom. I could, of course, oblige Mr. Mosher and tell her to piss her pants next time, or get catheterized so she can be there for his calls. I so badly wanted to say this, but decided discretion is the best part of valor, so I responded with, "She must have stepped away. Did you leave her a message? She will call you back."

He exploded. "I will not leave messages! I expect you to answer the phone, you will answer the phone, I do not know how you got this damn job approved anyway. I would not approve it. Justice did not want it. I don't know how you did it!" He sounded psychotic and he was screaming at the top of his lungs. However, I didn't hear anything after that one very important bit of information—the Department of Justice did not want this.

I told him that I had my own phone line. He asked why he didn't have that number. I explained that I gave it to Melanie Hartley (my counselor) as I was supposed to and that I had followed the rules. He didn't care, he rambled on, screaming, and then hung up.

The next day I talked to Melanie and she confided in me that I had gotten the worst probation officer and that he treated all residents badly—but I was being treated worse than anyone she had seen. She told me to follow the rules and that she had my back. She was a good person, and I believed her.

My thirty-sixth day passed and I was in the final stages of being approved for home confinement. Everyone gets home confinement if you follow the rules. I think even Jack Abramoff did. This meant no more roundtrips and I could save gas money; I could live with Kayla, Adam and the baby; I could escape the scabies breakout in the halfway house; I could escape seeing a resident beaten with a telephone receiver by another resident because he was on the phone too long; and I could escape the temporary Bunkie who relapsed on opiates, was out of it and literally bled on the floor in our room. (He was about twenty years old, had gone out for a visit with friends and somehow managed to get drugs. My roommate Jacob and I told the front desk about it. The next day they talked to him, but nothing was done. He eventually ran away.) Yes, there were a lot of reasons to be "home" on my thirty-sixth day. Two days before I was to be on home confinement, Melanie, my counselor, called me in and said, "Mr. Ney, I am not sugarcoating this—D. C. called and said, and I quote, 'The hell he's going home.' I'm sorry. You deserve it, but we cannot let you go."

This was too much. At this point I needed psychological counseling. I was suffering PTSD and a near first-time mental breakdown because of the relentless Mr. Mosher and the Feds. I was at a breaking point. If I had realized it would be like this, it would have been better to serve my time in prison.

I lived through the harassment of Resident-hater making fun of me when I called to report that I had arrived at my 12 Step meetings (this employee, who was supposed to be helpful, made fun of us a lot—making a difficult situation even more so); I lived through, as did the others, scabies, bed bugs, fights, filthy conditions, and a cook who would show up drunk and mess up our food. (When she came in drunk, the food was half cooked and she would sit and laugh about senseless incidents that she found hilarious, while holding our meals hostage.)

I talked with my lawyers briefly about all this, just to fill them in, but there was little they could do. I brought it up at 12 Step meetings and was reamed out, appropriately so, especially by Old Bill, who said that I was under people like this because of what I did, and to sober up and get with the program to keep it from happening in the future. I, of course, realized that "Old Bill" was correct and on point with his comment.

Chapter 34

NEW BEGINNINGS

*"Resentment is like taking poison
and waiting for the other person to die."*

—Carrie Fisher

It was June 2008 and although I was still in the halfway house, I needed to rent a place that was larger than Adam and Kayla's space for all of us and my possessions. I was able to go "home" on the weekends when I was given a pass. I found a house to rent through my friend Glenda Hampton. We are not allowed to rent or make any contracts while still in the halfway house, so Kayla rented it in her name. We stumbled upon it because Glenda knew someone who had a house that needed to be rented right away. As things happen in life, I met Glenda through kind and gracious Melody Ghiloni, who rented office space to me. Glenda came by the office one day and Melody introduced us. Glenda was so helpful. I could get my possessions out of storage where they had been since December of 2006.

The late George Carlin was popular not only because of his sarcastic wit and out-front, vulgar, blunt, everyday language, but also because we could relate to the everyday subjects he talked about and say, "Yes—that's me!"

I remembered his funny routine on "stuff." One acquires "stuff," then you have to get a place to put your "stuff," then additional storage places for your "stuff." That's where I was—I wanted my "stuff" and it was all in storage at a fee that I could not afford, paid out of what was left after cancelling my thrift savings plan, and the money would soon have to come out of my pocket. I absolutely could not afford the 300 dollars a month (which was half of what I used to make in a day).

So, out from storage in nearby Reynoldsburg, Ohio, came my "stuff." The house I rented was about 1,500 square feet. It had four bedrooms and a rec room. All three of us, Kayla, Adam, and I, were working and sharing the costs. The truck arrived, loaded with my previous 5,000 square foot-home "stuff." Some of it fit, some did not. I sold 7,000 dollars' worth of furniture to a halfway house resident's wife for 1,200 dollars. They eventually stiffed me and didn't pay. Even after placing the furniture that was left, including the pool table, foosball table, and so on, it left me with a garage and the attic area above it piled high and deep. However, I was happy to have a place, because it is tough for any felon to rent after release, and . . . I had most of my "stuff."

When we were opening box after box, suddenly Kayla yelled, "Dad! The key bowl!" In our house in Barnesville, then in St. Clairsville, and then in Heath, Ohio, we had a "key bowl." It was a small, brass bowl that held everyone's keys, all the time. With so many people, cars, and keys in our busy house, the key bowl was a symbol of stability. By putting our keys in the bowl, there were no massive "house hunts" for keys, the stress level was taken down a peg, and it brought tranquility no matter what else was going on. Anyone staying in our house had to faithfully put their keys in the key bowl. (Try it. It works.)

I looked at the key bowl, thought of Bobby, Kayla, the years that had passed, our home and the good times we had in it, and I smiled. Somehow, this one little piece of our "stuff" wrapped it all together and brought everything into perspective. Later as we unpacked box after box after box, I looked at Kayla and said, "We just had too many things." (Four yard sales later, some early giveaways to Kayla, Adam, Bobby and his wife, Julie, I am now at "stuff nirvana.")

I was transitioning back into the world. More and more friends were contacting me—friends like Brock Miskimen, a former staffer, who would take me to lunch and talk about life and the Congressional days. Rob Ellsworth, a friend and former staffer at House Administration also reached out to me and invited me to spend a day with him and his family in nearby Columbus. I met Justin Jasper playing racquetball and he was so helpful in my recovery. We spent many hours talking about our direction. I had wonderful visits from Diane and Ward Giannini, who are longtime friends. We spent many hours contemplating future directions and careers that we would take advantage of as we transitioned through the midlife options of our lives. Other friends and family made me feel whole once more. I continued going to 12 Step recovery meetings and met a fantastic new friend, Michael Decker. He overcame many odds and situations to bring his life to a fresh, new place. These wonderful friends and many others were the glue that was putting me back together.

★ ★ ★

I was finally released from Alvis House on August 15, 2008. I was now allowed to travel. I was also now directly under Charles Mosher's supervision. I did my scheduled visits with him and did community service, which I requested to do at the 12 Step recovery central office under the supervision of Denny McCort and Jan W. They were wonderful people, and so helpful in my recovery. Jan's husband, John, has been working and helping people in recovery for years. A side benefit of doing my community service at the office was to learn so much from Jan about 12 Steps. She provided comfort and an ear. Denny McCort was invaluable for guidance, and he also helped me trudge through four storage rooms full of Congressional and campaign boxes! He was with me when the Independent Film Channel came to Newark to film my opening the storage bin for the first time since my incarceration, and seeing my former Congressional life in boxes. The film that producer Zena Barakat talked me into was titled *Media Matters*. Denny called me "Congressman" and I dubbed him "Governor of Newark, Ohio," and we still use those "titles" for each other.

Mr. Mosher inspected the 12 Step office. I understood this, but he made a comment to me about how this was good, but since there were mandatory 12 Step meetings once a week and community service, it did not count for a meeting if at the same time I was cleaning the 12 Step office. I concluded that he simply did not understand 12 Step, AA, NA, Sex Anonymous, Overeaters Anonymous or anything else anonymous or of that nature. I went to over seven meetings a week; the mandated number was insignificant to me—but then I had already told him that.

We also had a bizarre conversation about police. During one of my visits to his office in Columbus, Mosher asked me if I had any run-ins with the police over the years. I wondered if he actually read my case or thought I was a member of a Columbian drug cartel. Sorry, but you've seen my pictures—I don't fit the stereotype of a street thug. Politician, yes—thug, no.

I told him of my reverence for police and law enforcement, how I was a safety director for the city of Bellaire in 1979–80, how I oversaw the over 1,400 Capitol Hill police, and how I had many friends who were in law enforcement.

He looked at me and said, "Oh, so you think you can get away with things with the Newark police?" There was just no winning with him.

I shared with Ellen that he was making what should be routine travel very difficult. Periodically, I would not get his approvals back in time. This caused a nightmare in pre-planning work trips, and the added expense of my not being able to book travel arrangements in advance. On occasion, I would plan a trip, arrive at the airport, but because I had not received Mosher's approval I had to call to see if I could leave or if I would have to turn around and go home. He or his secretary might give an okay at the very last moment, but not always.

I really could not function anymore. I also shared this with Mr. Ritter, my federally assigned psychological counselor. Of my entire prison and halfway house time, Mr. Mosher was (or I should say, I was letting him) about to take me down the tubes. I talked to my 12 Step sponsor, Russ P., about it, as I should. It was ironic that with all I had been through, my recovery from alcohol was most threatened by Mr. Mosher.

It came to a head one day when my former neighbor Lynne Ziants lost her father. I wanted to drive down to Belmont County for the funeral. I didn't need permission to do this, as it was in the realm of the Southern Federal District Court. I could go there and that area only without permission. By this time, I could also have a cell phone if Mosher needed to call me. He called me while I was at the 12 Step recovery office in downtown Newark, just as I was ready to leave for the funeral. He said he wanted to see me. I told him I was headed to a funeral. He told me to wait. He showed up two hours later than he said he would be there, said he had to run, but just wanted to check on me. I missed the funeral. I could only assume that he did it on purpose—because he could.

Possibly, Mr. Mosher was a "dry drunk," a person who didn't use alcohol but either had severe control issues or was the type of guy whose mom made him wear knickers as a kid and the other kids regularly taunted and kicked the shit out of him, thus creating an adult who needed revenge. (The "knickers" theory is my favorite fantasy about

why some men have control issues.) Or, it could be that he was just carrying out the D.C. Justice vendetta to the end, waiting for me to make
one mistake, blow up, fight back. I was on probation, so I could be sent
back to prison.

I was drug-tested and alcohol breathalyzed from February of 2008 to
September of 2010 over 416 times. (Lest you think I am exaggerating,
every day when returning from work I was breathalyzed; every evening
upon returning from the 12 Step meeting next door, I was breathalyzed;
when returning from 12 Step meetings in Columbus, at least two times
a week, I was breathalyzed; returning after every weekend at home, I
was breathalyzed; every day that I walked outside to exercise around
the building, I was breathalyzed upon reentry; twice a week that I went
to the gym and the one trip to the grocery store per week, I was breathalyzed upon returning; I was breathalyzed at random weekly screen-
ings, and there may be others that I have forgotten.) Every single test
was clean. I did not make their day. The tests probably cost more than
my trip to Scotland with Abramoff.

For me to continue to do my job, I had to fight weekly. Mosher had
told me my first week in the halfway house, six months earlier, that after
I was out of Alvis House, I would have to get permission of the Attorney General himself to go on radio. This was a lie, but a threat I felt. I
confronted him on one of the very last days of my halfway house confinement about my being able to go on radio and he flippantly said, "Free
country."

My attorney Bill Lawler petitioned Judge Huvelle to release me after
one year of probation. Everyone who has a perfect record gets his or her
probation reduced. On a visit to my house, Mr. Mosher's supervisor said
that I needed to be released and Mosher agreed, which is half the battle. However, Judge Huvelle would have no part of it. In the interest
and safety of the citizens, Bob Ney, the dangerous ex-con, the scourge
of the country, the Machiavellian manipulator of the lobby community,
the man who possibly started the Iraq war and the rise of gasoline prices,
needed to be contained. (Actually, I expected this. I was high profile and
my early release could potentially cause some heartburn and press
stories for me as well. I was not angry or upset with Judge Huvelle's
decision.)

My release from probation was denied but I did get an important con-
cession. For work purposes, I only had to tell Mr. Mosher where I was
going—but his permission was not required. Mr. Mosher didn't interpret

it that way and wanted clarification from Judge Huvelle, requesting that I get the judge herself to clarify it. This type of action on my part for something so clear would have been an irritation to the court. Bill Lawler, my lawyer, could hardly believe this one. He pushed back via a phone call to Chuck Mosher and I finally could do work properly for Talk Radio News Service. I was able to travel for my job to D.C. and New York and parts thereabouts for work without the "Mr. Mosher hassle."

I also got my passport back and most important, in 2008 I was able to cast my vote for Obama or the "Maverick" Senator John McCain. You decide where my ex-con, felony-laden vote went. I philosophically agreed more with McCain, but knew he would start another war; it is in his neocon blood. The biggest regret I had as a Member of Congress was being lured into the George Bush "big lie" (Weapons of Mass Destruction theory) that caused the invasion of Iraq and the death of many. As I stated in the Independent Film Channel's documentary, I lied, no one died; he lied, many died. I did appreciate voting again. It made me feel that I was nearing some normal status as an American once more. I regret to say that when I was a Congressman and oversaw federal law on voting issues through the House Administration Committee, I opposed felon voting restoration rights to be nationally imposed. This was a huge mistake on my part, and I hope that I can be part of the process someday to make felon voting restoration a reality. I am fortunate to come from Ohio, which is a bit more progressive. Some states forever ban the right of former felons to vote. This is simply wrong.

As far as the press part of my job went, Ellen was correct. Getting "back in the saddle" with semi-public exposure seemed to be a good fit.

The day after I was released from the halfway house was my first day on the radio, making the call-ins to various radio shows for Talk Radio News. Ellen did the calls with me that day. I was nervous—it was a tense time for me. *How would I be received?* Some of the radio show hosts that Ellen worked with were liberal. *Would I be accepted . . . or not?* The first show we did was with a prominent radio show host, Thom Hartmann. It went well. Thom was gracious, asked good questions about me and we had a solid interaction. That day the rest of the show hosts made me feel not only comfortable, but that I could once again, in a modified way, express my views of the political world. Ellen's show hosts that I have worked with are a politically diverse group across the spectrum. They are bright people, dedicated to debating information and bringing news that is important to people. They have been wonderful to me and I have enjoyed being on their shows over the past four years.

Six months after that first day on radio, I had my own radio show on WVLY Wheeling, West Virginia, thanks to the generosity of the owner of the station and my longtime friend, Howard Monroe. Howard has been a talk show host for decades and has a very sharp political mind.

The opening of my show went well. The media was invited and I thought they were fair, under the circumstances. My first guest was Roxanne Koteles Smith, formerly from the Ohio Valley. She devised a *cooking for health* regimen after her mother passed away from cancer.

Earlier that day, Eric Minor from WTOV in Steubenville, Ohio, showed up. He is a local television celebrity newsman. When he extended his hand to say hello, I knuckle-rapped him and laughed. (Knuckle rapping is done in prison in place of shaking hands.)

John McCabe from the Wheeling Intelligencer newspaper dropped by, as did D.K. Wright from Channel 7, who wrote to me while I was in prison. During the interview, it surprised me when she quoted one of my quotes back to me—one I paraphrased about good and bad moments in life. I usually ended my letters, and a few to D.K. when she wrote to me in prison, with: "At the end of the day, people have good and bad moments, but the moments that count are the ones that take your breath away. May you have many."

That evening, Howard threw a reception at Ye Olde Alpha, a local Wheeling restaurant. It was well attended with well-wishers and a couple of curious people. The day was good, the company wonderful, and Howard Monroe did a great job of putting it together.

The year I did that show was therapeutic for me and quite interesting. It gave me a new appreciation for Howard Monroe and all the other talk show hosts. Doing two hours daily on radio is not as easy as it may seem. Howard is a seasoned veteran of radio and has an uncanny sense about politics. I knew him for years and listened to him on radio. He was so smooth and interesting that I just naturally assumed it wasn't difficult.

★ ★ ★

Two big events took place in 2010. On August 14, my two-year federal probation period was officially over, and on September 1, I was heading to incredible India for a battery recharge, and to look into the efficacy of meditation and breathing for people with post traumatic stress disorder (PTSD) and substance abuse. It was Ellen Ratner's idea for me to go after she had spoken with my friend Dr. Deborah Akers, who was headed to Sarah College in India on behalf of Miami University (Ohio). It was a good suggestion for me personally at that time of my life.

Even though I had received a "verbal" okay to be off probation, there was no way I would risk leaving the United States without written confirmation—not with the threat of Obama's Justice Department, which contained Bush "holdovers," potentially sending me back to prison for a violation of probation. Endless calls to Mr. Mosher's office remained unreturned. Calls to his Assistant were met with "He is out. He says you are off probation."

Two days before I was to leave, on a Monday morning, my friend and attorney from Columbus, Ohio, Jim Owen, who is a premiere attorney in many areas but also nationally known in the area of wrongful convictions, went to Charles Mosher's office personally. Jim related to me that Mosher said, "Don't you have something better to do?"

Jim answered, "No, not till I get the letter." With that letter safely in Jim's possession, I headed to Newark, New Jersey, and then on to India. "Namasté" would be the next greeting I would hear in Delhi, India, and then the ten-hour journey to the land of Dharamsala, that western retreat for so many and the home of the exiled fourteenth spiritual head of Buddhism, HH (His Holiness—a Western rendering) Dalai Lama.

Thinking back on Charles Mosher today, for my own sake I can't afford to hold resentment, but I do feel bad for the many people who leave prison and are trying hard to reenter his or her life and society, but fall victim to a system that has no one watching the overseers. No one is there as an ombudsman for the felon who is trying to do the right thing. Maybe society has no sympathy for them because "they made their own bed." However, I think that when we head down that path we crumble the constitution, discard human rights, and as a society become no different from the felons we disdain.

There has to be a second chance for the lawbreaker embodied in "They did their time and paid their debt to society." Degrading a human being for no reason serves no purpose. Through my experience, I found that it is the small things—the subtle, psychological darts thrown at felons who are trying to recover that are significant roadblocks to their psyche and recovery. We have done wrong; we are trying to make amends; we seek forgiveness and grace, and we want to belong again. An example of one of these *darts* remains with me in my drawer at home. Trying to rebuild my life and regain some sort of dignity, I dressed in my suit and showed up for my first day at Mr. Mosher's office. He had me pose for my official ID—the one that would be shown many, many times throughout my two-year probationary period—in front of a picture of a Mail Pouch Barn. (A Mail Pouch Tobacco Barn, or Mail Pouch Barn, is a barn with an advertisement for West Virginia Mail Pouch chewing tobacco painted on the side of it.) Everyone on Federal probation has to have the ID while in custody. The picture of the barn was in the outer lobby of his office, in the waiting area. He specifically told me to stand by it, and he took my picture. I imagine he thought it was funny to ridicule the "big shot politician"—that I would look like a hick, an Appalachian hillbilly—who knows? He may have been amused and I may have been embarrassed for two years when I got comments from people who saw it, but actually, Mr. Mosher gave me a *gift*. May I always remember what he did to embarrass me so that I will always strive to have compassion for others who are down and need a second chance. And if I become a bit hardened, I will pull out that ID, take a breath, think about my behavior and attitude and treat others as I desire to be treated.

Recollections from Matt Parker, Former Chief of Staff

I started working for Bob in 2002; I was twenty years old. I would not be where I am today if it weren't for Bob giving me a chance.

I remember a time early on when I thought I was going to get fired. Bob, others from the staff and I were at the Capital Grille in Washington, D.C. Nearly everything we did, especially after normal business hours, revolved around alcohol. I ordered a beer and the bartender asked to see my ID. I quickly came up with an excuse that I did not have my ID with me, so I didn't get served. Aaron Poe, another staffer, was sitting next to me and he said, "Why didn't you just give him your ID?" I confided in Aaron that I was only twenty years old. Aaron quietly told Bob why I wasn't drinking. Bob said, "Come with me." I was scared to death. He took me outside and said, "What the hell is the matter with you?" At this point, I thought I was fired for sure. Bob continued, "I had a fake ID when I was fifteen!"

The year 2004 could not have gone any better. I was in Ohio running the campaign and I had just gotten elected Chairman of the Belmont County Republican Party. Bob and I took an active role in helping the Bush-Cheney reelection effort in Eastern Ohio and Bob was always deploying us to help candidates all over the state and country. Will Heaton, Chris Krueger, and everyone else on the staff worked extremely hard. Neil Volz, Bob's former Chief of Staff, had even taken a leave of absence from his lobbying firm to help with the effort.

Election night ended well. Bob won 66 percent of the vote in his reelection campaign, President Bush won reelection, and we helped to elect many Republican candidates all over the state and the country. We even helped Chris Berhalter, at 33 years old, become the first Republican Prosecutor in our home county in 78 years. Out in D.C., many leadership options were opening up for Bob, including Majority Leader of the House. He was the twelfth most popular House Member and he wielded that power wisely, getting several projects funded for the district. Bob is one of the hardest working Members I have seen—and he expected as much from his staff.

We first heard of the Abramoff scandal in 2004, but none of us thought anything about it. Then, in 2005, the press stories really began to escalate. On January 2, 2006, I was at the Sugar Bowl with my wife, Marina. The venue had been changed to Atlanta, Georgia, because of Hurricane Katrina. The West Virginia Mountaineers were playing the Georgia Bulldogs. My Blackberry was *blowing up* throughout the game. A major story about the Abramoff scandal had broken and I had to get home ASAP to begin getting talking points out to all of our supporters throughout the district. Marina and I left as soon as the game was over and drove straight through the night to the campaign office in Hebron, Ohio, where I worked from 7 a.m. until 11 p.m. that night.

That same month, we took a poll to test the waters before the primary. The numbers were dreadful. In fact our pollster, Glen Bolger, said they were the worst poll numbers he had ever seen for an incumbent member of Congress. The poll showed that anyone with a heartbeat could beat Bob.

Glen is one of the most, if not the most, respected pollsters in Republican politics. However, Glen is a pollster who always leads with the bad news. This is a smart thing for a pollster to do, because the worst thing a candidate can do is act overconfident. Bob and I always jokingly referred to Glen as the eternal pessimist, but Glen's polls are impeccable, so we definitely had reason to be concerned; yet things seemed to be going well in the district. We were constantly receiving positive e-mails, letters, and phone calls. All of our top district contributors were sticking by Bob through the scandal.

If someone is diagnosed with cancer, he or she sometimes seeks a second opinion. We were diagnosed as "terminal," so we hired another pollster to give us another look at the numbers. Unfortunately, their numbers were even worse than Glen's! Bob was faced with a tough decision. Most everyone in the inner circle felt that Bob needed to retire because there was no path to victory. I was twenty-four years old, young and dumb, and I wanted to fight. Bob and I shared this sentiment. Bob and I shared a bond because we were both born and raised in the Ohio Valley, both came from blue-collar families, and we never backed down from a fight.

With the polling numbers looking so bad, we decided to convene a meeting of all the political movers and shakers in the district at the Zanesville Holiday Inn. Prior to the meeting, Bob, Will Heaton, Brian Walsh and I had a meeting of our own in the hotel bar. Bob said, "We'll talk about the scandal, the challenges to getting reelected, and if there is any hesitation from anyone here to stand behind me, I will probably get out of the race." There was great support at the meeting and everyone in attendance endorsed Bob's campaign. In fact, we ended up getting nearly every Republican Party and Republican official in the district to endorse Bob's reelection campaign.

We were excited when we left Zanesville and instantly made plans to announce our candidacy in Tuscarawas County, the largest county in the district. Bob hit a homerun with his campaign announcement speech. Every local media outlet covered the event, and C-SPAN and Fox News even aired Bob's speech. There were hundreds of people at the rally. The image of that rally also helped keep some other elected officials out of the primary. Throughout the scandal, we heard rumors of a state representative and a county commissioner who were considering challenging Bob. I am convinced that our ability to lock down so much local support foiled their plans.

Bob had grown somewhat complacent, however, in regard to campaign resources. He was a decent fundraiser, but he used campaign funds in many ways that weren't prudent for someone running in a tough reelection campaign. Also, Bob's legal defense fund was not big enough to fund all of his legal fees, so we were bleeding cash and unable to do the television ads that we needed. Instead, we used a lot of shoe leather, made a lot of phone calls, and took Bob to many local events. Against all odds, Bob won the primary with almost 69 percent of the vote.

Bob had become very convincing in all of his media interviews that he was not guilty. We created the media as the enemy. It wasn't that hard to do since the media's tactics were so deplorable. They would stake out in the woods behind our houses, harass our office staff, and follow us around at every event we did. Bob was becoming a master at claiming the Abramoff scandal was nothing less than a government and media witch-hunt, and that he was completely innocent.

There was another poll taken by Glen Bolger after the primary, and Glen compared Bob to Rocky Balboa. Bob had taken *haymaker punches* to the head, but somehow he was still standing. The poll showed us with a lead over Zack Space, the Democrat nominee, and showed that we had a chance to win. Given our cash flow problems, however, I was worried that we would not have the money to win. The National Republican Congressional Committee and the Ohio Republican party were not on board. They did not believe that he could win. They also believed that Bob only added to the "Culture of Corruption" mantra that was coming out of the Democratic Congressional Campaign Committee and Democrat National Committee. The Republican Party was not willing to stand by him.

By the middle of 2006, I was spending twenty to thirty hours per week gathering information to fulfill Justice Department subpoenas, which meant I was working eighty to ninety hours per week and regularly sleeping in my office. The press and the Justice Department dug into other things not related to Abramoff. They smelled blood and they were on the hunt. Morale in the office was plummeting by the summer of 2006.

Paula, Bob's scheduler and Dave Distefano's sister (Dave was Bob's first Chief of Staff), had already left in 2005. It was bizarre; she was very loyal and a good friend of Bob's, but she left so quickly. She had worked for him since the first campaign in 1994. Paula and I ran the District Office. We were Bob's eyes and ears. We worked well together, although it was a sort of love/hate relationship. I always felt Paula and I had the same goals, but I was young and aggressive and she was more set in her ways and change was not something Paula appreciated. Even though the job was stressful, I could never understand how Paula could walk away so abruptly after eleven years. It was tough to replace her. As far as I know, she and Bob haven't spoken since she left. I have only spoken to her once or twice.

After the primary, the inner circle began to drop like flies. For example, Chief of Staff Will Heaton left town to get married and never came back to work. He never said goodbye to anyone; he just left. Will and I were very close and I stayed at his house when I was in D.C. and he stayed at mine when he was in Ohio. We learned later that Will cut a deal with the Justice Department and even wore a wire for the Justice Department as part of his plea agreement. It is believed that Will wore a wire while in our office and even in my house. That hurt because I thought we had a good friendship. I have put it behind me and don't hold a grudge. I don't know what I would have done if I were in Will's position, and I feel badly that things ended the way they did. I have tried, on multiple occasions, to reach out to Will since 2006, but have had no response. After Will's plea deal became public, Will's lawyers tried to paint him as an altar boy who was completely manipulated by Bob. Bob clearly wasn't innocent, but neither was Will. Will was no altar boy. All of us in Bob's inner circle deserved to take some blame. We had become completely consumed with politics and greed, losing our sense of right and wrong.

The district staff in Ohio remained intact and we continued to work hard. Most of the district staff had been with Bob since 1995, and they wanted to keep their jobs. There was also a sense of loyalty to Bob. The press stories, the investigation, and Bob's reckless lifestyle were going to make it very difficult to win, but the staff continued to volunteer time on weekends and evenings. With such a large possibility of losing, it was tense—but no one had given up.

Over the Fourth of July, we went to New Philadelphia for the First Town Days Festival and marched in the parade. This was always the biggest parade in the district and there were thousands of people lining the streets of the parade. Ahead of us was the *Times Reporter* truck giving out newspapers. That day, there happened to be a front-page story about our senior staff departures and reporting about the recent subpoena that had been handed down to yours truly. The people were very polarized. Some people were yelling, "Give 'em hell, Bob!" and some were shouting things that weren't so pleasant. I vividly remember going up to one man and trying to give him a campaign flier. The man just held the newspaper in my face. He told me to "get lost" without saying a word. People either loved Bob or hated him—there was no middle ground.

The trip to Scotland was at the center of the Abramoff scandal and the discussion of just about every single negative news story. At the time of the trip, I had just been hired as Bob's Executive Assistant. During a meeting in the spring of 2002, Will told Bob about the golf trip and tried to talk Bob into going. Bob said that he didn't want to go. Bob is not a golfer and that is well known to anyone who knows him. With that being said, I couldn't believe he didn't want to go on this trip to play at St. Andrews, the oldest golf course in the world. As an avid golfer myself, I was incredulous! Bob and I were on our way to the floor of the House for votes after the meeting, and as we walked, I questioned him about it. He said that he didn't want to spend the time away, he didn't like to play golf, and he was a lousy golfer. Will persisted, and eventually Bob decided to go. I took Bob down to Oglebay Park in Wheeling, West Virginia, and tried to help him with his swing before the trip, but his golf game was hopeless. I remember jealously thinking about what a waste it was for Bob to play St. Andrews because he was such a horrendous golfer!

In June of 2006, at 10 p.m. on a Friday night, I received a call from the FBI. I immediately hung up and called Bob. I ended up talking to House Counsel on Monday regarding the matter. This is a service of the Office of General Counsel of the U.S. House of Representatives (OGC) that provides legal advice and assistance. I was assigned a young, fresh-out-of-law-school attorney. I flew out to D.C. to meet with him and to learn why the FBI called me so late on a Friday night.

I was subpoenaed by the Justice Department for my testimony only. I was told that I wasn't a target of the investigation; they just wanted to talk to me, and I was told that the questioning shouldn't take long at all. I didn't prepare anything, because I had nothing to hide—I was questioned for nearly five hours. The question of the Scotland golf trip came up. While telling them what I knew about it, and the fact that Bob had not even wanted to go, I got the date of the meeting confused and the mood of the meeting took a drastic turn. They started calling me a liar and said I was protecting Bob. I was indignant and pushed back. I was arrogant and I got into a shouting match with an FBI agent. Kendall Day, an attorney for the Justice Department, calmly looked at my attorney and said, "You should advise your client to keep his mouth shut." This was definitely not my finest moment.

Due to my arrogance and ignorance, I became a target of their investigation for *perjury* and *obstruction of justice*. The young attorney could no longer represent me, as the OGC doesn't defend House staffers in criminal cases. I was forced to seek private counsel. Fortunately, my attorneys did great work and found e-mails that proved my innocence.

What worried me even more than possibly going to prison was that the Justice Department had been threatening to release all of our e-mails to the public. They threatened to do this to Bob and to us as an attempt to squeeze more information out of us. I am glad I never went to prison, but I am even happier that those e-mails never became public. I said so many things as an arrogant, young, political operative that I am not proud of. Those e-mails would have been embarrassing to all of our families. It was finally decided that the e-mails would remain private. Nevertheless, I owed forty-nine thousand dollars for attorneys' fees and I didn't have enough money to cover the bill. In the end, the law firm defending me did it pro bono, which kept me from filing for bankruptcy.

When I first started working for Bob, we all drank too much, but Bob was always up and at 'em the next day. I don't know how he did it, but he never let drinking interfere with his work. In 2005, however, Bob went from being a functional alcoholic to a raging alcoholic. He smoked multiple packs of cigarettes a day and would drink beer all day long—starting with beer in his coffee cup early in the morning. He would drink wine, not out of wine glasses, but out of beer glasses. One night at a political fundraiser, I watched him drink seven cognacs after dinner. He would become belligerent and often screamed at me over minute details; he arbitrarily said no to attending certain events; when Congress wasn't in session, he would take off two or three days a week, say he was "working from home," and would drink and smoke all day. Because most of us also drank too much, we accepted this behavior as the norm—but this was beyond the norm. I feel bad that I never did press the issue with him and that I allowed myself to pick up many of the same bad habits.

He came to my house the night he decided to plead guilty and we went out on my deck in the back. Bob was in a bad way—he was very drunk, which was normal, but he was also very emotional, which was not normal for him. Crying, he said, "I'm going to prison. My life is over. I'm worth more dead than alive and my kids would be better off." I knew that he was suicidal. My wife and I monitored him closely that night because Bob's wife and kids were not home, and I wasn't completely sure that Bob wouldn't do something stupid. That night Marina cooked us a big meal and Bob began to sober up. He went home with a much better attitude, but I called him twice that night to make sure he was doing okay.

Bob went into rehab before he went to prison, and I knew that rehab was exactly what Bob needed. His health and life had really deteriorated.

He was roughly sixty pounds overweight, he was smoking so much that he had a habitual cough, and he was ruining many relationships with his drunken, temperamental outbursts. I was at a football game in Morgantown, West Virginia, on a Thursday night when I got a call from Bob. He was in rehab in Cleveland, Ohio, and he was demanding that I come and get him. I refused. Bob was pleading with me on the other end of the phone, claiming that he clearly didn't belong in rehab with all of those drunks and addicts. He was begging me to come and get him. I didn't always make it a habit of standing up to Bob. In fact, 90 percent of the time, I just did whatever he told me to do. Not this time, though. I knew that he needed to get help, and there was no way that I was going to continue to stand by and let this man kill himself with booze. I really cared for him, and I knew that if I went to Cleveland to pick him up, I would be enabling him to keep drinking.

Bob was scheduled to come home that weekend, and I expected him to be furious with me. There had been some tense moments between us in the past. I remember a time in December of 2004 when we almost got into a fistfight. Bob had to go to D.C. for the day and he wanted me to sit at his house to wait on the UPS guy. It was a Saturday, I had rented a sander and I was redoing my living room floor. I politely told him that I could not go to his house, and Bob became furious on the phone. Later that night, I picked him up from the airport. I was on time, but his plane was five minutes early, and he was standing out in the cold, drunk and full of rage. He got in the car and did not say a word. I said, "Why are you so quiet?" He proceeded to scream at me, call me an ungrateful little prick, and he even punched his car stereo and broke the screen. We were driving down I-279 in Pennsylvania and I had had enough. I pulled over and said, "If you don't knock it off, I will physically pull you out of this car and whoop your ass!" There were quite a few other words exchanged and Bob finally said with a smart-aleck tone, "You can't hit a Member of Congress. That's a felony and you will go to prison." Truth was I didn't want to hurt him physically; I just wanted him to pass out so I could drive home in peace. He calmed down, I drove him home—and he did indeed pass out in the front seat. When we arrived home in St. Clairsville, I pulled him out of his car, but instead of beating him up, I simply dragged him into his house and laid him down on the couch.

I don't know what happened in that rehab clinic in Cleveland, but Bob was not angry with me. Bob was changed. He and I never talked much about his time at the Cleveland Clinic, but as far as I know, he has not drunk a drop of alcohol or smoked a cigarette since that day. He began to go to 12 Step meetings religiously and he quickly became healthier. I am convinced that those few days in Cleveland, Ohio, and the follow-up rehab at Woods at Parkside, Gahanna, Ohio, saved Bob's life.

When Bob went to prison, he gave me his power of attorney. I had no business taking care of his finances; I could barely take care of my own. In fact, my whole life was in shambles by then. I was definitely drinking too much, I had a smoking habit, I had stress-induced acid reflux that required heavy doses of medication, my wife and I were having marital problems and my financial situation was terrible.

In the five years I worked for him, work and alcohol were all that mattered to Bob and me—we were consumed with politics and partying. We had no perspective and no balance in our lives.

My friend Casey did an intervention of sorts with me over my finances in 2007. He was able to show me how I was only one disaster away from bankruptcy and that I was living very irresponsibly. He gave me a copy of Dave Ramsey's book, *Financial Peace*. My dad had given me a copy of this book when I was in college but I disregarded it and tossed it aside. This time I read it, and it turned my finances around. Today I have a business of my own, Front Porch Strategies. We provide state-of-the-art voter contact technology to Republican campaigns and conservative causes. We employ ten people and have done work in forty-one states and four Canadian provinces. In 2010, I was named a "Rising Star" by *Campaigns & Elections* magazine for my work as a Republican political consultant. When Bob got out of prison, I was able to help him with his finances by teaching him about Dave Ramsey's principles. I have been amazed at how well Bob has stewarded his money and his time since leaving prison.

By the grace of God, I have returned to my Christian roots and have submitted my life to the Lordship of Jesus Christ. Through the reading of the Bible, I came to understand the depths of my sinfulness and the infinite holiness of God. I put my faith in Jesus Christ because He alone is mighty to save. My relationship with my wife is better than ever, and we are in the process of adopting two children from Ethiopia. Recently I helped plant Christ Redeemer Church in Newark, Ohio, where I serve as the pastor for missions and administration. I am finishing my seminary degree at Liberty Baptist Theological Seminary and I serve on board of directors of World Help, a faith-based humanitarian organization that serves the physical and spiritual needs of people in impoverished communities around the world.

As I finish writing this chapter, I am on a plane to Guatemala with other pastors and World Help board members. We will be touring facilities that we have helped raise money for, meeting with Guatemalan pastors for a pastors' conference, and we will spend time touring villages that need our help desperately. Most of the villages we will tour have no access to clean water, adequate schools, medical facilities, roads, or any of the modern conveniences we so easily take for granted. Dozens of children die every single day in Guatemala because of basic sicknesses like diarrhea. The people in the villages we will visit survive on less than two dollars per day. It is so exciting to be part of the global church of Jesus Christ and to be his eyes, hands, and feet in the world. Jesus was definitely right when he said that it is more blessed to give than to receive.

I am a firm believer in the sovereignty of God. Just six years ago, I was a borderline alcoholic on the verge of bankruptcy and divorce. Bob Ney was on his way to prison and completely unsure of God's plan for his life. It is hard to believe that God has accomplished so much in our lives over the past six years.

Today, we are both fulfilling God's calling on our lives. I am helping to pastor a church and running a successful business. Instead of using my profits to pursue my old devotion to pleasure and self-gratification, I am using them to plant churches, distribute Bibles, and to help the extremely impoverished around the world. God has not blessed my business so that I can fall back into my old lifestyle. My life now has an eternal purpose.

Bob spends countless hours mentoring drug addicts and alcoholics. He has helped so many people and the press will probably never know about it. While he was a Congressman, he worked hard to steer millions of tax dollars to projects and people would name roads and buildings after him. Now, as he works to save lives from the depths and despairs of drug and alcohol addiction, works that will outlive him and last for eternity, it is truly ironic that this hard work is *anonymous.*

I am thankful for Bob Ney. I am even more thankful that we all suffered through the Jack Abramoff scandal. If Bob were still in Congress, we would both be miserable. God had a much better plan than we did.

PART V

★ ★ ★

MOVING ON

*"I may not have gone where I intended to go,
but I think I have ended up where I needed to be."*

—Douglas Adams,
The Long Dark Tea-Time of the Soul

Chapter 35

☆ ☆ ☆

INCREDIBLE INDIA

"There is more to life than simply increasing its speed."

—Mahatmas Gandhi

"Incredible India" is indeed an appropriate slogan for the tourism bureau. It is fitting that as I write this chapter I am on a train bound to Udaipur, a stunning city on the water in Rajasthan, the Indian state in the Punjab. I have just left the gorgeous, tourist oriented beaches of Goa, the "Hawaii" of India. My stay in a charming room at the Baia Do Sol Hotel, North Goa Beach, provided the "Ernest Hemingway" kickstart I needed to complete a large part of these writings. (Because of my semi-seclusion and the prolific writing coming out of India, my editor, Shari Johnson, gave me the "Ernest" moniker—it gave me a chuckle and pushed me onward.)

India, although far from my beloved America in distance and culture, for decades has had ties to the United States. In recent years some Americans and Westerners have been lured to India not just for tourism, but in many cases in search of themselves. India is both mystical and magical. Someone with weaknesses and fears who seeks answers for strength and inner peace in India will not be the seeker, but the sought. India will find *you*. She will allow *you* to find the answers.

The first Asian ever to be a U.S. Congressman, Dalip Singh Saund, who was in office from January 3, 1957–January 3, 1963, was an Indian/American from the Punjab. India and America are naturally aligned in many ways. After having been in India four different times,

I have concluded that we should totally abandon all trade with China and make agreements with India. If the status quo of U.S. jobs lost to foreign countries continues, India would be a better choice than China. India is the world's largest Democracy—and unlike the "Commie Red" Government of China, whose hierarchy privately loathes Americans, the Indian people actually like us. In addition, India would do fair trade, unlike the thieving Chinese manipulators.

The Indian community, not only numbering millions in the U.S. but many of them successful professionals, have integrated well into American society and are well liked in America. My doctor (and friend) is Dr. Ren DeLaCruz (who is Filipino/American), and before him was Dr. Buhlar; neighbors in St. Clairsville included Dr. Naba Goswami's family. Many people in America have positive experiences with Indians. It is no different in India. The poverty is abundant, but the spirit of the people remains hopeful. They are friendly and curious about us, often wanting to talk. They often ask, "Where are you from, my friend?"

The sights, sounds, smells, food, and people of "Mother India" call most people back for a return visit. My relationship with India started quite a while back. My mother, Dorothy, used to have what were called, Jewel Tea parties. People sponsored a Jewel Tea party where friends would come and order items. Jewel Tea was a "store" in a truck that came around once a month to homes and the salesmen/drivers sold just about every little thing one could think of. My mom had a party in our apartment. I was seven years old at the time and I saw a silver cup—a mini chalice that I became obsessed with. I wanted it in the worst way. We lived happily, but we were poor—I just didn't know it. Mom explained that she didn't have the money for the cup at that time. I was disappointed, but sure enough, Mom saved some money here and there and bought it for me later on. Mom and Dad were, and are, the best at sacrificing for their kids. They are quite incredible.

When the cup came, I was so excited. I held it in my hand and examined it carefully, running my fingers across the raised, hand-made designs. Although only about six inches tall, the silver and brass colors swirled into magical designs that captivated me. I then turned it upside down and saw the word "India." I wasn't sure what that was, or where it was, but I looked it up at the Bellaire Library. Thus began my infatuation with India. I didn't find India, India found me—at a Jewel Tea party far, far, from Mumbai or McLeodganj in the foothills of the Himalayas. Throughout the years, whenever I had the option to pick a topic to write about for school, "Bapu" (father) Mohandas Gandhi was my choice.

Eventually, the stunning classic movie of Gandhi's life came out, starring Ben Kingsley. One particular scene in the movie made an impact on me, where the unarmed people were gunned down for no reason at the Jhalawar Wall. Upon orders of the British general, the men fired on innocent men, women and children until their guns became hot. What lasted for fifteen minutes became the rally point that allowed the non-violent Gandhi to propel his movement to rid India of the British stronghold. (In the American Revolution, we did it with guns; Gandhi did it through non-violence.) The scene in the movie goes on and on. I believe it was the intention of the director to demonstrate the intensity and brutality of that event. I was at the theater with my college roommate and friend from Bellaire, Tim Ritter, and we sat there watching this horrific, senseless, murderous, seemingly endless bloodbath. The movie stopped suddenly and the screen went blank. It was intermission for this long epic. My emotion got the best of me and I yelled out, "Screw the royal family!" I did get some applause for it in the theater. Now I love the UK, but I was young, impassioned, driven, and quite intemperate in those days. Not that I got much better with age—until now.

As years passed, I met Mother Teresa, was in the Indian Caucus, supported Indian issues and had literally ten requests to go to India, but had to decline them all for various reasons. Over the years I had traveled to over fifty countries, but never to Mother India.

(The term Mother India was coined by my good friend, Gulam Ahmed. Gulam is a wonderful man with a great family and he works in Saudi Arabia. He is from Hyderabad, India. One day in 1983 when I was working in our Amerigard's office in Saudi Arabia, Gulam walked in, looking smart. In India, "looking smart" does not mean that he looked intelligent, which he is, but he looked, as we might say, "dapper."

Gulam walked up to me and said, "Hello, I think you are American, I would like to work for your company. I will work free for two weeks. If you think I am deserving, you can hire me. If not, I leave."

I was so impressed with him that I said, "Deal!" That started our almost thirty-year friendship. Gulam told me the things I didn't know about India; he filled in the flavor, fun, humor, and diversity. Later in life, I learned the political side. Of course, our own Martin Luther King Jr. patterned his civil rights movement on Gandhi's efforts of nonviolence.)

Congress came and went for me—as did prison, life changes and jobs—but up to that point I had not one thought about going to India. India and Ellen Ratner had different plans. Perhaps India called to Ellen—who knows.

Geshe Kalsang Damdul la (la is an honorific title in the Tibetan language) is the number two man at the Institute of Buddhist Dialectics (IBD). He is a Tibetan Monk, and now a Member of the Parliament of the Tibetan Government in Exile. I had not met him, but he had met Columbus, Ohio. Geshe la was involved in a multi-year experiment utilizing meditation in lieu of medication only for stress and life problems.

The administration of former Governor Bob Taft, Ohio, had spent a hefty (and wise, I might add) 200,000 dollars for the comprehensive study of the effects of meditation, and the State of Ohio became sold on the project. Ohio State University researchers were monitoring this important study—the brainchild of my college friend, Dr. Deborah Akers. (I was best man in her wedding to Sami Al Shubaily.) Deb put all the elements of this study together, which included bringing a monk (Geshe la) halfway around the world to add an incredibly important component. (See the link to this study in Resources.)

Geshe la came to Columbus periodically to teach and practice meditation with women who were residents in Amethyst House. This is a very successful entity that, through trauma and addiction treatment, supportive housing, and reconnecting them with their children, helps homeless women take back control of their lives. When I heard about this project from Dr. Akers, I was provided the opportunity to meet Geshe la. He is a wonderful, kind, intelligent and compassionate Tibetan monk who escaped across the Himalayas as a child when His Holiness the Dalai Lama did. We talked about meditation and its therapeutic ability.

At the time, in 2010, I was working for Talk Radio News and had my own radio show on WVLY in Wheeling, West Virginia. Dr. Akers came on the show as a guest and discussed meditation and her study at Amethyst House.

The inception of the project came about from a chance visit by Dr. Akers to Dharamsala, the home of the Dalai Lama and the Tibetan Government in Exile. While there, she saw monks soon after they had fled Tibet who had been tortured in hideous ways by their brutal occupiers, the Chinese Communist Government. (The Chinese overtook Tibet in 1959 and were on their way to kill the Dalai Lama when he and others fled and were welcomed, against the wishes of China, into India.)

One particular monk Dr. Akers saw while on that visit to Dharamsala was in a very bad mental and physical state, due to the torture. A year later she returned and recognized the same monk, only he was amazingly rehabilitated. When she asked him how he did it, he gave a one-word answer—meditation.

I also interviewed the women at Amethyst House. Their stories were tough. Some were similar and others were far worse. However, one theme emerged—the meditation had made a huge difference.

Having been in rehab at three different facilities and entrenched in a 12 Step program, I became fascinated with the concept of meditation. I meditated in prison, so I know the value of it when life becomes stressful, unbearable, or out of one's control. My 12 Step program emphasized many ways to recovery; meditation and a person's higher power were part of it.

I believe that a pill-popping America is manna from Heaven for the pharmaceutical companies. Having a bad day? Pop a happy pill. As television commercials tell us, "If your prescription isn't working, try this one." America has gone prescription crazy. There are those cases when medication is the answer, but there are also times when *meditation* is the better answer.

Ellen Ratner and I talked about meditation versus medication. She has been into deep breathing for quite a while and is beyond knowledgeable about rehab and PTSD. As previously mentioned, I had my own radio show on Howard Monroe's station WVLY in Wheeling, West Virginia. I was happy there and I think the show could have grown, but something else was calling me. Call it karma, the universes colliding or whatever, Ellen suggested I go (where else?) to India. She said I could ". . . view this meditation process up close, and on a personal note, you can recharge your own batteries."

September 1, 2010, I was finally off to "Mother India" with the Miami University of Ohio Tibetan Studies Abroad. I was fortunate to be able to travel with their group, which was arranged by their anthropology professor. The stay at Sarah College spanned six weeks. It was located thirty minutes down from McLeodganj where HH Dalai Lama actually lives. It is a Tibetan Studies College for monks, nuns and lay people, including Indians. The principal of the college is Geshe Jamphel Dhakpa and the manager is Passang Tsering la, both very capable individuals. Passang la is not a monk and he was a graduate of Tibetan Children's Village (TCV), founded fifty-one years ago by the sister of His Holiness

Dalul Lama (who also played his mother in the Brad Pitt film, *Seven Years in Tibet*). Passang la is quite a success story. He was raised in TCV, became a Fulbright Scholar in Montana, and is now managing the school.

We arrived in Delhi, and then we were to make the 10.5-hour bus trip to Sarah College the next day. The one night in Delhi was spent at the Tibetan enclave, or settlement town, which is a crowded cluster of shops, tiny rooms, small guesthouses and restaurants. Most Tibetans and many visitors stay there when in Delhi. Some Tibetans live there, somewhat isolated from the Indian community. It could be comparable to a Native American Reservation, yet poorer in many aspects. The students were split up into rooms and I was included in that room draw. I shared a room (one dresser, two beds, and one small bath, but clean) with a student named Sean Kennedy. Because of his level of maturity I thought he was an older student, but he was only nineteen. A television was not to be found, so we spent the time the old-fashioned way—talking. We bonded quickly and we are still friends. He is quite a visionary for someone so young. Sean is full of life, has his priorities in the right order and is eager to learn. In December of that year his mother, Sally, her twin sister, Sue, and Colinda, a wonderful friend of theirs, visited for seven days in McLeod. We laughed, ate, did some paragliding off the mountains and had a great time with one another.

Sally left for Ohio and Sean remained for another month. I was able to spend some time talking with him. India had "grabbed" him, and our days were spent at Ali Baba's Mandala Coffee Shop talking about life, philosophy, plans for the future, and the universe. It was therapeutic for me.

At the coffee shop I met countless wonderful Tibetan and Indian friends like Imran Khan, Lobsang Yarphel and an abundance of Tibetan monks and nuns. One of the employees at Mandala was Anil Kumar. He is my Indian "Buyya" (brother) and we remain best friends. His buddy, Vaibhav Khulbe from Mumbai taught me priceless lessons about life in India and the classic, philosophical books that deal with self-help.

Shelley McBreairty and Carole Marks (Carole hosts a national radio show, "A Touch of Grey") visited India and I arranged days of interviews for them. As we traveled and spoke to people, I became even more fascinated with India and the Tibetan culture that was so intertwined in Dharamsala. It brought me peace, understanding and above all, taught me that my struggles, imprisonment and trials were minor compared with the daily economic struggle for the Indians, and the decades of strife for the exiled Tibetans who are unable to return to their homeland due to China's continued occupation of Tibet.

It was a time of rethinking my path and dealing with losing that anchor called stress.

There were monkeys at Sarah College. Ever since my Grandmother Ricer bought me a "Zippy" musical monkey, I have had a fascination for this wonderfully entertaining animal. Not only was I surrounded by the monkeys at Sarah College, but I also learned how to handle them. If you grin at them, pick up a rock or instrument, or stare at them, you may suffer their aggression by getting bit, losing a tooth, or worse.

When I went to McLeod, following the six-week stay at Sarah College, I didn't do the "Tibetan home stay" that the students did. There were Tibetan families who have been providing these home stays for Westerners for years. Most of the time, the Westerners live in one room with the families and continue their studies. Westerners like space; Tibetans only dream of it. I took a guest room for 500 rupees a day, which is about 10 dollars. That included tax and utilities. It provided clean sheets, a balcony view overlooking the gorgeous Moon Peak Mountain that towers above McLeod, India, a hot shower, and electricity (most of the time). At no extra charge came the 24-hour per day, three-day-long weddings the Indians are famous for. In India, there is no calling the police because the "neighbor's stereo is too loud"!

There is also the "Dharamsala Dog Opera," so named by Dr. Akers. In this area of India, as in most of India, dogs, dogs and more dogs roam the streets. However, there are more in Dharamsala because not only will the Tibetans not squash a mosquito (they cringe when the Westerner's roll up a newspaper), but they are kind to animals as well. Therefore, the dogs get fed and are in abundant supply. At around two a.m. the presence of a night leopard or some other animal might set off a barking chain that starts in McLeodganj and goes all the way down to Dharamsala, for a period of about forty minutes —thus the "Dog Opera" of Dharamsala.

In McLeod, I would walk the kora path. It is a small religious/spiritual path behind the Dalai Lama Temple. The Tibetans walk it clockwise, then end up in the Temple. Very religious Tibetans do it three times. (I find that there are a lot of "threes" in various religions; such as, Father, Son, and Holy Ghost.) For Tibetans, the walk is religious, and for me, a Catholic, it is spiritual.

One day I walked the kora path with my friend Tsering Choney.

Choney, as he is called, is one of the more commonplace Tibetans these days. He was born in Dehradun, South India, but has grown up like tens of thousands of Tibetans in India, and has a "foot in both worlds"—the country from which his people were exiled, and India where he was raised. Choney is the IT manager at Sarah College. Due to his five years of exposure to Emory University (Atlanta, Georgia) and Miami University of Ohio students, he has become savvy to Western ways and has related well to Westerners. We became friends at the speed of light. He is an easygoing person, and enjoys the small things of life. His passion is photography and he manages a Web site that deals with Tibetan issues: tibettoday.com

This particular walk on the kora path with Choney resulted in *Mother India* discovering my fears, as she does with many, and addressing them. I had become fearful of monkeys, due to stories and my personal observations of their becoming aggressive. As we proceeded along the path, suddenly three monkeys appeared—two to the right of the path and one to the left. These were not tiny, tree monkeys. These were actually from the ape family and had no tail. They were not ape-sized, but were definitely in the chimpanzee category for weight and strength. I immediately panicked and wanted to turn back, but Choney, calmly and without missing a step, said, "Don't show aggression, don't show fear and don't stop." Of course he gave me no choice, as he kept walking. In my thinking at the time, I could follow him or be left with the King Kong Trio.

My heart raced and I looked straight ahead, held on to the back of Choney's backpack, and walked between the monkeys that were about six inches from me on each side. If they had heard my pounding heartbeat and had construed that as fear, I would have been attacked in about two seconds. I took a deep breath, confronted my fears and we passed by safely, which enabled me to walk comfortably past these fascinating creatures in my future visits. In the Buddhist cave areas of Ellora and Ajanta, I actually hand-fed the more trained langurs, when we lured them to take biscuits from our hands.

Other fears, uncertainties, insecurities, wounds, and mental anxieties that had developed post-Abramoff were also found and healed by "Mother India."

I soon realized that there was much more to India than cows roaming the streets, dogs, monkeys, chaotic, noisy streets and the like. It is a multi-cultural melting pot and there is an acceptance of the vast differences of those cultures. There is a do-not-give-up spirit that endures despite some lack of opportunity. There is almost a child-like innocence in many adult faces. In the midst of adversity, most are not depressed or turning to artificial substances for a way out. Throughout the Tibetan community, from those who were and continue to be repressed and tortured by the Beijing Communist hard hand, there is sadness due to being in exile, but a continuing spirit of hope. As HH Dalai Lama says, "Never, never, give up" and "If there is a problem and you can solve it, don't worry, and if there is a problem and you cannot solve it, don't worry."

I'm not sure if it is Buddhism, Hinduism, Christianity as practiced with the Indian mindset, or a combination of all, but India is spiritual, alive, and peaceful in a strange sort of mystical way. I continued my stay through most of December, missing my family but torn with the desire to stay just one more month. The last twelve days before I left were spent on a wonderful "on the cheap" travel journey with Sean and Choney across Rajasthan, on desert camel safaris, and to the Taj Mahal, the gem of India.

As Sean and I entered the airport, the goodbye in Delhi was tough for us, especially seeing Choney leave. Then our thoughts turned to savoring our travel, our time in India and the friendships made. I returned to my loved ones in time for Christmas. The present I was given by Ellen Ratner, who made my venture possible, was the spirit of meditation, the learning of patience to survive India's lack of instant American necessities (electricity always on, buses always running, water always hot) and a total re-charge of my batteries—I was dramatically changed in many ways.

In 2011, I worked for Talk Radio News, was collecting a $1900 (gross) per month pension (and glad to have it!), making what I made in 1982. I did not own a home, have healthcare, or life insurance. Nevertheless— I was a healthy 64 pounds lighter than when I entered prison four years before and I was happy.

Even though I was in a good place emotionally, I was still driven to do more. No matter what people think of me and other Members, most Members like to help people. I was no exception. I was adamant with the staff when it came to helping people. My zeal to know what was going on with constituent cases was laborsome for the staff. The reports and information flowing to me on constituent cases was constant. I was obsessed with keeping up with the district and its people.

Neil Volz writes in his book, *Into the Sun*, of working for me first as a volunteer who was made to think that his clipping of constituents' news stories was one of the most important tasks in our office. I believe he thought I was just trying to make him feel good. That was not the case; it was important to me then and it would be important to me today if I were still in office. Yet there was that period of time in my life when that part of who I was melted away like butter left laying out on the table in the hot summer sun.

I returned to my non-officeholder life in the U.S., but was searching for guidance, a path, a purpose—my purpose. January through March brought some work with Talk Radio News then I was back to India for part of March, April, and halfway through May. I spent my time just *being* there. I was a tourist and continue to be one whenever I go there. I take the time to meditate. I also watch for any projects anyone I know in the U.S. might be interested in helping with. Subsequent trips back in the fall of 2011 and spring of 2012 have all been my *recharge* stays. I enjoy the chai houses—in particular, Mandala's Coffee Shop in McLeodganj, or visiting and trekking with Sonu Kumar at Billings Travel. I have made countless friends, like Kaasim Robber, my Hindi tutor and a college student who has come from a very humble background, but as many modern day Indians do, has managed to excel in college and now has a bright future; Sheehan Osborn who is a "mountaineer" from Seattle; Anthony Féoutis, a composer from France (who, by the way, has forgiven me for Freedom fries), and Gerry Becker, an actor from New York.

Ellen has returned to Dharamsala yearly. I have always been there when she comes, and we have been able to spend some time together. On the last trip she made, Ari Zoldan of Quantum Computers came with her. Not only was he delightful, but during his short visit, India *grabbed* him and he felt the lure of "Mother India," as so many do.

I can see why Elizabeth Gilbert in her book *Eat, Pray, Love* makes India the *Pray* part. Incredible India shares the compassion of Gandhi, the friendliness of a broad smile, and the stillness of a glistening moon on a dark river that has bends and curves yet to be sailed upon.

Chapter 36

☆ ★ ☆

ONE DOOR CLOSES, ANOTHER OPENS

"Keep your thoughts positive because your thoughts become your words. Keep your words positive because your words become your behavior. Keep your behavior positive because your behavior becomes your habits. Keep your habits positive because your habits become your values. Keep your values positive because your values become your destiny."

—MAHATMA GANDHI

I am not sure what lies ahead. I continue to check the Google alerts and "Bob Ney" on Twitter to see what is being said. The comments or opinions are not as frequent as they once were, but my name still pops up quite often. Sometimes I ignore them, sometimes I respond in earnest, and sometimes I simply respond to be sarcastic or, frankly, to irritate someone if I think I can get under their skin. My friend Anne Gehman, an internationally known spiritualist and medium, reminds me often when I visit with her and her husband, Wayne, "What someone else thinks of you need not be your business."

I have adjusted to life without Congress. Continuing with Talk Radio News Service has allowed me to be at arm's length from the Hill, but still within reach through opinion. Ellen Ratner has a lot of great host stations and those dedicated radio personalities of all philosophies try to make a difference in their communities. Being part of the opinion and analytical side is a comfortable role for me.

After readjusting to life and realizing that "significant" income was not going to be a reality or a goal of mine, I was able to see what is really important and how to achieve it.

I had to avoid the merry-go-round that John Lennon talked about in his song "Watching the Wheels." Some of my friends are disappointed that I am not trying another run at Congress. It was tempting in 2012, as I saw that people in the District were fed up with the system, period. However, the motivation and the timing for me to run just weren't there. If I were to make another run I would need to focus on good things, as I did originally in my career. For me, it was all about service—until I got sidetracked on what was not important.

Since prison, I have been able to watch my grandbaby, Aaliyah, grow from an infant to a kindergartener at this writing. I walked my daughter, Kayla, down the aisle when she and Adam Kidd married. I was able to attend my son Bobby's wedding to Julie Pitt in September of 2011. I had the privilege to attend both weddings as a free man and to enjoy my family and many friends that attended. (Ellen received the longest distance award for both weddings, coming in from somewhere else in the world.)

I have not been in a position since before going to prison to buy another house, but I am happy having settled into a small house that I rent with a roommate. Living with a roommate allows me to spend my money on other areas and stay on a budget. I've been tempted to buy another house, but I have come to the realization that "needs" and "wants" are two different things.

In losing so much financially, I certainly woke up to an America that has become just a bit too consumer-crazy: buying more and more upgraded cell phones, the latest laptops/notebooks/iPads, a bigger plasma screen TV, another "needed" car, and every other tempting electronic "toy" that is out on the market.

As America has been on its current collision course with debt, we have seen the Bush Administration and, even more so the Obama Administration, promote personal "spending" to solve the dilemma we are in. The opposite should occur for individuals *and* the government.

Matt Parker gave me a great book when I got out of prison that shed light (and hope) on how we need to live. *Financial Peace* by Dave Ramsey was the best book I have read for my own financial peace. I have passed it on to many people.

These days as I awaken, I have no needs. I still have wants, but I've been able to separate those from what really counts. I constantly check myself through conversations with friends. This revives my creative energy for ideas and goals and allows me to proceed without fear of failure. I have come to realize that if I have the desire, dreams, goals and passion for what I want to do, success will find me—perhaps not in dollars, but in personal satisfaction.

Broadening my horizons and not limiting myself to strictly political literature or one-sided views (Jon Stewart has replaced some mainstream news for me) has allowed me to have a more open view of politics and life in general. I am now uplifted by watching Judge Judy, Judge Mathis, Oprah, and Ellen DeGeneres versus reality shows and endless, twenty-four hour news. These new venues teach me more about people, their lives, my life, and learning about change than my old myopic, mindless entertainment shows ever could have.

For my health, I have undertaken a changed eating regimen of mainly vegetables, very little red meat and a greatly reduced intake of processed foods. I also force myself to find time to exercise. It started ever so slowly with my 234-pound, 5' 8" frame, to today's 160-ish-pound weight. I didn't do it because of vanity; at my age, I'm beyond that. My improved physical health has improved my mental health. I donate time to 12 Step programs as I can, I enjoy a good book now and then, and through Facebook, e-mails, and good old-fashioned telephone conversations (I prefer not to text), I maintain contact with friends and savor the increased time I have with my family.

My purpose in mentioning my finances and any sacrifices or adjustments I have had to make is certainly not an attempt to gain sympathy. I don't deserve it, nor do I need or want it. I bring up the subject of finances and lessons learned for one reason. If I could leave with you any of my thoughts, suggestions or bits of wisdom from my experience and all that I have written in this book, it would be the following:

Realize now, at whatever age you are, whatever your life's position, whatever your economic situation, that money is necessary, but unless it is placed in the proper perspective, it becomes the slave master that tells us how to live and conduct our lives. Life and pursuing what is truly important as we make this brief stop in these short-lived, earthly shells is the key to happiness. Living within means and utilizing the free time to be with people we love, need, and appreciate is the only "overtime" we need. If you have money to burn, pursuing the next electronic toy, the best new car, the biggest home, the ever-changing wardrobe is one thing, but burning your time to have it just never pans out at the end of the day.

The other clear message I can deliver is about ethics. I know what you're thinking—*This guy is going to tell me about ethics?* You would be right to wonder. I failed the ethics course, broke the mold, "screwed the pooch," crossed the line, and put myself and others into ethics hell. Yet I have learned firsthand what it is to run off course. If I had to analyze the system and comment on the honesty, integrity, and transparency of our government and how it functions in the U.S., I would have to give it a C-. It receives a grade that high because we are America, still the greatest bulwark of freedom and the best *living* available on the planet. If we didn't have these factors going for us, the grade would be lower. We can do so much better.

Small numbers of people control the future of this country. People from the "Left" love to complain about the Citizens United case (the Supreme Court overturned long-standing campaign finance laws restricting corporate political expenditures, which allowed groups to raise and spend unlimited amounts supporting or opposing candidates), while in one night, one actor, George Clooney, whom I happen to like both professionally and personally, can bring in twelve million dollars.

The Right love to rant about the socialist billionaire George Soros, who with his wealth controls the shadowy MoveOn.org and influences politics and government, sometimes for personal gain—such as the foreign steel he flooded into our market. Yet the mega-rich, conservative Koch brothers and power brokers like Karl Rove can raise large dollars at the snap of a finger.

American workers are put on the back burner and the middle class shifted to the back of the bus—achieved by both the Right and the Left. Money is money, power is power, and a small group of billionaires deciding the course of America is just plain wrong. Were Jack (Team Abramoff) and me (Ney World) the rotten apples or was the barrel corrupt? I know that Alex Gibney's important film *Casino Jack and the United States of Money* can provide an answer to this question. It is irrelevant if the entire barrel is rotten in how "history" or you choose to portray me, but it *is* important that you hear this—don't let your feelings about Jack Abramoff or me cloud your vision. Pay attention to your political world before it bites you hard. In today's America, PhRMA (Pharmaceutical Research and Manufacturers of America), big oil, and the "Soros" and the "Kochs" of the world, rule.

You need to be diligent, questioning, and thorough—not just about whether your Member took a trip or a dinner—that is peanuts compared with that Member voting away your rights and your money for *big influences*. It happens today, and it has happened to our top political leaders on both sides of the aisle. If the spokespersons of our systems—if the leaders of our parties are in the pockets of *influence peddlers* that pale Abramoff, then we are in serious trouble. The corrupt barrel is cracking in America. There are good people, but the system needs a makeover.

I hope my story awakens you and makes you aware that there are others who need to be watched closely by you, the voter, to avoid other "Casino Jacks" and "Justice Departments" laced with inside personal interests, lobbyists and friends, all waiting to line their pockets for purely personal gain. The Dave Distefanos, Barry Jacksons, Alberto Gonzales's and Alice Fishers of the world are still at large, and it is up to you to do your own due diligence and arm yourself with the right questions for your Congressional Members as they seek your vote every two years.

This *free course* in ethics and human behavior techniques and analysis I'm offering you isn't concerned only with those running for, or currently in, political office. It applies to the average citizen who is employed or not, has a family, has friends, volunteers, is active in their community with social and fraternal groups, belongs to a volunteer fire department, works at the local youth center, is retired . . . and the list goes on. When dealing with other people in any capacity, if the situation doesn't feel right, doesn't look right, doesn't smell right, gives you any hesitation or bad feeling—if it tugs at your conscience, your moral compass, or scares you legally, ethically, or emotionally—say "no" and move on. Using your common sense, doing the right thing when nobody is watching, and following your heart with what you know deep down is right, will give you a personal freedom to excel and move through any situation, knowing that you have done the right thing. Follow your gut and your conscience and you will be free to explore curves and bends yet to be seen. Otherwise, you might be sideswiped; and it could be at your own hand.

One last thing—although I have mentioned my adaptation of this quote before, keep in mind that it's not the good and bad moments that count, but the moments that take your breath away. May you have many!

Afterword

IS THE BARREL
STILL CORRUPT?

I have always been, and even more so now, a person who loves to learn from self-help books and quotes. Out of the thousands of motivational and inspiring quotes I have viewed over the years, one of my all time favorites comes from my friend Tim Hannon. It is simplistic but says volumes about where we have ended up and what journey lies ahead. Tim says, "God puts people in our paths."

In my case, God—for you, the higher power of your choosing—puts people in our paths. Our interactions with those people may be brief, of long duration, good, bad, or sometimes even unnoticed, but they will still have meaning for us in ways yet to be revealed.

I could not end this book without saying some interactions that crossed my path seemed to be dark, bleak, and without value at the time—yet they had meaning. I'm not only talking about lessons learned, but about what I did—and the system in which I did it. I have certainly changed, but has the system changed? You will determine that for yourself as time goes on in our political/governmental process. Let me share with you my thoughts about whether we have progressed from the Ney/Abramoff days:

Is it still bribery if it's legal?

Today, even with all of Nancy Pelosi's 2007 efforts to "drain the swamp" after Jack and I hit the press, legal influence peddling exists. While the days of lobbyists dropping off tickets to local sporting events and casual lunch and dinner invitations at Washington's finest restaurants have largely stopped, Members, staff and lobbyists have found

339

SIDESWIPED

more meaningful loopholes. Under Congressional ethics rules, a lobbyist cannot invite a Member or staffer to dinner or an event on a social basis, but (get this) they can invite them if it's a fundraiser! So to recap,
• watching the Redskins play in a lobbyist's luxury box: illegal. Watching the Redskins play in a luxury box with a handful of folks who also write you a $2,500 individual contribution check and a $5,000 PAC (Political Action Committee) check at the lobbyist's request: TOTALLY LEGAL.

Lobbyists can host fundraising events for Members in their homes, at restaurants, on golf courses, sporting events, and so forth, and Members can host them, too. Members frequently host PAC events in exotic locations. Just last year, Members hosted events for lobbyists interested in just about anything (even at a bondage club, for Young Republicans).
• As long as a lobbyist or businessman can pony up $5,000 from their PAC, they can party with the Congressman and his/her chief of staff in Beverly Hills; they can grouse hunt, golf & fish in Sun Valley; ski in Aspen; attend the Grammys or Country Music Awards in L.A. or Vegas; go big-game hunting in Alaska . . . you name it! And bring your kids! Both parties do it—this is not exclusive to one.

The fact that money influences Washington isn't news. What *is* news is just how much time Members and their chiefs of staff spend raising money and how little money it takes to influence the process. To be clear, Members and staff don't view contributions for legislative acts as a "quid pro quo." They rationalize it. Because the fundraising is legal and rarely
• clear-cut, money doesn't always buy you a direct vote, but it gets you access. If you show up at a Congressman's event and give him or her a check for $500–$2,500, and then request a meeting in his or her office a few days later (on any topic), you'll get a meeting. Access is what it gets you (and often times considerably more quickly than a Member's constituents can gain access).

Granted, a contribution of any size, even if it gets you access, isn't going to change a Congressman's vote on a big-ticket issue with his constituents. Even a $30,000 fundraiser won't guarantee that a Member changes his position on a gun vote, abortion vote, healthcare vote, or anything incredibly popular/unpopular in his/her district that could cost the Member reelection. However, regarding 90% of other legislative
• areas that get little publicity, it can absolutely buy an outcome (even if that outcome is murky).

Members can submit record statements that garner a good bit of press or internal company/trade association backslapping. A Member can insert language in appropriations bills or larger authorization vehicles without anyone knowing what it is and who it is for. A Member can initiate a letter to an agency, co-sponsor legislation, start a caucus (for just about anything), say positive/negative things to the press on a given topic, give statements on the House/Senate floor, give VIP tours of the White House and Capitol to key donors, speak at events or on conference calls at a lobbyist's request, and vote certain ways on items that are totally inconsequential to the Member's or constituents' priorities.

And . . . just about all of them do this or some form of it without even realizing it. Because . . . it's legal. Maybe it's not within the "spirit of the law," but it's certainly within the letter of the law—as long as the actions taken aren't implied, understood or in writing. Only one person in history has ever been convicted of an LDA (Lobbying Disclosure Act) violation and his name wasn't Jack Abramoff, Bob Ney, Duke Cunningham or Tom DeLay. You wouldn't even know his name. This gentleman failed to fill out registration forms for his clients for years, and even ignored slaps on the wrist and small fines to avoid getting into trouble.

If most constituents knew how much time Members of Congress spent raising money, they would storm the Capitol. After countless efforts at "Campaign Finance Reform," the system is even worse. A perfect example was the effort to cap contribution sizes at small amounts.

No, we don't want a system where a handful of donors can write unlimited amounts (ironically, they can now write unlimited amounts to "Super PACs," thanks to Citizens United), but what we've done has required Members to raise the same amounts of money (because the campaigns cost more every year) in smaller increments. The net effect is a $1,000 check now has more value than ever before and a lobbyist who can find a Member thirty of them in one lunch hour is a King!

If a Member in a tough race still needs to raise $3 million, that's a lot of little individual checks and PAC checks to get there. More pressure is added by the threat of a Super PAC (which doesn't have any limitations placed on the amount of monetary contributions they receive), or I.E. (independent expenditure) coming into a Member's district. So, if there are 300 business days a year, divide $3 million by that number of days and a Member of Congress needs to raise about $10,000/day for his or her campaign every workday. That can become the biggest focus of a day or week—not testimony before an important committee hearing.

To do this, the Member in a tough race and the chief of staff walk from their Congressional offices down the hill (literally a block away) to either the NRCC (National Republican Campaign Committee) or DCCC (Democrat Congressional Campaign Committee) to sit in large rooms divided into cubicles to "dial for dollars." They and their staff are handed call-sheets from their paid finance director who works on their campaign and coordinates with a D.C.-based PAC fundraiser. Maybe 50 to 100 Excel spreadsheets lay in front of them with names of personal friends, past contributors, lobbyists, trade associations, etc. These lists include how much the person has given to the Congressman before, when they gave, and any personal notes about the person: "How's your wife recovering?" or "Congrats on the promotion!" It's not atypical for this to go on for several hours a day between votes or committee hearings or other fundraising breakfasts, lunches or dinners every single day of the week.

Senior Members of Congress on top tier Committees (especially if they are chairman of that committee), may not have a tough race of their own to raise money for, but they are expected to pony up for their party to maintain the majority. These senior members often receive a "bill" of sorts from the NRCC or DCCC, letting members of leadership and key committees (like Ways and Means, Energy and Commerce, Appropriations, and Financial Services) know what they are expected to raise/transfer from their personal campaign/leadership PAC accounts to the party. It can be $50K–$100K for a plum seat, or $500K–$1 million for key chairmanship, and well beyond that for members of the leadership team. "Pay-to-Play" isn't rhetoric. It's reality.

When the Supreme Court made its decision on Citizens United in 2010, it is a fact that some House Members' chiefs of staff coordinated a call with the Member, fundraisers, and top strategists to produce a list of their best donors and contacts to counteract a "worst case scenario"— if a Karl Rove-type group came into their district. Instead of legislating, they were making a mad dash to find limitless cash (even though in some cases, they already had millions more in the bank than their underfunded challengers).

While Super PACs weren't decisive in the 2012 presidential race with two well-known, well-financed candidates, they can be lethal in House and Senate races.

There's a huge misperception about lobbyists and campaign contributions. Most Americans today view lobbyists as holding sacks of money, roaming the halls of Congress. However, lobbyists hate giving their own money, especially if they don't control a large PAC. Members have such a large appetite for campaign money that they spend hours a day on the phone, calling lobbyists and asking for money. One lobbyist told me he hides from certain Members and avoids phone calls from numbers he doesn't know. One time he was driving home and got a call from a random (212) area code and accidentally answered the phone. It was a U.S. Senator requesting he come to a $2,500 dinner the next day.

"It's awfully hard to tell a U.S. Senator no, especially when he's helping your client with something."

With 535 members doing the same thing, there's only so much cash in a PAC or lobbyist's budget.

There have always been lobbyists and money has always been a part of politics—probably always will be. Lobbyists first got their name from a group of "advocates" for various companies who caught wind that President Grant hung out at the Willard Hotel for cocktails at a certain time each night. They would hang out in the lobby, so he started calling them the "lobbyists."

The art of lobbying is a noble one—and a constitutional one. Every American (and in the Supreme Court and Mitt Romney's view, corporation) has the constitutional First Amendment rights to free speech, peaceable assembly, and to petition their government for a redress of grievances. And, there's no way a single Member of Congress and their small policy staffs (often four or five fresh-faced twenty-somethings) can know or keep track of every detail of every issue under the sun.

Congress and lobbyists need each other and rely on each other. If a lobbyist lies or hurts a member, they get shut out for good. But the onus is on the elected official to seek out all information and listen to all sides (especially his/her constituents, who may not be totally informed) before making a decision. What skews this is money. That's why we should bite the bullet and have public-financed campaigns. Yes, the Chamber of Commerce and Labor Unions will hate it; yes, it is expensive to taxpayers; but it will save the country more in the long run. Our current campaign finance system is legal bribery and bankrupting the country—plain and simple.

I had a drug of choice; a substance that I abused. There is a current situation in the Congress that needs an intervention in a different arena. Every politician's drug of choice is campaign funds. An intervention by the public demanding that it be different is the only cure.

Appendix 1

☆ ☆ ☆

IN ADDITION . . .

I suppose everyone who writes a book still has some things to say and nowhere to put them. This is the reason for this Appendix. These are thoughts, incidents, anecdotes, and so forth that you might find interesting. There are many more I could have written, but alas, page limits are just that—limits.

PUSHY WIVES (AND OTHER CONGRESSIONAL HEADACHES)

To avoid being accused of misogyny, let me start this with a quote from Barbara Walters: *"If it's a woman it's caustic, if it's a man it's authority. If it's a woman it's too pushy, if it's a man it's aggressive in the best sense of the word."*

In 2000, the year I took my children to Italy for the Pope John Paul II Papal Mass, there were several members of Congress on that trip. It was a yearly event. This particular trip became memorable because Republican Representatives Bill Thomas (R-California) and Phil Crane (R-Illinois) were on the trip, and they were both vying for Chairman of the Ways and Means Committee. It was a huge battle.

Phil Crane had a serious drinking problem, but there had been an intervention, he had sobered up and quit drinking. His wife was his other problem. The late Mrs. Crane (Arlene) was extremely bossy. When we arrived in Italy, our large group was divided into two hotels. One was the Excelsior. We were told that if we were going to be staying at the Excelsior, we were to identify our bags and they would go to the right. If we were in the other hotel, they would go to the left.

There was some confusion and Mrs. Crane all of a sudden turned around and said, "When *I'm* running Ways and Means, it's not going to be like this!" Bill Thomas, who was from California and a prickly type of Congressman, seized upon this and a lot of chatter made its way around the Republican Delegation in the realm of, "Well it's very obvious that if Phil Crane becomes Chairman, his wife is going to be running it!"

Mrs. Crane was a strong personality. After the Italy trip, I remember being on a boat in Antigua with her and Congressman Crane. There were some Democrats on the trip with us; Donald Payne, a U.S. Representative from New Jersey at the time, was one of them. We were guests of Allen Stanford, of Stanford Financial *(who is now in prison serving a 110-year sentence for a massive Ponzi scheme and fraud)*. Mrs. Crane was furious because Phil didn't get the Chairmanship of the Ways and Means Committee. She proceeded to drink quite a lot, became angry and then said in a loud voice that the Speaker of The House's staff were "perverts (gay) and Scott Palmer, his Chief of Staff, knew that they were all sleeping with each other in a house they shared in D.C. This came right out of the blue and shocked everyone. We were trying to quiet her down because she was saying it in front of the Democrats. She just said anything bad she could think of about the Speaker's people. Mrs. Crane was a factor in costing Philip Crane his chairmanship. His former drinking wasn't helpful, but Phil Crane was a nice guy.

Some of the Congressional spouses were interesting and aggressive. There was the late Mrs. Young (Lu), wife of Republican Representative Don Young from Alaska. Don was a big, burly, teddy bear-type of guy, but he was also really, really tough. He was Chairman of the Transportation Committee, famous for the Bridge to Nowhere. (This was $223 million earmarked for building the Gravina Island Bridge from Ketchikan, Alaska, to Gravina Island that contains Ketchikan's airport. There is a small car and passenger ferry that travels the quarter-mile in three to seven minutes and runs every half hour. Critics assailed this as pork barrel spending at taxpayers' expense and dubbed it the "Bridge to Nowhere." The bridge was defunded and the money was funneled to Alaska's Department of Transportation. I had constituents who said I should vote against the Highway bill because the Bridge to Nowhere was in there. I said, "No! I have fifty-eight million bucks in there." I was hoping that if the constituents realized the possibility of losing millions in highway funds, it would help them understand why I would go along with the Chairman.)

Don Young was a gregarious type of guy. One time, due to a committee staffer error, I didn't get a needed amendment into a transportation bill. I wanted that noted for the public purpose of getting it in somewhere along the line as the bill headed to the Senate, so in the committee I said, "Mr. Chairman, I just wanted to note that hopefully I'll have a chance in the Conference Committee." Chairman Young sat in the Chairman's seat, in the middle of the dais, a row above me. He looked down at me in front of the entire Transportation audience and said, "Mr. Chairman of the House Administration Mayor Ney [I used to be called the Mayor of Capitol Hill], you control my drapes, you control my carpeting, you make my wife happy or not and therefore you can have anything you want."

The audience laughed. I used to get calls from the late Mrs. Young when she wanted certain things changed, or there were some spots on the carpet in her husband's office. (She voluntarily managed the office for him.) Jay Eagan, who was a very uptight CAO (Chief Administration Officer) of the House Administration Committee, was under my jurisdiction. Jay went by the book, dotting every "I" and crossing every "T." I wanted the carpet replaced, Mrs. Young wanted the carpet replaced, but Jay said that it just wasn't *weathered* enough. We pushed Jay pretty hard, and because of Mrs. Young, we replaced all the carpeting in Congressman Young's Office. Lu Young was a sweet woman who loved Don dearly—she also loved Alaska and the constituents.

The wife of the late Democratic Congressman Tom Lantos from California nearly always travelled with Congressman Lantos. She was actually a cousin of Zsa Zsa Gabor and she was a character, in the good sense of the word. She wore a lot of makeup, was very stylish and flamboyant, had a heavy Hungarian accent and talked quite a lot—about everything. She would be hard to forget.

Former Republican Representative Ben Gilman from New York was a quiet guy. After his first wife passed away, he remarried and this Mrs. Gilman wore great big glasses with Hollywood-style frames. My exasperated staff would many times say, "Oh my God" and referred to her as "Congresswoman Gilman," which she wasn't. She could be quite demanding on the trips. On a trip to Germany where we were meeting with Helmut Kohl, the Chancellor of Germany, Mrs. Gilman demanded that she be in that meeting. Ben just couldn't tell her no. He was a nice guy and said, "Well, honey . . ." and in her New York accent she said, "No, Ben! The spouses need to be in that meeting!" Finally, the German authorities told Ben's staff that if she continued, no one was going to be in the meeting. It was for Members of Congress only—no spouses. On the trip, she had all the specialty items and food she wanted. She was catered to more than Congressman Gilman was.

As for the Congresswomen, one spouse that stands out in my mind was Paul Pelosi, the husband of Minority leader, Nancy Pelosi (D-California). At one particular dinner function, Paul was seated at a table with the Republican Representatives. Nancy was on the dais, and was to give a speech. Paul was charming, funny, and we all got along well. After a bit, one of the Members said, "Hey, why don't you take Nancy's place and she can run the business in California?"

He smiled and said something to the effect of, "Don't go there!"

Female spouses, no question, were catered to by staff, by the Capitol Hill Police, by everyone, including me, because we knew these women had so much influence on their husbands that it could actually affect how they operated. If a spouse were to get mad at someone, the Member of Congress would probably go to that person and say, "Hey! You know you're pissing my wife off?" Therefore, yes—they absolutely had a lot of power—and they made life on the Hill fascinating.

DIRTY WORK

When I was Vice Chairman of the House Administration Committee (1995–2000), among my duties was carrying bills to the floor of the House on behalf of the Chair. The person who does this is commonly called the Floor Manager, or the Manager of the Bill. Another duty involved those times when Chairman Thomas's staff would ask me to represent the Chairman if he were "not available."

One memory that stands out was in 1998 when I was asked by Chairman Thomas's staff to represent him at a high-powered budget meeting between Newt Gingrich, then Speaker of the House, and Dan Burton, who was a "quirky," unpredictable Member. Dan had a tendency to be volatile and exaggerate, which added drama to whatever he happened to be working on. He was quite animated and had a sense of emergency about him, as though some intricate plot was in the works and about to descend upon him.

I naively felt that I was summoned by the Chairman to fill in at the highest level because he was detained.

I went into Speaker Gingrich's office, past the large, authentic, skeletal

Tyrannosaurus Rex head that took up a tenth of the space, and into the conference room. Newt's first love, as he told us many times, was dinosaurs. (I guess if you have a name like Newt, you might feel akin to the prehistoric.)

We sat at the table and Dan Burton immediately began lobbying for more money. He headed an investigation into Democratic Party campaign finance abuse. Dan had been given a budget to go after the Clintons and "abuses" in their administration, including looking at the Whitewater investment scheme that involved President and Hillary Clinton. As a member of the House Administration committee, I knew that it was headed down a dead-end road. Many subpoenas had been issued and there was nothing clear-cut coming forth. The Republican staff that had pored over tens of thousands of documents said that there was nothing shocking there. The government had gone after James and Susan McDougal, Webb Hubbell, and now the Republican Congress was trying to nail the Clintons.

Dan said that he was close to nailing the President and this could lead to his impeachment. Newt asked pertinent questions, as Newt does, concerning the facts of the case and proof of Dan's intent. He wanted more than just Dan's feeling that he was close to nailing the President.

Newt said, "Look Dan, I want to get to the bottom of this and I think there is something here, but we have spent so much money and don't have anything of direct substance that could be used to legally pursue the President in the Whitewater affair."

Dan responded with a plea: "Newt, the people of the United States want the truth and I need to provide it."

The conversation turned to me and I followed House Administration Committee staff *script* of not giving in: "We have just so much money allocated for this. House Administration oversees and allocates the budgets of the standing committees and select committees and at this time we will not be able to sell the idea, especially with this *new Congress*." (This is what we called the 104th Congress with the new Members due to Newt's Contract with America.)

Dan then pled directly with me: "Bob, you know there is something here; you know the Clintons are involved, and you know that we can nail them if we just have more money."

I asked, "How much more?"

Dan said, "I believe I can do this with around five million dollars more."

I looked at Newt, he looked at me and I said, "I just don't see it in the cards. House Administration will not appropriate more money. We have done enough, and followed the game plan."

Dan exploded. He said, "You people are not doing the will of the country, just because of money!"

Newt and I knew that we were all headed down a political rat hole. We could spend millions and millions more and find nothing. If we gave Dan Burton more money, he would return for more—again being "ever so close."

Newt said, "Dan, there is a process, and I cannot solely decide this."

I spoke up and said, "There is no more money and I cannot see any forthcoming."

Dan's tone then went from saving the country with the truth, to a personal rant and said, "You people are screwing me, dismantling my career, making me look like an idiot. I cannot believe that you, Newt and the Republicans are f——ing me. I will be thinking about resigning. Shove this! I don't need it."

He then started crying. I am sitting there with Newt Gingrich who is third in line for the presidency, I am being used by House Administration Chairman Thomas to do his dirty work, and the chairman of a Select Committee to go after the sitting President of the United States is in tears, storming out of the room saying, "You people are f——ing up my career!" It was a moment that will probably not be included in a chapter of Profiles in Courage II. Newt and I looked at each other, said nothing, and I left.

Later, after debriefing the staff of Chairman Thomas, I was told, "Good job. The Chairman appreciates your filling in for him, as he had a schedule conflict."

I then went about my business, and got death stares from Dan for a while. (In January of 2012 Dan Burton retired from the U.S. Congress, citing personal family health reasons.)

HUMAN RIGHTS

Congressman Frank Wolf (R-Virginia)

Congressman Wolf has traveled the globe extensively in the name of human rights for those who suffer. He has spoken out over the treatment of the Bahái's, human trafficking, and the Chinese human rights record. He tried to prevent the Clinton/Gingrich 1999 Chinese Permanent Trade Bill, and has trumpeted human rights issues in the Sudan.

In a major move, Congressman Wolf was successful in passing a clause in a U.S. spending bill in 2011 that prohibited NASA and the White House Office of Science and Technology to do any joint scientific ventures with China. His quote was "We don't want to give them the opportunity to take advantage of our technology, and we have nothing to gain from dealing with them. And frankly, it boils down to a moral issue . . . Would you have a bilateral program with Stalin?"

Congressman Chris Smith (R-New Jersey)

Congressman Smith is another great Member of Congress who has stood up for the Right to Life movement and has been a very fair Member when it comes to working people and labor issues, and has done extensive work in the area of human rights and human trafficking. In 2005 he was appointed Chairman of the House International Relations Africa, Global Human Rights and International Operations Subcommittee.

Congressman Wolf and Congressman Smith were prohibited by Chinese Security forces in 2009 from meeting with Chinese human rights lawyers in Beijing. Both of these Congressmen continue to be leaders in the U.S. Congress on this important issue of human rights.

HONEST SERVICES FRAUD CHARGE

As a note of interest concerning one of the charges against me, honest services fraud, it was unanimously ruled by the Supreme Court on June 24, 2010, in the cases of Black and Skilling to be too vague to constitute a crime unless a bribe or kickback was involved.

Stepping Down in New Orleans

In January of 2006, I was in New Orleans as Chairman of the Housing Sub Committee of the Committee on Financial Services, and Congresswoman Maxine Waters, (D-California) was the Ranking Member. Our goal was to have a hearing on Hurricane Katrina. It was actually the first hearing by a Congressional Committee to be held. The *Picayune Tribune*, after we arrived, rebuked both Speaker Hastert and Nancy Pelosi, the Minority Leader, for not having a hearing or paying enough attention to devastated New Orleans.

When Maxine became my Ranking Member, some said that she would be impossible. Our relationship was not impossible—it was perfect. Maxine and I had worked together on housing issues, trying to get people into affordable housing. I was Chairman of the Housing Subcommittee (a subcommittee of the full Committee on Banking). I visited her homeless shelters in Los Angeles. She was particularly concerned with social engineering, and was a pleasure to work with. Although controversial, particularly among white conservatives, she is able to frankly and openly discuss race issues, give a different perspective to the issues, and resolve differences. We may have disagreed, we may have taken aggressive positions, but at no time were we uncivil. We were totally honest with each other, just as Steny Hoyer and I had been. There were even two articles written, one by the late and wonderful journalist for the *Washington Post*, David Broder, and the other by *Roll Call*, highlighting Maxine and me, and Steny and me. One of the articles by Broder said essentially that Congress would be a better place if more people got along as we did.

The hearing was in a good-sized auditorium and it was packed. My office tried in vain to get Mayor Ray Nagin at the hearing, but he was under fire in New Orleans for siding with some people who, it was alluded to, didn't want to help the poor people relocate and were "red tagging" areas for other development, not for homes. However, Maxine's office got Mayor Nagin there.

The night before the hearing, Maxine, her husband, some of the staff and I decided to eat in the French Quarter to provide some positive publicity about eating there again. It seemed like an eerie ghost town.

The next morning as I was getting ready for the hearing, Brian Walsh, who worked for me and was a top-shelf Press Secretary, called me on the phone and said he had to come to my room ASAP. Scott Palmer, Speaker of the House Dennis Hastert's Chief of Staff, had called Brian having a bombastic, fit and said, "Denny [Speaker Hastert] is going to get a bad article and Bob needs to step down [as Chairman of the House Administration Committee]." Brian then asked about what direction the article was going on me.

Scott said, "The article is not about Ney, but about criticizing Denny for being weak so we have to 'save the Speakership' and make Denny look strong." He continued, "Ney has to step down now [as Chairman of the House Administration Committee] so Denny can mention it in the *Washington Post* article."

I told Brian, "I serve and have always known due to my 'Speaker's Chairmanship,' which was a special one, that I could be called upon to step down any day any time, so I will." (*The chair is chosen strictly by the Speaker, as are the Chairs of the Intelligence Committee and the Rules Committee. All the rest of the Chairs are chosen by a voting process of a committee of various Members and approved by the entire Republican Conference of Members. My Chairmanship was designated by the Speaker only, and I could be removed the same way.*)

I added, "Tell Scott I need an hour as I am headed to the hearing and want to tell my family before it hits the media [before Scott Palmer leaked it out] and my kids hear it on a CNN blurb."

Brian responded, "Sure." Then I heard Brian raising his voice to Scott, who was raising his voice to Brian. Brian said, "Scott, you have to be kidding, we just need an hour. . . . Okay, fifteen minutes."

Scott Palmer was the ultimate drama queen and would wildly flip his hands in the air and scream at anyone in his path. I observed this behavior many times and he was famous for it on the Hill. He was also notorious for calling the Speaker of the House, "Denny." We all knew they were friends and roommates, but Scott seemed to have to prove that he ran "Denny." Behind Scott's back, people referred to him as "Lurch" from *The Addams Family*.

Brian said Scott's response was, "Absolutely not!" and he hung up. I thought about refusing to step down, but instead accepted what I could not control. I arrived at the hall, had to greet people immediately and prepare for the hearing. I had no time to make calls to prepare my family, so I asked David Popp, my Executive Assistant to call my mother and father, wife, sister, and my children, Bobby and Kayla.

Before the hearing in New Orleans got underway, Louis Farrakhan (religious and social leader, and head of Nation of Islam) stepped into the room and a buzz ensued. One of the other committee members, we had about nine present, asked me not to let him testify or it would cause Mayor Nagin to come unglued. Minister Farrakhan had been criticizing the mayor for how he was handling the city business after Hurricane Katrina.

I greeted Minister Farrakhan by saying in Arabic, "Salaam alaikum" He looked surprised, and responded, "Alaikum, salaam." He then said,

"Congressman, have we met before?" I told him that we had, once in Saudi Arabia in 1987 at a hotel restaurant.

(I was on an ACYPL [American Council of Young Political Leaders] trip as an Ohio State Senator. I and about five other members of a bipartisan group from around the United States were at a dinner table in Jeddah, where I had lived in 1983. A white councilman from Phoenix, Arizona, was talking about Louis Farrakhan to an African American leader from the Democrat National Committee. The councilman said he found him to be "bizarre; a bit scary." The Democrat he was speaking to basically agreed. A man then approached us and said, "The Reverend Farrakhan would like to invite you to his room to clear up any misconceptions." There, sitting at the next table was Minister Farrakhan. The two men who were discussing him looked as though they had seen a ghost. We spoke with the minster and ended on good terms.)

When I told Minster Farrakhan that we had met in Saudi Arabia, I think that incident had been long forgotten. I began by saying, "Minister Farrakhan, we are pleased to have you here. I would like to recognize you, but unfortunately the witnesses and the order are preset. Had I known, I would have liked to accommodate you."

He responded, "I am fine, I am here to be of support."

I proceeded to the Chairman's seat and began the hearing. After a few minutes into some introductions, Maxine nudged me, showed me her Blackberry and said, "What the hell is this?" It was a news flash that I was stepping down as Chairman of House Administration (not the Housing Sub Committee—even Scott Palmer couldn't take both away; it would be like hitting a dying man). Maxine said, "I will do whatever you need, stand with you, make statements, help you fight this." I so appreciated her sincere words. I said, "Thanks, but it's done."

(Later in 2006 after I announced my plea deal, the pressure was on for me to resign my Congressional seat—but not by all. Until I actually entered a guilty plea with the Justice Department, John Boehner understood the rationale and legal fact that until sentencing, a plea could be changed or dropped, and that nothing would be final until sentencing. It would have been a quagmire for Boehner to get into a pissing match with me after his involvement in a "resign for job and money" scheme—the one where he told me if I stepped down I would get a job and he would raise money for my legal bills.)

Scott Palmer in Hastert's office was not of the same mind. Statements were made by Speaker Hastert, calling for me to resign as a Congressman now. The Democratic side was silent, with no calls from Nancy

Pelosi or Steny Hoyer. The Republicans, not all, but many, joined those calling for my resignation.

There were several reasons I opted not to: The Press focused on my staying in until December to get my paycheck, and I admit that was one reason; but I was closing my office down, working feverishly on last minute cases where I had more power with the bureaucracy to help my constituents as a sitting Member of Congress (a disgraced, prison-bound Member is still a Member). However, the main reason was that I cared, and always did—despite my behavior—about what happened to staff. I was afraid there would be terminations of the "tainted Ney people" in my personal D.C. office and possibly the District Office staff as well.

One of my biggest regrets concerning how all this went down was that I couldn't call the staff personally and tell them what was going on. With everything exploding in my life, it was impossible to do it. However, my larger concern was that there would be a repeat of what happened when I stepped down as Chairman of the House Administration Committee.

(We supposedly had a deal that my staff in House Administration would be protected. However, when Vern Ehlers, a nice man and the only nuclear scientist in the House, became the Chair to replace me, his chief of staff made the St. Valentine's Day massacre look like a Roman love orgy. He even fired the student interns whose class grades depended on their jobs. I was angry anyway, as they were firing my staff right and left for no reason—people who would not know what Jack Abramoff looked like if they had not seen him on television. I called Vern, and at that time in January of 2006, my anger fueled by alcohol sent me into a tirade that made it clear I would call the national media and launch into him, the Speaker, Scott Palmer, and anyone else I needed to and would say anything I had to in order to stop what they were doing. They stopped some of the bloodletting, and at least the innocent college interns were hired back.)

Knowing what *butcher* Scott Palmer and his *protégé* Ted Van der Meid were capable of, I was staying as long as possible to protect my staff in the personal office to give them time to maneuver into other jobs. The calls for my resignation lessened and I lost *front page status* in late September of 2006 when it was revealed that sitting Congressman Mark Foley had been inappropriately texting male pages and an investigation was about to ensue.

I stepped down right before the election in November of 2006 without anyone really paying attention.

RIGHTING WRONGS

An outstanding Member of Congress, Chaka Fattah (D-Pennsylvania), pointed out that there was not a portrait of an African American on the House side. In the years that I had walked through the corridors of the House, I had never realized that. I thought that the callousness from 1793 all the way up to the 2000's was indeed evident with not one portrait of an African American. My office did some research and Lynne Crow, who is from Ohio and worked for House Administration, took the lead. We discovered that the first elected African American to the House was not seated. We then found out that the first seated African American was Congressman Joseph Rainey, in 1870. I commissioned a portrait and it was painted from a picture that the House Historian found of the Congressman on the first floor of the capitol near a fireplace.

We invited his relatives to the unveiling of the portrait, as well as many prominent African Americans, including the black caucus and Jesse Jackson Sr. Oprah Winfrey was invited but could not attend. I hosted the event with the late Juanita Millender McDonald (D-California), the Ranking Member of House Administration and an African American Member herself. As I read my portion of the program, I asked the relatives of Congressman Rainey to stand. There were African American relatives standing on the right and the Caucasian relatives on the left. They looked at each other and waved—some of them possibly seeing each other for the first time. We had a reception afterward, and it was a great day.

This idea of Chaka's led to several more great ones. Xavier Becerra (D-California) requested a portrait of the first Latino, and Marcy Kaptur, Congresswoman from Toledo Ohio, asked for a portrait of the first woman elected. Prior to this we had NO portrait of a woman hanging in the House. I was proud, as a matter of principle, that the first portraits to be hung in the House of an African American, a Latino, and a woman was done under my time and under the Republicans.

I worked with Jesse Jackson, Jr. to expedite the Rosa Parks statue and we commissioned the Helen Keller statue, which is the first statue of a person with disabilities to be placed in the capitol.

During my time as Chairman, it was a pleasure and honor to carry the legislation for Congressman John Lewis (D-Georgia) to create the African American Museum. He had tried to get it passed for sixteen years, and it finally became law.

CONGRESSIONAL BIGOTRY

One of the most appalling calls I received as Chairman of House Administration came from House Majority Leader Dick Armey's top staffer.
(Each party had four main elected positions. For the Republicans, who
were in the majority at this time, the positions were Speaker of the
House, Majority Leader, Whip, and Conference Chair. The Democratic
side had the same setup with the substitution of Minority Leader for
the Speaker's position.) These leaders had a lot of power, and a "secret"
in the House was that none of them were monitored by House Administration—they were not accountable to House Administration for lost
equipment, nor were their newsletters approved by House Administration. Actually, they were "free to roam" as they pleased. When they
called me, they called with authority. I could do little to them over-
sight-wise.

Congressman Armey's staffer had called to complain about the House
considering some changes that would deal with equity for gay and lesbian staffers. She said that we did not want to do things for these "fags."
I told her sarcastically that this was the 21st century and we call the
"fags" gays these days! I was just surprised at the blatant slurs used
by the Majority Leader's office and by Dick Armey himself, although it
wasn't the first time. Dick and his staff talked that way in front of me
and others on many occasions over the years—such as Dick Armey's
famous so-called slip of the tongue when he called openly gay Congressman Barney Frank, Barney Fag.

David Duncan was my Assistant Staff Director for the House Administration Committee. David did a remarkable job and although he was
young, his organizational ability was amazing. Will Heaton, my Chief
of Staff, was leery of him and said he was "on a power trip." Some
staffers also grumbled about David, but most of it was pure jealousy of
his abilities. Jennie Vollor, my scheduler, and David were great friends
and as co-workers, they got a lot done for us.

One day a staffer asked me if David was gay and I said yes. (David
was once a board member of the Republican Gay Staffers Association
and was quoted in a *Washington Post* article: *"You have to separate the marketing from the reality. The reality is, these members are not homophobic. For
the most part, they're using this marketing to play to our base and stay in power.
They have to turn out the vote."*)

When the staffer frowned I said, "If that's a problem, get over it. And by the way, if you can find ten more 'gay staffers,' let me know—the House can run much better.'"

However, when it came to how it played in the District, I was not the most upstanding about this issue myself. When my general election opponent in 2006, who also campaigned against gay marriage and made it known that he was a "Conservative Democrat," went on Rachel Maddow's Air America show, I connotated that he was a liberal because he went on the show of a "cross-dressing Liberal from New York City." It sells in the conservative Democrat seats, but I think if I were to redo that today, I would stick to "the Liberal from New York." Not only do I apologize to Ms. Maddow, I watch her show.

The Republicans in general need to be a bit kinder and keep the inflammatory language down.

In general, the award for bigotry and intolerance went to Tom DeLay and Dick Armey for the most insensitive workplaces.

JOE, CHET, AND BOB

Joe Rose, Chet Kalis, and Bob Olexo were all bright spots in our office and in my life. We had many great staff people who served the District constituents—these three passed away far too early and within three years of each other.

I was introduced to Joe Rose through Dan Lipperman of Bellaire. "Danny," as he was called, ran our toughest field operation in 1994, which was the Belmont/Jefferson County area in the southeastern part of the district. He met Joe, who was the Assistant Manager of a convenience store in Steubenville, Ohio. Joe and I later realized that we met when we were kids. We got a kick out of "who would have dreamed then that we would be working together."

Joe was a real success story. He came from a wonderful family, was a devout Christian, and had a lot of common sense. He was a hard worker and a local supporter of the Ohio Republican Party. He had no plans to run a Congressional office, but fate stepped in. (Joe would have called it the will of God.)

Joe had the innate ability to read people and sense situations. He was really an amazing person. After we won the campaign, Joe came aboard and eventually ran the Zanesville, Ohio office. Constituents constantly raved about Joe. He used his vacations to help with the kids at church camps. A constituent told me one day when I was in the Zanesville office and Joe was out that Joe donated money to people in the district who came to us for help with their electric bill. When he was unsuccessful in keeping their electricity on, he gave them money from his pocket to help them.

Joe called one day and told me that he was marrying Jessica, a woman he had met through the church. He said, "This will be my first and only marriage, God has let us find each other." I felt humbled that Joe asked me to be his best man in the wedding. Less than one year later, on Easter Sunday 2003, the Lord called Joe home. When his wife awoke that day, she found that Joe had passed away due to a heart attack. The pain of losing Joe was nearly unbearable for all of us in the office and within our family. He was the only son of Joan and Ed, brother to Tracy Kline, and a beloved friend to us and many more in the district.

On the heels of losing Joe, came the unexpected illness that befell Chet Kalis. I wrote about Chet earlier. He and Payam Zakipour (American name, Kyle Washington) were roommates of mine on my boat in D.C. Chet and Payam developed a wonderful friendship. Chet was also my next-door neighbor in St. Clairsville. He would come over to my house and we would joke about when he ran Bob Olexo's campaign against me in 1984 for the Ohio State Senate. I told Chet, "That's why I like you so much—you messed up the campaign and I won."

Chet's part with HAVA (the Help America Vote Act) was invaluable. He dogged the bill, wrote many parts of it, massaged it, and made all the players come together—HAVA was his masterpiece. As a Democrat, Chet was able to bring groups to the table that I could not.

Chet and I both took our children to the signing of the bill. President Bush 43 signed it. I remember receiving a personal, stern warning from Barry Jackson that day—the president would sign it and he had no time to talk to people. Chet and I plotted, then took our kids and Pat Leahy, a staffer of mine who was blind, to meet the president. We all rushed the stage, including Pat's guide dog, Nina. After that, the stage area was bombarded with others. Barry let me know later through Dave Distefano how pissed he was. I, of course, didn't care. Chet was happy and his daughters Ali and Jillian, plus my daughter, Kayla, got to meet the president.

Chet was a caring person; he cared about his family and about how the political process worked. Then he began acting strangely, and a few people noticed, including me. Chet was getting a bit forgetful. He normally had a razor sharp mind. His mood changed from easy going to a bit irritable, and for the first time, he was making some mistakes.

The job offers he had after HAVA were amazing. I told him it was time to move on. He had three children and this was now the financial opportunity of a lifetime. He said he didn't want to leave House Administration and my office. I was sincere when I told him that he would force me to dismiss him for his own good to take one of many job offers. We finally agreed that he would help me get things on track in the office with HAVA as we implemented it, and then he would move on to take another job.

Chet was quickly offered an amazing job with a firm and was in the process of accepting it. I told him that I was sorry to lose him, but delighted that he was doing something he liked and was tripling his salary, which would really help his daughters.

It was 2004, and I was asked to give a series of HAVA-related speeches. Pat Sweeney, a staffer and former Ohio Democrat State Senator, was traveling for me across America, and Chet went to Chicago to give a speech for me that same week. I recall the day when my receptionist told me that Chet was on the phone for me. Chet said, "Hello" and nothing more.

I said, "Where are you?"

He sounded frustrated and responded, "I am in Chicago, at the airport. Where am I flying to?"

In those days, our schedules were unbelievable and I assumed he had not written down his schedule as he bounced from D.C. to St. Clairsville and all over the country. I said, "You are flying to Pittsburgh, and going home, I will see you this weekend sometime when I return from D.C."

"Where is home?"

I was alarmed and asked, "Are you okay?"

He said, "Yes, I just can't remember where home is."

With a terrible feeling of foreboding and trying to keep as calm as possible, I told Chet to get on the plane to Pittsburgh, knowing that his girlfriend, Jennifer, would be there to pick him up.

On Monday, I was back in D.C. and at the National Republican Campaign Committee offices making fundraising calls when Chet called. He had been to the doctor.

"I have a lump, a lump on my brain."

Even as he was losing his ability to communicate, he would still react when he saw television reports on the HAVA Bill and the Abramoff controversy, Jack's amendment for the Indians, and about me. He knew that we would not jeopardize the bill with Jack's amendment—Chet's part of HAVA had been the most intricate. He was also aware that we had not introduced the amendment. Chet's perseverance with the HAVA Bill is one of the main reasons we have an improved U.S. elections system today.

On my birthday, July 5, 2005, Chet lost his battle with a brain tumor.

Chet's funeral and seeing the devastation of his daughters, family, and his many friends, was painful for all of us. Congressman Steny Hoyer (D-Maryland) spoke at a D.C. memorial for him.

The third shocker came when Bob Olexo, Chet's best friend and my former opponent in the 1984 Ohio State Senate race, passed away in his sleep in February of 2006.

Bob was a wonderful, long-time public servant. When we ran against each other in 1984, it was a fierce election. Later I read where Bob, unsolicited, said that he felt I was doing a better job in elected office than he could have. I called Bob, we met for lunch and it was the beginning of a wonderful friendship.

After my election to U.S. Congress and Bob's retirement from a job that he had, I asked him to be the Development Director for our Congressional office. He did a remarkable job and helped to improve the lives of so many in the Congressional District.

As I went through my trials and tribulations, he was always there to provide support for my family and for me.

The personal pain over the loss of these three friends was not overshadowed by the government investigation—it was just the opposite.

Appendix 2

☆ ☆ ☆

THE CASE OF
DON SIEGELMAN—
A POLITICAL PROSECUTION

While you have been reading this book, you may have doubted, discounted, or disbelieved some of the things I have related regarding politics, judicial misconduct, and possible conspiracies. There is a current travesty of justice unfolding as this book goes to print that underlines what I have written on these pages. You have probably heard the saying that "absolute power corrupts absolutely." I think there is no better evidence of that than the ongoing case of Don Siegelman, an ex-governor of Alabama who at the age of 67 is serving a seven-year sentence for nothing more than being a popular Democrat in a Republican state.

According to Alabama Congressman Parker Griffith, "Karl Rove's hands are all over this. This is absolutely, one of the most unjust things I've ever encountered. The Karl Rove southern strategy is a racist strategy, it pits people against one another, it splits us apart and he was very successful in vetting judges."

This case is best described by Mimi Kennedy in her Huff Post Politics Blog dated September 3, 2012.

Don Siegelman should be a star in the Democratic Party. Instead, he's a former elected official sentenced to prison by a right-wing judge in Alabama.

Siegelman had the temerity to be a popular Alabama Democrat who'd won every statewide office by 1998, when he first became governor. With Jewish and Catholic roots, and empathic appeal to minorities, he threatened the GOP "southern strategy" for a domi-

nant one-party Republican nation. To the GOP, Siegelman was potentially Another Clinton—as repellent to them as Another Cuba.

U.S. Attorney Leura Canary, a friend of Karl Rove's, incited Siegelman's prosecution for bribery, destroying his political career and
hurting his family. [There is a letter referenced in the article signed
by 113 former attorneys general and other national leaders, both
Democrat and Republican that assert the prosecuted "bribe" wasn't
one, and that, if this conviction stands, it threatens every public official and contributor at every level of government.] Such routine
transactions, if prosecuted, would choke our courts.

The "bribe"? Don Siegelman wanted to create a state lottery that
would provide funds for Alabama youth to attend state college for
free. Richard Scrushy, CEO of HealthSouth, donated $500,000 for a
campaign to convince Alabamans this was a good idea. The lottery
referendum went on the ballot. The half-million didn't benefit Siegelman's gubernatorial campaign or him personally . . '. The referendum lost. It was opposed with money pouring in from nearby
Mississippi, where Indian casinos, represented by Jack Abramoff
were threatened by the idea of Alabamans spending gambling money
at home, for education.

Siegelman's first indictment from federal prosecutors came in
2004. Already, in 2002, rumors of alleged "crimes" had circulated during Siegelman's campaign for re-election as governor. But he almost
won anyway; he went to bed as the announced winner on election
night. The next day, [opponent] Bob Riley announced that he had
won. A sudden redistribution of gubernatorial votes in Baldwin
County had reduced Governor Siegelman's totals by 3000, giving the
win to Riley. No other Baldwin County results shifted during this
odd event. Republican Attorney General Bill Pryor denied a recount
of the paper ballots.

The 2002 indictment was thrown out immediately. Federal Judge
U.W. Clemon called the case "unfounded" and dismissed it with prej-
udice. In 2006, Don Siegelman sought to regain his stolen governor-
ship—and was indicted again. This time the prosecution was brought
by U.S. Attorney Leura Canary. *Leura's husband, Bill Canary was running Bob Riley's re-election campaign.* [Italics mine.]

Federal Judge Mark Fuller didn't throw out the indictment,
though it was brought after the 5-year statute of limitations had run
out on the crime alleged. Fuller ignored this, and disallowed all evidence of political and legal corruption in the case, including witness

and jury tampering. Siegelman was convicted. His appeals have run nearly six years and his prosecution has cost the taxpayers millions. It ended with the U.S. Supreme Court's refusal to hear the case this summer and its decision to send the case back to Judge Fuller "without comment."

Judge Fuller ruled that ex-Governor Don Siegelman shall resume serving his remaining sentence—five years—and chose for Don to report to prison on September 11.

What did Mr. Scrushy "get" in return for donating to Siegelman's lottery campaign? Re-appointment to a state board for hospital oversight. It's a position that doesn't pay and Scrushy didn't want it. He'd served on the board for twelve years for three preceding governors. According to Governor Siegelman's intrepid daughter, Dana, her father implored Scrushy to re-join the board to make it bipartisan and attract more business to the state. Some bribe! Scrushy gives, and gets what he doesn't want in return, along with an indictment and prison, too. [There were stated reasons], but he also said yes to a popular, targeted Democrat.

Dana Siegelman has launched a presidential pardon petition for her father, who was taken in shackles from a courtroom ten years ago. Don Siegelman served nine months before release on appeal, moved among prisons in various states, making it difficult for family, friends and media to see him. He was recommended for solitary confinement, and put there often. When a warden in Louisiana finally asked, "What's with the recommendation for solitary?" Don replied, "I have no idea." And that warden put him in the general prison population . . .

I rest my case!

☆ ☆ ☆

RESOURCES

Chapter 11—Cry Me a River

http://www.veteranstoday.com/2011/01/08/matt-taibbi-the-crying-shame-of-john-boehner%E2%80%8F/

http://www.politicspa.com/john-boehner-brings-his-corporate-special-interest-backed-agenda-to-pennsylvania/16779/

Chapter 13—Freedom Fries

http://en.wikipedia.org/wiki/Freedom_fries

Jacques Chirac, 2003 People in the News — Infoplease.com http://www.infoplease.com/ipa/A0908009.html#ixzz228UP3sHV

Chapter 14—MEK: Terrorists Among Us

http://www.cnn.com/WORLD/9801/07/iran/interview.html

http://www.cfr.org/iran/harnessing-irans-role-afghanistan/p19562

http://en.wikipedia.org/wiki/People%27s_Mujahedin_of_Iran

http://www.huffingtonpost.com/steve-clemons/what-did-rove-do-with-200_b_41472.html

http://www.guardian.co.uk/world/2012/sep/21/iran-mek-group-removed-us-terrorism-list?newsfeed=true

http://www.guardian.co.uk/commentisfree/2012/sep/22/barack-obama-terrorism

http://www.guardian.co.uk/commentisfree/2012/sep/23/iran-usa

http://www.csmonitor.com/World/Middle-East/2011/0808/Iranian-groups-big-money-push-to-get-off-US-terrorist-list

http://www.iran.org/news/pr_970723.htm

http://www.sarbaz.org/000english/earticles/mujahedeen.htm

Chapter 16—Presidents

http://www.washingtonpost.com/wp-srv/politics/special/clinton/stories/decided121798.htm

Chapter 18—Encounter of the Best Kind (Sonny Bono)

http://en.wikipedia.org/wiki/Budget_impasse#United_States_federal_government_shutdown_of_1995_and_1996

Chapter 19—What a Tangled Web We Weave

http://thinkprogress.org/politics/2007/02/26/10643/parsi-iran-offer/?mobile=nc

http://www.dispatch.com/content/stories/editorials/2007/12/09/sudd09.ART_ART_12-09-07_G5_OL8N4MP.html

http://www.dallasdancemusic.com/awareness-politics/208337-bush-admin-denies-ties-abramoff-but-his-accountant-visited-white-house-97-time.html

Chapter 20—"Let's Go to London, Bob!"

http://www.theatlantic.com/magazine/archive/2008/09/what-did-bush-tell-gonzales/7064/

http://fouadalzayat.com/controvercies

Chapter 21—"Fore!"

http://en.wikipedia.org/wiki/Monetary_influence_of_Jack_Abramoff

Chapter 22—SunCruz

http://www.cbsnews.com/2319-100_162-1451868.html

http://www.cbsnews.com/elements/2006/03/29/in_depth_us/timeline1451868.shtml

Chapter 23—Foxcom

http://www.zdnet.com/blog/government/house-rescinds-wireless-hill-deal-cut-by-abramoff/2618

http://en.wikipedia.org/wiki/Robert_Ney#License_to_a_telecommunications_firm

Chapter 24—A Contract, a Conspiracy, and a Cover-up?

http://www.projectcensored.org/top-stories/articles/12-mysterious-death-of-mike-connell%E2%80%94karl-roves-election-thief/

http://discuss.epluribusmedia.net/content/ohio_attorneys_seek_protection_mike_connell_his_family_against_alleged_threats_karl_rove

http://www.alternet.org/story/93330/gop_computer_guru_controls_key_congressional_websites/

http://www.bradblog.com/?p=7652

http://www.prisonplanet.com/mike-connell-was-warned-not-to-fly-before-plane-crash.html

http://nomadicpolitics.blogspot.com/search?q=Mike+Connell

http://en.wikipedia.org/wiki/Michael_Connell

http://en.wikipedia.org/wiki/Ken_Blackwell

Chapter 25—The Case of the Non-Amendment

http://www.cbsnews.com/8301-504803_162-57319068-10391709/jack-abramoff-inside-capitol-corruption/

Chapter 26—The Press á la Abramoff

http://www.politicsdaily.com/2009/10/29/bob-neys-redemption-after-jack-abramoff-scandal/

http://indiancountrytodaymedianetwork.com/2012/03/08/abramoff-scandal-secrets-tribal-confrontation-sparks-journalist-mystery-101902

http://www.washingtonpost.com/blogs/in-the-loop/post/tom-delay-jack-abramoff-seen-dining-together/2012/12/05/610c7ab4-3efa-11e2-a2d9-822f58ac9fd5_blog.html (via shareaholic.com)

Chapter 27—Pretty Alice

en.wikipedia.org/wiki/Dismissal_of_U.S._attorneys_controversy

http://lonestarproject.net/Permalink/2007-04-10.html

http://en.wikipedia.org/wiki/Alice_S._Fisher

http://www.youtube.com/watch?v=Wz_qq2ZcjzY

http://www.nytimes.com/2007/04/19/washington/19cnd-gonz.html

http://downwithtyranny.blogspot.com/2008/05/good-riddance-to-more-bush-rubbish.html

http://christyhardinsmith.firedoglake.com/2009/09/14/has-anyone-asked-alice/

http://blogs.wsj.com/law/2008/09/10/latham-hearts-the-doj-alice-fisher-to-rejoin-firm/

http://www.washingtonpost.com/wp-dyn/content/article/2006/09/14/AR2006091402051.html

http://www.justice.gov/opa/pr/2006/September/06_crm_622.html

http://www.huffingtonpost.com/jane-hamsher/flippin-jack-and-heckuva-_b_13243.html

Chapter 28—Boehner: The Rest of the Story

http://www.youtube.com/watch?v=KXpeCAVgCcg

Chapter 29—The Perfect Storm

http://susanbradfordpress.wordpress.com/2011/01/04/indian-chief-defends-abramoff-demands-investigation-of-mccains-hearings/

http://www.redstate.com/susanbradfordpress/2012/03/11/tribal-chief-who-participated-in-mccain's-sham-abramoff-hearin

http://en.wikipedia.org/wiki/Jack_Abramoff

http://en.wikipedia.org/wiki/Monetary_influence_of_Jack_Abramoff

http://www.blogforarizona.com/blog/2008/06/the-cover-ups-2.html

http://abcnews.go.com/blogs/politics/2008/05/obama-hits-mcca-3/

http://www.dailykos.com/story/2008/02/23/462347/-Jack-Abramoff-John-McCain-rsquo-s-other-Lobbyist-problem

http://firedoglake.blogspot.com/2006/01/heckuva-job-alice.html

http://en.wikipedia.org/wiki/Alice_S._Fisher

http://en.wikipedia.org/wiki/Recess_appointment

www.rense.com/general69/neo.htm

http://www.sourcewatch.org/index.php/Iran-Syria_Operations_Group

http://www.justice.gov/opa/pr/2006/September/06_crm_622.html

Chapter 30—Altar Boy Will

http://tpmmuckraker.talkingpointsmemo.com/mark_foley/

http://www.washingtonpost.com/wp-dyn/content/article/2007/08/12/AR2007081201287.html

http://www.washingtonpost.com/wp-dyn/content/article/2006/10/19/AR2006101901931.html

http://tpmmuckraker.talkingpointsmemo.com/dennis_hastert/

Chapter 31—One Day at a Time

http://www.guardian.co.uk/world/2011/feb/10/republican-congressman-resigns-craigslist

http://cityroom.blogs.nytimes.com/2010/03/09/i-tickled-aide-but-that-was-all-massa-says/

http://en.wikipedia.org/wiki/Scooter_Libby

http://en.wikipedia.org/wiki/Webster_Hubbell

http://en.wikipedia.org/wiki/Duke_Cunningham

http://www.washingtonpost.com/wp-dyn/content/article/2006/09/14/AR2006091402051.html

http://en.wikipedia.org/wiki/Mark_Foley

http://en.avaaz.org/843/remember-to-make-time-for-the-really-important-things-in-life

Chapter 32—Morgantown Federal Correctional Institution

http://thehill.com/homenews/news/9205-channeling-garth-brooks-ney-sends-farewell-e-mail

http://fedsgotme.com.whoisbucket.com/

http://badlawyernyc.blogspot.in/2011_04_01_archive.html

http://en.wikipedia.org/wiki/Emmanuel_Onunwor

http://www.tmz.com/2011/05/02/celebrity-apprentice-star-richard-hatch-tax-evasion-prison-stint-survivor/

http://en.wikipedia.org/wiki/Bill_Clinton_pardon_controversy

http://triblive.com/x/pittsburghtrib/opinion/columnists/qa/s_745886.html#axzz2ItywGPzn

Chapter 34—New Beginnings

http://www.foodwisdomrx.com/

Matt Parker:

http://www.washingtonian.com/articles/people/when-the-boss-gets-busted-survival-stories-from-the-front-lines-of-political-scandal/index.php

Chapter 35—Incredible India

http://www.amethyst-inc.org/index.php/About-Us

http://www.dispatch.com/content/stories/life_and_entertainment/2007/
12/13/RELAX.ART_ART_12-13-07_D1_968N85M.html

http://tibetoday.com/team_members.htm

http://www.billingvalley.com/

http://arizoldan.com/bio/

Appendix 1—In Addition . . . (Stepping Down in New Orleans)

http://usatoday30.usatoday.com/news/washington/2006-09-14-ney-
corruption_x.htm

http://articles.cnn.com/2006-10-14/politics/abramoff.ney_1_bob-ney-gop-
leaders-guilty-plea?_s=PM:POLITICS

http://qz.com/25295/think-youre-a-republican-or-a-democrat-i-bet-that-
would-change-if-you-hung-out-with-more-politicians-or-their-staffs/

Dirty Work: http://en.wikipedia.org/wiki/Dan_Burton

Appendix 2—The Case of Don Siegelman: A Political Prosecution

http://www.huffingtonpost.com/2012/12/12/don-siegelman-karl-rove_
n_2285174.html

http://www.huffingtonpost.com/mimi-kennedy/don-siegelman_b_1851909
.html

Miscellaneous

2012 article about Barry Jackson/lobbyists

http://www.buzzfeed.com/andrewkaczynski/top-boehner-aide-used-
private-email-address-to-com

Jack Abramoff: http://www.politico.com/news/stories/0712/78865.html

INDEX OF NAMES

☆ ☆ ☆

ABOUT THE AUTHOR

Bob Ney was born in Wheeling, West Virginia, and raised in the Ohio Valley. Shortly after graduating from the Ohio State University with a B.S. Education Degree, he taught English in Iran, where he developed a lifelong interest and love for international travel and cultures in addition to his own.

His 25 years in political office began at the age of 26, when he was elected to the Ohio House of Representatives, then to the Ohio State Senate, and his final 11 years in office as a U.S. Representative from Ohio's 18th District.

Ironically, Bob's life was forever changed for the better through a prison sentence that included a 12 Step program. Sober and healthy, he was a talk show host for WVLY, Wheeling West Virginia, and is a political analyst for Talk Radio News Service.

Today Bob spends his time writing, is involved in humanitarian endeavors, and is committed to people in recovery through 12 Step programs.

Bob is devoted to his granddaughter, Aaliyah, as well as to his children, Bobby and Kayla, and their spouses, Julie and Adam. He divides his time between two of his great loves—Ohio and India.